The Giant Guide to Golden Retrievers

DR ALEX LLOYD

The Giant Care & Training Manual
for your Golden Retriever

CM
YOUR DOG. YOUR LIFE

CANINE MEDIA

First published in Great Britain by Canine Media 2023

ISBN: 978-1-913586-47-8

TABLE OF CONTENTS

1. Greetings from the Golden Retriever

'The face of a golden retriever feels like home.'

~ David Rosenfelt ~

Sturdy, muscular and hard-working, golden retrievers are among the most popular dog breeds due to their attractive golden fur and amenable disposition. Frequently trained as sight and support dogs, these Scottish gundogs have a versatility which makes them suitable for most dog owners, whether you're looking for a hunting companion or family pet.

These medium-sized dogs are known for their dense, beautiful golden coat, which gives the breed its name. Males can reach a height of 56-61cm (22-24 inches) with a weight of 30-34kg (66-75lb) when fully grown, while females are slightly smaller at 51-56cm (20-22 inches), weighing in at 25-32kg (55-71lb). Their hefty build can give them the appearance of a larger dog - and don't underestimate their strong pulling power when taking them for a walk!

With their dense, double coat of medium fur, golden retrievers are easily identified. Their intelligent, expressive eyes belie their eagerness to learn and work. Natural swimmers, they were bred to retrieve waterfowl, meaning they're happy to go into the water to play fetch for hours. Their webbed paws make it easy for them to move about in the water. When combined with their oily, water-repellent coat and bushy, shaggy tails, it's no wonder they love swimming around.

Unlike Labrador retrievers, a similar sporting dog, goldens have a much smaller range of coat colours, ranging from light to dark golden. One thing's for sure though – whatever colour coat your retriever has, it'll be a very attractive dog.

Typically, golden retrievers take around three years to reach maturity. While they can reach their full height by around 9-12 months, it takes longer for them to fill out to their adult weight and even longer for them to mentally mature. Expect a bouncy, exuberant, puppy-minded dog for the first few years. The average life expectancy of a Golden is 10-12 years, although some make it to 17, 18, or even 19. The oldest known golden retriever lived for 20 years.

Goldens make great family dogs if you meet their need for plenty of exercise and training. These dogs are bred to be working dogs, so they thrive on being given things to do, particularly retrieving. It's all in the name! The amount of exercise they need varies with the different lines: if your retriever comes from a working field line, they'll need anything up to 2 hours' exercise per day. If you get a pup from a show line, they don't need quite as much. As an average guide, expect to have to walk your dog for at least 20-30 minutes twice a day if you want a chilled, calm house pet.

As a rule, golden retrievers get on well with other dogs, pets, and children, particularly if they've been trained well. They're powerful dogs and benefit from obedience training at an early age, or you might find yourself being walked by your dog instead of the other way around. Since they're high-energy dogs, don't expect to be able to leave your retriever alone all day or neglect their exercise routine. Otherwise, you'll see your delightful dog turn into a terror, chewing, digging, or barking excessively. There's nothing worse than coming home to find your golden retriever waiting for you, tail merrily wagging, while they sit in the middle of a ton of destruction. Divert their strong retrieving instinct by giving them plenty of toys and guidance.

Nevertheless, retrievers are consistently one of the most popular dog breeds in the United States and the United Kingdom. They're intelligent and love to learn new tricks, due in part to their drive to make their owners happy. They are prone to becoming overweight if they're not exercised, so watch their food portions to make sure they get the right amount. Golden retrievers do best in homes where they can spend plenty of time with their family. They quickly become an important member of the household.

Since they build such close bonds with their families, retrievers are often protective of them. Their friendly nature means they're usually happy to make new friends too! Be careful that your retriever doesn't develop a habit of 'mouthing' people – not everyone will understand your dog doesn't have bad intentions. Giving them a toy to carry to fill their mouth is a good way of stopping this habit.

Be warned – their luscious double coat, which enables them to retrieve birds from icy water, comes with the downside of shedding. A weekly groom is enough for most of the year, but during shedding times, you'll want to give your retriever a daily groom. Even then, be prepared to end up covered in golden hairs when they hug you!

History

The golden retriever and Labrador retriever aren't just the most popular breeds for waterfowlers. They're also one of the most common breeds chosen as family pets and service dogs. Their intelligence and versatility mean they aren't just impressive hunters. They're also wonderful for those who just want some company or are looking for the perfect family pet.

The Golden Retriever breed originated in Scotland in the nineteenth century. Sir Dudley Marjoribanks (pronounced 'Marchbanks'), who would become Baron Tweedmouth, crossed flat-coated retrievers with tweed water spaniels. The resulting pups were then bred with lines which included Irish setters, bloodhounds, St. John's water dogs, and black retrievers to create the much-loved breed we know today. In 1952, the Marjoribanks' highly detailed stud book was published. This put paid to the various rumours which had been circulating about the breed's origins.

Marjoribanks' motives were simple. He wanted to create the ultimate retriever to work at his Scottish estate, Guisachen. He chose a yellow flat-coated retriever named Nous as the perfect dog to start his new breed. Nous was whelped in June 1864 and had been the sole yellow pup in a litter which was otherwise completely black. This was unusual, although two black parents could produce all manner of colours, including liver, brown, golden, and yellow. This striking colour is what gave rise to the romantic fantasies surrounding the origin of golden retrievers. For example, one early story claimed that Nous had been bought from a Russian circus trainer in Brighton. Other versions stated that Nous had been acquired from a cobbler or a gipsy. The more mundane truth was that Nous had been bred by Lord Chichester at his Stanmer Park estate near Brighton.

In 1868, Nous was mated with a tweed water spaniel bitch. Belle is mentioned in the studbook as having been born in 1863 and coming from "Ladykirk breeding." Belle had four yellow pups named Primrose, Cowslip, Crocus, and Ada. Marjoribanks picked Cowslip as the best bitch and mated her with a tweed water spaniel called Tweed. Cowslip then had a bitch pup named Topsy.

Subsequent matings saw Cowslip matched with a red setter named Sampson, which saw her produce a dog pup named Jack. Meanwhile, Topsy was mated with a black flat-coated retriever called Sambo. Their daughter, Zoe, was then mated with Jack. Marjoribanks kept a bitch called Gill and a dog named Nous II from that litter. Gill was mated with a black Golden retriever, Tracer, and one of the resulting bitches, Queenie, was then mated with Nous II. All existing golden retrievers can be traced back to this mating.

While there were other pups produced by these various matings, ranging in colour from jet black to light cream, Marjoribanks only retained the golden-coloured ones to form the foundation stock of the golden breed. In later years, he was also known to have brought in a sandy-coloured Bloodhound and a Golden to improve the stock.

All this information came to light thanks to the work of Marjoribanks' great-nephew, Giles Fox-Strangways, the 6th Earl of Ilchester. He worked with Elma Stonex to study Marjoribanks' stud book before publishing their research. This put paid to all the rumours of more exotic origins to the breed. The studbook, detailing the period from 1868-1890, is now kept in the library of the Kennel Club in London.

Initially, golden retrievers were known by the more unwieldy name 'flat-coated retriever, golden.' They were considered simply a colour variation of the existing breed. In 1903, the first examples were recorded by the Kennel Club, including them in the same register as flatcoats. The following year, a golden retriever won a field trial and then in 1908, the first goldens were exhibited at confirmation shows.

A breed club was established in England in 1911. Known as the Golden Retriever Club, they named the breed the yellow or golden retriever. This marks the moment when the breed was considered to be an individual breed, distinct from the flat-coated retriever. However, it took until 1913 for the Kennel Club to record them as a breed distinct from flat-coated retrievers, and it wasn't until 1920 that they were officially dubbed the golden retriever.

Winifred Charlesworth was an early twentieth-century champion of the breed. She played a major role in establishing the breed club and securing recognition of the breed by the Kennel Club. She defined the first breed standard, which the Kennel Club accepted with minor adjustments. The standard remains mainly unchanged to this day. She was the first to breed and exhibit a golden retriever Show Champion, advocated keeping the working instincts of the breed and is seen as the one responsible for popularising the breed at show trials and among shooting sportsmen.

In the years following the First World War, the golden retriever enjoyed a boom in popularity, becoming more widespread in the Western world during the 1920s and 30s. The Canadian Kennel Club acknowledged the breed in 1927, followed by the American Kennel Club in 1932. France started to register them in 1934, as did Australia in 1937. The worldwide appeal of the breed meant that it was unaffected by the Second World War when many British dog breeds suffered from British wartime restrictions on the breeding of larger dogs. This meant that there was plenty of quality breeding stock available around the globe to maintain the standards and characteristics of the breed.

After the end of the war, the breed's popularity has only continued to grow. It is now one of the most recognized and registered dog breeds in the Western world.

FACT ***Marjoribanks was interested in dog breeding from an early age – at least from his teens. Back then, dog breeding was seen as an admirable hobby for the well-to-do and socially influential. While his older brother inherited their father's banking partnership, Marjoribanks inherited a hefty sum, enabling him to pursue his hobby.***

While golden retrievers are highly popular breeds and do well in agility and obedience shows, to date, a golden retriever has never won Crufts in the United Kingdom.

Breed Standards

United Kingdom Breed Standard

The breed standard details the desired temperament, characteristics, and appearance, including details such as the correct colour of a breed. This is all to ensure the breed is fit for function. A good example of the breed requires absolute compliance. Both breeders and judges should avoid any deviation from these standards, particularly if this would cause problems for the health, welfare, or soundness of the breed. Occasionally, some conditions or exaggerations may be considered to have the potential to adversely affect dogs in some breeds. Further information can be found in the breed watch section of the United Kingdom's Kennel Club website: www.the-kennel-club.org.uk.

These are the current standards for the British golden retriever:

General Appearance. An ideal golden retriever should move with symmetry, balance, and power with a level gait. It should have a kindly expression.

Characteristics. A golden should be biddable and compliant with above-average intelligence. It should have a natural working ability.

Temperament. Golden retrievers should be kind, outgoing, and confident.

Head and Skull. The head should be balanced and well-chiselled. A retriever should have a broad skull absent of any coarseness. It should sit well on the neck. The muzzle should be powerful, wide, and deep.

The length of the foreface should be roughly equal to the length from the well-defined stop to the occiput. Ideally, the nose should be black.

Eyes. Dark brown and wideset with dark rims.

Ears. Moderate size at the same general level as the eyes.

Mouth. Strong jaws with a perfect, regular, complete scissor bite. The upper teeth should closely overlap the lower and all be set square to the jaw.

Neck. Good length, clean and muscular.

Forequarters. The forelegs should be straight with good bones. The shoulders should be well laid back with long blades. The upper arms should be equal in length so the legs are well under the body. The elbows need to be close-fitting.

Body. A retriever's body should be balanced, short coupled and deep through the heart. The ribs should be placed deep and be well sprung. The topline should be level.

Hindquarters. The loin and legs should be strong and muscular with good second thighs and well-bent stifles. The hocks should be well let down and look straight when examined from the rear without turn-ins. Cow hocks are to be avoided.

Feet. Round and catlike.

Tail. Set on and carried level with the back, reaching out to the hocks. There should be no curl at the tip.

Gait/Movement. The retriever's stride should be long and free without any Hackney action in front. (Where a dog lifts its front feet up and out with a bend at the wrist while driving from behind.) It should move powerfully with a good drive with a gait straight and true in front and read

Coat. Flat or wavy with good feathering with a dense, water-resistant undercoat.

Colour. Any shade of gold or cream. Red and mahogany are not permissible, although a few white hairs on the chest are acceptable.

Size. Ideal height at withers: 56-61 cms (22-24 ins); bitches: 51-56 cms (20-22 ins).

Faults. Any deviance from these stipulations qualifies as a fault. The seriousness of the fault will depend on the extent, any impact on the health and welfare of the dog, and whether it impacts the dog's ability to carry out its traditional work.

Note. Male retrievers should have two seemingly normal testicles which are fully descended into the scrotum.

American Breed Standard

The official breed standards for the American golden retriever, as laid out by the American Kennel Club, vary slightly from those for the British golden retriever. They are given below. If a dog does not conform to these standards, it will be automatically disqualified if presented for show in an AKC-sanctioned event:

General Appearance. A golden retriever should be symmetrical, powerful, and active. It should be solidly built and well put together. It should move gracefully but not be long in the leg. It should have a friendly expression with a keen, alert, outgoing personality. Since they are predominantly hunting dogs, they should be shown in hard-working condition. In shows, appearance, balance, gait, and purpose will be given more weight than individual components. Any deviation from the prescribed ideal will be deemed a fault. How serious a fault is will depend on how much it impacts the breed's purpose or character.

Size, proportion, and substance. Males should measure 23-24 inches in height at withers, with females coming in at 21½-22½ inches. Dogs which are up to an inch above or below this standard will receive a proportionate penalty. If they are more than an inch away from the standard height, this will result in an automatic disqualification. The length from the breastbone to the point of buttocks should be slightly more than the height at withers, following a ratio of 12:11. The weight for golden retrievers should be between 65 to 75 pounds for dogs and 55 to 65 pounds for bitches.

Head. The skull should be broad with a slight arch laterally and longitudinally without any prominent bones in the forehead or occipital bones. The stop should be well-defined without being abrupt. The foreface should be deep and long, almost the length of the skull. The muzzle should have a straight profile with a smooth, strong blend into the skull. It should be slightly deeper and wider at the stop than at the tip when viewed from the side or above. While it is permitted to remove whiskers, this is not preferred.

Eyes. These should have friendly, intelligent expression. They should be medium in size, set wide apart and reasonably deep with dark, close-fitting rims. Ideally, they should be dark brown, although medium brown is acceptable. Dogs which show signs of a functional abnormality of eyelids or eyelashes are to be disqualified. In addition, faults will be given for slant eyes or narrow, triangular eyes.

Ears. Short with the front edge attached just above the eye and well behind it. They should fall close to the cheek. If you pull them forward, the tip of the ear should just cover the eye. If ears are low and hound-like, this will attract a fault.

Nose. The nose should be black or brownish-black in colour, although if it's cold, a fade to a lighter shade should not be penalised. However, faults will be accrued for pink noses or a nose severely lacking pigmentation.

Teeth. There should be a neat scissor bite, with under or overbites disqualified. If teeth are misaligned, or there is a level rather than a scissor bite, this is undesirable but does not merit disqualification. All teeth should be present, with obvious gaps being a serious fault.

Neck, Topline and Body.

The neck should be medium long, gradually blending into well-laid-back shoulders to give a sturdy, muscular appearance. There should be no throatiness. The backline should be strong and level from the withers to a slightly sloping croup, and this should be the case regardless of whether the dog is standing or moving. Any slope in the backline, a flat or steep croup or a roach or sway back will be faulted. The body should be well-balanced and deep through the chest. The chest area between the forelegs should be at least as wide as a man's closed hand (including the thumb). The forechest should be well developed. The brisket should reach the elbows. Ribs should not be barrel-shaped. Instead, they should be long and well-sprung. They should extend well towards the hindquarters. The loin should be short and muscular with minimal tuck-up. Any signs of slab-sidedness, a narrow chest, a shallow brisket or excessive tuck-up will all attract a fault.

The tail should be thick and muscular at the base and be well set on. It should follow the natural line of the croup. The tail bones should reach but not go below the point of the hock. The tail should be carried with a bright action, either level or with a slight upward curve. It should never curl over the back or between the legs.

Forequarters – These should be muscular and well-coordinated with the hindquarters. They should move freely. Shoulder blades should be long and well laid back, the upper tips placed fairly close at the withers. The upper arms should be roughly the same length as the blades, placing the elbows back beneath the upper tip of the blades, close to the ribs, without being loose. When viewed from the front, the legs should be straight with good bone without coarseness. Pasterns should be short and strong, having a slight slope but no sign of weakness. Dewclaws may be removed from the forelegs but are usually left in situ. Feet should be medium size, round, compact and well-knuckled with thick pads. It is acceptable to trim away excess hair to display the natural size and contours. Faults are incurred for splayed or hare feet.

Hindquarters – These should be broad and strongly muscled. The croup profile should have a slight slope with a greater slope at the pelvic bone approximately 30 degrees from the horizontal. When standing naturally, the femur should join the pelvis at roughly 90 degrees. The stifles should be well bent, and the hocks well let down with strong, short rear pasterns. The feet should be the same as the front. The legs should look straight when examined from the rear. Any cow-hocks, spread hocks or sickle hocks will be faulted.

Coat. The coat should be dense and water-resistant with a good undercoat. The outer coat should be firm and resilient with neither a coarse nor silky texture. It should lie close to the body and can be straight or wavy. There should be an untrimmed natural ruff. The forelegs and underbody should have moderate feathering with heavier feathering on the front of the neck, back of thighs and underside of the tail. The coat on the head, paws and front of legs should be short and even. Any open coats, limp, soft coats, or overly long coats will attract a fault. While feet can be trimmed and stray hairs tidied, the natural appearance of the coat or outline should not be interfered with by cutting or clipping.

Colour. Acceptable colours for golden retrievers are any shade of gold. It is permitted for the feathering to be lighter than the rest of the coat. While greying or whitening of the face and body due to ageing is permissible, any white markings (except for a few hairs on the chest) will be penalised depending on how much there is. Allowable light shadings should not be confused with white markings. The dominant body colour shouldn't be very pale or dark. Some allowance can be given to a light puppy if its colour looks like it'll darken with age. If there is any visible black or other off-colour, this will be considered a serious fault.

Movement. Golden retrievers should trot with a free, smooth, powerful, well-coordinated gait, demonstrating good reach. Legs should not turn in or out, and the feet should not cross or interfere with each other. As the dog moves faster, the feet will converge towards the centre line of balance. It is a good idea to show your dog on a loose lead to best show off its true gait.

Temperament. A golden retriever's temperament is as much a representation of the breed as its appearance. A retriever should be outgoing, reliable, and trustworthy. If there are any signs of aggression towards dogs or people or the dog appears timid or nervous, these are not typical golden characteristics and should be penalised depending on the severity.

Disqualifications.

1. Any deviation from the standard height in either direction.
2. An undershot or overshot bite.

Intelligence

If you want to assess your golden retriever's intelligence, you might like to get a copy of "*The Intelligence of Dogs*". This book has become the standard for rating the intelligence of different canine breeds.

"The Intelligence of Dogs" was written by psychology professor Stanley Coren, a researcher and writer who specialises in the intelligence, mental abilities, and history of dogs. He identified three main categories for judging canine intelligence:

- Instinctive Intelligence – this is a dog's ability to carry out the tasks it was specifically bred for, e.g., guarding, herding, hunting, pointing, retrieving or companionship.
- Adaptive Intelligence – how well a dog can figure out problems by itself.
- Working/Obedience Intelligence – how fast a dog can learn from humans.

While every dog is different, and there are variations within the same breed, the golden retriever is one of the most intelligent breeds. This is why it's used for so many diverse purposes, such as hunting, seeing-eye dogs, search and rescue, etc.

Coren places the golden retriever as the fourth smartest breed for obedience and working intelligence. They're also very good at communicating with their human owners and reading their emotions. Coren's research found that goldens could learn a new command with less than five repetitions. This means you could teach your dog a new trick in 10 minutes. They'll also obey a known command on the first try at least 95% of the time, making them one of the most obedient dogs out there.

British vs American golden retrievers

While golden retrievers are popular around the globe, there are definite differences between British and American goldens, as well as working and show dogs. The reason for this is that although all goldens descend from Sir Dudley Marjoribanks' original stock, once they crossed the Atlantic to America, changes started to evolve. North America and Europe are separated by an ocean, so dogs on the two continents were generally bred with each other. The American and British Kennel Clubs have laid down different standards for the breeds, so breeders in their respective countries are trying to conform to different requirements. In addition, the purpose of a line would also create differences. A dog bred specifically for working will have different priorities than one bred for show.

So, while a golden retriever is still a golden retriever the world over, there will be variations within the breed depending on its origin and purpose. How important are these variations? Well, it depends. An English cream golden retriever fan will claim that these are healthier, calmer dogs than other retrievers. But the Golden Retriever Club of America will counter this by saying that there's no such thing as an English cream golden retriever, and the term is just a marketing ploy. What's more, most English golden retrievers found in America actually derive from other countries like Denmark, France, Ukraine, Hungary, Spain, New Zealand, Australia, and the Netherlands.

Depending on your reason for getting a golden retriever, it may not matter what type you go for. Ultimately, the most important thing is you get a happy, healthy dog sourced from a responsible breeder. If you have a specific purpose in mind, it's useful to be aware of what to look for when choosing a retriever type.

Similarities. Whether you get an American or British golden, working or show, be prepared to deal with shedding. These dogs moult a lot, so be prepared to deal with a lot of fur all over your home.

Retrievers are bred for their even temperament, so you know you're getting a sweet-natured dog when you choose a golden. What's more, they're all intelligent dogs, making them easy to train. They love working and thrive on learning new tricks. They respond well to positive reinforcement and adore earning a treat for making you happy. Be aware that goldens do love their food, though. They can become obese if you allow them to eat too much. This can cause health issues, so make sure you give your dog an appropriate number of calories taking to account any treats given during training.

Differences. Each dog is an individual, so there are always going to be some differences between dogs, even within the same litter. However, there are some consistent variations between the lines. One main difference between British and American goldens is that Americans are more prone to cancer. According to an article on Mercola.com, 60% of American goldens will die from cancer compared to 40% of their European counterparts. As the article states, "Their genes are significantly different, which suggests the risk of cancer in American Goldens is the result, in part, of a fairly recent gene mutation."

According to the standards laid out by the respective Kennel Clubs and detailed earlier in this article, British retrievers can be slightly shorter than their American equivalents. Also, American goldens have to conform to a weight requirement, while British dogs don't. These standards have also resulted in shorter, stockier dogs in the UK and taller, lankier dogs in the States. British golden retrievers are bred for blockier heads than their American cousins with ears sitting lower. American goldens usually have a more sloping topline when compared to British dogs, with shoulders a little taller than the hips.

Another difference between the two continents is the colour. The subset of English cream golden retrievers came about because British retrievers can be light golden or cream, while the American Kennel Club has a preference for dogs which are genuinely gold.

While it is by no means a scientific observation, many British golden retriever owners and breeders claim that their dogs are calmer than American breeds. This is also influenced by whether a dog was bred for show or work. While they're all still retrievers, field-bred golden retrievers were bred to hunt. They're designed to be on the go all day, out in the field retrieving fowl. As such, personality and drive are the most important factor for field breeders.

In comparison, show-quality retrievers are bred to conform to a specific look as laid out by the appropriate Kennel Club. As such, stamina and energy are less important. Field retrievers tend to be smaller and slimmer with wedge-shaped heads. Show retrievers tend to be bigger and stockier with blocky heads. Be aware that just because you get a show golden retriever doesn't mean your dog won't have lots of energy. They still come from a working line and will have that drive to work.

Pet-quality and show-quality

Pet-quality and show-quality are labels used by breeders to describe the type of puppy they produce, but there's a lot of overlap. Experienced breeders will take years to evaluate, select and study their dogs. This helps them identify their expected growth patterns, so they have a certain ability to predict how their litters will turn out.

Don't feel that you're getting an inferior dog if you opt for one which is pet-quality. A lot of the time, the differences between pet and show are so tiny that only a qualified breeder or dog show judge would be able to spot any minor flaws your dog may have.

Most golden retriever owners care more about getting a healthy, well-adjusted puppy than whether their dog could win a dog show. There are some traits which will automatically render a pup 'pet-quality' because it has faults that do not conform to the written standard for the breed. These may include:

- Underbite.
- Overbite.
- Eye colour.
- Coat colour, texture, or markings.
- Height.
- Weight.
- Sold on limited registration so are not allowed to participate in conformation.

Whether your retriever is 'show-quality' largely depends on how closely it matches the breed standards. If you're considering getting a show-quality golden retriever puppy, you'll need to consider many factors, including:

- You may have to wait longer for your pup. Reputable breeders tend to have long waiting lists.
- They cost more.
- Your breeder might require you to sign a contract committing you to show the dog.
- You'll need health clearances.
- Your breeder may be entitled to partial ownership or breeding rights.
- You cannot neuter or spay a show dog.
- You may need to attend conformation classes to learn how to show your dog.
- Your dog will have to conform to a specific look.

- Your dog will have to conform to a specific personality and character.
- Your breeder may require you to hire a professional handler.

20 Golden Retriever Secrets

To round out your knowledge about the golden retriever breed, here are some interesting facts, trivia, and secrets about them:

1. You can usually get an idea of what shade your golden retriever puppy will be by looking at its ear colour. While goldens change colour as they grow, the adult coat rarely strays far from the colour of the puppy's ears.
2. Goldens are one of the few dog breeds that can develop "snow nose". This is when pink spots form on the nose during the colder months. This is down to the breakdown of an enzyme called tyrosinase which produces pigment.
3. If you're looking for a guard dog, you're probably better going with a different breed. Since they're so friendly, retrievers are more likely to bring their ball to an intruder to play than do anything to stop them coming in. Studies suggest that goldens are the sixth least likely breed to display aggression.

4. According to research carried out by the University of California, your golden can get jealous if you don't spend enough time with them. Since they develop strong bonds with their human family, they don't like sharing you with other pets. This also means they can get depressed and suffer separation anxiety if you leave them alone for too long.
5. While golden retrievers are generally healthy, they can suffer from hip dysplasia, elbow dysplasia, hypothyroidism, skin conditions and eye diseases. If you want to keep your dog healthy, feed your dog an appropriate diet and give them plenty of exercise.
6. A golden retriever can take up to 300-400 breaths per minute. If overheated or stressed, they can breathe more heavily to cool themselves.
7. Golden retrievers tend to be at their most active very early in the morning. This is believed to be because they were bred to wake up early to hunt.
8. A golden retriever is capable of something known as 'soft mouth', which enables them to carry lots of things in their mouth without breaking them. They can even carry raw eggs without cracking the shell. This is great because you don't want your retriever to bring you back waterfowl covered in bite marks!
9. Golden retrievers are natural-born actors because they're so biddable. They enjoy showing off and don't feel self-conscious. Combine that with their intelligence and they're the perfect canine movie star. Films featuring golden retrievers include "The Parent Trap", "Homeward Bound", "A Dog's Purpose", and "You've Got Mail".
10. Goldens are often used on search and rescue teams due to their keen sense of smell and excellent tracking abilities.

11. For a long time, the Guinness World Record for a dog holding the most tennis balls in its mouth was held by Augie, a golden retriever from Dallas, Texas. Not only did he hold five in his mouth, but he also gathered them all himself. Since then, another golden, Finley, has been recorded as holding six tennis balls.
12. Another Augie holds the record for being the oldest golden retriever. Born on April 24, 2000, Augie (full name August) passed away peacefully at home in Oakland, Tennessee, aged 20 years and 11 months. Not only was she the oldest golden, but she was also the 19th oldest dog ever.
13. Famous golden retriever owners include Betty White, Ronald Reagan, and Oprah.
14. Goldens are the third most popular dog on Instagram according to hashtags. They're only outperformed by chihuahuas and French bulldogs.
15. A golden called Murphy survived on its own in the California wilderness for almost two years. He went missing while his family were on a camping trip. He was found when someone spotted him and told the family.

16. Todd, a golden retriever, saved his owner from a rattlesnake but was bitten himself. The puppy jumped out in front of his owner when she was about to step on the snake, suffering bites on the nose.
17. While golden retrievers aren't known for being particularly noisy dogs, the loudest bark by a dog was measured at 113.1 dB. The pooch responsible was a retriever called Charlie, who lived in Australia.
18. The LCC K-9 Comfort Dogs is a team of dogs set up to spread love and peace. They are taken to tragic events such as Hurricane Sandy and the Sandy Hook Shooting to give emotional support to those affected.
19. While you might see dogs which look like miniature golden retrievers, there's no such thing as a mini version of the breed. If you do find a mini golden, they're either a cross with a smaller breed or the dog suffers from dwarfism. It's also possible they were bred from runts of the litter, in which case it's best avoided for health reasons.
20. Goldie Palooza, 2018, was held in Huntington Beach, California, on October 14. This was the site of the unofficial world record for the most goldens in one place, with an impressive 681 retrievers attending. This smashed the previous record, which had been sent at a 150th-anniversary celebration in Scotland which attracted 361 goldens

There really is no question that the popular golden retriever has earned its place in the hearts of families the world over. Their attractive, friendly demeanour combined with their eagerness to learn makes them a perfect choice, regardless of whether you're looking for a working dog or a family pet. Now that you have the fundamentals about this adorable breed, it's time to learn more about how you can look after your furry family member so they can be the well-adjusted, happy dog they were born to be.

2. Preparing for Your Puppy

"My fashion philosophy is, if you're not covered in dog hair, your life is empty."

~ Elayne Boosler ~

Before you get your golden retriever puppy, you should consider several factors. Some may seem trivial at first glance, but they'll have a big impact on your decision if you get it wrong. If you've never owned a dog before, you may not realise how much they cost beyond the initial price of a pup. In this chapter, you'll get a full overview of what dog ownership entails.

Are you ready for a puppy?

It's not fair on anyone to take on a dog you can't care for. You won't get the full benefit of canine companionship, your family will struggle to cope, and the poor pup won't get the attention they deserve. That's why it is always helpful to take a serious look at your lifestyle, both currently and how it might look in the next ten to fifteen years. Start by asking yourself some important questions before committing to a puppy:

- Do you have the required time and patience to devote to a puppy who will grow into a dog needing lots of attention, training, and dedication?
- Are you physically active, or are your exercise levels low? For instance, do you go jogging every day and climb mountains at weekends, or would you rather spend your leisure time lounging on the couch?
- Are you a frequent flyer? Would you be better off choosing a dog small enough to travel in the plane cabin with you?
- Are you super tidy? A low or non-shedding breed might make more sense.
- Do you have allergies? Some breeds are more suitable for those who suffer from allergies.
- Do you have a young, growing family who needs your attention? A dog needs a lot of time. What's more, if your children aren't used to dogs, they may not act appropriately around them, which may lead to disaster.
- Are your children old enough to carefully handle a puppy?

- Are you physically fit and healthy enough to be out walking a dog two to three times a day, come rain or shine?
- Can you afford the extra expenses that come with being a conscientious dog owner?
- Is the decision to bring a puppy into your life a decision the whole family gets behind, or are you doing it just for the children, who might quickly lose interest?

- Have you thoroughly researched the golden retriever breed? Do you have a reputable breeder in mind?
- If you haven't raised a dog before, is there someone who can help you with this?
- If you plan to travel without your dog, can you afford to hire a dog sitter, or are you able to make alternative arrangements while you are away?
- Is a golden retriever compatible with your lifestyle? Are you only considering this breed because you had a similar dog when you were a child, or you like the way it looks?
- What is the main reason you want a dog in your life?

Once you've answered these important questions, you will have a much better understanding of whether adding a puppy or dog to your family is going to enhance everyone's life.

Cost of Ownership

If you decide to go ahead with getting a dog, it's time to discover what the true costs of dog ownership might be. While bringing home your new furry friend is super exciting, it is easy to become distracted and quickly skim over the reality of true expenses, so let us take a closer look.

FACT ***The pet industry is BIG business. According to Pet Industry Market Size and Ownership Statistics, dog owners worldwide spent approximately £168 billion ($232 billion) on their pets in 2021. It is estimated that this figure will increase to £254 billion ($350 billion) by 2027.***

Basic supplies, food, and clothing vary in price depending on where you live. In general, estimates have shown that while appropriate yearly canine upkeep can be as low as £2,310 ($3,180) if you're careful with your shopping habits, it could also be much more than you predicted.

To gain a more precise estimate of what the cost of owning a golden might be and whether it is an affordable dog for you, it might be helpful to break down expenses into 'one-off', 'monthly' or 'annual' categories. Note that the following cost estimates suggested are based on average pricing and exchange rates at the time of writing and are likely to change over time. Use this as a guide for you to do your own research.

Bear in mind that many of the noted expenses will vary in price depending on where you live, what is available locally, the age and size of your dog, etc. Some are entirely optional. For instance, canine clothing is quite pricey. However, you might want to sew your own doggy fashions or even avoid dressing your dog at all.

One-Time Cost of Ownership

The initial golden retriever puppy purchase price varies depending on whether you choose to rescue or search out a reputable breeder. Even between breeders, the cost of purchasing your chosen puppy can differ immensely depending on their reputation and experience, as well as market forces. During the lockdown for Covid-19, puppy prices soared, only to crash once restrictions were lifted.

Beyond breeder fees, some numerous hidden costs and expenses aren't always obvious at first glance when initially deciding if adding a dog to your life is an affordable option. Listing average one-time costs help to provide a more realistic picture and would include the following:

- Golden retriever breeder fee: Average £1200-2500 ($1000-3500 in the US).
- Rescue fee: Free to £200 ($250 to $550 in the US).
- Potty-training supplies: £15 to £220 ($20 to $300).
- Lead, collar, ID tags: £87 ($120).
- Bed and crate: £18 to £180 ($25 to $250).
- Food and water bowls: £7 to £36+ ($10 to $50+).
- First vaccinations: £30 to £60 ($40 to $80).
- Microchipping: £11 to £30 ($15 to $40).
- Neutering/spaying: £110 to £365 ($150 to $495).
- Obedience training (optional): £70 to £435+ ($100 to $600+).

Estimated Total One-Time Costs: £550 to £4000 ($750 to $5500).

Monthly and Annual Cost of Ownership

The monthly cost of dog ownership fluctuates significantly between those who choose to spoil their dogs with every available accessory and those who only buy the basics. However, even if you don't opt for any of the optional products or services, there are still many monthly costs to consider.

With the first-year expenses averaging about £1,900 ($2,530), subsequent years will cost £960 ($1,330/year) or £80 ($111/month) after that. Throughout your dog's lifetime, the average cost of owning a golden retriever is £14,000 ($18,160), including purchasing and set-up costs.

This covers all the essential costs. Additional costs, including medical expenses and services such as dog walking, dog boarding, and pet insurance, can all increase the overall cost of ownership.

To put this into perspective, if you use a dog-walking service five times a week for 50 weeks and a boarding service for one week every year, the overall cost of owning a golden retriever could climb to £44,000 in the United Kingdom and between $59,900 and $116,840, with an average of $86,675 in the United States.

The above are average estimates, and the actual costs might be more or less depending on which *optional* items are included and where you source your regular purchases.

Choosing a Breeder

So, you've done all your research, you've carefully considered your lifestyle, and you've decided that a golden retriever is the dog for you. Your next step is to locate a reputable breeder, and there are several ways to determine if you have made the right choice.

If you think you've found a breeder, you'll need to research their reputation. The internet is a valuable resource in this process. If you want feedback from people with first-hand experience, you can post on internet forums discussing breeders.

Carry out as much research as possible about the specific breeder you are considering before making initial contact with them. The more information you have about the breeder, and the more the breeder knows about you, the more successful the match will be. In the United Kingdom, it is advisable to contact your nearest regional golden retriever breed club.

Contact details for all these clubs are available at: www.goldenretrieverbreedcouncil.co.uk.

There is an online puppy sales list on The Kennel Club website with the details of breeders who have puppies for sale at: www.thekennelclub.org.uk/search/find-a-puppy.

Please note that The Kennel Club does not guarantee that breeders on the list are reputable, so bear this in mind and check the breeders out for yourself.

For the United States, a list of golden retriever breeders is available through The Golden Retriever Club of America at: www.grca.org/find-a-golden/where-to-find-a-golden. The club has puppy referral volunteers who can advise you on how to buy your retriever pup from a reputable breeder.

FACT ***Your puppy's personality and temperament are a combination of what they are exposed to during their first few weeks when they are in the breeder's care, the genes inherited from both parents, and how their new owners train and socialise them.***

Once you think you've found a breeder, make an appointment to meet them, either in person or through a video session. This is the best way to get a feeling about the cleanliness of the premises and the breeder's commitment to raising healthy puppies. Meeting the mother and father of your potential new golden puppy can tell you a great deal about what their likely temperament and demeanour will be when they're all grown up.

Visit the breeder several times, observe the parents, interact with the puppies, and ask plenty of questions. This will help you to get a true feeling for the legitimacy of the breeder. These are some questions that you can use as a starting point:

- Why did you decide to breed golden retrievers?
- How long have you been breeding?
- Do you ever show your dogs?
- What do you look for in a home for your puppies?
- Can I visit you and tour your facility?
- Do you own both breeding parents? If not, have you worked closely with both parents?

- How often do you permit your females and males to breed?
- Can I see the other dogs in the kennel?
- Can I observe the dogs and puppies socialising together?
- Are you registered with a local or national breed organisation?
- How old must the puppies be before they can go to their new home? (If the answer is anything less than eight weeks, they are probably more interested in making a profit than the health of their puppies.)
- Do you offer a return policy?
- Will you take a puppy back if it does not work out?
- Do you provide the puppy's pedigree documentation? (Be wary of breeders who ask for an extra fee for papers or those who offer to provide them later via mail.)
- Do you have testimonials from past clients?
- What is the procedure for collecting the puppy?

How a breeder answers these questions can tell you if they are genuinely concerned about the health and welfare of their puppies. If you find the breeder is patient when answering your questions and keen to provide you with all the information you require, this might be a breeder to consider.

Once you are satisfied you have located the right breeder and visited their facility, notice whether they limit the amount of time you are allowed to handle the puppies. A reputable breeder will only permit serious buyers to hold them for health and safety reasons.

Also, be ready to answer any questions the breeder might have for you. A responsible breeder will want to ask their own questions to satisfy themselves you're going to be a good owner for their puppy who will provide them with a loving, forever home.

Health and Medical Questions to Ask

Even the best breeders cannot guarantee the lifelong health of any puppy since once they're in your care, how you look after your dog will have a major impact on their health.

However, they should readily guide a prospective owner and provide plenty of information about the health of the puppy's parents. The breeder must be willing to give you pertinent medical information and answer the following health questions:

- What health conditions typically affect golden retrievers? (Beware if the breeder says there are no health conditions that typically affect the breed.)
- What health tests have been carried out on the parents?
- Have the parents been tested for hip, thyroid, eye, or any other health problems?
- Do the parents or grandparents have any congenital problems?
- Have there been any premature deaths?
- Have the puppies been seen by a veterinarian?
- Who is the breeder's veterinarian?

- Have the puppies been wormed?
- Have the puppies received any vaccinations?
- Can they provide the veterinarian's report on the puppies?

TIP ***Always ask the breeder what shots the puppy has received and when they were last dewormed. In most instances, the pups should have had their first round of shots before they leave their mum. If the breeder has not carried out any of these procedures or they are unable to tell you when the last shot or de-worming was carried out, you might be best advised to look elsewhere.***

Also, ask to see the breeder's veterinarian report on the health of a puppy you are interested in. If they cannot produce this report, again, it may be best to look elsewhere.

Temperament Questions to Ask

When the time comes to pick a puppy from a litter, your breeder should be able to tell you a little about each puppy's unique personality. They're ideally suited to help you make the right selection based on your needs. The following questions could help you choose:

- What are the parents' personalities like?
- Which puppies are friendly, easy-going, and eager to play?
- Which puppies are timid?
- Which puppies are more likely to push the boundaries?
- Have the puppies had any socialisation?
- Have they been introduced to children or other dogs?
- Have they been introduced to other animals?

Return Contract

Any reputable breeder will want you to contact them first in the event of a problem during the life of your puppy. They will also want you to return a puppy or dog to them if your circumstances change and you are unable to continue to care for it. They won't want to see your golden go to a shelter or rescue facility. If the breeder does not offer this type of return policy, think carefully before going ahead with the sale, as no ethical breeder would ever allow a puppy from one of their litters to end up in a shelter.

Reliable breeders offer return contracts since they have a reputation to protect. They want to be certain that if a puppy they have sold has an undetected genetic defect, it will not be allowed to breed and continue to spread the defect, weakening the entire breed.

You'll find that many breeders also offer return contracts because purchasing a puppy can be expensive. If you find your puppy has a worrisome genetic defect, this could cost you a great deal in unexpected veterinarian bills. If this happens, most honest and reputable breeders offer a return policy and will be happy to give you another puppy when available.

A good breeder has nothing to hide and should be more than willing to provide you with testimonials from previous clients. After all, the best recommendation is a happy customer. If you can contact some of the breeder's past clients or ask to have them contact you, this is a good way to ask about their experience with the breeder and the health and temperament of their dog.

Always ask if the puppy you are interested in has displayed any signs of aggression or fear. If this is happening from an early age, you might experience behavioural problems as the puppy gets older.

How to Avoid Puppy Mills

When a dog breed becomes popular, it is sadly common for disreputable, high-profit puppy mills (see picture) or commercial breeding farms to start breeding them. Frequently, a specific dog breed can shoot up in popularity due to what is called the Lassie effect. This is when a dog is featured in a popular movie and becomes highly sought after as a result.

Puppy mill breeding is especially prevalent with cute, smaller breeds, as it takes less space to mass-produce smaller dogs. This inhumane world of canine pregnancy for profit happens all over the world. Unless you are incredibly careful about where and how you purchase your puppy, it is possible to unknowingly end up supporting this disreputable practice.

FACT ***Puppy mills make a major contribution to overpopulation. They produce diseased and/or genetically flawed puppies who might suffer from behavioural and/or health-related problems. These issues cause untold grief and stress. In addition, there are unexpected financial costs due to the increased need to consult a vet. Sadly, a puppy-farmed dog may not live long.***

Puppy-farmed dogs suffer in ways most of us could never imagine. Most of the breeding dogs have never walked on solid ground or felt grass, spending their lives in cramped, wire cages. Females are bred repeatedly until they can no longer produce puppies. They're then sold to laboratories for experiments, killed, or dumped on the side of the road. Pet stores are the main source of these unfortunate puppies in America, who are taken away from their mothers far too young—at 4 to 5 weeks old—and sold to brokers, who pack them into crates to ship them off to pet stores. Many innocent puppies die during transportation. Fortunately, this despicable practice was outlawed in the UK in 2020. Now you can only buy a puppy from someone who has bred the dog themselves. This doesn't mean that you are completely protected from puppy mills though, so do your due diligence on any prospective breeder.

Just like the drug trade, it is difficult to shut down these mass-producing farming operations because of the large-scale, lucrative nature of the business. Although puppy mill puppies are sold in a variety of different venues, there are certain locations to be suspicious of, including:

- Pet stores.
- Flea markets.
- Roadside.
- Beaches.
- Back gardens.
- Newspaper ads.
- Fancy websites.
- Internet classifieds.

Almost all puppies sold in pet stores—whether the employees working there are aware of it—are the result of inhumane puppy mill breeding. The exception to this is "puppy friendly" stores, which source homeless pups from local shelters.

Every time someone buys a golden retriever puppy from a pet store that was obtained from a puppy mill, it encourages the store to order more from the same source. To a store, a puppy is just inventory, no different to bags of dog food. When one item drops off the inventory list, another is purchased to replace it.

The only way to put these reprehensible, commercial businesses out of business is to never buy a puppy from a pet store or any other source unless you've thoroughly checked them out by visiting the facility in person.

It is always sensible to be cautious when answering an advertisement for a low-priced puppy, especially if the person selling offers to deliver the pup. This could be a sign you are about to be involved in an illegal retriever puppy mill operation. Educating yourself and spreading the word to others about puppy mills is the first step towards ensuring no one is ever unwittingly involved in the suffering forced upon the breeding dogs and puppies trapped in a puppy mill or mass farming operation.

TIP ***Consider looking for a golden retriever at a shelter or rescue centre or a responsible puppy-friendly pet store that hosts animals from shelters/rescues for adoption. The shelter will have vet-checked the pup. Not only is it a more affordable option than buying from a breeder, but you're also rescuing a dog from a tough start in life.***

Since October 1, 2018, amendments to the United Kingdom Animal Welfare Act have introduced rules for anyone selling dogs. For example, the sale of two or more litters within the same year requires a licence and the keeping of clear, detailed records. There are also strict rules for advertising dogs for sale, which must include the breeder's licence. These changes are a very strong deterrent for back garden and puppy mill breeders and those illegally importing dogs across borders.

How to Choose a Puppy

Choosing the right golden retriever puppy for your family and lifestyle is probably the most important decision you can make about your dog. Get it right, and you make it easy for yourself to hit the ground running. It requires some serious thought before making your final decision. Although your breeder can often help select the right puppy for you and your family, you might feel particularly drawn to one puppy over another. Or rather, the pup might decide it wants to dominate your time! It's often said that the pup chooses you rather than the other way around. How you feel towards a specific dog in a litter is an important part of deciding which one to bring home, although it shouldn't be the only consideration.

Apart from your feelings, considering the following guidelines will help improve your chances of having a positive relationship with your new golden retriever puppy:

- Be objective when evaluating each puppy in the litter. Try not to let personal feelings get in the way. While looks might be important to you, it's much better to choose a pup for its temperament.
- Do not be exceedingly emotional when picking out your dog, as this could make you choose a puppy who displays extreme behavioural issues—overly shy or aggressive.

- Be aware that while extreme behaviour can sometimes be corrected, often it cannot. Don't rely on being able to coach a dog through it.
- Be careful not to choose a puppy simply because you feel sorry for them. They might have health or emotional issues.

Choosing the Right Temperament

Some people become incredibly emotional when choosing their retriever puppy and are attracted to those who display extremes in behaviour because they want to 'save' them. It isn't a good idea to choose a pup who shows signs of being very shy, frightened, or aggressive in the hope they might grow into a normal, well-behaved dog under your guidance.

It is certainly great that there are people with the capability to raise and care for puppies which might be afflicted with health or behavioural problems. However, these decisions mustn't be undertaken lightly, as such challenges can put you on a rollercoaster of highs and lows, creating emotional and financial problems for both canines and humans alike.

Many minor behavioural problems can indeed be modified with early training. However, be aware that the time and effort required to get your pup to lose a bad habit is difficult to predict. 'Rescuing' a dog with behavioural problems may require the services of a professional dog trainer or psychologist.

Male or Female?

Everyone you ask will have an opinion about whether you should choose a male or a female golden. It does make a difference, so it's worth being aware of a few considerations that could help you make a more informed choice:

- Male dogs tend to want to mark or pee on anything upright when they're on a walk—trees, telegraph poles, tall grass, a stranger's leg. However, a dominant female will also wee to mark territory.
- Even a house-trained male dog can try to lift their leg on furniture when visiting a home where other dogs are present.
- Some breeders will not sell you a female puppy unless you sign a contract promising to have them spayed.
- Compared to spaying a female, neutering a male dog is a less invasive medical procedure and tends to be cheaper as a result.
- Some people choose the sex of their golden retriever because they attribute human characteristics to their chosen dog. You may feel a female dog will have a sweeter temperament, or a male dog could be more independent. This doesn't always follow. Don't confuse your dog with a human. They're still canines and will behave like a dog, no matter how much they're part of the family.

One or Two Pups?

Adding two puppies to your family at the same time may be twice the fun, but it usually results in more than twice the work. You'll need to be doubly alert and patient. Be prepared to lose more sleep than you bargained for during the toilet-training phase.

All puppies need constant attention and guidance. Two puppies mean you'll need to be on the alert even more. Before taking the plunge and committing to two, ask yourself the following questions:

- Do I have the time and energy to give constant attention and guidance to two little retriever puppies who could be running in opposite directions?
- Why do you think two puppies are a good idea?
- Am I choosing two puppies for the right reason, or is it just that I think they'll be cute?

You need to be careful that your reason for getting two puppies isn't so they'll always have someone to play with or your puppy won't be alone while you are at work. While having two puppies *can* be double the fun, it may make more sense to get just one. Some things you might not be aware of include:

- Two puppies are often too much work for a family to handle.
- When they grow up, there might be continual sibling rivalry. As each puppy vies for attention from you, they might not get along with each other as well as they did when they were younger.
- Two puppies who spend all their time together do not always socialise as well with people and other animals because they've had each other for company.
- Each puppy requires individual attention during toilet training as well as when you teach them commands. Having two golden puppies can make it difficult for them to concentrate or focus. For instance, teaching one puppy to '***Sit***' while the other is trying to bite its tail is going to be challenging, to say the least.

- When two puppies grow up together, one will always be more dominant. This could mean neither fully develops their personality.
- Two puppies in the home can focus on one another more than they do you. This results in them bonding far less with you, making it more difficult to train them or establish your leadership.

Most professional trainers or psychologists advise that if you want two puppies, you at least avoid getting them at the same time or from the same litter. This enables you to house train and teach basic commands to one puppy before you introduce another into the home.

Which Puppy from a Litter?

When looking for a stable and well-balanced golden retriever puppy from a litter, consider the following:

- Find one who is friendly and outgoing rather than overly aggressive or fearful.
- Take note of the puppy's social skills when they are still with their littermates. Puppies who interact well with their littermates are far more likely to become easy-going, happy adults who play well with other dogs.
- When the puppies are playing, see which ones are comfortable both on top and on the bottom when play-fighting and wrestling with their littermates. Observe which puppies prefer only being on top. Puppies who do not seem fine with either position usually play well with other dogs when they become adults.

- If the pups have toys to play with, see which ones try to keep the toys away from the other puppies and which ones are happy to share. Those who want to hoard the toys and keep other puppies away might be more aggressive with other dogs over food, treats, or toys as they become older.
- Notice which puppies seem to like the company of the other pups and which seem to be loners. Puppies who like the company of their littermates are more likely to be interested in spending time with other dogs as they mature.
- Observe the reaction of puppies who get yelped at if they nip another puppy or roughhouse too hard. Puppies who ease up when another puppy cries are more likely to calm down if they play too roughly as adults.
- Check if the puppy you are considering is happy to socialise with people. If they will not come to you or display a fear of strangers, this could be an issue when they become adults.
- Notice if the puppy you are considering is comfortable being handled. If not, they may have problems with adults and children during daily interactions, grooming, or visits to the vet.

How to Check if a Puppy is Healthy

One of the most important things you need to do is check whether your prospective golden retriever is both emotionally and physically healthy.

First, ask to see veterinarian reports from the breeder to satisfy yourself that the puppy is in good health and doesn't have any congenital conditions. Once you've decided to share your life with a specific puppy, make an appointment with your vet for a complete examination.

To help you choose a healthy puppy from a litter, here are the common signs of good health:

Ears – Check for any signs of redness and make sure the ears are clean. Dirty ears can mean mites or infections. A healthy puppy with good hearing should react if you clap your hands or snap your fingers behind its head.

Eyes – A healthy golden puppy has bright, clear eyes without crust or discharge. They should react if a ball is rolled past them within their field of vision.

Nose – A healthy puppy breathes quietly without coughing or sneezing. There will be no crusting or discharge around their nostrils.

Body – They look round and well-fed, with an obvious layer of fat over their ribcage. The body should be strong, with good muscle definition. The belly should not be protruding, which may indicate worms or other health issues.

Skin – Part the puppy's fur and check that its skin is clean and smooth without any redness from scratching or flea bites.

Coat – A healthy golden retriever puppy has a clean, full, soft coat with no dandruff, dullness, greasiness, or bald spots.

Genitals – There should be no discharge visible in or around their genital or anal regions. Constant licking of the area might indicate a problem.

Poos – If possible, check the puppy's stools are firm. Loose stools can indicate diarrhoea from sickness.

Energy – A well-rested puppy is alert, energetic and keen to play.

Mobility – A healthy retriever puppy runs and walks normally without wobbling, limping, or appearing to be weak, stiff, or sore.

Considerations for Allergy Sufferers

In the United Kingdom, approximately 10% of pet owners suffer from allergies. Since the Asthma and Allergy Foundation of America has noted that 'as many as 30% of Americans have pet allergies', it is common to be allergic to the pet dander found in cats and dogs. The good news is those who find owning a dog challenging because it might trigger sneezing, wheezing, watery eyes, or even hives in more severe cases, could still enjoy sharing their lives with a retriever by taking a few precautions.

FACT ***It is important to remember that no dog is 100% allergy-free, despite some breeds being dubbed hypo-allergenic.***

It is common knowledge that breeds with non-shedding coats produce less allergy-causing dander. Therefore, choosing a dog with a non-shedding coat and not a golden retriever might be a good option if this is an issue for you. If your heart is set on getting a golden, regularly hoovering and keeping your pooch well-groomed can reduce the amount of dander to an acceptable level.

Canine breeds have quite different coats, and for anyone suffering from allergies, the type of coat a particular breed has could have a significant effect on the severity of any allergies. For instance:

- Curly, woolly coats tend to shed minimally— e.g., Bedlington terrier.
- Shorthaired, thin-coats which are easy to keep clean— e.g., Italian greyhound.
- Soft, curly hair which sheds minimally and tends to produce fewer allergens— e.g., poodle, cross breeds including poodle.
- Hard, wiry coats which don't shed much— e.g., wire fox terrier.
- Straight, silky hair which is less likely to produce high amounts of allergens— e.g., Yorkshire terrier.
- Water-repellent coats. If your golden retriever swims regularly, it will have lower allergen levels and fewer allergen concentrations in its hair, despite its shedding.

For those individuals who suffer from allergies but still want to share their lives with a furry canine friend, there are many purebred terriers and other breeds of various sizes known to produce less dander. While some are hairless or have coats that shed minimally, many breeds fall into the category of being 'allergy-friendly'. The following is a list of some of the most common allergy-friendly breeds:

- American hairless terrier.
- Australian terrier.
- Bichon frisé.
- Bolognese.
- Border terrier.
- Brussels griffon.
- Cesky terrier.
- Havanese.
- Irish terrier.
- Golden retriever.
- Maltese.
- Norwich terrier.
- Poodle.
- Schnauzer.
- Scottish terrier.
- Shih Tzu.
- Tibetan terrier.
- Welsh terrier.
- Wire fox terrier.
- Yorkshire terrier.

Some crossbreed dogs are considered to be 'allergy friendly', particularly mixes with poodles. However, they are not listed above, as it is more difficult to predict the type of coat or amount of dander that might be produced when mixing two or more breeds.

If you are uncertain whether you have dog allergies, an allergist can evaluate you and provide a proper diagnosis. A skin-prick test is the most common way to diagnose a dog allergy. During this test, a small amount of an extract of dog allergen is put on your skin, which is then pricked with a sterile probe allowing the liquid to seep under your skin's surface. You are then monitored for swelling and redness or other signs of a reaction, signalling an allergy. Typically, results are available within 15 to 20 minutes. If you think your symptoms are caused by your dog, it is always a good idea to be tested since they could be the result of another environmental exposure.

If you suffer from severe allergies, the best way to find out your triggers is to have specialised medical tests as well as immunisation therapy.

How to Choose a Puppy That is Better for Allergy Sufferers

If you have allergies to pet hair and dander, how you react around a specific dog can vary greatly. For example, someone with a severe allergic reaction to a Maltese may experience little reaction to a Yorkshire terrier. Every dog is different, as is how an allergic person reacts to a specific dog.

When considering a breed, your reaction will be the deciding factor. It is helpful when searching for the right match to make a shortlist of the allergy-friendly breeds you are interested in and then test each of them to establish which one gives you the mildest allergic reaction.

If you suffer from allergies, before you bring home your golden retriever puppy, you need to find the right match. This means physical interaction by petting and being around the breed to discover how much they trigger your allergy. For example, if you have a friend with a golden retriever, try to visit them and spend time with their dog. Play with the dog, rub their body, and touch your face multiple times. Then, note whether you get any type of allergic reaction shortly afterwards.

Another good idea is to try to interact with the litter when you visit your breeder. Again, touch and play with your chosen puppy and then rub your hands on your face as much as possible. Take an old T-shirt, rub it over the puppy's body and then wear it for a few hours when you get home. If you do not observe any allergic reaction over the next couple of days, then this could be the puppy for you.

Before committing to your golden puppy, check that you can return the dog if it sets off allergies. A responsible breeder or shelter should allow this. Many shelters let you spend one-on-one time before going through with the adoption of a four-legged friend.

Can I Have a Golden Retriever Without Suffering?

Ultimately, the only person who can answer this question is you. Whether you can share your home with a golden retriever without suffering depends on how severe your allergic reaction is to the breed.

Golden retrievers are not considered a hypoallergenic breed due to their shedding. They have a double coat, which is short and dense. The topcoat or guard coat has a wirier texture than the undercoat, which is denser and softer. While not all golden retrievers lose the same amount of hair, they do shed heavily throughout the whole year. During the shedding seasons—autumn and spring—they shed more than normal. This excessive shedding during the year can trigger allergic reactions in many owners. In addition, dogs' fur and dander production change with age. The same adorable puppy which was fine when you first brought them home may trigger severe allergies when it reaches adulthood. This is why it's important to spend time with adult dogs as well as potential pups before deciding if this breed is right for you.

FACT ***Interestingly, for most people, it's not the dog hair or fur that's the trigger. It's usually the dander (flakes of dead skin), saliva and urine that's the problem. This means that any dog can potentially cause an allergic reaction.***

If you have your heart set on a stunning retriever, there are things you can do to determine whether it is feasible. First, you need to evaluate the severity of your allergy. When you have close, physical contact with a golden retriever, you soon find out how quickly or severely your allergy is triggered. Next, if you decide that your symptoms are manageable, taking steps to reduce pet allergens per the advice below should make it possible for you to share your life with this popular dog.

Reducing Pet Allergens

People with highly sensitive immune systems can react in various ways when their allergies are triggered. Symptoms may include:

- Sneezing.
- Postnasal drip.
- Coughing.
- Chest tightness.
- Difficulty breathing.
- Red, itchy eyes.
- Stuffy, itchy, runny nose.
- Itchy skin.
- Rash on the face, neck, or chest.
- Hives.

If you give your golden retriever a daily groom, this will eliminate most of the extra hair that would otherwise end up being shed throughout your house.

All dogs shed dander. A combination of dead skin cells and hair can trigger allergies and asthma attacks. However, there's a lot you can do to reduce pet allergens in your home. These suggestions may make bringing home a golden retriever a viable option:

HEPA Air Purifier – The HEPA filter is a specific type of high-quality air filter that meets the HEPA filter standard. This means it removes at least 99.97% of particles from the air which are at least 0.3 microns in size. These filters are a common component found in air purifiers that filter the air to clean it. A HEPA air purifier (see picture) traps pet dander rather than allowing it to circulate throughout the home.

HEPA Vacuum Cleaner – Regular vacuum cleaner filters aren't designed to trap and hold allergens, so they will circulate them back into the air. Use a HEPA filter vacuum cleaner for a cleaner home.

Closing Air Vents – If your home has air conditioning or forced-air heating vents, closing them can reduce the amount of circulating animal hair and dander. If you can't close all the vents, shutting the ones in rooms where you spend most of your time—especially bedrooms—will help.

Dusting – Dusting as often as possible helps minimise dander, hair, dust mites, and other allergens.

No Dogs in the Bedroom – Ban your dog from your sleeping quarters if you have asthma or are allergic to pet dander. (This is a good rule in general, even if you don't have allergies.)

No Dogs on Furniture – Training your retriever to sleep in their doggy bed rather than lounging on your sofas, chairs, or beds will limit your exposure to dander.

No Dogs in the Car – Most vehicles are relatively small inside. If you have pet allergies, letting your dog travel in your car could trigger a reaction. Keep pets out of vehicles if possible, or at least restrict them to non-upholstered areas where they are farthest from the allergy sufferer.

Hard Floors Instead of Carpets – Replacing wall-to-wall carpets with wood or another hard flooring makes it easier to keep these areas clean.

Frequent Washing of Pet Materials – Regularly hoovering and washing your dog's bed, pillows, blankets, or rugs will reduce allergens.

Personal Hygiene – Changing your clothes after playing with your golden retriever or washing your hands after petting them helps reduce allergic reactions.

Pet Bathing – A study reported in the *Journal of Allergy and Clinical Immunology* compared levels of allergens found in dog dander before and after a five-minute bath and discovered the bath 'reduced the dog's allergen levels by about 85%'. Unfortunately, allergen levels recover quite quickly, returning to normal in about three days. While bathing your dog twice a week is probably excessive, if you use a mild shampoo that does not dry out their skin and coat, washing them once a week will significantly help.

Pet Saliva – If you're unaffected by dog dander, you could still be highly allergic to your dog's saliva. If this is the case, training your dog not to lick people will prevent an allergic reaction. Besides, it's just good manners!

Clothing – If you know you have allergic reactions to pet dander, but you absolutely must have a retriever regardless of your allergic response, you might want to consider putting clothes on your dog, such as a T-shirt or Lycra body suit. Clothing your dog makes their skin less accessible while also containing shedding hair and dander.

Antihistamines, Decongestants, Nasal Steroids – Dog allergies can be treated with these common drugs that block the effects or reduce swelling and calm inflammation.

Allerpet – You could try Allerpet dog dander remover (see picture). This is a liquid, damp-wipe product you apply to your dog, giving you an easy way to remove allergens without having to bathe your dog to remove dander. Additionally, it softens your dog's skin, unlike bathing with shampoo, which may dry or irritate it.

Allergy Shots – While a course of treatment can help some who suffer from dog allergies, these shots do not work for everyone and may take a long time to become effective.

As you can see, being allergic does not necessarily mean you cannot have a golden retriever or that you need to give up one you already have. Learning about minimising pet-related allergens and making some minor adjustments can resolve your problems.

People with allergies can live happily with a dog if they make a concerted effort and commitment to regularly clean and care for their dog and home.

3. Bringing Your Golden Home

"If you don't own a dog, at least one, there is not necessarily anything wrong with you, but there may be something wrong with your life."

~ Roger A. Caras ~

Bringing your new puppy home is extremely exciting. You've probably been dreaming about the arrival of your new furry friend for months—or even longer. Or maybe you fell in love with a retriever pup who needed a home, and now they're suddenly joining your household. Regardless of how you decided to get your new companion, the first weeks with your golden retriever puppy will be a period of adjustment for everyone.

TIP ***Moving to a new home with a new family can be stressful for both you and your golden puppy. You can make the transition easier for everyone by doing a little advanced planning and preparation.***

When you bring your new puppy home, most of the time, dog insurance isn't at the top of your to-do list. With the best will in the world, your pup may have an undetected problem or have an accident. It is always reassuring to know that, in the event of an accident or illness, you won't have to cover large medical bills, so you can stay focused on making sure your retriever puppy feels better. Research dog insurance options and find out what is and is not covered before you buy a policy (see more about insuring your puppy in Chapter 16).

17 Must-Have Puppy Supplies

There are many essential supplies you'll need when you get a puppy. The best way to prepare for their arrival is to get your shopping list in order and go shopping in advance of the happy day when you bring your new family member home. That way, you can know your puppy's needs will be in place so you can just enjoy getting to know them.

Use the following list to ensure you don't miss out on any of the essentials:

1. **Pee pads** – No matter what type of house-training routine you plan to follow, it is always useful to have a package of pee pads on hand while your new puppy is learning where to toilet.

2. **Food** – Most breeders will give you a couple of weeks' supply of the food your puppy has been eating. If you plan to change your golden puppy's food, do it gradually over 5 to 7 days so you do not cause a stomach upset. Begin by mixing a ratio of 25% new food with 75% old food on day 1. On the 3rd day, increase the proportions to 50% new with 50% old, then on the 5th day, change to 75% new and 25% old. Finally, by day 7, your puppy can fully transition to its new food.
3. **Food and water bowls** – Always make sure your retriever's food and water bowls are small enough for them to get close to so they can comfortably eat and drink.
4. **Treats** – Every puppy loves special treats. They are an important part of encouraging good habits during house training or when teaching commands or tricks. The best treats are those with a single ingredient, such as chicken or liver. Freeze-dried ones are easier for your puppy to chew.
5. **Crate or Sherpa** – Every retriever puppy or dog should have their own hard-sided crate. This gives them a quiet haven to retreat to when a busy home is too much or if they need a nap. It is also a good idea to purchase a soft 'Sherpa bag (see picture) for transporting your puppy. Any dog up to 7 kilograms—15 pounds—or less can be easily trained to enjoy travel inside a Sherpa bag.

6. **Collar and lead** – As your puppy grows to full adult size, you'll need to buy a few collars to fit. However, you will probably only need to purchase one lead. Make sure it fits comfortably in your hand, is lightweight and has an easy-to-operate clip on the end that attaches to your puppy's collar.

7. **Soft beds** – While your retriever puppy should always have a hard-sided crate to nap in, it is advisable to give them access to a soft bed (see picture) or two in other areas of your home where they might spend time near you.
8. **Blanket** – When puppies are young, they can get cold. They often appreciate the comfort of a little more warmth, especially when they're adjusting to being away from the rest of their little. A small, soft blanket that is easy to launder is a marvellous addition to your puppy's list of essential items and can be used in their crate, Sherpa, or bed.

9. **Soft toys and a ball** – Your puppy will love a few soft toys (see picture) to play with and snuggle up to in their bed or crate. Most puppies delight in chasing a ball or favourite toy.
10. **Canine shampoo and conditioner** – Your golden puppy will need to get used to having a regular cleansing bath, especially if you have allergies. Familiarising them with baths early on means buying shampoo and conditioner that are specially formulated with the correct pH for your retriever's skin. Be sure not to make the bath water too hot—test it on your wrist—and keep it just above warm.
11. **Non-slip mat** – Since having a bath might not be your retriever's favourite pastime, it is especially important when starting out that you do everything to make the process as comfortable for them as possible. Sinks and bathtubs get very slippery when wet. Putting down a non-slip mat will help keep your puppy's feet stable and make them feel less nervous.
12. **Towels** – Just as we need towels to dry ourselves after a bath, your puppy needs towels, too. It's a good idea to keep two small hand towels and a couple of larger towels to squeeze out excess water and rub your puppy as dry as possible before using a hairdryer to finish the job.
13. **Hairdryer** – If you do not have a hairdryer in your home, buy one, so you can dry your puppy. Puppies and older dogs often get cold very quickly after a bath and begin to shiver. Thoroughly dry their fur immediately after their bath with the hairdryer to prevent this. Keep the temperature

moderate, and do not blow air into their ears or directly into their face. If you can get your puppy used to a hairdryer early in life, they come to enjoy it and might run up to ask you to blow dry them when they hear you drying your hair.

14. **Soft bristle brush** – Brushing is a normal part of keeping your golden's coat in good condition. Establishing a brushing routine with your puppy when they are young will train them to enjoy it.

15. **Daily moist wipes (see picture)** – These are specifically made with the correct pH balance for your dog so you can wipe off dust and debris from the day before bedtime or freshen their face and eyes in the morning.
16. **Nail scissors** – It is important to trim your golden's nails regularly. Starting this routine when your dog is young helps them to accept nail trimming as a regular part of their life. A simple way to introduce your puppy to nail trimming is by buying an easy-to-use pair of nail scissors. All you need to do is snip off the curved tip of each nail. Once your retriever is a few months old and its nails stronger, you can buy a pair of medium-sized, plier-type nail clippers.
17. **Finger toothbrush (see picture)** – Dental health is extremely important for every dog. Getting your puppy used to brushing when they are very young helps them accept this essential healthcare throughout their life. Begin with a soft, rubber finger toothbrush that fits over your finger to get them accustomed to having your fingers in their mouth while you rub their teeth and gums. Once their adult teeth have come through—at approximately 28 weeks—you can graduate to a soft, child's toothbrush and then, for the best clean, a child-size electric brush.

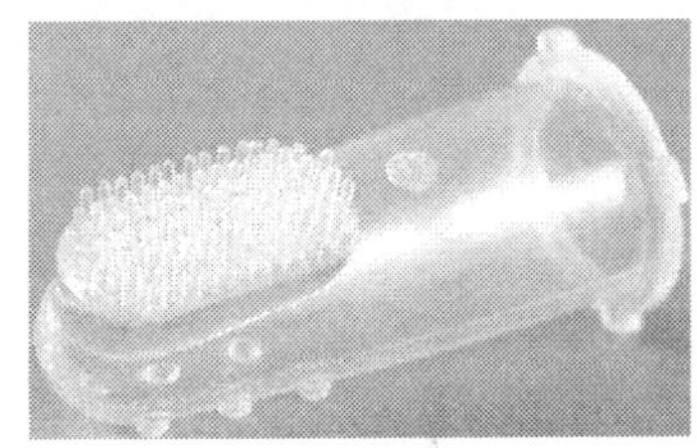

Dogs and the law in the U.K.

Owning and caring for your golden retriever can be great fun and incredibly rewarding. However, it's essential to understand the relevant dog laws to protect yourself, your dog, and others. Here's a basic introduction to your responsibilities:

Animal Welfare

If you are responsible for a dog, even if only temporarily, by law, you must properly care for it and take reasonable steps to ensure its well-being. The Animal Welfare Act 2006 requires owners to provide their animals with a proper diet, a suitable environment, the ability to exhibit normal behaviour patterns, protection from suffering, pain, injury, or disease and meet their need to be housed with, or apart from, other animals.

Taking your dog out

Transport – The U.K. Highway Code states that dogs must be properly restrained when in a vehicle so they cannot distract you while you are driving or injure anyone if you stop quickly. Ensure that you have a seatbelt harness or other suitable method for restraining your retriever in your car, such as a dog guard or crate.

Dogs in hot cars – Never leave your retriever alone in your car on a warm day. In hot, stuffy cars, they cannot cool themselves down – and cars can get deathly hot very quickly. Opening a window or having a sun shield on your windscreen will not be enough to keep your dog cool. Leaving your dog in a hot car could be considered an offence under the Animal Welfare Act 2006. Each year, dogs die in hot cars. Don't risk it.

Keeping them on a lead – It is an offence to have your dog off their lead on all motorways and designated roads. You are advised to you always keep your dog on a lead when on the road to comply with the law and to keep your retriever safe. Several local authorities have made it a statute for dogs to be kept on their leads in certain areas like public gardens and parks. For information on any restrictions in your area, contact your local council.

Cleaning up – In England and Wales, there are laws requiring you to clean up after your dog. Failure to do so could result in a fine. Even if it wasn't the law, it's always a good idea to clear any mess your dog makes for health and safety reasons. Make sure you have plenty of poo bags whenever you and your golden retriever are out. Ensure you dispose of the bags properly and don't just leave them on the ground.

Identification

Collar and tag – The Control of Dogs Order 1992 stipulates that your dog needs to wear a collar and tag when in public. The tag must have your name (not your dog's!) and address on it. (Your house number and postcode are sufficient.) Your telephone number is optional but could make it easier for you to get your dog back if you lose it. If your dog goes out without a collar, it may be caught and treated as a stray. Keep your contact details on the tag up to date. You may be fined if you don't. If you move home or change your telephone number, you need to update those details as soon as possible.

Stray dogs – If your golden retriever goes missing, inform your local authority as soon as possible. They are responsible for strays and might charge a fee to reclaim your dog if they find it. If your dog is not claimed within seven days, they have the right to rehome or euthanise them. Telling them you've lost your dog increases the chances of you being reunited. Up-to-date identification makes it easier for anyone finding your dog to contact you. If you have pet insurance, your insurance company may require you to inform your vet practice as well. Check your policy.

Microchip – Since 2015 in Wales and 2016 in England, by law, all owners must have their dogs microchipped if they are over eight weeks old. Your breeder should arrange this before they send your pup home with you. If you adopt from a shelter, they may also sort this out for you.

Control of dogs

Livestock worrying – Your golden retriever must never be allowed to worry livestock—you, or whoever is responsible for your dog while out, are committing an offence if your dog chases, attacks, or causes suffering to livestock. Your dog could be seized by the police if they're suspected of worrying livestock. If convicted of an offence, you could be liable to a maximum fine of £1,000. There is also the possibility that your dog may be shot by the farmer. The law allows for this if there's no other way of stopping your dog from bothering livestock. Keep everyone safe, and make sure your dog is on a lead whenever they're around livestock.

Dangerously out of control – Under the Dangerous Dog Act 1991, it is a criminal offence to allow your golden retriever to be 'dangerously out of control' whether out and about or at home. A 'dangerously out of control' dog is a dog who has injured somebody or it might be reasonably believed it will injure someone. Ensure your retriever is always under control. Something as seemingly benign as your dog chasing, barking at, or jumping up at someone could lead to an investigation. If your retriever injures someone, they could be seized. If convicted of having an out-of-control dog, you may face a lengthy prison sentence and/or a fine. There is a possibility your dog could be euthanised unless you can convince the courts that your golden is not a danger to the public. In this instance, your dog might be subject to a control order. You should also be aware that it is a criminal offence for your dog to attack an assistance dog.

If you live in Germany, be aware that dog ownership is taxed instead of requiring a licence. Breeds held to be 'dangerous' are subject to higher taxes.

Dogs and the law in the U.S.

Most American states and municipalities have licensing laws in place. If you live in Australia, Canada, Ireland, or New Zealand, you also need a licence for your dog. Legal regulations in the U.S. vary between states. Many fines are issued for violating the legal regulations relating to:

- The transport of dogs.
- Behaviour in public.
- Having an escape-proof fence around your dog's exercise area.
- Providing safe access to your front door.
- Putting a collar and lead on your dog in public.
- Safely controlling your dog in public.
- Mistreatment, cruelty, or failure to properly care for your dog.
- Cropping your dog's tail or ears.
- Not cleaning up after your dog.
- Putting a muzzle on a dangerous dog.
- Owning a banned breed.
- Excessive barking.
- Chasing livestock or wildlife.
- Destroying property.

You can verify the local dog laws for the state you live in here: www.animallaw.info/content/state-dog-laws.

Puppy Proofing

Most puppies are a delightful bundle of exuberant energy, keen to explore and experience the world around them, which means they'll soon find their way into everything around them. Before you bring your golden puppy home, take time to assess the safety of its new environment.

If you're going to provide an appropriate environment for your new puppy, you'll need to take a serious look around your home from the perspective of a curious puppy.

TIP ***A young puppy has a much lower vantage point than you. There might be things in their new home that are potentially harmful. You might not immediately notice these hazards unless you get down on the floor and have a good look around.***

Crawl around the floor to identify and eliminate any sources of danger. Take the same precautions you would for an inquisitive toddler. If you have children, it can be fun to get them involved in doing this.

For example, power leads can be found in every room in the home. To a curious, teething retriever puppy, these look like irresistible, fun chew toys. Tuck all electrical leads securely out of your puppy's reach or put them inside a chew-proof PVC tube.

Puppies and dogs familiarise themselves with their environment through sniffing, touching, or tasting things. Your young golden retriever will want to investigate every electric cable, closet, shoe, and dust bunny. In short, they're going to want to experiment with anything left on the floor. You'll need to take care to remove anything that could be a choking hazard for an adventurous young pup.

When you first bring your puppy home, you can close off some rooms to let your fur baby slowly get used to their new space.

Kitchen –many human foods are harmful to dogs. Your kitchen should always be off-limits to your puppy whenever you're preparing food. Calmly send them out of the kitchen any time you are in there, and they will quickly get the idea that this area is out of bounds.

Bathroom – bathroom cupboards, drawers, and any low surfaces such as the side of a bathtub can hold many dangers for your golden puppy. Tissues, cotton balls, cotton buds, toilet paper, razors, pills, soap, or other materials left within your puppy's reach could result in an emergency visit to your veterinarian. Family members need to keep shampoos, soap, facial products, make-up, and accessories out of reach or safely tucked away in a cabinet or drawer.

Bedroom – if you do not keep your shoes, slippers, and clothing safely behind doors, you could find that your puppy will use them as chew toys. Be vigilant about keeping everything safely in containers or drawers, including items small enough to swallow, like jewellery, hair ties, bank notes, coins, etc.

TIP ***If you have children, make sure they understand the importance of keeping their bedroom tidy, especially when your golden retriever puppy is teething. Be vigilant that they don't leave anything that may pose a choking hazard to your puppy within their reach.***

Living Room – Many of us spend hours watching TV or playing games in our living areas. Often, these rooms have many enticing items for a nosey, teething puppy, including books, magazines, pillows, tablets, mobiles, TV remotes, etc.

Office – if you spend a lot of time in your home office, your puppy will want to be with you. They'll be interested in the contents of your office, such as papers, books, magazines, and USB cables. Although your puppy might think that elastic bands or paper clips are fun toys, leaving them within their reach could result in a fatal game if your puppy swallows them.

Plants – plants can be a very tempting target for your puppy's teeth, so keep them well out of reach. If you have plants on the floor, move them to a shelf or worktop or place them behind a closed door until your golden grows out of chewing everything in sight. You should also know that many houseplants are poisonous to dogs (for more information, see Chapter 15).

Garage and Garden – there are many dangers for your golden puppy lurking in your garage or garden. These include antifreeze, petrol, fertilisers, rat poison, weed killer, paint, cleaners and solvents, grass seed, bark mulch, and insecticides.

If you store any of these toxic substances in your garage or garden shed, make certain you keep them inside a locked cabinet or stored on high shelves so your golden puppy cannot get to them. Even better, go organic and don't use toxic chemicals anywhere in your home or garden.

As you can see, time spent wandering through your home to identify potential dangers is a good investment. Here are some additional tips for puppy-proofing your home:

- Put cleaning products in a locked cabinet or store them where your golden retriever puppy cannot get to them.
- Store all rubbish in a bin with a tight-fitting lid or keep it out of sight in a cupboard.
- Store open food containers in a fridge or cupboard—put a lid on anything left out.
- Keep the floor clear of small objects—they're a choking hazard for your adventurous retriever.
- Cover open sources of water—the toilet, bathtub, outdoor ponds, swimming pools, etc.
- Put all medications and other toiletries out of reach.

- Keep windows and external doors securely closed while your puppy is roaming about.
- Use baby or pet gates to keep your retriever away from out-of-bound places (see picture).
- If you have a cat, keep their litter box where your puppy cannot reach it so they do not eat the poo.
- Dispose of all food waste properly so your puppy cannot get it. This is particularly important for chicken bones and any food that can be harmful to your golden.
- Store lawn and garden tools where your puppy cannot get to them. Make sure they won't fall over if your retriever knocks into them.
- If you have a garden, consider securely fencing it to keep your puppy in.
- Never leave your golden alone in your back garden. Even a fence may not stop a motivated, inquisitive puppy who could be smart enough to figure out an escape route.
- Avoid the use of toxic chemicals such as fertilisers, pesticides, or herbicides anywhere your puppy could encounter them—this includes toxic carpet and floor cleaning products.
- While your puppy is very young, if you cannot closely watch them—for example, when taking a shower—confining them in a safe place such as their crate is a good idea.

Naming Your Puppy

You might have decided on a name for your new golden retriever puppy before you bring them home.

If you haven't picked a name, this is one of the first things you need to deal with, so you can get them used to responding to it.

While choosing a name can be fun and involve the whole family, you might want to think about what the puppy will look like when they are fully grown rather than letting the children call them 'SpongeBob' after their favourite childhood cartoon.

As you get to know your pup better, certain traits will emerge as their personality emerges. This might give you inspiration for a name. For example, they might love running up and down the hallway as fast as possible. You might then call them something like 'Racer'.

Their name is going to be with them for life, so avoid choosing one you'll later regret. For instance, calling them 'Nipper' when they are going through their teething stage or 'Fluffy' when they are still in their fluffy, puppy coat might not be appropriate.

Ultimately, the name you choose will depend on your puppy and your preferences.

Introducing Your Golden Retriever to Your Home and Children

Even the most outgoing golden retriever puppy will be nervous about new and unfamiliar faces, smells, and surroundings. They'll also be missing their mother, siblings, and the environment they were used to during their first 8 to 10 weeks of life.

Don't overwhelm your new puppy by exposing them to too much all at once. Closing off rooms they do not need access to and encouraging your puppy to stay with you as you wander about in a smaller space might be less stressful for them.

Even before your golden puppy comes home, you can help make introductions go smoothly by explaining to your children that they must be calm, quiet, slow and gentle until the puppy gets used to them.

If your children are very young, they may want to pick up your little puppy and carry them around like a stuffed toy. Discourage this for the safety of your golden puppy.

Toddlers can sometimes squeeze a puppy too tightly or drop them. They might also scream in excitement, which can scare your puppy and make them afraid of children. When introducing your small puppy to your small children, monitor them closely and limit exposure to very young toddlers.

Introducing Your Puppy to an Older Cat or Dog

When introducing your golden puppy to an older cat or dog, take care and be ready to protect them from sharp cat claws or a bigger dog who might feel jealous.

TIP ***Most puppies are extremely excited when greeting another animal and can be naturally boisterous. A cat who has never encountered a puppy before or just does not appreciate their bouncy nature could retaliate with hissing and sharp claws. This is where you need to be vigilant to make sure nobody gets upset or suffers an injury.***

Introducing your small golden retriever puppy to an older dog requires a slow and steady approach until the puppy has been accepted into the pack and is not in any danger. Often, it is your puppy who will be over-excited to see another dog. If the older dog has little tolerance for an energetic puppy, they might respond with a growl or a snap if your puppy gets too close (for more tips on how to introduce your pup to another cat or dog, see *Behaviour with other pets* in Chapter 6).

The First 24 Hours

Before you pick up your golden retriever puppy from the breeder, there are a few last-minute tasks to consider:

- Hoover your floors.
- Do a final sweep of every room in your home to make sure every potential puppy hazard is carefully tucked away out of sight and nothing is left on the floor or on easily reached areas where your inquisitive puppy might get into trouble.
- Close most of the doors inside your home, giving your puppy access to just one or two rooms. Keep it like this for the first few days while your golden gets used to their new home.

- You should already have been shopping for everything you need, so lay out some puppy pee pads for when you bring your new furry friend home.
- Place your golden's soft bed in an area where you spend most of your time and where your puppy can easily find it.
- Take your puppy's first toy with you when you pick them up.
- Have your hard-sided crate or soft-sided 'Sherpa' travel bag—lined with pee pads—when you go to collect your puppy. Securely fasten it to the seat of your vehicle with a seatbelt. Even though it is tempting to hold your new puppy in your lap for the drive home, not only is this a dangerous place in the event of an accident, but it is also illegal in the U.K. and other countries.
- Ask a friend to drive you, so you can sit with your puppy in the backseat. If your puppy cries during the journey, soothe them by talking in a soft, reassuring voice.
- Before taking your golden puppy inside, bring them to where you want them to go to the toilet and wait long enough for them to at least wee. Praise them when they do.
- Once indoors with your new golden retriever, this routine will help them to get used to their unfamiliar surroundings:
- Show them where their food and water bowls are in case they are hungry or thirsty.
- Let them wander around, having a good sniff of their new surroundings. Encourage them to follow you where you go.
- Show them where you've put the puppy pee pad. Make sure you place it either near the door you will use to take them outside to wee or poo or near their indoor toilet. Many pee pads are scented to encourage your puppy to wee.
- Show them their hard-sided crate and put them inside with the door open while you sit on the floor in front of it. Quietly encourage them to relax in their crate. If possible, practise this crate exercise several times throughout the day. If you give them a little treat each time you entice them to enter their crate, this will help encourage them to go inside.
- Take a break from exploring and sit quietly with them. This is a good time to allow your children to slowly approach and gently greet your puppy. The puppy will probably be tired out and feeling sleepy.

After your pup has had its evening meal, roughly 20 minutes later, take them outside to go to the toilet. When they do, make sure you praise them enthusiastically and give them a small treat.

Sleep time – Before it is time for bed, take your puppy outside for one last short walk. Go to the same place where they last went to the toilet and make sure they wee before bringing them back inside. Before your pup settles down for the night, prepare a hot water bottle for your retriever puppy and wrap it in a towel so it is not too hot for them and place it inside their crate. Remember, they are used to snuggling up to their warm mother and other puppies, so the water bottle might help them fall asleep. You can make their crate even cosier with a soft lining, blanket and/or a toy.

Turn the lights down and encourage them to go inside their crate. Let them walk into the crate by themselves, then give them a little treat. Persuade them to settle down while you sit on the floor in front of their crate. Once they're comfortable, turn all the lights off, close the door, and leave them. Quiet, soothing music playing in the background might also help your puppy to sleep on their first night home.

If they cry or whine, be patient. This is the first time in their young lives that they're alone, away from the comfort of their mother and siblings. Do not immediately let them out of the crate. Instead, reassure them with calm, soothing words, so they know you are with them, and go back to sleep.

Unless you want your dog to sleep on your bed as a large adult, bringing their wet or dirty feet with them, now is the time to use a little tough love. Don't be tempted to let them sleep outside their crate, even though they might prefer sleeping next to you.

It is not recommended, but if your pup isn't settling in its crate, one option is to place it on your bed if you have space. This could help your puppy get to sleep because they've got you next to them, but they're still safe inside their crate. Over time, they will become used to their crate so you can move it to the floor.

BEWARE: If there is any danger of the crate falling off the bed during the night, do NOT use this technique. You will traumatise your puppy and make them afraid of its crate.

How Can I Help My Scared Puppy?

Understandably, your golden retriever puppy might sometimes seem afraid or nervous about its new surroundings when they first come home. If your family stays calm, this fear usually passes quickly. In the meantime, there are a few things you can do to help your anxious puppy deal with these feelings:

- Use a soothing tone when you speak to them.
- Engage them with a distracting game or toy.
- Keep them close to you until they begin to relax.
- Play relaxing music.
- Do not shout, and avoid making any sudden, loud noises.
- Keep interaction with other animals and people to a minimum until they've had a chance to settle down.

The First Few Weeks

The first week with your new golden retriever puppy is the best opportunity to establish a routine that works well for both of you. You should take this time to get used to your puppy's needs while they become familiar with your usual schedule.

TIP ***Try to be consistent with your waking and sleeping routine. Getting up and going to sleep at the same time each day makes it easier for your puppy to establish a routine in their new life.***

First thing in the morning, take your pup from their crate. Immediately go outside so they can relieve themselves in the same place as before. Do this quickly, as they might not be able to hold it for very long after waking up. If you are training them to use an indoor toilet, take them there.

If you are teaching them to ring a bell to go outside, lift their paw to ring it before you go out the door with them, whether you are carrying them or they are walking.

Before you bring them back inside, attach a lead to their collar and let them follow you, so they get used to being on a lead. Be careful not to drag your puppy if they stop or tug on the lead. It will take a while for them to get used to being on a lead.

Now your pup can enjoy its first feed of the day. Twenty minutes after they have finished eating, take them outside or to their indoor toilet to relieve themselves.

When your retriever puppy isn't eating or sleeping, it will want to explore and play with you. When you play together, you start building a close bond. As their new owner, it is your responsibility to keep a close eye on them throughout the day, so you can spot the signs of their needing to go to the toilet.

You need to ensure your pup eats and drinks enough, so establish regular feeding times four times a day. In addition, set specific times in the day to take your golden out for a little walk on their lead. This way, they don't just go outside for toilet breaks but get to explore their neighbourhood and become familiar with new scents and sights. Meeting new people and other animals will also help socialise your pup.

Don't walk your puppy for long when they're still very young since they tire easily. Similarly, too much exercise when they are young can stress growing joints and bones. Keep walks to no more than 15 or 20 minutes during the first week. If your puppy seems tired or cold, pick them up and carry them home. Next time, have a shorter walk and put a coat on them.

Within the first few weeks, your golden puppy will change so much. You'll notice how they've adapted to their new routine and how much you have already accomplished together.

First milestones might include their first visit to the vet, their first bath and teeth brushing, their first full night's sleep in their crate, and the first time they rang the bell to let you know they wanted to go outside.

FACT ***Whining and crying are your puppy's ways of letting you know they need something or are unhappy.***

Show patience, compassion, and understanding when your puppy is upset. Working out the root cause of the crying and then solving the problem is the best way to help them. There could be many reasons why they are whining or crying, including:

- They need time to adjust to being taken away from their mother.
- They are lonely.
- They do not want to be alone in their crate.
- They are afraid or nervous.
- They are hungry or thirsty.
- They want affection.
- They want a walk or playtime.
- They want a toy.
- They need to go to the toilet.
- They are bored.
- They feel unwell.

It will take time for your retriever puppy to adjust to its surroundings and learn the new rules and expectations. While their crying or whining can be annoying, yelling or becoming frustrated will only make things worse. The good news is that whining and crying do not usually last long, as dogs are fast learners and want to please their owners. Staying calm and patient during this early stage is the start of developing a strong bond between you and your golden retriever.

During the next few weeks, there will be many new things you need to familiarise them with, including:

- Different sounds, such as the doorbell, telephone, hairdryer, hoover, music, etc. This should be a positive experience. Introduce new sounds slowly, if possible, play with your puppy so they will not be frightened when they hear the noise, and offer a treat reward when they do not run away.

- Stairs and other terrains. These can be difficult for your golden retriever puppy. Gently encourage them to work out how to tackle obstacles without injuring themselves.
- Travelling in a vehicle. At first, this might be daunting for your young puppy. Get them used to being inside their crate in the car before you go anywhere. Then start the engine and leave your car running for a while. Next, take a short trip around the neighbourhood until you are sure they are comfortable in the car.
- Being handled by people. Getting your puppy used to being handled is important as they must be taught to accept being picked up and handled during grooming, or it's time to go to the vet. Get them used to being on a table or worktop early on, so they will not be afraid when they receive an essential treatment.
- Bonding with family members is also important during the first few weeks of your golden puppy's life. Each family member should spend time socialising with the puppy and get involved in the daily care of the dog.

4. Crate & House Training

"When the dog looks at you, the dog is not thinking what kind of a person you are. The dog is not judging you."

~ Eckhart Tolle ~

A dog crate is an enclosure made from metal, wire, plastic, or fabric where your golden retriever can be kept for protection or transportation. Dog crates are designed to resemble a dog's natural den and provide a safe place for them in their home or when travelling.

Although some people can feel guilty about crate training their canine friend, enclosed spaces form a haven for your golden to relax and rest. Most dogs instinctively hunt out small spaces as a protective shelter. Crates are useful training aids for puppies, safe refuges for senior dogs, and lifesavers for many emergencies.

FACT ***Most vets, dog trainers, and breeders recommend crate training golden retrievers from about 8-10 weeks old.***

Crate training is an essential part of house training your puppy. Dogs, like people, do not like to soil their sleeping quarters. Being in their crate helps them to learn to hold their bladder, so you do not have to clean up their mess. Once your puppy has learnt to accept sleeping in their crate at night-time, this will accelerate their toilet training.

Contrary to what some people believe, a crate is not a canine prison cell. When appropriately trained, a crate will give your puppy or dog a calm, secure, relaxing space where they feel safe and comfortable. They'll love it the way you do your special chair or favourite place to relax.

Early crate training is always a good idea for any puppy because it can be used in various situations. There are so many benefits for both owner and puppy, including:

- A refuge from a noisy or busy home.
- A secure place to sleep at night.

- Safe aeroplane transportation when small.
- A quiet haven for a relaxing daytime nap.
- Protection from harm when home alone.
- A safe place while travelling in a vehicle.
- A protected area for post-surgery recovery.
- A helpful tool for house training.

Choosing a Dog Walker or Daycare

Much as you love your dog, there will be times you'll need to leave them, such as when you go to work. If you need to regularly leave your golden retriever alone for more than 4 hours and do not have a friend or family member to help, get a dog walker to break up their day. Alternatively, you could put them into doggy daycare. Left unattended for more than three hours in a crate can be considered animal cruelty under RSPCA guidelines.

A dog walker comes to your house, takes your dog for a walk, and brings them home again. They will usually need a key to let themselves in and out of your home at the agreed time(s).

A dog walker allows your golden to get out and go to the toilet, enjoy some fresh air and exercise, and give them company before you come home.

If you are looking for a dog walker, start by asking for recommendations from other dog owners in your area. Here is a checklist of questions to ask a potential dog walker:

- Are you independent or part of a company?
- Can you show me proof of insurance? Do you have any relevant qualifications, such as dog first-aid?
- Can I see reviews or references from other clients? If the walker or organisation has a website, you may be able to find reviews there.
- What do you use to transport dogs if you need to? Check these are clean, secure, and well-ventilated. In addition, each dog should have a separate compartment.
- What alternatives do you have in place should you be unable to walk my dog for any reason?
- How do you plan to safeguard my keys and home security?

If you think you've found a suitable, reliable dog walker:

- Introduce your dog one-on-one to the walker. Your golden retriever must trust the walker. In turn, the walker needs to be familiar with how your dog usually behaves.
- Clarify whether your dog needs to be walked alone or would prefer being walked with either a couple of dogs or a large group of dogs.
- If the latter is the case, check if the other dogs are vaccinated and up to date with flea and worming treatment.

If you enrol your golden retriever in a daycare centre, your dog might receive less one-to-one human attention. The flip side is that they will have the opportunity to interact with other dogs and won't be bored. If they are already familiar with other dogs at the daycare, this can help them adjust and settle in. Here is a checklist of things to ask a potential dog daycare centre:

- Do you have any reviews or references I can look at? Check online for reviews and ratings as well.
- Can I see your local authority licence? Since 2018, dog daycare providers in the U.K. have been required by law to be licensed by their local authority. This guarantees they are trained to a minimum of an OFQUAL-regulated Level 2 qualification in a relevant subject, such as canine behaviour, or have clear evidence of knowledge and experience.
- Can I visit your facilities and get a tour? As you look around, consider whether they are spacious, clean, and well-organised. Do they have water readily available? There should be separate play and rest sections so your dog does not become over-tired. If there are any dogs there, they should appear contented and upbeat.
- Are all attending dogs checked for up-to-date vaccinations and insurance?

In turn, the daycare centre should ask you about your dog's behaviour. For example, how does your golden retriever interact with other dogs and new people?

Choose a day-care which offers professional, friendly service. A love of dogs is important.

Check the centre's policy about what to do if a dog fight breaks out. With several dogs playing together, occasional altercations will break out. They should be happy to let you know their procedure.

Crate Training

There are different sizes, styles, materials, and types of crates (see picture). If you enjoy interior decorating, you could integrate a custom-built dog crate into the design of your home, perhaps underneath a staircase or in a built-in cupboard or cabinet.

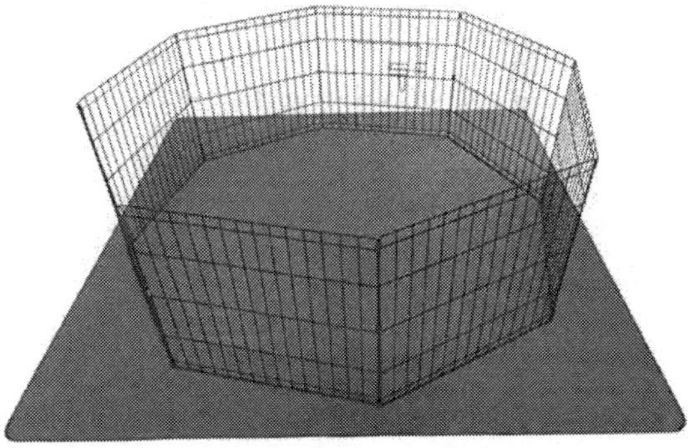

Dog crates are available in a variety of sizes. The most common are 60, 75, 90, 100, and 120 centimetres (24, 30, 36, 42, and 48 inches). Some brands offer slightly different sizes, but these are the standard sizes.

The best type of crate for the home is a wire crate. These are easy to store because they are collapsible, provide great puppy visibility, and typically come with a metal divider allowing you to adjust the crate size to fit your puppy as they grow. Once you have your crate, slowly introduce your pup. Rushing the crate-training process could create trauma or puppy anxiety that will take a long time to heal.

Top 20 Crate Training Tips

The following steps will help train your new golden puppy to see their crate as somewhere they want to be:

1. Choose a crate where your puppy can stand up and easily turn around inside or lie down with outstretched legs when they are fully grown. For a fully grown male golden retriever, a 100-centimetre (42-inch) one would probably be most suitable. If you have a female retriever, you

may be able to use a 90-centimetre (36-inch) crate. Note that placing your tiny puppy in a very large crate might encourage them to use a corner away from their sleeping area to do their business. If the crate is large enough to accommodate your puppy when they are an adult, simply block off the back half of the crate to make it smaller until they need the extra space. Some crates are adjustable for precisely this reason.

2. Place the crate in a quiet place away from family activity, heating vents, direct sunlight, cables and plants.
3. Place a vet bed in the bottom of the crate and put soft bedding on top of it. Vet beds are tough and durable mats vets use in their post-surgery recovery and treatment rooms. They are made from double-strength polyester. They are designed to allow extra warmth and increased airflow around your dog, so they don't get overheated or uncomfortable.
4. When you first start using the crate, sit on the floor beside the open crate door to keep your puppy company.
5. Leave the door open and place a favourite chew toy and a treat just inside to encourage them to go in—you can also hold these in your hand to entice them to enter the crate.
6. Praise them when they enter the crate on their own. Next, persuade them to step inside to get another treat and give them lots more praise.
7. Feed your puppy their meals inside the crate. If they seem anxious about entering, initially place their food bowl close to the door and then gradually move it farther and farther inside the crate.
8. When your golden puppy is happy to eat their meals inside the crate, close the door while they eat and open it when they finish.

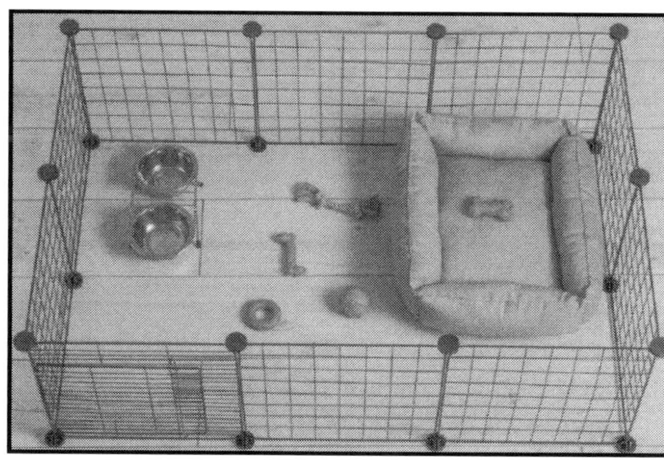

9. Gradually increase the time your puppy spends in their crate with the door closed. Place a treat, toy or food puzzle inside and close the door behind your pup for about 15 to 20 seconds.
10. If there are no signs of stress—crying, whimpering—and they seem happy to play with their toy or puzzle, increase the time to 30 seconds and slowly build up to 1 minute, 5 minutes, 10 minutes etc. Always stop if your puppy seems anxious and stay within sight.
11. When you open the door to let your puppy out, don't let them rush out of the crate. Tell them to stop and sit at the entrance, so they relax before slowly emerging.
12. Once your puppy is content with being in its crate for several minutes, you can start to move farther from it. Your ultimate goal is to go to another room for a few seconds before returning to where they can see you.
13. If they do not make a fuss or start to whine or bark when they see you return, open the door, and give your puppy a treat.
14. Slowly increase the amount of time you are out of sight while your puppy remains calm, quiet, and comfortable in its crate.
15. Further, increase the time when your puppy is alone in the room in their closed crate. Aim to eventually leave them for up to 60 minutes.

16. Always remove collars, clothing, and anything that may be a choking hazard before putting your puppy in the crate, so there is no chance of it getting caught on anything that might cause discomfort or fear.
17. When your dog is used to spending time in the crate, you can use it for longer periods, such as overnight or while you are out. Leave them with an enrichment feeder or safe toy to keep them occupied. This will prevent your dog from getting bored. However, never leave your golden alone in their crate for more than three to four hours at a time during the day.
18. Avoid emotional and prolonged departures. Give your retriever praise and a treat for entering their crate, then leave without a fuss. If your dog is acting excited when you return home, do not reward them by responding enthusiastically. Ignore them until they calm down.
19. If you are on a budget and prefer to buy just one crate, go for one big enough for an adult dog and reduce the size for your puppy by using crate dividers or a box in the crate. As your dog grows, you can adjust the size of the crate.
20. Your golden puppy can safely be left in the crate for a certain amount of time, depending on their age. Consult your veterinarian for a specific recommendation, but here's a general guide to the amount of time you can leave your puppy in a crate:

Age of the Puppy	Maximum Time in Closed Crate
9 – 10 weeks	30 to 60 minutes
11 – 14 weeks	1 to 3 hours
15 – 16 weeks	3 to 4 hours
17 + weeks	3 to 5 hours

A crate is not a magical solution to behavioural problems. If used inappropriately, your golden retriever will feel trapped and frustrated. For example, if your dog is left in the crate all day while you are at work and then all night while you sleep, they are spending too much time in a confined space. If you need to use a crate to keep your dog safe during the hours you are at work, try to go home for visits or consider hiring a dog walker. Make every possible arrangement to accommodate their physical and emotional needs. Not only is this best for your dog, but you are also legally obligated to provide them with an appropriate environment and could get in trouble if you don't.

You should practise crate training after your golden has been exercised and is tired so they are ready to relax or sleep inside their comfy crate. By now, you should know the signs of your dog unwinding and looking forward to being in a safe place where good things happen. They might even choose to rest in the crate of their own volition if they feel content there.

While they're in their crate with the door closed, give your dog tough, rubber toys that can be filled with food they can slowly lick out or long-lasting, tasty chews to give them different reasons to enjoy spending more time in their crate.

The more you invest the time to get your dog accustomed to their crate, the more you will be free to attend to other household activities while your dog is inside their crate. This will also come in handy when you have visitors who are worried about dogs, and you need to pop your golden inside their crate while they are in your home.

It is also important never to use a crate as punishment. Your golden retriever will not understand the reason for this and might start to resent being in their crate, excluded from the fun they were having moments earlier. This will undermine all your hard work.

House training

Whether you call it 'toilet training' or 'house training', teaching your golden retriever not to do their business inside the house is an important first step in their education.

When you initially bring them home, they will rely on their new family to teach them what they need to learn. When you are kind and understanding, puppies are capable of learning quickly at a very early age. House training is all about establishing a routine. As with any new experience, it takes time and patience. Remember to use plenty of calm, compassionate understanding while your golden puppy learns their new toilet rules.

House training your puppy requires diligent supervision. The more watchful you are, the quicker your puppy will learn where you want them to go to the toilet-and where you don't. While it's nice if all family members can get involved in recognising your golden's 'need to go' body language, younger children or children with special needs are often distracted and not always up to the task.

Some people allow them to roam freely during the day rather than confining them to a limited number of rooms. This is called free training and is not recommended because it requires far more attentiveness. If they are not closely watched during the day, the chances are high that they will have an accident when first learning their toilet routine and take longer to understand what you need them to do.

While it would be wonderful if your puppy could always 'tell' you that they need to go to the toilet, this does not usually happen until they have already learnt exactly where their toilet is. Until your retriever puppy can ring a bell or bark and scratch at the door to let you know they need to go out, it is up to you to watch for the relevant signs and take them outside for regular toilet breaks. Pay attention if they start:

- Sniffing around.
- Circling.
- Looking at or approaching the door.
- Whining, crying, or barking.
- Scratching at the door.
- Acting agitated.

Remember, puppies are puppies, not people. Your golden is bound to make mistakes during the toilet training process. While it's upsetting when they pee on your nice, hardwood floor or expensive Persian rug, never get angry or scold your puppy for having an accident inside your home.

Yelling at or punishing your puppy could result in them becoming frightened or sneaky, only relieving themselves in dark, hidden, or secret places when nobody is watching. All you need to do if you notice your puppy making a toilet mistake is stay calm, firmly say, '***No***', scoop them up, and take them to their designated toilet area.

Puppies are particularly sensitive when first introduced to their new home environment. Any loud admonishment when they have an accident will be especially upsetting. They will know something is wrong and may become afraid, making it harder to train them. It is vital you show compassion and patience during this house-training time in your young golden retriever's life so their education is as stress-free as possible for both of you.

It is imperative to pay attention to the signs that mean your puppy needs to wee. This will reduce the possibility of a toilet mistake in the first place.

How Often?

As your golden puppy grows, it can usually wait to go to the toilet for about one hour for every month of its age.

For example, if your two-month-old puppy has been quietly snoozing for two hours, once they wake up, they will likely need to relieve themselves.

Paying close attention to your puppy's sleeping, eating, drinking, and playing habits allows you to predict when they need to relieve themselves. Your golden will normally perform their duties at regular times during the day:

- Straight after waking.
- After being in their crate.
- After intense, exciting situations with dogs, people, or toys.
- Approximately 20 minutes after a meal or drink.
- After playing.
- Before going to bed.

How often your golden retriever needs to go will vary from puppy to puppy. While the number of toilet breaks your puppy requires will reduce as they grow, on average, you can still expect your puppy to need to relieve themselves eight or more times daily until they are six to seven months old. By this time, your puppy's bladder and bowel control will be much greater, so they can wait longer before needing to relieve themselves.

Indoors or Outdoors

The difference between indoor and outdoor training is simply a matter of convenience. If you live in a 40-floor high-rise building, you might prefer to house train your dog inside rather than take the lift 8 or 10 times a day to get your puppy outside for toilet breaks. On the other hand, if you live in a home with a garden, or easy access to the street, you'll probably prefer to train your puppy to go to the toilet outside from the start.

Indoor Instructions

Toilet training your puppy can be challenging if you do not know what to do. Luckily, there are several aids you can use to support indoor training. Pee pads, potty patches, and litter boxes can all be used to train your puppy to use an indoor toilet.

Pee pads (also known as potty pads or training pads) These square or rectangular pads are made from layers of absorbent material designed to contain any sort of puppy mess. Whilst there are various kinds of toilet training pads, the most basic is a leak-proof paper pee pad (see picture). There are also washable fabric pads if you prefer something reusable, as well as pheromone-infused ones to encourage your pup to use them.

Litter Box. Although most people indeed associate litter boxes with cats, it is also possible to train your puppy to use them in the same way.

TIP ***When your puppy is little, it may need a ramp or step to help them get into a litter box (see picture). Also, it should be at least 7.5 centimetres (3 inches) deep and large enough for your puppy to comfortably turn around inside it.***

For anyone considering a litter box doggy toilet, you need to decide on the type of litter you want to use. Puppies eat anything, which means you should never leave them unsupervised in a box full of litter crystals in case they decide they look like a tasty snack. A safer choice of litter for a puppy would be natural, paper fibre litter infused with a pheromone attractant to help entice your puppy to use the box.

Potty Patches. There is a range of potty patch-type systems for house training your puppy, including:

- Basic synthetic turf with mat and tray (see picture).
- Synthetic turf with removable waste bin.
- Natural grass in a tray.
- Plastic grate in a tray.

These patches can be used in the same way as pee pads. They're more substantial than pads and designed to mimic the feel and smell of being outside in a grassy area, which may support the transition to outdoor toileting.

If this is going to be their permanent toilet, just as you needed to pick the right size crate, your pup's litter box needs to be large enough to accommodate them when they are fully grown.

You can choose any of the above three options to housetrain your puppy indoors. Here are the steps you need to follow if you select to use a potty patch:

- First, decide on the best place for your puppy's indoor toilet. It must be somewhere easily accessible for your puppy. This might be in a spare room or the bathroom. If possible, choose a room with a hard floor surface, such as tiles, linoleum, or hardwood. This will make it easier to clean if they miss the mark.
- Place the potty patch in your chosen areas. Place pee pads or newspapers all around it.
- Keep some tasty treats in your pocket or close at hand, so you can reward their good performance whenever your puppy uses their toilet area.
- Positive reinforcement using treats can work wonders with a golden. Retrievers love making their owner happy and take to positive, reward-based training very quickly.
- The moment you notice your puppy telling you they need to go—or when it is one of their regular times during the day, as detailed above—pick them up and take them to their toilet area. Encourage them to relieve themselves by saying, 'hurry up', or something similar. Using a voice cue reminds your easily distracted golden puppy why they are there.
- The moment they have done their business, give them a treat and praise them, so they start to associate using their toilet location with receiving a reward for good behaviour.
- After they have used their toilet for the first time, their scent will linger. Next time it will be easier for them to identify the toilet area as the right place to relieve themselves.

- Do not allow your puppy to play in their toilet space. They need to learn they are there for one specific purpose.
- If they wee on a pee pad near their toilet area, don't scold them. Simply move the soiled pee pad closer to help emphasise the familiar toilet scent they left previously.
- Soon, your golden puppy will learn that when they feel the urge to relieve themselves, they must go to the toilet area and do their business on the potty patch. When this happens, celebrate! You don't have to be so attentive about looking for the 'signs' or cover the whole floor with pee pads or newspaper because your retriever has now learnt where to go.

NOTE: Use the same positive reinforcement training process outlined above for teaching them to use pee pads or a litter box. The only thing you need to change is to use pee pads or a litter box instead of placing a potty patch in the designated area.

Depending on how well your puppy sleeps when they are young, it might not be able to hold it all night long. You have the following options for night-time training:

Option 1: Set an alarm and get up at 3:00 in the morning to take them outside. This reinforces the message that your puppy shouldn't go to the toilet inside the home.

Option 2: Section off part of the room where they sleep and lay a plastic sheet in a corner of that area with a pee pad on top. Soak a tissue in your puppy's pee and place it in the centre of the pee pad to encourage them to go where you want them to. This will be less disruptive to your sleep pattern.

Outdoor Instructions

Once you become familiar with the signs associated with your dog needing to go to the toilet, most golden puppies are not hard to house train. The following steps will get your golden off to a good start when starting to use their outdoor toilet:

- Place several pee pads on the floor near the door your puppy usually uses when going outdoors just in case they're not able to make it outside in time.
- Always use the same door when taking them outside, so they start to associate the door with their urge to urinate or defecate.
- When they begin showing the signs that they are looking for a place to go, or it is their scheduled time, quickly put on their lead (if need be) and take them outside.
- Take your golden to the same spot in the garden or the same street corner every time you take them out for a toilet break. There will be familiar scents from when they last did their business or where other dogs might have relieved themselves. This will further reinforce the message that this is the time and place to do its business.
- Let your puppy explore and sniff the area. Exercise and sniffing help stimulate the urge to go to the loo. If you can, let your puppy out in the garden without a lead on as it is too restrictive. However, if this isn't possible, an extendable one will give them the freedom they need to go to the toilet.

- Say, '***Good boy/girl***' and give them a treat the moment they have finished doing their business. This helps reinforce the message that when they perform their duty outside it is a positive occasion. You can further encourage their good performance by giving an extra reward—enthusiastic praise, a chest rub, or a scratch behind the ears—every time they perform in the right place.
- Do not let them become distracted from the task at hand when they are taken out for a toilet break. They must know this is not a play session. If they seem preoccupied, help them focus by moving them along to areas that potentially contain scents encouraging them to pee, such as a corner with a pole or tree, or a patch of grass. Keep using your chosen voice cue to remind them why they are outside.
- Once they have used their outdoor toilet, bring them back inside straight away rather than allowing them to play or greet other people or dogs. This reminds them they were outdoors for the sole purpose of relieving themselves.
- Being consistent with your voice cue during this early training teaches them to go on command. You'll be grateful for this skill when time is short or it's a dark, rainy night when you all just want to get back inside as soon as possible.
- Once they are regularly using their outdoor toilet, you can slowly stop giving them a treat and instead use vocal praise, physical pat, or wait to give them a treat when you get back home.

Doggy Doors

If you live in a home with a securely fenced back garden, you might like to consider installing a doggy door— or pet flap—as this can speed up the house-training process. Once you have installed the doggy door, you'll need to teach your golden how to get to their outdoor toilet. Place a pee pad beneath the doggy door to catch any mishaps until they have learnt to exit and enter on their own. This is how you teach your pup to use a doggy door:

- Show your puppy the door. Open it to the outside with your hand, so they can smell the intriguing outdoor scents that will make them want to investigate.
- If you can, get someone to help you teach your pup to use the pet flap. One of you should be on the outside of the doggy door and the other on the inside. The person on the outside can then have a treat in their hand as an extra incentive and reward for your golden once they push their nose through the door.
- It might help if you put your puppy's lead on. The outside assistant can then draw it through to provide a gentle tug towards the outdoors. At the same time, the inside person can lightly use their hand to guide your puppy through the flap.

TIP ***It is important not to rush the process, especially if your puppy is nervous about the door. If they're going to get comfortable using a pet flap, they need to feel confident enough to go through the door of their own volition rather than being forced.***

When you approach doggy door training in a relaxed, fun manner, it can become an entertaining game, which your golden puppy will quickly learn to enjoy, especially when they get praise from you and tasty treats. Once your puppy is a little older and fully house-trained, it will be able to go in and out without needing your assistance.

Bell Training

To introduce your golden retriever puppy to house training, it can be helpful to teach them to let you know when they 'have to go'. Teaching them to ring a bell whenever they need to go outside is a handy alarm system for both of you and can prevent toilet accidents. It is also fun and easy to teach.

There are many types and styles of commercially manufactured bells to choose from. These range from the elegant '***Poochie Bells***' that dangle from a leather or nylon strap attached to a doorknob (see picture below) to the simple '***Tell Bell***', which is like an old school bell that sits on the floor. There are also various high-tech door chime systems available that function similarly to a doggy intercom. All your golden puppy has to do is push a pad with its paw to ring a bell.

TIP ***You also have the option of building a bell system yourself. All you need is a bell with a loud ring. Attach it to a piece of ribbon or string and hang it from the handle on the door you use to take your puppy out. Make sure the string is long enough for your puppy to reach the bell with their nose or paw.***

Okay, so the big question is how you get your puppy to ring the bell when they need to go to the toilet. This is a very simple process:

- Every time you take your puppy out, say, '***Out***' and go to the door with the bell.
- If your bell is hanging from the handle, lift its paw and knock it against the bell to make it ring. If you have chosen the type that sits on the floor, press their paw on it to ring it.
- Praise them for following your command and say, '***Out***' again as you immediately open the door and go outside.
- Once outside, say your cue word, and when they go, reward them with praise and a treat.
- Go back inside straight away, so they associate ringing their bell solely with going outside to the toilet. Otherwise, they'll start ringing the bell when they want to go outside just to play or explore.
- If they ring their bell because they are bored and want to go for a walk, you will still need to take them outside. If you ignore them when they ring the bell, they'll ignore the bell when they need the toilet.

When you consistently use this method, your smart golden puppy will soon start ringing their toilet bell by itself.

12 Top Tips for Working Dog Owners

Golden retrievers are social animals who love to be in a pack. For a family pet, their pack includes their humans. If you work full-time, you will probably need to juggle your workday schedule around your dog to make sure your pup's needs are met. If your dog suffers from separation anxiety, it'll develop all manner of destructive behaviours that will need to be addressed before they become a serious problem. If you cannot hire a dog walker or use a day-care facility for whatever reason, here are some helpful tips to smooth the process of leaving your golden alone at home:

1. Before you leave for work in the morning, take your dog out for a walk. Make sure they have enough exercise to burn off their natural morning energy. If you've got time, include a game of fetch. If you exercise your golden, it will keep them happy. The adage that a tired dog is a happy dog is true.
2. Dogs thrive on habit and routine. Try to maintain a consistent workday routine where you leave home in the

morning and come home at night at the same time. Avoid staying late if possible. The more predictable you are, the more your golden retriever will become used to the time of day and hours you will be away.

3. Goldens need stimulation to stave off boredom. Before going out in the morning, make time to interact with your dog. When you're gone, leave them their favourite chew toy or stuffed toy.
4. Ensure there is a soothing ambience while you're gone. Research suggests soft jazz or classical music will help relax your dog. Leave some soft music on to keep your dog company.
5. Keep your home temperature at a comfortable level. Make certain there is enough daylight coming through the windows.
6. If you choose to let your golden roam free around the house, make sure you puppy-proof your home. If they're bored or feel separation anxiety, most dogs will chew or exhibit unwanted behaviours.
7. Some employers allow employees to take their dogs to work with them. Many believe that having pets around improves productivity and the overall wellness of their staff. It's always worth asking if this is an option for you.
8. Unfortunately, barking s unavoidable. All dogs will bark from time to time. To reduce the chances of your golden's barking becoming a nuisance, keep your dog in a confined space in the innermost part of your home, away from shared walls or the front door.
9. These days, many companies offer a flexible working policy where you can either work from home or take an extended lunch break to nip home and see your dog.
10. So your retriever doesn't feel like they're being abandoned every time you leave, pop in and out of sight for a minute or two while your golden is in another room. They will soon learn it is okay for you to be out of sight for a while because you will always come back.
11. If possible, consider using drop-in services. You might have a retired parent or a friend who works from home who can check on your pup and give them a little company during the day. There are also paid-for drop-in services available.
12. Finally, don't beat yourself up over having to work full-time when you decide to get a golden retriever. They are wonderful life companions who lower stress levels, give you a reason to get more exercise, and are big fluffy bundles of fun. Most of us have to work, and it is entirely possible to have both a retriever and work full-time. Put your mind at ease, and don't feel guilty.

Dealing with Accidents

In some ways, puppies are like human babies. With the best will in the world, toileting 'accidents' will happen while your pup learns to manage its urges.

When dealing with puppy accidents, following the following tips will help gradually reduce their frequency:

- Always stay calm. Your golden puppy has no hidden agenda. They don't want to upset you. They simply don't have fully developed bladder, bowels, or the muscles that control them. They need time to learn their toilet rules.
- Remain empathetic. Remember that your puppy does not understand yet that doing their business anywhere they like is unacceptable behaviour.

- Remember that they are young and need to learn from you. You're there to teach them the location of their toilet.
- If they are caught in the middle of an accident, simply use a firm tone and say something like, '***Uh-oh***' or '***Oops***', followed by a firm, '***No***'. Then take them directly to the place where they should go to the toilet.
- If they have an accident without you seeing, and you discover a puddle some hours later, it is pointless taking them to their toilet location. It is too late for them to associate this with having made a mistake they will have long since forgotten about. All you can do is thoroughly clean it up and forget about it.
- Never yell, scare, or punish your golden retriever puppy for having a toilet accident. This only frightens them and might teach them to avoid going to the toilet in front of you.

FACT ***You might have heard about rubbing your golden's nose in any mess they make or taking them to the scene of the crime and admonishing them. Unfortunately, such training methods are extremely damaging and disconcerting for your puppy. Avoid them at all costs.***

If you want to train your puppy quickly, they need to be calmly told when a mistake is made and praised when they get it right.

It can be confusing and frustrating when your puppy continues to use the wrong place in the home for their toilet, especially after you've repeatedly cleaned the area. Any leftover smells will attract your golden to return to the same spot to relieve themselves. It's essential to thoroughly scrub the area.

Your retriever's sense of smell is up to 2,000 times more sensitive than yours. In other words, whilst the area you just cleaned up might look and smell clean to you, it probably still has an odour that will attract your puppy to the same spot.

Proper Clean-up. Sourcing a product that effectively and completely removes all smells from house-training accidents can be challenging. Many products that supposedly remove smells and stains are not as effective as you need. **Choose a professional-grade oxy-charged enzyme cleaner (see picture).** This won't just mask the scent with another but completely remove it. These contain professional-strength odour neutralisers and urine digesters that bind to and completely absorb odours on any surface.

Marking

There are many reasons why dogs use their urine for 'marking territory' or 'scent marking'. Though marking behaviour is more often displayed by male dogs who lift their leg to pee on the corner of a sofa or chair, females may also occasionally mark their territory.

Dogs are notorious for marking territory when out on a walk. You'll find they'll frequently stop at trees, corners of buildings, tufts of tall grass, and other upright objects to leave their scent.

Dogs have a deeply ingrained evolutionary urge to mark their territory with their scent. The most effective way to do this is to urinate. Dogs do not begin to engage in marking behaviour until they reach adulthood.

When your golden retriever smells a urine mark left by another dog, it'll feel compelled to 'overmark' or place its scent on top of the earlier mark. This leaves a dominance message indicating the previous dog who peed there is now subordinate to the one who peed most recently. The reasons why a dog marks their territory in the home include:

- A female dog coming into heat might pee inside the home.

- A dog going into a building where there are—or have been—other dogs present often marks furniture to display authority over the smell of the other dogs.
- Dogs might start marking when a new animal or person starts living in the home or when something changes—e.g., furniture, carpet, curtains, wall colour.
- Visiting guests may have the scent of another dog on them.

To avoid a marking problem, stay vigilant when your dog's environment changes or other dogs come over. Promptly interrupt this undesirable behaviour. Keeping a visiting dog on a lead using a loud '***No***' or hand clap could be all you need to get your golden to stop marking. If your dog persists in marking its territory inside the home, there are ways to help prevent this unwelcome activity, including:

- Spay or neuter your golden retriever—50 to 60% of males stop marking once neutered.
- Thoroughly clean previously marked areas with an enzymatic cleaner to eliminate any scent.
- Use bitter sprays on furniture or other items your golden tends to mark.
- Play calming music.
- Diffuse calming essential oils, such as lavender.
- Have your dog wear a belly band to contain any urine. These wrap around your golden's midsection and have a removable, absorbent inner liner. They can also be used for toilet training or if an older dog becomes incontinent.

Excitement Urination

As with all breeds, some golden retrievers urinate when excited, especially when they are puppies. Puppies pee when over-stimulated, as their young muscles cannot hold back the flow of urine. Just the joy of seeing their owner is often enough to make them lose control of their bladder. This is purely reflexive behaviour, so your puppy will be unaware of what they've done. Any punishment will only confuse them. Usually, your golden will outgrow the problem as they mature and gain command of their bladder.

Never punish or scold your dog for excitement urination. This will only make the situation worse because your puppy will start to urinate out of fear. If you become angry with your golden puppy for excitement urination, it can easily develop into submissive urination.

If the issue does not diminish as your puppy gets older, try the following tips:

- Ask visitors not to be overly enthusiastic when approaching your puppy.
- Keep your voice gentle and non-threatening when greeting.
- Ignore a boisterous, bouncy puppy until they settle down.
- Try a new greeting routine. Ask your golden puppy to sit and wait for a treat when you first come home.
- Make sure your pup isn't suffering from a bladder infection or other medical issues.

ve Urination

scary situation, even if a house-trained golden retriever could display submissive urination. mmonly seen in golden puppies who roll on their back when approached by a larger or more og or are with someone who makes them feel nervous.

o dominant and strict, it will reinforce submissive urinating. Stay calm and be kind to your ver. Keep your temper under control. Never scold or punish your golden for submissive ur dog will not understand why you are angry. They will only urinate more because to them, ttempt to calm and appease you.

In most cases, submissive urination is an instinctive reaction to another dog or person whom they find intimating. It is typically a behaviour they'll grow out of as they mature.

our golden retriever puppy might have a temperament which means they continue to be ly timid into adulthood. If this is the case, submissive urination could become an issue in are other signs of submissive behaviour, such as tail tucking, crouching, and rolling be many reasons why your dog engages in submissive urination, including:

- ly shy nature.
- iate punishment in the past.
- have been treated harshly or
- be confused about the rules.
- ing to avoid punishment.
- be nervous when meeting
- be unclear about how to being greeted.
- noise or disturbance.
- ot have been properly

ever demonstrates this ny steps you can take to boost their confidence to prevent submissive urination:

- alise them with different people, dogs, and situations.
- r nervous golden.
- w-key.
- ntain a calm, quiet home environment.
- Use positive reinforcement and rewards to teach commands.
- Make new experiences happy and positive by playing games and giving treats.
- Never use a loud voice or dominant posture with your timid or apprehensive golden retriever.
- Let your nervous dog come to you and sniff the back of your hand rather than approaching them.
- Avoid direct eye contact and keep your body language calm.
- Spend time sitting together while your golden retriever is on their lead.
- Encourage them to respond to simple commands such as '***Sit***' or '***Stay***' to earn a treat reward.
- Do not pat the top of your dog's head. Rub them under the chin instead.

- Avoid taking your golden into loud, noisy, or unpredictable situations that you cannot control until they develop more confidence.

Helping your golden gain confidence requires patience. It will take time for them to overcome their fears. Excitement or submissive urination is instinctual rather than behavioural in golden retrievers. They aren't doing it to be disobedient or punish you. They can be excited, frightened, or show submissiveness to any person or animal they perceive to be dominant.

5. Golden Puppy Care

"Dogs have given us their absolute all. We are the centre of their universe. We are the focus of their love and faith and trust. They serve us in return for scraps. It is without a doubt the best deal man has ever made."

~ Roger Caras ~

Whether you are getting your first golden retriever or just need to refresh your memory about caring for them, here's what you need to know to get your puppy on the right track to adulthood.

Development Stages

Let's start with the development stages they go through before they become fully grown adults:

Neonatal Stage: Birth to 2 weeks – The neonatal stage is the 'newborn' time between birth and two weeks of age. Puppies have the senses of touch and taste but are still blind and deaf. At this age, a puppy can only crawl slowly and is entirely dependent on its mother for food and grooming.

Transitional Stage: 2 to 4 weeks – This is when the puppy's eyes open, their hearing begins to develop, and their milk teeth emerge. During this time, puppies start to walk, wag their tails, and make those cute little barking noises.

Weaning Stage: 5 to 8 weeks – By the end of four weeks, puppies can urinate and defecate without needing stimulation from their mother. They will play and wrestle with their littermates and are ready to start eating solid food.

When they reach eight weeks old, they should have fully transitioned to solid food and no longer need to nurse. Towards the end of this period, a puppy is emotionally mature enough to form strong bonds with its new human family.

New Home Stage: 8 to 10 weeks – This stage is known as the 'fear period', as this is when a puppy is highly impressionable. It is important to make any new experience with people, places, and other animals, fun and positive. It is helpful to make less pleasant events—such as vaccines—more like a game with abundant praise.

First Learning Stage: 8 to 16 weeks – This is when your golden puppy will have a fervent desire to be near its owner. Many people enrol their puppy in their first training class during this time. This is a good way for them to encounter other puppies in a fun group setting. During these weeks, it is imperative to get them out in their new world. Every puppy needs to be in lots of places where they can meet and greet new people of all ages and ethnicities and have a positive experience with different situations.

Pre-Adolescent Stage: 4 to 6 months – During this stage, you will see a gradual increase in confidence and independence in your puppy as their curiosity drives them to explore farther afield. This is a good time to step up training routines and make sure they understand and obey basic commands.

TIP ***When your golden retriever puppy can go everywhere with you, this will broaden their horizons and help build a strong bond of trust and respect between the two of you. This is useful as you become more advanced in your training sessions. You should consider whether you wish to have your puppy neutered or spayed towards the end of this timeframe.***

Adolescent Stage: 6 to 18 months – This 'terrible teens' period in your young golden's life is when they have attained sexual maturity and start to test the boundaries of their environment. This is also a high-energy time when your puppy might become bored more easily. Their need for mental and physical stimulation can manifest through lapses in obedience as their personality asserts itself, and they test your limits to see what they can get away with.

While it might seem that the obedient puppy you had just a few short weeks ago has all but disappeared, when you are consistently patient, find ways to engage them in vigorous play and exercise, and do not expect perfection, you will both make it safely through this stage.

Emotional Maturity Stage: 18 months onwards – (Note that some goldens don't reach emotional maturity until two or even three years old.) When your golden retriever is approaching emotional maturity, any inclination towards dominance or wanting to climb the social ladder within their human household might start to show. When your dog begins to exhibit dominant traits within the family, you need to increase the time and energy spent training so they understand they must remain a follower. Should this behaviour become aggressive, you may need to consult a behaviourist.

Weight Table – It can be helpful to understand how your golden puppy might grow and how long it could be before they attain its adult weight. Your golden's weight could vary as certain factors influence their adult size, such as:

- Parental size—you can usually tell the size a puppy will reach when you see its parents.
- Gender—male dogs are usually larger than females.
- Time of spaying or neutering—when spaying or neutering, the chemical signals that tell the bones to stop growing are cancelled, which means dogs neutered earlier in life tend to be taller.

Regardless of the above factors, the following weight table can be used as a general guideline. It outlines the expected variances in weight from birth to two years for a golden retriever puppy:

Age	Male Expected Weight (kg)	Female Expected Weight (kg)
1 month	1.4-2	1.4-2
2 months	1.4-12	2.3-7.7
3 months	4-15.5	5.5-10
4 months	6.8-25	7.3-19.5
5 months	9-30	11-26
6 months	17-34	12-30
7 months	17-34	12-30
8 months	18-35	18-30
9 months	20.5-35	20-31
10 months	22.7-35	22.7-31
11 months	25-34	23.5-32
12 months	29-34	25-32
2 years	29-34	25-32

Bonding with Your Puppy

Bonding with your golden retriever puppy begins the moment you bring them home from the breeder.

At this stage, your role is to guide your puppy and make sure they stay safe. You need to be extra patient, kind and gentle with them while they get used to their new surroundings. They'll be learning all about their human family, which is now the centre of their universe.

Daily interactions during disciplined exercises, including going for walks on a loose lead, teaching commands and tricks, as well as establishing routines (see Chapter 11), are all wonderful bonding opportunities. There are endless ways to strengthen the connection with your puppy. The best times usually occur while teaching your puppy new things.

Playtime is a fantastic time to bond with your puppy. Some puppies want to play the second they step inside your home. Others might need time to adjust to their new environment. Having their favourite doggy treats to hand can coax them into playing with you. Games such as 'Hide and Seek' and 'Find It' offer both training opportunities and quality time for you and your puppy.

TIP ***Cuddle sessions are also important. They provide your puppy with the sense of safety and comfort they crave. The ideal time to snuggle up with your golden puppy is when they're sleepy.***

To encourage your retriever puppy to relax with you, have some food or treats in your hand to coax them, and use them to reward them when they settle beside you. Gradually eliminate food treats over time and replace them with your love and affection. Cuddling, massaging, and hanging out together are all good ways to get your puppy to unwind at the end of the day and get them used to having their paws, muzzle, ears, tummy, etc., handled. You can also use this time for some light grooming practice, such as brushing their fur or cleaning their eyes. Working these sessions into your puppy's daily routine every evening teaches them this time of the day is when they should be settling down.

Teething and Play Biting

How to Help with Teething – When your puppy is teething, they naturally want to chew on everything and anything to try to alleviate the pain of new teeth pushing through their gums. Thankfully, there are many simple ways you can help your golden puppy through the teething stage, such as:

- Having compassion. Teething is painful!
- Keeping items you do not want to be chewed safely out of reach.
- Having plenty of chewable items to hand. You may like to have chew toys and treats, rope toys, stuffed and frozen Kong, hard rubber toys, cold carrots, or a knotted tea towel soaked in water and placed in the freezer.
- Making chicken broth ice cubes. These can be messy, so only give them to your pup outside or somewhere you can easily clean after them.
- Rubbing their sore gums with your finger. This is a good time to introduce your retriever's teeth brushing routine.
- Buying them teething toys designed to be frozen.

Every puppy is different when it comes to teething. Some are more upset or bothered than others. For example, it is not unusual for a puppy to lose their appetite or even have a low-grade fever when its new molars are pushing through. If they are reluctant to eat, offer warm, soft foods that are easier on their sore gums.

How to Stop Play Biting – Sometimes, puppies get into the habit of biting and nipping at human fingers or other body parts when they are young. This is how they play with their littermates, so your golden puppy might try to do the same with you.

While there are many things you can do to discourage this type of behaviour, it's best not to encourage it in the first place. This means not engaging in rough play, which includes tussling with your puppy and sliding them across the floor. It might be entertaining to see them scramble and run back for more, but this type of behaviour can teach them to bite at people.

The following simple steps can help stop your young golden retriever from play biting:

- Loudly say, '***Ow!***' in a high-pitched voice, so your puppy knows they are getting over-excited and biting too hard.
- Do not shout. This can create more excitement. Instead, firmly say, '***No***'.
- If they are biting your fingers, make a fist as you firmly say, '***No***'.
- Lightly tap the end of your puppy's nose with your finger.

- Give another light tap on their nose, with a firm '*No*' if they continue to bite your fingers or toes.
- Exchange your fingers for a doggy chew toy.
- Praise your puppy when they choose the chew toy.
- Stop the play session when they start nipping, so they know there is no reward for biting.

Puppies need to learn how to moderate the force of their bite so that when they are playing or biting out of excitement or pain, they don't hurt anyone.

The 7 Common Mistakes to Avoid

It is easy to make a mistake that could have been avoided when first bringing home your adorable new golden retriever puppy. You can get so excited to have a new, furry family member that you might not consider how today's actions might bring future unwanted consequences. While it's ultimately up to you to decide how you want to handle your dog, the following section outlines some of the common mistakes that a new owner can make.

1. Sleeping in Your Bed

It is often tempting to allow your crying puppy to sleep in your bed to settle them down. Whether this is a good idea depends on your golden and what sort of relationship there is between you. Of course, while this can help to calm and comfort your new golden puppy, this might not be the best idea in the long term:

- It can set a precedent that results in behavioural problems later in life because it may lead them to believe they're in charge.
- You may accidentally crush your small puppy in your sleep.
- Your puppy could hurt themselves if they fall off the bed during the night.
- It might aggravate allergies.
- If your puppy suffers from separation anxiety, it could make them feel even worse when you have to leave them alone.
- It might encourage your puppy to be overly clingy.
- Sharing a bed with your puppy could bring hair, fleas, dirt, and anything else your pup has encountered into your bed.
- Your squirming puppy can interrupt your sleep cycle, especially if they are a restless sleeper, barks at every little noise they hear, snores, or has wind.
- Your puppy could accidentally wee in your bed.
- They might growl when you move or your partner comes to bed because they believe this is their domain. If they are already a bossy dog, this can exacerbate this tendency.
- Once your puppy has been permitted to sleep in your bed for some time, it will be difficult to discourage the habit.

TIP ***As much as it might feel awful to hear your new puppy crying for the first few nights in their crate, a little tough love at the beginning will keep them safely confined while helping them to learn to love and respect you.***

2. Picking Up a Puppy at the Wrong Time

There can often be a strong urge to pick your puppy up when they are displaying nervousness, fear, or aggression—such as growling or barking—at an object, person, another dog, or animal. While it's easy to scoop up your pup when they are still little, and picking them up can help relieve their anxiety or stop them barking, this might not be the best course of action:

- Picking up your puppy or dog rewards unwanted behaviour.
- It teaches them that the behaviour they just displayed is acceptable to you, and they could learn to continue to do it.
- It teaches your puppy that they are in charge.

Anyone who wants to teach their puppy to be well-behaved, and default to their owner's rules any time they react inappropriately, will want to gently correct their unbalanced behaviour. This is easily accomplished with a firm '***No***' followed by standing in front of them (between your puppy and the dog or person they growled at), so their attention is now focused on you, their owner. They need to learn to listen to you and not react to new people, dogs, or situations with fear or aggression.

When a golden retriever puppy or dog is small, many owners get into the habit of carrying them far too much. Sometimes, it is necessary to pick your puppy up to help them, such as getting them into their crate inside your car. However, you should try to keep your pup on the ground walking on their own most of the time, so:

- They don't think they have the 'top dog' position.
- They can properly meet and greet other dogs.
- They do not decide they are the leader.
- They do not become an armpit alligator (see below).

TIP ***Carrying your golden around can create an 'armpit alligator' situation. This happens when your dog becomes overly possessive of you because you carry them everywhere. As a result, when another adult, child, or dog sees your cute little dog and approaches to say hello, your golden retriever might lunge, snap, and/or growl because they think they're the boss.***

Even dogs who are friendly or not naturally wary or suspicious of strangers can learn to become intolerant of other people and pets if they aren't properly socialised. This means it is always possible for any dog to become protective or possessive of its owners. You are advised to help your puppy when needed but not to overdo it by carrying them all the time.

3. Playing Too Hard, Too Long or Too Often

The average puppy needs between 16 and 20 hours of sleep a day. While this may seem a lot, this rest is essential for the healthy growth and development of your puppy's muscles, brain, central nervous system, and immune system.

Puppies are naturally playful and bouncy. A healthy puppy is always ready to play. However, sometimes people play too much, too long, or too roughly with their young puppy. As much as you may want to have fun with your cute little furry friend, it is important to remember your young golden tires easily and needs their rest. Just like you established regular eating and toilet times for your new puppy, they also need to have regular resting times while they are growing and developing.

It is perfectly normal for your puppy to take a nap roughly every hour. Young puppies burn a lot of energy when they are awake because exploring all those new places, people, sights, and sensations is exhausting, and that's before you include teaching them your rules.

The world is a stimulating place for your young golden, and they might not always know when it is time to take a break. Thankfully, there are a few simple steps you can take to create a routine that allows your puppy to get enough rest throughout their exciting day:

- Establish a routine where play sessions or walks are always followed by a rest period.
- Make sure they know where their crate or bed is kept, and if they seem tired, encourage them to go to bed.
- Make sure they are left undisturbed. Children need to learn to leave the puppy alone when they are asleep.

Puppy Play and Rest Routine – Here's an example of an appropriate routine to ensure your puppy receives the regular rest they need:

Morning Routine

- When they wake up, take them out for a toilet break.
- Feed them breakfast.
- Take them out for another toilet break shortly after eating.
- Play, or a walk and socialise until they tire.
- Rest time (puppies tire easily and can sleep most of the day.)
- Take them out for a toilet break as soon as they wake up.
- Give them lunch.

Afternoon Routine

- After lunch, take them out for another toilet break.
- Indoor play or explore until they are ready to nap.
- Rest time.
- Take them out for a toilet break when they wake up.
- Training or a walk.
- Rest time again.

Evening Routine

- Feed them dinner.
- Take them out for a toilet break and a short walk.
- Let them spend time playing and interacting with family.
- Take them out for a toilet break before bedtime.
- Settle them into their crate with their favourite toy for their night-time sleep.

4. Free Feeding

Free feeding is usually associated with how most people feed their cats. Most cats know when to stop and do not overeat. However, the same is often not true of dogs who tend to eat whatever is in their bowl.

FACT ***If there is food in your golden puppy's bowl 24/7 so they can eat when they want, they will almost certainly eat too much.***

As golden retrievers love food and are an exceedingly food-oriented breed with a tendency toward obesity, free feeding is not recommended for them. When training, their love of food can be used to your advantage since they are highly motivated to work for it. However, overdo the treats and their waistlines suffer, as they would eat until they burst if given the chance.

5. Treating Your Dog Like a Human

Often, we get into the habit of treating our dogs more like small, furry humans than dogs. This is called 'anthropomorphism', and this tendency usually begins when they are a small puppy, still needing supervision and protection from harm.

Like anxious parents, we worry and ask all sorts of questions to make sure our puppy is okay, just as we would a child:

- Are they getting the right amount of exercise?
- Are they warm enough?
- Are they eating and drinking properly?
- Are they getting enough sleep?
- Are they feeling okay?

While you want to do your best for your golden retriever, remember, no matter how much you might like to think they are a small, fur-covered human, your relationship will be better if you treat them like the incredible dog they are. If you don't, you can confuse your dog, leading to behavioural problems.

It is very human of us to interpret our canine counterpart's behaviour based on human emotions and the belief our dogs think and reason the same way we do. When you combine this attitude with your golden's awesome ability to read human cues and adjust themselves and their way of life to integrate with ours, it's easy to kid ourselves that our dogs do think like us.

We should not blame ourselves for attributing to our dogs our human ability to feel, reason, and think. We were brought up on the idea. We were indoctrinated into this mostly misguided view of animal psychology through popular children's books about talking rabbits and bears. Then you have cartoon series featuring loveable dog characters, such as Pluto, Goofy, and Lady. As if that wasn't enough, well-trained dogs such as Lassie, Rin Tin Tin, and Benji starred in Hollywood movies, encouraging us to delve even further into anthropomorphism.

As tempting as it might be to believe our dogs can think and reason like us, expecting your dog to be able to match human reasoning can cause difficulties in the relationship, such as:

- Expecting your golden to 'know better' or 'feel guilty' when they pee on the floor.
- Creating confusion about who is the leader in the relationship.
- Overfeeding or feeding them an unhealthy diet.
- Making them uncomfortable, e.g., dressing them up in human clothing.
- Causing them to feel anxious or stressed when they do not react the way you want.
- Not allowing them to behave like dogs, e.g., being overprotective by carrying them or putting them in pushchairs and wheeling them around like a baby.

Even though our dogs certainly have their own set of emotions, they do not show them or understand them in the same way we do. Ascribing our human emotions and feelings to our dog does a disservice to our canine companions.

Perhaps a more accurate explanation for why dogs are so good at appearing to understand us and do what we ask is that they have learnt how to be expert opportunists. You could say dogs do what works best for them so they get what they want. The priorities for most dogs include:

- An owner who will guide and lead them.
- A predictable, standard schedule.
- Consistent rules, boundaries, and praise.
- Spending time with their owner.
- Learning routines and tricks.
- A regular feeding programme.
- The occasional treat.
- Plenty of daily exercise.
- A chest rub or physical affection.
- A toileting schedule.
- Opportunity to play with their toys.
- Socialising with old and new friends.
- A quiet, comfortable place to sleep.

6. Waiting Too Long Before Socialising

When first bringing home your gorgeous golden puppy, you will want to spend as much time as possible playing with them and keeping them all to yourself. However, sometimes you can have so much fun you forget your puppy needs to be socialised.

Part of the socialising process is interaction with other dogs from an early age. It is advised not to introduce your golden retriever to other dogs until they have been fully vaccinated, which is about 13 weeks old. Unfortunately, the critical time for canine socialisation is between 3 and 16 weeks of age.

One option is to attend a puppy class as soon as you bring them home, but this involves the risk of your puppy catching a virus from the other pups. While there might only be a minimal risk of your puppy contracting a deadly virus, since most will have had at least one vaccination, you should weigh the benefits of early interaction against health risks.

Until you're able to take your pup out and about, focus on things you can do at home to make your puppy as confident, inquisitive, and brave as they can be. This should give them a great head start. Expose them to as many everyday things as you can within the confines of your home, garden, or garage.

TIP ***Once your puppy is fully vaccinated, you should wait another two weeks before giving them full access to the outdoors. When going to new places where they might be nervous, you***

might like to keep some treats with you to reward them for not displaying anxiousness or a favourite toy to distract them and make the new experience a pleasant one.

There are detailed instructions about socialising your puppy later in the book (see Chapter 10).

7. Waiting Too Long Before Establishing Basic Manners

You need to start guiding your golden retriever's behaviour from the moment you bring them home. Teaching them basic manners, phrases, and commands is the cornerstone for having a well-behaved companion and makes them a joy to be around. If you wait too long, you can end up going down the difficult road of re-training unwanted behaviour.

Rather than having to fix a problem you created, it is much easier and less stressful to teach basic commands to your golden puppy before they are five months old, which is when they are most impressionable. As soon as your puppy's paws cross the threshold of their new home, they are ready to start learning. With just 5 or 10 minutes a day, they will already know the following basics by the age of 4 to 5 months (see Chapter 11 for details on how to teach these commands):

- Come.
- Sit.
- Stay.
- Down.
- Ring a bell to go outside.
- Loose lead walking without pulling.

Many puppies are ready to learn far more than just a few basic commands long before six months of age. If your golden retriever puppy seems eager to learn more, perhaps begin with some simple tricks—shake a paw, roll over, sit up—or begin teaching them a fun canine sport.

Keeping Your Pup Healthy

Choosing an appropriate veterinary clinic is very similar to choosing the right doctor or healthcare clinic for yourself. Caring owners want to ensure that their golden retriever receives the quality care they deserve, and this means taking time to find the best possible vet.

This is one of the most critical decisions you will ever make for your puppy's health. Your vet plays an important part in making sure your retriever lives a long and healthy life. When deciding, you must think about what's essential to you, such as their hours and location.

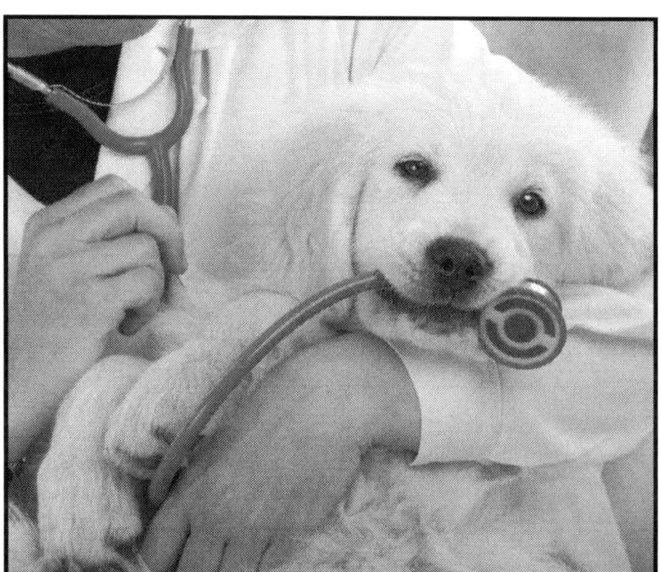

Word of mouth is by far the best way to find a vet. Ask your friends and family for any recommendations. Online reviews can also be helpful, but suggestions from people you know and trust are even better.

Ideally, you will have found a veterinarian before you get your pup. Within a few days of taking your new puppy home, take them to your vet for a general exam. You will be seeing a lot of your vet in the first few months for vaccinations, health checks, and later spaying or neutering. If you decide to neuter your dog, wait until puberty, which will be at around six months old.

Your veterinarian will identify any potential health issues early on and advise you about caring for your golden long-term. The initial visit also opens the door to communication between you and your vet. Some vets offer a puppy club so your retriever can have positive experiences with the vet as well as more negative ones.

Puppy's First Vet Visit

It is a good idea to have your new golden retriever puppy checked over by your vet as soon as you buy or adopt them. It is recommended that you do this as part of the buying process and agree with the breeder that if there are any health issues, you can take the pup back within a set time, usually 24-48 hours.

Some veterinary clinics specialise in caring for smaller pets, others in larger animal care, while some have a wide range of expertise and care for all animals, including livestock and reptiles.

Your vet will give your pup a thorough examination to ensure they are in good condition. This includes checking for signs of worms and fleas and weighing them. If your golden puppy has not already had their first vaccinations to protect them from serious infectious diseases, these will also be done during their initial vet visit. Not only will this benefit your puppy, but it will also give you peace of mind that your golden retriever is healthy.

Beyond these standard procedures, the vet will usually discuss your puppy's history, such as the name of the breeder, any prior treatments that might have been initiated by the breeder, and confirm your puppy's birthdate. This is when you should review future vaccination plans, ask questions about feeding or other future care, and even talk about pet insurance.

Vaccinations

Puppies – Puppies can be vaccinated to protect them against four common and serious diseases. These are parvovirus, canine distemper, leptospirosis, and infectious canine hepatitis. If your puppy has not been vaccinated and encounters a virus, they might quickly become sick. Even when treated, there is no guarantee they will survive.

FACT ***The Royal Veterinary College in London recommends that dogs should be vaccinated from nine weeks old onwards, with a second vaccination given four weeks later. Approximately one week after your golden puppy has received all their vaccinations—called 'core' vaccines—they are fully protected from those specific diseases.***

Adults – It is common practice to vaccinate adult dogs every 1 to 3 years. If your veterinarian is adamant about vaccinating your dog yearly, ask why, because 'over vaccinating' has the potential to cause other health problems. Rather than getting unnecessary vaccinations or boosters, you could ask the vet to give your golden a blood test first because this is a straightforward way to determine whether they need a booster. (See Titre Testing below.)

You may also decide to give your dog additional non-core vaccines— 'lifestyle vaccines'—which are optional and often depend on your retriever's lifestyle and where they live. Besides your dog's general health, your vet will also take into account the following when considering boosters or non-core vaccines:

- Whether your retriever attends a daycare facility, boarding kennel, or groomer.
- Whether certain diseases are known to be present in the area where you live.
- Whether your retriever's lifestyle includes travelling across borders, hiking through heavily wooded areas, or regularly swimming in bodies of water.

Non-core vaccines offer protection from the following viruses/diseases:

- Bordetella bronchiseptica.
- Canine influenza H3N2 virus and H3N8 virus.

- Lyme disease.
- Parainfluenza.
- Rabies.

Titre Testing – Titre testing is an easy way to minimise the possible side effects inherent in multiple vaccinations by avoiding unnecessary boosters. A titre test is a blood test that measures antibodies in a blood sample. This can indicate whether a previous vaccine is still producing antibodies and protecting your golden retriever's immune system.

For instance, some dogs are protected for their entire life just from their initial puppy vaccinations and a one-year booster. So, why give your dog a booster if they do not need one? That said, if you are travelling internationally, be certain to check a country's specific requirements to make sure your dog's vaccinations are up to date.

The People's Dispensary for Sick Animals (PDSA) has reported that side effects from vaccines can vary widely and include:

- Allergic reactions.
- Autoimmune problems.
- Lethargy.
- Mild swelling around the vaccine site.
- Lack of appetite.
- Fever/high temperature.

While we certainly need to protect our dogs from harmful diseases, it is also true that giving a vaccine when not needed can expose dogs to unnecessary hazards that could have been avoided.

Worming

Worms are a common parasite in dogs and live mainly in their intestines and respiratory system. Every puppy is susceptible to worms, which they can get through their mother's milk or placenta. The most common worms affecting golden retriever puppies are roundworms, tapeworms, lungworms, and hookworms.

Roundworms are intestinal parasites found in the gut. They look like spaghetti. They can cause diarrhoea and intestinal irritation. Puppies are affected more than adult dogs. The microscopic roundworm eggs are frequently passed in apparently normal faeces. The worms infect the puppy through their mother's placenta, which is why many golden puppies have contracted worms at birth.

Tapeworms are another kind of intestinal worm. Its lifecycle relies on an intermediate host, which is usually eaten by your golden, infecting them. Fleas are the intermediate host for the most common tapeworm affecting dogs. Dogs get tapeworms when nibbling or grooming, often in response to a flea bite, thereby ingesting the tapeworm-infected flea.

As their name implies, lungworms live in your retriever's respiratory system. Like the tapeworms, their lifecycle requires an intermediate host, in this case, normally slugs and snails. Dogs tend to contract lungworms through eating slugs, snails, or grass with snail trails on them. They can also acquire it through playing with toys that have been in direct contact with snails.

Dogs can also be infected with hookworms, whipworms, and heartworms. Hookworms are dangerous as they rob your puppy of nutrients, which can lead to anaemia. If there is a heavy infestation, they can also spread to the lungs. Heartworms are not indigenous to the United Kingdom but can be contracted when travelling abroad.

As worms are common in puppies, you must know how to treat them. Puppy worming should first be done at five, eight, and twelve weeks old. Then, it should be repeated at least every three months for the rest of their lives to ensure they do not get infected by worms.

Most worming products stay in the body for no more than 48 hours as the liver metabolises them. They kill and remove any worms present in your golden's system during that period. However, your dog can become re-infected soon afterwards. It is not uncommon for dogs to be re-infected with worms within a month of treatment.

If your golden retriever puppy has come from a reputable breeder or rescue centre, they should be worm-free because they will have been wormed before you take them home. Make sure you keep any paperwork in a safe place so you can keep track of your puppy's worming treatment.

Since fleas often cause worms in puppies, you should regularly check and treat your retriever for any flea infestations.

Although it is rare, worm-related diseases can be a risk to humans. Children can be in contact with tiny roundworm eggs when playing in soil and sandpits, causing infections. The worms migrate from the intestine and travel around the body, damaging organs such as the liver, heart, brain, and eyes. If you suspect your child has been infected by worms, seek immediate medical treatment.

Using a veterinary-prescribed prescription-only product is the best way to treat worms. These come in the form of tablets, spot-on treatments, and palatable chews. If you suspect your golden retriever puppy has worms, contact your vet straight away. They will recommend the best course of treatment and wormer to treat multiple species of worm to ensure your dog does not suffer any ill effects. If you prefer, you can also buy conventional and natural worming treatments at pet supply shops.

Should you wish to limit the number of worming products your golden retriever is exposed to, there is a new method called Faecal Egg Count. This provides an evaluation of the number of worm eggs in your dog's faeces. This gives an idea of the number of adult female worms in your golden's gut. Having identified each species of worm egg present, where appropriate, they are quantified to give an indication of the level of infestation.

If you choose to use this method, you'll need to send in a sample of your dog's poo every three months. If a worm infestation is detected, you'll need to de-worm your dog, but if there's no sign of worms, no treatment is required. If you are in the United Kingdom, you can use diagnostic vet goldens such as Wormcount: www.wormcount.com. There are similar services in the United States as well, including www.zeroeggcount.com.

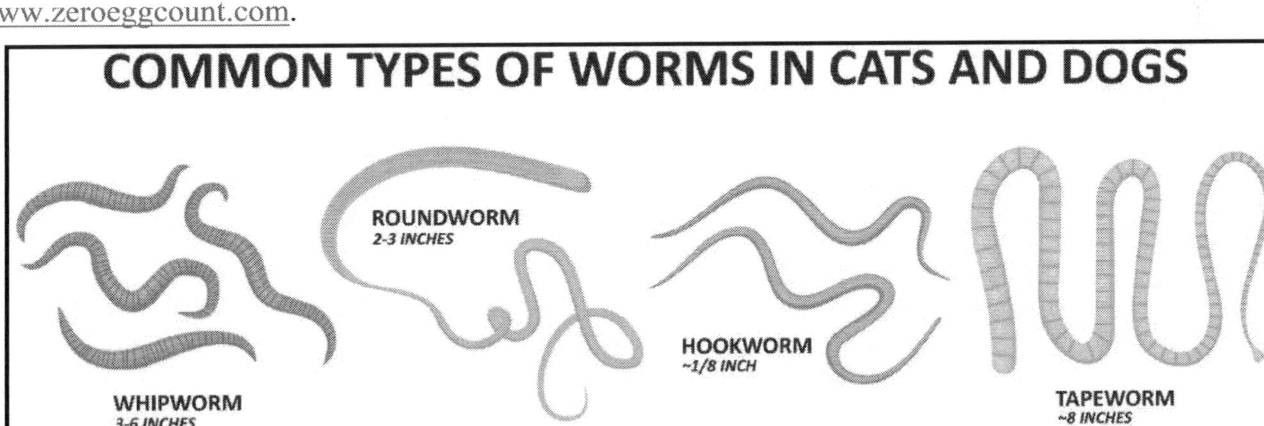

As you can see, there are many types of worms that can cause a variety of health issues for puppies, and just as many deworming products designed to tackle infestations. Your pup needs to be treated with a suitable de-wormer as soon as possible after an infestation has been identified. Your vet will advise what products are licensed for use at each puppy age, how much to give, and how often.

Worm Prevention – Thankfully, there are effective deworming medications and many natural remedies for treating and preventing worms. While various chemical medications are quite harsh, if given to your dog in small enough quantities, the poison will not be fatal for your golden retriever. This is why it's important to consult a vet over dosing.

Conventional Worming Medications – Many chemical or pesticide-based products are conventionally used to eliminate or prevent worms. Some of the most popular include:

PRO-Wormer 2, Nemex-2 – The active ingredient in these products is 'Pyrantel Pamoate' (paralysing agent). These medications treat roundworms and hookworms in puppies and adult dogs. They are recommended for small dogs and approved for use on pregnant females. They can be administered directly or mixed with your dog's food.

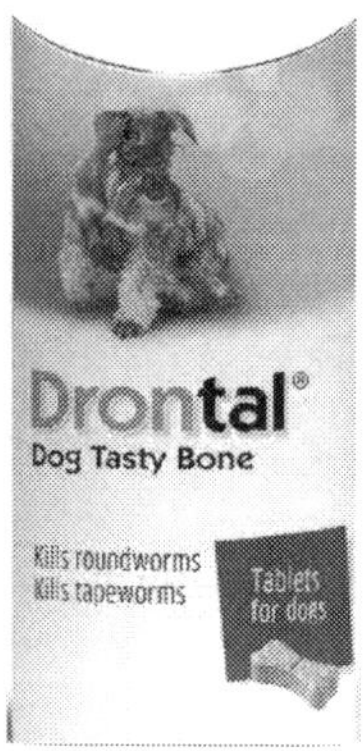

Panacur and Safe-Guard – The active ingredient in these deworming medications is 'Fenbendazole' (anti-parasitic). These drugs provide an effective treatment for dogs to eliminate several gastrointestinal worms, including roundworms, tapeworms, and lungworms.

Droncit, Drontal (see picture) – These are highly effective treatments against all common species of tapeworm that infect dogs. They are developed with praziquantel as the main active ingredient and target both the immature and mature forms of tapeworm by damaging their normal functions.

Natural Worming Products – If you are concerned about the possible side effects of conventional worming products, you may prefer to choose from many natural alternatives to treat and prevent parasites from invading your golden's body, such as:

Pumpkin Seeds. These contain an amino acid that paralyses the worms to get rid of them. Just one teaspoon of raw seeds per 4.5 kilograms (10 pounds) of body weight twice a day is very effective.

Carrots. If you coarsely chop up carrots and add them to your puppy's dinner, they will scrape the walls of the stomach during digestion, removing mucus and any parasites contained within it. Since carrots are a source of vitamin A, they also boost the immune system.

Coconut. This is a 'vermifuge' or agent that destroys or expels parasitic worms. When dried and sprinkled on your golden's dinner, coconut can easily kill off any worms. It also helps to prevent further invasive parasitic infections. A recommended daily dosage depends on your dog's weight, as follows:

- Puppies and small dogs: ½ to 1 teaspoon.
- Medium-sized dogs: 2 teaspoons.
- Large dogs: 1 tablespoon.

You can also regularly give coconut oil to your dog to clear out any internal parasites. As an added bonus, it also helps your dog develop a lovely shiny coat, eliminates bacteria, improves digestion, and reduces inflammation.

Turmeric (see picture). This is an antibacterial, antifungal, anti-inflammatory super food that contains four compounds to help eliminate worms as well as boost the immune system. It also assists in repairing any damage the parasites have caused to the intestine. If you combine turmeric with coconut oil, it will be easier for your puppy to absorb.

Cider Vinegar. This can be an effective worm treatment. Fermented vinegar increases the alkaline levels in the intestines, making it an inhospitable environment for parasites. You should add ¼ to 1 teaspoon of raw organic vinegar to your dog's water bowl. It's important you dilute cider vinegar so it doesn't damage your dog's teeth enamel.

Diatomaceous Earth (see picture). This is made from the remains of microscopic, one-celled plants—phytoplankton—that used to live in the oceans and lakes and are now mined from underwater beds or the bottom of ancient, dried lakes. If you were to look at diatomaceous earth under a microscope, these crushed particles would look like tiny shards of broken glass. When the sharp particles touch a parasite, they pierce the protective coating dehydrating the pest dehydrate and killing it.

FACT ***Diatomaceous earth is packed with many beneficial minerals—calcium, copper, magnesium, iron, phosphorous, potassium, selenium, silicon, sodium, and zinc—making it an effective nutritional supplement.***

Food-grade diatomaceous earth is inexpensive, easy to use and deadly to any parasite, yet completely harmless to animals. It's a natural way to eliminate all intestinal worms and parasites in both dogs and humans. The recommended daily dosage to sprinkle on your retriever's dinner will depend on their weight. For a golden retriever puppy, the suggested dose is ½ teaspoon.

6. Golden Retriever Behaviour

'The average dog is a nicer person than the average person.'

~ Andy Rooney ~

What is fascinating about our dogs is that they must learn the language of an entirely new species so they can communicate with us. You could even say they try to understand how we think better than we understand how they think.

Our dogs are highly capable of observing behaviour and understanding subtle differences. While we try to communicate with them as if they are humans, they do not try to communicate with us like we are dogs. They only understand that the differences between the species are vast, so they develop ways to communicate with us so we can understand them. Golden retrievers know there are some things they can't do, such as reaching the top shelf where the treats are, or opening the locked door to the back garden, so they devise clever ways to get their messages across to their owners. For example, how many times have you seen a dog sit at a door and bark or sit in front of the cupboard where their favourite treat is kept? Without saying a word, you know exactly what your retriever is asking for.

Since goldens will never learn how to talk, they communicate what they are thinking through their body language and behaviour. If you are observant, you will soon develop unspoken communication with your golden retriever. For instance, if your dog wants to play, they will signal this message with their play bow body language (see *Body Language Messages* in Chapter 7).

While the dog brain is smaller than ours, it has similarities to the human brain in that the left hemisphere is associated with language for both dogs and humans. Scientists have established that a dog's brain is capable of the following:

- Vocabulary recognition equivalent to that of a preschool child.
- Memory skills—they can remember familiar people, places, and animals.
- Sensing danger.
- Learning search patterns.
- Learning to discriminate smells, signals, and sounds.
- Establishing routines.
- Anticipating people's habits.
- Problem-solving.
- Reading human behaviour.

Though our canine companions may be highly accomplished, there is a greater difference between how dogs and humans think in the part of the frontal cortex associated with higher-level reasoning.

Okay, so we can't expect our dogs to do our tax returns for us. However, even though dogs are an entirely different species from humans, they are capable of so much more than we give them credit for.

Canine Emotions

For millennia, dogs have been considered 'man's best friend'. Today we view our canine companions in much the same way as any human family member. We can do our best to learn how to be a 'dog's best friend', and this includes being aware of canine emotions.

FACT ***Even though the range of canine emotions remains a bone of contention, science has proven that both dogs and humans have the same hormones and undergo the same chemical responses during various emotional states.***

Did you know that dogs also generate the hormone 'oxytocin' that creates feelings of affection and love for others in humans? Since both species possess similar brains, neurology, and chemical reactions, it's not unreasonable to assume that the ability to experience emotions is similar for both humans and dogs.

However, before we go too far with anthropomorphising our furry friends, recent scientific evidence has shown that a dog's mind is not as fully developed as that of an adult human. It is believed a mature dog's mind is approximately equivalent to the mind of a 2 to 2 ½-year-old child. This suggests your retriever's mind can experience emotions like a toddler who has not yet developed a full complement of emotions. Therefore, the emotions your golden will feel are the basic ones, such as:

- Anger.
- Anticipation.
- Anxiety.
- Contentment.
- Disgust.
- Excitement.
- Fear.
- Frustration.
- Joy.
- Love.

Current research tends towards the idea that the more complex emotions, such as feelings of shame (for having peed on the floor), pride (for winning a dog show) or guilt (for stealing a biscuit from your plate), will simply not exist in the mind of a dog.

Emotion and the Senses

Your golden's nose dominates their brain as the part dedicated to scent is forty times greater in a dog than in a human. There is more emphasis on information they get from scent and smell rather than focusing on emotions. Nevertheless, the evidence suggests your golden retriever's emotional experiences might be even greater than we ever imagined.

Has something you smelt ever evoked a memory? When you or your golden inhale, scent molecules stimulate chemical messages, bypassing other areas of the brain and going straight to the amygdala, the brain's emotional centre. This passes emotional judgments to other structures that put together memories that are then passed on to the cortex. Emotionally appropriate hormones that affect mood are then released into the body. Since your dog's dominant sense is smell and a large portion of the brain is dedicated to processing scent, it is further evidence that dogs might be more driven by their emotions than we've ever acknowledged.

The Food/Brain Relationship

Understanding the connection between the food your dog eats and brain function provides us with crucial data not only about how the brain works but also how we can use that information to help dogs learn and modify behavioural states such as anxiety and fear. For example, stimulating your retriever's sense of smell with food will not only motivate your dog to learn but is also a valuable tool in changing the way their brain works.

Many people think using food as a reward is tantamount to bribery. What they do not understand is how powerful food is as a motivator. Giving your dog food reduces the impact of fear.

When your retriever is frightened, several changes happen in their body. Their heart beats faster, their blood pressure rises, and blood flow is diverted to their muscles to prepare for fight or flight. If food is offered before your retriever reaches a high level of stress, a positive emotional response can take place instead, thanks to the presentation or anticipation of the food.

Some circuits in your dog's brain encourage seeking or hunting behaviour, while others elicit the fear response. Giving your golden retriever a tasty treat or a toy filled with food will activate their seeker system and shut off fear. In turn, this encourages them to play a game in the presence of something they are afraid of.

As such, activities like scent work are incredibly valuable for frightened dogs. Turning on your golden's thinking brain deactivates their emotional brain, enhancing your dog's attention with positive motivation. It allows your dog to move into a calmer state where learning can take place. This is one reason why most canine trainers consider positive reinforcement with treats to be the most effective training method (see more details in Chapter 11).

Canine Personalities

Golden retrievers are full of character, and every dog has their unique traits, but did you know there are just five basic personality types? They are:

1. Shy.
2. Confident.
3. Independent.
4. Adaptable.
5. Happy or laidback.

While most puppies fit into one or more of the categories listed above, a large factor in influencing how your golden retriever's personality develops is usually related to the people, places, and situations they encounter during their first six months. When you understand what personality type is more dominant in your puppy, you receive valuable insight into how they view their world and important clues about the best way to raise and train them.

The Shy or Timid Personality

Some golden retriever puppies can be naturally timid, nervous, or shy, especially when meeting new people and dogs or being introduced to new places or situations. Introducing a shy puppy to new experiences requires a patient, slow, and careful approach, so they do not feel overwhelmed. When they are learning about their new world, it is important not to force them into situations that could frighten them because they could start to mistrust you.

Your shy or nervous puppy will learn best at a slow pace that includes plenty of treats and enthusiastic encouragement. If your puppy has a naturally timid and sensitive personality and does not enjoy loud or chaotic environments, they will flourish better in a calm home where there is harmony between family members and there are no small children to startle them.

The Confident Personality

A confident golden retriever has no worries when venturing out into the world. However, since this kind of puppy is happy to take charge of a situation, they may display dominance towards another dog. Nevertheless, they are generally comfortable as a team player. This outgoing pup does well at the side of an equally confident owner who trains with positive reinforcement, and they could be a great candidate for learning many canine sports and tricks.

The Independent Personality

A golden retriever with an independent personality is a one-person dog who is often standoffish with strangers and does best with an owner who can provide firm leadership. This dog might be a challenge to train for new dog owners because they prefer to think for themselves. However, if the owner has the skills, understands the independent mind, and establishes a relationship of trust and respect, there is no limit to what such a team might accomplish together.

The Adaptable Personality

The adaptable puppy easily fits into any type of situation, as they are willing to do whatever their owner asks of them. A puppy who has a naturally strong desire to please is easy to train and usually a friendly, yet not overly boisterous, retriever who will get along well with everyone while paying attention to their owner. This type of loving, calm personality will often be the perfect candidate for a therapy dog.

The Happy, Laidback Personality

The happy, laidback golden is the one with the ever-wagging tail who loves everybody, whether human or animal. So friendly are these types of dogs that they will gleefully welcome any intruders into the home and even help them carry their ill-gotten gains to the get-away vehicle!

FACT ***The golden retriever's personality usually falls under the happy or adaptable category. However, every dog is always unique, so your golden might easily have traits from the other personality types too.***

They are a highly enthusiastic greeter who cannot resist bouncing all over everyone in their excitement to make a new friend. Though laidback dogs are easy to train, take care to teach them to be calm around toddlers or unsteady seniors whom they could accidentally knock over.

Top 13 Golden Retriever Traits

While a dog is still a dog regardless of breed, so there will be some traits you can expect from all canines, each specific breed has characteristics that are associated with them. Golden retrievers have some very breed-specific and unique personality traits all their own, and as you are considering owning one, or already do, it is important to know all about these:

1. They are generally open and welcoming to strangers. They also enjoy being petted by people whom they have only just met.
2. These dogs have a strong reputation for being kind and tolerant of children, which is why they're so popular with families. They will often bond strongly with your children and be happy to play with them – and share their biscuits! You need to make sure your children are taught the correct way to handle and play with them and know when to leave them alone.
3. These dogs tend to be very receptive and trusting of their owner once they know what is expected of them. They take new challenges and situations in their stride without excessive levels of fear.

4. Golden retrievers are a very sociable breed who don't like being on their own for hours at a time. As such, they are more prone than other breeds to developing separation anxiety. It is important to start training your golden from a young age to willingly use a crate or go to their bed to chill out, so they learn they cannot be around people all the time. The golden is a real people pleaser and typically works hard to achieve what you ask them to do when training.
5. The golden is typically very placid and forgiving of children's mistakes, but when pushed too far, they will eventually growl or snap.
6. These dogs are intelligent enough to learn quickly and repeat commands reliably. They will love working one-to-one with you and picking up new skills.
7. Golden retrievers easily learn to perform tricks as well as a range of higher-level commands, which is why they're such good candidates for therapy dogs. They work well on the praise and reward structure of positive reinforcement training while being given treats they like for successful responses.
8. Calm, kind, but firm handling is the best approach with golden retrievers. Their lively natures, high intelligence, and eagerness to make you smile will make training them a very pleasant experience.
9. As a working dog breed, the golden was traditionally bred to be confident, bold, and calm in most situations when faced with the unknown. While they are now more commonly kept as pets at home than as working animals, they have retrained these traits, so it is unusual to find a golden retriever who is more shy and reserved.
10. As a general rule, golden retrievers are naturally calm and non-aggressive. However, there are some instances when your golden may display aggression. If they are afraid, sense danger, have been abused, have been poorly trained, or come from a puppy farm, they may display signs of aggression in certain circumstances. Take the time to get to know why your dog is being aggressive so you can work to resolve the problem.

11. As a working breed, golden retrievers were bred to spend most of their day outside running around and staying active in both body and mind. These dogs are tenacious hunters, but they can also be trained to suppress their natural hunting instinct when inappropriate. They are lively, active dogs who need regular daily exercise and are certainly not one of the more sedentary breeds.
12. You should provide lots of play, stimulation, and exercise to keep your golden entertained within the family home.
13. Golden retrievers are very affectionate dogs who will never say no to a cuddle.

20 Ways to Avoid Unwanted Behaviour

It's always best to avoid developing unwanted habits rather than trying to fix them after the fact. Sometimes, we are unaware that it's our actions which encourage a dog to behave badly. For example, it is easy to think that a good way of distracting your misbehaving dog is to pick them up or give them a treat. However, any sort of reward—treats, picking them up, talking soothingly, petting them, undivided attention—given to your dog when they display unwanted behaviour is likely to send an unspoken signal to your golden retriever that their behaviour was a good thing.

Now and then, an owner inadvertently blurs the lines of communication between themselves and their dog. For example, you might be playing fetch at the park. If your golden is excited about chasing the ball, when they bark at you to throw it, you will probably throw the ball in response. Now your retriever has learnt that if they bark, they get what they want.

FACT ***How dogs learn is mainly through associating an action with a result. For instance, a dog quickly learns to connect the action of picking up their lead with the result of going out for a walk.***

To take preventative action and avoid unwanted behaviour from your golden retriever before it occurs, do the following:

1. Never give a treat or life reward—picking them up, petting, talking soothingly—as a distraction for unwanted behaviour such as barking, growling, or lunging. No matter what your retriever does, you need to stay calm. Be careful. Even angry shouts or upset gestures could be misinterpreted as play or encouragement, which is something your dog will take as an encouragement to continue. Instead, keep your gestures slow and deliberate, your voice low and level, and all your actions placatory to help calm your dog.
2. Extensively socialise your retriever, so they learn not to overreact when meeting new people and dogs or being introduced to new situations.
3. If they become overly excited in any situation—such as meeting new dogs or people—remove them from the source of excitement, so they learn being overly excited is unacceptable.
4. If they do display unwanted behaviour of any sort, be assertive by firmly saying, 'No.' They need to learn from you what is acceptable.
5. Teach your golden to be patient by not giving them what they want, for instance, if they barked for the ball or pulled harder to get to the park. Slow down, so they start to understand being

impatient does not get them what they want. It can be helpful to have an interrupt command your retriever will obey when they do something bad. You could use 'Stop', 'No', 'Drop it', or 'Leave it' to get your dog's attention and let them know their behaviour is unacceptable. A harsh, loud tone of voice helps reinforce the meaning of your command and teaches your golden to cease and desist.

6. Praise them for good behaviour. If they are excited when they see a stranger, teach them to sit when meeting new people and then treat and/or praise them for being good.
7. If you're noticing consistently bad behaviour, consider increasing the amount of exercise your retriever gets. A bored and/or under-exercised dog is more likely to act up than a tired dog. Some bad behaviour, such as digging or chasing, could be the result of pent-up energy. Giving your retriever more exercise lets them use that energy in more positive ways. They are then less likely to misbehave. It also reinforces your bond with your dog, so they are more likely to pay attention to you and obey your commands.
8. Give them mental as well as physical exercise. Teaching them a trick, command, or routine as mental exercise is even more tiring than a good walk.
9. Teach rules and boundaries, so they learn to respect you and follow their commands.
10. Teach basic commands before they are 4-months old, so you establish a relationship of trust and respect (see how in Chapter 11).
11. Desensitise them if the prospect of going for a walk makes them overly excited. For example, put on their lead but then wait to go out until they are calm and listening to you.
12. Teach them to be quiet when someone knocks on the door. When someone arrives, have them sit and wait at least 3 metres from the door and ask visitors to ignore them until they are calm.

13. Teach them not to pull on their lead when on a walk. The second the lead is tight because they are not beside you, stop walking, so they learn that feeling tension on the lead means no forward movement.
14. Teach them to bark on command if they bark too much. Often, training your dog to bark with hand signals stops excessive barking because they will wait for the command to speak.
15. Get to know all the things they love, and then use those things as rewards for their good behaviour.
16. Teach your dog hand signals for all their commands. Hand signals make them more attentive as they must pay attention to you to know what they are being asked to do (see details in Chapter 11).
17. Ensure your golden has their own space at home where they won't be disturbed by family members or guests. Give them a quiet place they can escape to whenever they need. This will help them feel safe, even if they don't use it very much. Having the option to get away will often make your retriever feel more comfortable and less likely to misbehave.
18. Consistency is key. You need to make sure everyone uses the same approach with your dog. Even if you do not feed your dog treats from the table, if your spouse or children secretly do, they will

soon learn to beg. Or if you don't let your retriever jump up on you, but others encourage it, inevitably, they will think this is permissible. Everyone must follow the rules to set the standards for your retriever's behaviour.

19. In extreme cases, it can be necessary to work with a trainer to try to curb your golden retriever's bad behaviour. A good trainer will offer you several options for controlling unwanted behaviour. They will also help identify what will work best for your golden to stop their unwelcome actions and encourage more positive behaviour instead.
20. Some instinctual behaviour, such as chewing and digging, might be impossible to stop completely. Instead, redirect your golden to more appropriate choices, like providing safe chew toys or allowing digging in one specific spot to spare the rest of your garden from unwanted attention.

Many types of bad behaviour are purely attention-seeking, such as jumping up, barking, or begging. If you ignore their behaviour, your golden retriever will not receive the attention they are seeking, and their behaviour will eventually change. This means you shouldn't shout at or punish your retriever, as even negative attention is still the attention your dog craves.

Behaviour with Children

Teaching children the proper way to interact with your golden retriever is very important, especially at an early age. Toddlers might not understand how easily a small puppy can be injured during rough play, while older children should already know they must be careful.

TIP ***When introducing your golden puppy to younger children, keep a watchful eye on both children and dog, so everyone remains safe. Some situations can potentially create problems with a new canine family member, such as if a child squeezes your puppy or yanks their ears.***

We all love our children and dogs unconditionally and want them to live in harmony together. The best way to avoid problems between younger children and your golden puppy is to teach children the difference between an inanimate stuffed toy and a live puppy. Children can easily be taught to interact appropriately with the puppy, so your retriever is not afraid and does not feel the need to protect themselves with a growl or a nip. It is a good idea to provide a safe and secure refuge for your puppy, such as a crate, so they can get away from children when they want to.

There are many fun activities children can play with their golden retriever without any rough play, such as:

- Fetching a ball.
- Gentle playing with puppy toys.
- Simple tricks with treat rewards.
- Playing hide-and-seek.
- Going for a walk.
- Giving the puppy their dinner.

Always be extra safe and vigilantly supervise when there are young children around your puppy, as accidents can happen that might not be anyone's fault.

How to Keep a Baby Safe

Even though most adult dogs are generally tolerant of babies as they can sense they are young and helpless, the same is not true of puppies who might have no prior experience. Puppies can learn to both love and to be afraid of babies, which is why properly introducing your puppy to a baby will help them become friends. The following suggestions will make your golden's introduction to the baby a positive experience:

- Allow your puppy to see, sniff, and gently touch the baby, so they understand there is nothing to fear.
- Always associate something good with the baby. Give your retriever a treat to reward them when they calmly approach for a sniff.
- Do not make a big fuss when the puppy is around the baby, as you want your puppy to think the baby is just a normal part of their world.
- Always closely supervise any interactions between baby and puppy and never leave them alone together.
- Do not force your puppy to approach the baby, especially if the baby is crying.

How to Keep a Toddler Safe

The best way to keep toddlers safe around puppies and older dogs is to teach them the proper way to safely interact with all dogs, whether it is the family puppy or a strange dog they meet when they're out and about. Here are a few things to teach your toddler:

- Never run up to a strange puppy or dog, as this might startle or scare them.
- Never approach a strange dog without first getting permission from you and the dog's owner.
- Always go up to a dog slowly and quietly.
- Let the dog approach and sniff the child's hand.
- Tell them not to put their hands on top of the dog's head. It is better to stroke them under the chin or the chest.
- If the dog appears nervous about the child, do not force an encounter.
- Never approach a dog that is focused on a treat or a toy.
- Never approach a puppy or dog when they are eating.
- Never approach or try to wake up a sleeping puppy or dog.
- Never tug on a puppy's ears, tail, or feet.
- Do not hug puppies or dogs. They are not humans and usually don't enjoy it.
- Do not yell, scream, or run around a puppy or dog.
- Do not pick up a young puppy—most toddlers will want to—as they could accidentally squeeze too tight or drop it.
- Eat food where the puppy cannot reach it because puppies can be tempted to grab food that is easily within reach, and this could scare a child.

Never expect all dogs to like or accept children, especially those who have never experienced them before or have had negative encounters.

Behaviour with other pets

A golden retriever puppy will not usually harbour any ill intentions towards other household pets and is curious and excited to meet them. However, your puppy might not have previous experience with other dogs, cats, birds, or other pets, and will not understand how to meet and greet in a safe way that does not upset anyone. As a retrieving dog, you should also be aware that sometimes instincts might overrule training, especially where birds are involved.

Introducing an Older Dog

Some older dogs will welcome a new puppy, while others can feel that their turf is being invaded and might react by growling. Of course, much of how an already established canine member reacts to your puppy will depend on how respectful or boisterous your golden retriever is when meeting the older dog.

Here are several steps to take that can make their first meeting less traumatic and more pleasant:

- Let them meet outside your home on neutral ground and/or with a fence between them.
- Take the puppy and the older dog for a walk side by side.
- Go to a local park, and if it's safe and they have good recall, allow both to be off-lead.
- Let them sniff each other.
- Give both dogs a treat as a reward for calm behaviour.
- If they decide to play together, do not let it get too out of control.
- Walk home with both dogs.
- Stop in the garden and let them sniff about.
- Offer them both treats again for calm behaviour.
- Have the older dog enter the home first.

Once these two new companions have spent some time together in an unthreatening space, it should be much easier to integrate your new golden retriever into the home environment. However, until you are certain your puppy and older dog have learnt to be considerate of each other's space, always keep a close eye on both.

Introducing a Cat

Many golden retrievers love their feline friends. However, it can take some careful planning to make sure your golden puppy does not end up with a scratch, and the cat is not overly stressed during first encounters. The following steps will help keep everyone safe:

- Place the cat in another room with the door closed.
- Place a blanket with your puppy's scent on it next to the cat.
- Put a cat-scented blanket where your puppy can find it.
- Encourage your retriever to sniff under the door where the cat is.

- Let them hear and smell each other without direct contact.
- Place the cat in a pet carrier.
- Place the cat carrier in the middle of the room.
- Allow your puppy to walk around and sniff at the carrier. If your pup starts becoming over-excited or barking at the carrier, take them away to calm down before continuing.
- Place your puppy on its lead and open the carrier door.
- Let the cat come out of their carrier of its own accord.

At this point, when the cat slinks out of its carrier, they may want to run away from your puppy and hide or gain higher ground by jumping up on a worktop or sofa. Keep a tight hold of your puppy's lead, as they will probably be curious and might try to chase after the cat.

TIP ***If the cat does not immediately run and seems to want to get a little closer to check out your puppy, let them slowly greet. The moment it seems your puppy is going to become too excited or the cat hisses, put some space between them, so the cat does not become scared, and your retriever learns to be calm around them.***

Once it is clear the cat is not worried by your new puppy, you can let the dog off their lead. However, always keep a close eye on them both, so you can step in to create some space if anyone gets too aggressive or over-excited.

Introducing a Pet Bird

Most dogs naturally view birds as prey especially breeds like the golden retriever that were specifically bred for hunting birds. Even so, if they are introduced slowly and carefully, they can learn to get along. Thankfully, most pet birds usually live in a secure cage well out of reach of a puppy. When the bird is in its cage, simply let them hear and observe one another. If the bird is occasionally allowed to fly outside its cage, the following steps will help to make them comfortable together:

- Place the bird's cage near your golden puppy.
- Let them take a while to observe one another.
- When they are calm, give them both a treat.
- Move the bird's cage closer to your puppy.
- When both remain calm, give each another treat.
- Place the bird's cage next to your pup and let them be eye to eye.
- If they both stay calm, give each one more treat.

Practise this type of exercise every day for several days, paying close attention to how excited the bird and your retriever puppy are. Your eventual goal is to remove the bird from its cage and allow it to sit on your hand or shoulder while your puppy is nearby. However, you should be prepared for this to never be a possibility.

You can never predict how your puppy will react to a bird, especially if the bird suddenly squawks or flaps its wings. No matter how carefully you introduce them to each other, remember golden retrievers retain an instinct to hunt birds. Despite how friendly you think they may be, always be vigilant or you might be faced with a tragedy.

Introducing a Small Mammal

Many smaller pets are natural prey for a dog, including rats, mice, gerbils, hamsters, and rabbits. When introducing a small mammal to your golden, even when they are young puppies, you should be extra careful, as most retrievers are hard-wired to seek and destroy these tiny creatures.

Prey drive, which is the urge to hunt and kill small creatures, will usually be strongest in breeds that have a working history of being hunters, such as the golden retriever.

Encouraging your golden to make friends with a pet rodent could be expecting too much of your dog, and it might not be possible to completely trust the two to get along. If you decide to go for it and introduce your little pet to a retriever puppy, the following steps might come in handy:

- Put your puppy on a lead and place your pet's cage a metre or two away. Let them observe one another and get used to how they both smell.
- If both remain calm, give each of them a reward.
- Move the cage closer to the pup.
- If they remain calm, give another treat to both.
- You might like to put a muzzle on your golden retriever at this stage.
- Open the small animal's cage and let them out.
- Keep a tight grip on your puppy's lead.
- Allow the small mammal and puppy to come close to one another.
- If your puppy tries to nip or becomes aggressive, take them away.
- If your little pet starts to become agitated, fluffs up its hair, chomps its teeth, or tries to bite, immediately place it back in its cage.

While some small pets and retrievers can learn to become friends and even enjoy playing together, closely observing any interaction is essential.

Common Behaviour Issues

Many canine behaviour issues are more common than you might think. The 10th PDSA Animal Wellbeing (PAW) report in 2020 revealed that 75% of dog owners would like to change their dog's behaviour. So, if this is how you feel, you're not alone! Dogs pick up bad habits in the same way humans do, which can create problems for their owners.

Behaviours like jumping up and pulling on the lead are both annoying and frustrating. However difficult it is not to become annoyed when your dog does things you do not want it to, bear in mind that no dog is perfect. If you would like to change some of your retriever's habits, you must remain calm and teach your dog a better way to behave. After all, infuriating as they can be, I'm sure you wouldn't swap your canine friend for the world! Read on to see how to eliminate these bad habits.

Excessive Barking

Barking is your dog's natural way of communicating. Depending on the breed and its history, some dogs are more prone to vocalise than others. The golden retriever is not known to bark a lot, but occasionally may bark for reasons such as:

- If they need to warn you about intruders.
- If they're excited or happy to meet another dog or person.
- If they're bored or anxious.
- If they're protecting property or family.
- If they're eager to go for a walk.
- When playing with other dogs or children.

- When playing fetch.
- If they're feeling dominant.
- Attention-seeking.
- If they're feeling afraid.

When your golden retriever becomes a member of their human family, excessive barking is not going to be appropriate behaviour. Once you've determined the reason for their excessive barking, stopping this unwanted behaviour will involve communicating to them that this is not acceptable to you. There are three simple steps to make your retriever stop barking:

- Firmly say, '***No***' and tell them to '***Sit***' whenever they bark.
- Remove them from the source of whatever is making them bark.
- Let them see what it was that made them bark.

By following these steps, your dog will view this as you are taking charge of the situation since; (1) they were given a command, and their attention was diverted back to you; (2) space was created between them and the provocation for their barking; and (3) they were allowed to see it was nothing to get upset about. You can read more about canine barking in the *Canine Sounds* section, Chapter 7.

Destructive Chewing

Chewing objects is natural, normal, and necessary for a puppy or older dog because it is how they explore their world. Golden retrievers are known to be especially prone to chewing compared to other breeds because they were bred to carry things in their mouths.

A young puppy will chew everything in sight to relieve the pain of teething and help their adult teeth push through. An older dog also needs to chew, and their reasons for doing so include:

- To relieve boredom.
- To offset mild anxiety.
- To help keep their teeth clean and their jaws strong.
- To stave off hunger pangs.

FACT ***If your golden retriever is chewing to relieve boredom, they are not getting enough attention. If you spend more time with them engaging in outdoor adventures, training, socialising, and involving them in more physical and mental activities, this type of chewing usually disappears.***

If your dog is chewing to relieve themselves from mild anxiety, this tends to happen when they are left alone and feel frustrated and upset. It may also be accompanied by whining, barking, or escape attempts. If your retriever is chewing inappropriate items when left alone, this is their way of saying they are unhappy being by themselves so much. There are several ways to alleviate this type of mild anxiety:

- Vigorously exercise them before they are left alone, so they are tired and more likely to sleep while you're away.
- Re-visit crate-training methods until you have established how long they're comfortable staying in their crate.

- Find ways to keep them occupied while you are away. Give them interesting chew toys and food puzzles.
- Put on soothing, calm music while you are away.
- If you can, take them with you when you go out.
- Shorten the length of time you leave them alone.
- If you really have to be away for a long time, have someone else stay with your dog.

Dogs need to chew to keep their teeth clean and their jaws strong. If they do not have chew toys that satisfy this natural chewing urge, they may turn to shoes, the corner of a carpet, or the furniture.

Each dog is different in terms of what they like to chew and how gentle or tough a chewer they are. This often means a little experimentation before finding the right chew toys.

For instance, if your golden retriever has a strong bite, giving them a chew toy designed for a soft chewer could mean they quickly destroy it. They may even accidentally ingest some. Chew toys are identified according to whether they are for soft, medium, or heavy chewers. Here are some examples:

- Firm rubber toys—these can be any shape.
- Rope toys—good for tug-of-war games.
- Balls or durable, stuffed toys—for fetch games.
- Interactive toys—these can be stuffed with treats.
- Treat dispenser or puzzle toys.
- Self-amusement toys—they can play with them when alone.
- Comfort toys—soft, plush toys your retriever likes to sleep with.
- Synthetic bones—there are many types, sizes, and strengths.
- Real bones—choose organic and avoid cooking them, as this can cause shards to break off.
- Antler pieces—if they are not processed with chemicals and additives, these are great for a heavy chewer.

From time to time, your golden retriever might begin to chew on unacceptable things because they are hungry. If your dog is regularly underfed or they are on a restricted-calorie diet, they could start to chew objects to add more sustenance to their diet. If this is the case, there are a few steps you should take:

- Weigh your retriever to determine if they are the right weight for their age and size.
- Take them to the vet for a complete check-up. They might have worms that are eating their food before it is digested.
- If they are receiving plenty of daily exercise and are not overweight, feed them more.

When your retriever is engaging in destructive chewing behaviour, resolving this problem can be as simple as teaching them what they **are** and what they **aren't** permitted to chew. The following tips will help:

- If you haven't already, dog-proof your home. Place items your golden might want to chew out of reach and off the floor.

- Give your dog plenty of things they are allowed to chew, and praise them when they choose one.
- Use a deterrent spray on objects you can't move out of reach—i.e., furniture.
- Make a note of when they are more likely to want to chew and provide an interesting chew toy, treat puzzle, or walk to keep them occupied at those times.
- Do not give your puppy an old shoe, pair of socks, or another article of clothing to play with as they will not be able to differentiate between an old trainer and your new pair of expensive shoes.
- Often, destructive chewing is a direct result of your retriever's frustration and boredom from lack of exercise or mental stimulation appropriate to their age and activity level. Make sure they get regular exercise and have plenty of toys and games to occupy them.

Digging

Digging is a primal urge for almost every dog, large or small, just like barking is part of being a dog. Some breeds are more prone to dig as they were bred for their ability to dig and search for their prey in underground dens. Golden retrievers are among these breeds. Many dig simply because they enjoy it, while others do it due to relieve boredom, anxiety, and more. (See below.)

FACT ***The instinctual need to paw at the carpet or the cushions on the sofa before settling down is likely a throwback to the times before dogs were domesticated. When it was time to settle down for the night, they would often circle and dig as a way of disguising their scent.***

Today, there are other reasons why your dog might dig, including:

- Hunting rodents tunnelling just under the surface.
- Burying a bone to save it for later.
- Wanting to find cooler ground on a hot day.
- The denning instinct when pregnant.
- Digging under a fence to escape captivity.
- To relieve boredom or anxiety.
- It's fun!

Although it can be difficult to curtail your retriever's urge to dig, especially as the breed has a particularly strong instinct for this activity, there are ways to control it so your back garden isn't filled with craters.

First, think about why your retriever might be digging. Next, consider whether they are getting enough exercise or interesting mental stimulation throughout their day. If they aren't, they could simply be digging to relieve boredom. An easy fix for that would be to take them for more walks or set aside time to teach them a new trick or command. Other things that can minimise the destruction of a perfectly landscaped garden include:

- Always supervising your dog when they are in the garden.
- Providing interesting puzzle toys.
- Sectioning off an area for a sandbox and burying toys in it, so it's the most fun place to dig.
- Playing fetch.

- Setting up an agility course.
- Placing rocks along fence lines.

Ground Scratching

Many dogs, including the golden retriever, scrape the ground with their hind legs after peeing or pooing. While this is a natural and healthy activity, it can destroy a neatly manicured lawn.

The reason dogs do this is deeply ingrained and instinctual. Just like peeing on trees to mark their territory, when they scratch the ground after toileting, they're marking their territory. Canines have scent glands on their paws, and when they scratch the ground, not only does it leave a visible warning scar to other dogs, but it also transfers the long-lasting scent from the paw glands to the ground. Although it is difficult to completely curb this ground-scratching instinct, there are several things you can do to minimise the activity:

- When you're in the back garden, immediately interrupt your dog with a favourite toy before they start scraping.
- As soon as they finish their toilet routine, call them to you to get a treat.
- Section off a corner of your garden for your golden retriever's toilet so they don't scrape up the whole garden.
- Take them for on-lead toilet walks outside the home, so if they begin to scratch the ground, you can easily interrupt them.

When your dog is engaging in an activity that is simply part of their natural instincts, while you can redirect this behaviour by interrupting them, you need to be patient and reasonable about what you can expect.

Separation Anxiety (Separation Distress)

Many golden retriever puppies and dogs suffer from separation anxiety when they become hyper-attached to their owners. Some sensitive breeds that have been bred for close companionship tend to be more prone to developing this type of anxiety than others. Goldens were bred to have strong ties with their owners so they could be good at their job, which means they rely on their human family more than other breeds.

FACT ***Golden retrievers frequently suffer from separation anxiety, as they do not like to be left on their own and tend to become anxious or stressed when their owner leaves the house. It can get so bad that just seeing you putting your coat on or picking up your keys could trigger your golden's anxiety.***

Fortunately, there are ways to treat your retriever's separation anxiety and minimise stress. If you don't take the time to crate train or gradually get your puppy used to spending brief times alone, it can be harder to eradicate separation anxiety when your puppy is older. If your golden retriever puppy is suffering from the stress of separation anxiety, there are many behavioural issues they may engage in, including:

- Whining.
- Chewing.
- Howling.
- Barking.

- Crying.
- Pacing.
- Trembling.
- Drooling.
- Panting.
- Digging around windows or doors.
- Escape attempts.
- Pooing or peeing in the house.

If your golden puppy feels extreme stress, they can seem terrified, as if the end of the world is nigh, since they are so worried the person they rely upon might never return. The only way to support your puppy through this if they have not previously learnt to tolerate moments alone is to teach them as soon as possible that no harm will come to them if they are alone for a while. Here are some tips that can help your retriever feel far more relaxed about their alone time:

Exercise – The first thing to do before leaving your puppy by themselves for a while is to take them out for an energetic walk, so they are tired when you leave them alone. A good mental workout is equally taxing, so perhaps teach them a new trick or command. A tired puppy will always be less stressed and could simply fall asleep.

Haven – Your golden retriever should have a quiet place set up somewhere where they can settle and relax when at home. Think about things that might interrupt your dog when creating their special place. If your retriever gets frustrated, you might want to set this up in a room that does not overlook the garden or roads. Apprehensive or anxious dogs often prefer a crate covered with a blanket to hide in. Your retriever should always have free access in and out of their safe area, so if you use a crate, always leave the door open.

Mental stimulation – When you leave your golden, make sure they have plenty of things to keep them occupied and provide them with mental stimulation. Give them to your dog in the room where you will leave them, and make sure they are interested and engaged with them before you go.

Low-key departures – Avoid making too much fuss when leaving your home. Leaving should be a normal, everyday occurrence, so your retriever knows it is not something they need to be stressed about.

Low key arrivals – When you arrive home, quietly greet your golden retriever with gentle, verbal praise and encourage calm behaviour where possible. Try not to over-excite your dog, as you do not want to incite any more stressful behaviour.

Step-by-step – Gradually increase the amount of time your golden is alone. You should do this slowly over a period of a few weeks. Closely watch your dog for signs of stress as you increase the time you leave them and go back to shorter lengths of time if your retriever is starting to show signs of being unsettled.

Baby gates – If you can, instal baby gates throughout the house to allow you to move from room to room without your golden as your perpetual shadow. This will help train your dog to stay relaxed when you are not nearby. Scattering a few morsels of your dog's daily allowance of dry food on the floor when you leave a room will also help distract them.

Teaching to settle down – If your golden retriever is especially anxious and is struggling with you being away from them even for short periods, you can practise teaching them to settle on their own. This will help your retriever become more independent and will improve training in the future. To achieve this, fill a food toy such as a Kong and place it by your feet while watching television. Do this regularly over a few weeks and gradually place it farther away from you each time. This teaches your retriever to settle down and engage in activities without you. While your dog is occupied with the food, go in and out of the room as normal.

Reward independency – Reward any independent behaviour from your dog with gentle praise if they choose to settle down somewhere away from you.

Training – If your golden retriever is frightened or anxious when left alone, it may be down to a lack of confidence. Just like humans, the more you reward your dog and boost their confidence, the more relaxed and content they are to occupy themselves without you. Another way to help your dog to be less anxious about being left alone is by engaging in some basic training they already know to increase their self-confidence.

Calming Aids – There are many calming aids on the market designed to reduce the stress of separation anxiety, including:

- Calming sonic collars.
- Calming chews.
- Thundershirts.
- Calming sprays, essential oils, and diffusers.
- Pheromone products (DAP).
- White noise calming music.
- ZenCrates.
- DogTV.
- Edibles.

Shirts – There are several types of shirts that can help a dog suffering from separation anxiety. The idea behind these shirts is that they provide your retriever puppy with a hugging sensation that helps them feel safer and more secure.

Collars – Species-specific sonic collars are designed to play calming music at the perfect sound frequency to relax your stressed pooch. Copious amounts of research have been carried out recently in this relatively new field of sound behaviour. Clinical studies prove sound therapy is an effective method to reduce your retriever's stress levels.

ZenCrates –Every dog needs to feel they have a safe place to retreat to, and this is even more important when your golden puppy is nervous. Although this safe retreat could easily be your puppy's crate, the 'ZenCrate' (see picture) takes the haven concept several steps further. When your puppy goes into it, motion sensors automatically play soothing music accompanied by gentle airflow while also blocking noise from outside sources, all of which help to relax your dog.

TIP ***Calming, white noise music played in the home has also been shown to help reduce stress, especially for dogs who are nervous when they hear loud, booming noises, such as thunder or sirens.***

DAP Products – There are many pet calming products—sprays, collars, etc. —designed to calm your overstressed retriever puppy or dog using dog-appeasing pheromones (DAP). These products (see picture) contain a synthetic pheromone designed to reduce stress and anxiety by mimicking the 'feel good' pheromone released after a mother dog gives birth. They don't work well for all dogs. Some find them very effective, while others don't really experience any relief.

DogTV – This is the first cable television network created specifically for dogs. It broadcasts television programmes 24/7 designed to entertain dogs and is available in both the U.K. and the U.S. Dog behaviour trainers and specialists have helped to adjust the colour, so it has a particular appeal for canines. The 3 to 6-minute segments are designed to relax, stimulate, and expose your dog to scenes of everyday life, such as doorbells or riding in a car. If you have ever noticed your dog paying attention to your television screen, this could be a viable solution.

Essential Oils – It is known that aromatherapy has a profoundly calming effect on humans, as the molecules react with compounds in our bodies to elicit a physical, mental and emotional response. The same is true for dogs. Essential oils can be mixed into a spray for spritzing bedding or kennels. You can also spray your hands and give your retriever puppy a relaxing massage, apply diluted oils directly to the ears or tummy with a roll-on, or diffuse them through the air so your dog can inhale the calming scents. Some of the most popular essential oils (see picture) for calming your stressed dog include:

- Bergamot – anti-depressant.
- Cedar – reduces panic and repels pests.
- Chamomile – deep, calming, soothing pain relief.
- Cypress – soothes agitated emotions.
- Frankincense – quietens anxiety.
- Lavender –calming.
- Peppermint – mood booster, flea repellent.
- Rock Rose – relieves terror and panic.
- Star of Bethlehem – relieves shock or trauma.
- Sweet marjoram – calming, stress relief.
- Tangerine – soothes the nervous system.
- Vetiver – stress relieving.
- Ylang-ylang – anti-depressant, skin-soothing.

Although a lot of essential oils are safe to use on puppies and dogs, they should always be diluted with a neutral carrier oil—such as coconut or olive oil—so they are not too strong. If you mix your own, the dilution ratio for dogs should be no higher than 1%, for example, 3 drops of pure essential oil mixed into 30 ml (1 oz) of carrier oil.

It is important to be aware many essential oils, such as anise or birch, are NOT suitable for use on pets, as they might be either irritating or toxic if eaten. Before using essential oils on your dog, always check they are safe for your pup.

Edibles – There are many chews, bites, and treats designed to calm your dog if they are suffering from anxiety. These contain a wide variety of natural calming ingredients, such as hemp, chamomile, passionflower, and valerian root. As with DAP products, these edible products (see picture) work for some dogs but not others.

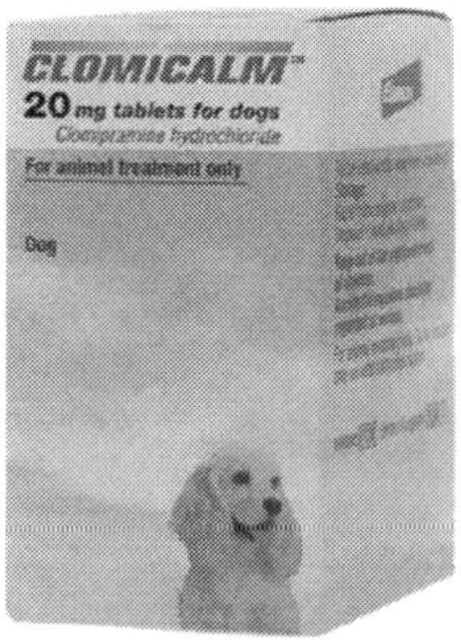

Medications – Your vet can prescribe medication for your golden if they are suffering from the effects of separation anxiety. However, you should do all you can to modify the behaviour more naturally, especially since medications often don't become effective until they have been given for approximately 30 days. The following medications are commonly prescribed for the treatment of canine separation anxiety:

- Alprazolam/Xanax.
- Amitriptyline.
- Buspirone.
- Clomipramine hydrochloride/Clomicalm (see picture).
- Dexmedetomidine/Sileo.

- Diazepam/Valium.
- Fluoxetine/Reconcile or Prozac.
- Lorazepam/Ativan.
- Paroxetine/Paxil.
- Sertraline/Zoloft.

As with any medication prescribed by a health professional, there can be side effects to these drugs, such as weakness or vomiting.

Despite your best efforts, some dogs are so strongly bonded to their owners that they might never truly be able to relax and deal with their feelings of anxiety when they are left alone. In these cases, you will have to try and avoid leaving them alone unless you absolutely have to, or consider having someone stay with them or leave them at a daycare facility.

Begging

Dogs are naturally predisposed to find food wherever they can, even if they are not hungry. When their owners are eating, it is only natural for many dogs to see it as an opportunity to get extra food. Begging is a biological, instinctive behaviour for all dogs who have no idea that humans think it's rude.

Being highly food motivated, goldens are prone to beg while you are eating. It is hard to say no when your sweet golden retriever gazes up at you with those loving eyes. However, unless you are careful, responding to their begging will soon have your intelligent puppy opening cupboards and stealing from the rubbish bin. It is important to nip this habit in the bud before it becomes a problem.

FACT ***Most dogs do not realise that eating everything in sight may not be a good idea and could give them stomach ache or diarrhoea. While many dogs appear to be hungry 24/7, they simply do not know when to stop eating.***

Also, we are often guilty of inciting begging behaviour in the first place. It is easy to do because a pleading golden retriever is usually quite comical and difficult to resist. They might dance about, perform tricks without being asked, closely watch your every bite with an intense stare and 'talk' to you with cute little growls. Those little foibles are so endearing you will often feel compelled to share food with your canine companion, who so clearly craves it.

The reality is your golden retriever begs for food because you probably unwittingly reinforced the behaviour. When your golden wants food, you might only need to give in once to reinforce their begging behaviour. However, when your dog has become skilled at manipulating you into giving them food, there are several things you can do to diminish or even eliminate the behaviour if you do not give in:

- Have your dog sit and stay at least 2-3 metres away from where people are eating.
- Send them to their crate when it is mealtime.
- Give them a puzzle toy to play with while you eat.
- Feed them in their normal place at the same time you're eating.
- Ignore whining, growling, or any cute acrobatics.
- Feed your puppy on a regular schedule.
- Do not give in under any circumstances because any success will encourage your dog to continue.
- Ask visitors not to feed your golden from the table as this will undo all your hard work on stopping their begging.

- Remember, your dog is not really starving, no matter how much they may give that impression!
- Teach yourself not to equate food with loving your dog.
- Give your dog a treat after you've finished eating to reward them for not begging.

When you find yourself falling prey to those manipulative doggy eyes, perhaps it would help to remember that over 50% of dogs are overweight. Over-feeding your dog can contribute to shortening their life.

Chasing

Chasing is an instinct for retrievers. There are many chasing activities dogs might engage in that might be just for fun or dangerous.

FACT ***Some breeds, such as the golden retriever, are more prone to engage in chasing activities because they were originally working dogs who were bred to chase.***

Most dogs like to chase a ball, toy, or Frisbee, as the fast movement is exciting to them and sparks their prey drive (the urge to chase after the object and catch or retrieve it).

The intensity of prey drive varies from extremely high in some breeds to almost non-existent in others. For example, some dogs only occasionally enjoy chasing their tail, while others with a strong prey drive might engage in dangerous activities, such as chasing moving vehicles. If your puppy is happy to just enjoy a game of fetch, there is nothing to worry about. However, if your puppy begins to show a desire to chase or herd other moving objects, such as vehicles, bicycles, joggers, children, skateboards, squirrels, cats, etc., this behaviour needs to be stopped to keep everyone safe.

How long it takes to teach your golden retriever to control their impulse to chase depends on how strong their instinct is. Following are some steps and suggestions for curbing the chasing behaviour and safely channelling this urge into other areas.

- Put your retriever on their lead and go out for a walk.
- Make sure you have some treats in your pocket.
- When your dog attempts to chase a bird, squirrel, or skateboard, firmly say '***No***'. When they switch their attention to you, give them a treat to reward their positive behaviour.
- You can also carry a small, squeaky toy and squeak it as a distraction whenever your dog lunges forwards to chase.
- Reward them every time they control their desire to chase.

Once your retriever has learnt impulse control and understands what they are and are not allowed to do when out on a walk, you can re-direct their desire to chase into a fun game, such as fetch, tug-of-war, or hide-and-seek inside the home. Also, several canine sports appeal to dogs with a strong desire to chase, such as:

- Herding trials—herding sheep.
- Disc dog—chasing and catching a Frisbee.
- Flyball—racing and retrieving a ball.

- Lure coursing—the pursuit of a mechanical lure (a plastic bag attached to a line that moves at speed on a track to simulate a hunt).

Jumping on People

There are different reasons why dogs jump on people. The most common one is that they are excited to greet someone and want to get closer so they can receive the attention they desire. Golden retrievers are sociable canines who enjoy the company of people. They can also be extremely enthusiastic when you return home or have visitors and often jump up. Although it is lovely to know your puppy is happy to see you, there are several reasons why trying to control this jumping behaviour is a good idea:

- They might knock over toddlers or unstable seniors.
- It can frighten young children.
- It might bruise or scratch someone.
- They might have muddy feet, which most people will not appreciate getting on their clothes.
- It encourages overly exuberant behaviour.

Instead of reprimanding your dog, you need to teach your golden retriever a more polite way of greeting people. The following suggestions will help teach an overly boisterous jumper to keep their paws on the ground:

- Remain calm and keep it low-key when greeting your dog.
- Don't give them any attention when they are excited, so they understand they need to be calm if they want to be noticed by people.
- Do not make a fuss, talk to them, or act excited in any way.
- If they start to jump up, walk towards them, so they must move away.
- When they calmly greet you with all four paws on the ground, give them a treat to help reinforce their good behaviour.

TIP ***Teaching your puppy to keep their feet on the ground requires patience, consistency, and help from other family members and friends. It is best to 'train' your family and any visitors, so everyone knows how to encourage this new, calm behaviour. Otherwise, they only learn not to jump on you while everyone else remains fair game.***

Excessive Excitement

An over-excited puppy can seem adorable, and most people will interpret this as your golden being happy. However, if they are learning to be overly eager all the time, this can have a negative effect on their health. When they become hyper-aroused by someone or something that makes them excessively enthusiastic, it releases a rush of dopamine that can become addictive. When you are unable to keep their excitement under control, it has the potential to lead to future behavioural issues.

For instance, an over-stimulated dog will find it hard to pay attention to their owner. When your golden retriever becomes used to a rush of dopamine in their system, this lack of self-control can result in negative reactions to other dogs or people when out walking. The problem is owners often do not know how to identify when their puppy is being overly zealous, so they can't calm them down or accidentally encourage the behaviour.

While it can be tricky to spot the difference between play, high energy and being overly rambunctious, there are certain signs to watch for, including:

- Uncontrollable running in circles or back and forth.
- Jumping up, nipping, and mouthing at people's hands.
- Barking and spinning in circles.
- Wildly running through the house and jumping off furniture.

Once you know the signs of their overwrought behaviour, the following steps can help calm your puppy and teach them to control themselves:

- Do not encourage their behaviour by giving it any attention or reacting with equally excited energy, as this can teach them to behave this way even more.
- Re-direct their energy towards something more structured or controlled, such as a toy, puzzle, or game of fetch.
- Do not kid yourself that they will soon grow out of it, as this is not just puppy behaviour and can continue into adulthood.
- Always reward your golden retriever's calm behaviour by giving a special treat, together with calm attention.
- Always remain placid and talk to your puppy in a slow, gentle voice.

Worktop Surfing

Keeping the kitchen counters clear of food might not be something to worry about when your puppy is too small to reach them. Nonetheless, it is still a good idea to be aware of this activity as some puppies can be amazingly acrobatic, despite their size, when there is food to be had.

Puppies and dogs are natural opportunists when it comes to scavenging for food. Whether surfing a kitchen worktop surfing or snatching from the family's dining table, it is still a natural golden retriever behaviour. Unfortunately, if your dog got away with it once, they will remember, and it is only natural for them to look for a chance to score again.

FACT ***Pilfering human food right off the table is very annoying for owners, and it can also be harmful to the dog if they steal something toxic to them.***

Thankfully, some steps can help prevent these 'worktop surfing' activities:

- Make sure you don't leave any food on counters and tabletops.
- Thoroughly clean all surfaces to remove any crumbs or enticing scents.
- Keep a closed door or gate between the kitchen and your retriever.
- Teach them to stay out of the kitchen.
- Train them to ignore a food item that has less scent than chicken or roast beef—such as a carrot—and when they ignore it, reward them.
- Slowly 'up the ante' by placing harder-to-ignore food items on a table or worktop, and when they ignore them, reward and praise them.

- Teach them to expect a treat when, for example, they sit and patiently wait or go to their bed or crate instead of jumping up at the worktop.

Never punish your retriever for stealing food from the worktop, as they might have already forgotten about it, or they might learn to be sneaky and only do it when nobody is around. Plus, if they are still young, you should show a little leniency, as they might not have yet learnt this is unacceptable behaviour.

Stealing Items

Although it is perfectly normal for a pup to steal food that is within reach, they might also steal other not-so-normal items. Your golden puppy will be curious while they get used to their new environment and steal anything they can reach. This includes such things as socks, underwear, sponges, tea towels, tissues, or anything else they might find on the floor.

The first step to stop your dog from stealing is to make sure there is nothing left within their reach that might be too tempting to ignore. What often happens is that a puppy steals something they shouldn't, and you chase after them to try to pry it out of their mouth. Most puppies love a good chase, and this will seem like a fun game. Therefore, you should resist the impulse to give chase—unless they've got something harmful in their mouth—as doing so will teach your puppy that stealing things is fun.

Normally, golden retrievers steal socks because they want to chew or play with them. There are two schools of thought about this. One is people believe retrievers love socks because it offers them a sense of comfort, while others say it is because they smell like their owners. Some golden retrievers will take things back to their bed or crate, including any socks you leave lying around.

Once your puppy has discovered an interesting activity that gets them attention and a good chase, they might start looking for other things they can grab that will get them desirable results. This is especially true when they are feeling bored or under-exercised. Making sure they get enough exercise and mental activities should also help counter this type of behaviour.

Patience and consistency will teach your curious golden retriever puppy not to steal people's belongings. Once your puppy grows out of their mischievous first year, they are usually no longer interested in the things that were so fascinating to their younger self.

Not Coming When Called

There are several reasons why your puppy will refuse to come when called. The most common ones are:

- They think they are in trouble.
- They might not understand what the word means. (Using too many words for the same thing can create confusion, such as '***Come Here***', '***Come Now***', '***Come Right Now***', etc.)
- They do not want to stop playing.
- They think your request to '***Come***' is not as much fun as what they are currently doing.
- The '***Come***' command has not been taught correctly (see Chapter 11).

If the '***Come***' command is always used to end a fun play session, your golden retriever might learn to ignore or associate the command with something unpleasant, so offer a treat reward instead, so they get something better for having to leave their play session.

Never use a frustrated or angry tone when asking your puppy to 'Come'. If they start to associate the command with getting into trouble, they will quickly decide that responding is not a good idea and deliberately ignore you. If you've noticed this already happening, you should restart teaching the recall command again, but using a different word that means 'Come', like 'Here,' so they connect the new word with a positive outcome.

TIP ***Expecting an easily distracted puppy to 'Come' when their recall isn't 100% reliable yet could be asking too much. When they are in the middle of an exciting activity, such as playing with another furry friend or pursuing a frightened squirrel up a tree, this is a huge distraction.***

The only way to ensure your golden puppy always comes to you when called is to make sure the '***Come***' command is always a positive experience.

Pulling and refusing to walk on lead

It is not natural for any dog to be tethered to you, so since walking on a lead is unnatural, time must be spent teaching your retriever how to walk properly without pulling. It is natural for goldens to be exploratory, curious, playful, and sociable. If they find that pulling on their lead will get them to a particularly interesting scent sooner, you can bet they will drag you along to get there. It's a simple equation in your dog's mind. If pulling gets them what they want, why wouldn't they pull?

Sometimes, you can encourage your dog to tug on the lead without even realising you are teaching them this behaviour. For example, when your golden puppy strains on their lead and you continue to move forwards, you've just rewarded them for pulling. Thankfully, even if your puppy has already learnt this habit, there are some tricks you can use, so everyone enjoys a comfortable, loose lead walking habit, including:

- Stop moving forwards the instant your puppy pulls.
- If they pull, stop and tell them to sit.
- Change direction when your puppy pulls.
- Walk in a circle or figure of eight.

When you first put a collar and lead on your puppy, this new, and potentially disturbing sensation of restraint, might cause several unexpected reactions, such as:

- Nipping at the lead.
- Trying to break free from their collar.
- Standing still and refusing to move.
- Lying down.
- Rolling on the ground.
- Bucking.
- Squealing or screaming.
- Pulling backwards.

When starting to acclimatise your puppy to their collar and lead, always remember to be patient and understanding, and above all else, never drag your puppy. See Chapter 11 to learn how to train your puppy to walk on a loose lead and teach them to associate pleasant experiences with wearing their lead and collar.

Running Away

There are many reasons why your golden puppy or dog could develop the habit of running away. What you might not appreciate is that it is in the DNA of every canine companion to be an energetic explorer. As a species, dogs are active, curious, and built to roam. A recent survey commissioned by the Blue Cross found Labrador retrievers are the most likely breed of dogs to run away, with the cocker spaniel and Jack Russell also in the top three. The pet charity's researchers compiled their list from the experiences of 2,000 British dog owners. When a dog becomes part of your human family, it is your responsibility to ensure they have plenty of opportunities to enjoy an exploring adventure. Some of the reasons why your golden retriever might choose to run away include the following:

- Their high prey drive—they cannot resist chasing a bird, squirrel, cat, etc.
- There's an easy escape route with no human supervision—a low fence, a chain-link fence that is easy to climb, a hole in the fence, a lock on a gate that can be opened, an open window, etc.
- The overwhelming drive to mate when not neutered or spayed.
- Boredom and lack of exercise.
- Frightening sounds—loud, sudden noises, thunder, car alarms, sirens, etc.

Most escape attempts can easily be prevented by never leaving your golden alone or unsupervised. Bear in mind the following tips:

- Give your puppy plenty of opportunities for exercise and fun activities to relieve boredom.
- If your retriever has a high prey drive, keep them on their lead while outside the home so they can't chase unsuspecting prey.
- Regularly check the back garden fence for holes and make sure gate latches are dog-proof. Keep windows closed when you leave your pup alone in the house. Doing this will remove possible escape routes.
- If your golden retriever has been desensitised to frightening noises, they will no longer feel the need to run away from those sounds (see *Fear of Loud Noises* in Chapter 10).

Aggression

Even dogs who are naturally friendly and loveable, such as the golden, have the potential to become aggressive if they are not socialised and taught how to interact appropriately in the human world. Also, some dogs will be more prone to developing aggressive tendencies than others, such as if they have been:

- Bred from parents with aggressive histories.
- Abused or mistreated.
- Bred for protection work.
- Bred from a long line of fighting breeds.

Whatever the reason, it is totally unacceptable for any dog who is going to be a family pet to display signs of aggression, such as biting, snapping, snarling, baring teeth, growling, or lunging. The following sections will examine the common kinds of aggression and how to correct this behaviour.

Fear Aggression

As the name suggests, this type of aggression comes out of fear. Dogs react with aggression when they are afraid because they feel like they are in a dangerous situation they cannot escape. If your golden feels trapped or unable to remove themselves from a seemingly dangerous situation, panic sets in, and they might be forced to defend themselves. This is usually when aggression comes into play. For example, if your golden believes they have no way out of an uncomfortable situation, they might growl or bare their teeth.

TIP ***If you are confronted by an aggressive dog, the simplest, safest way to deal with the situation is to slowly back away, so they no longer feel afraid. When you give the dog space, they no longer feel the need to protect themselves, and a tense situation that might have resulted in a bite can be defused.***

Dominance Aggression

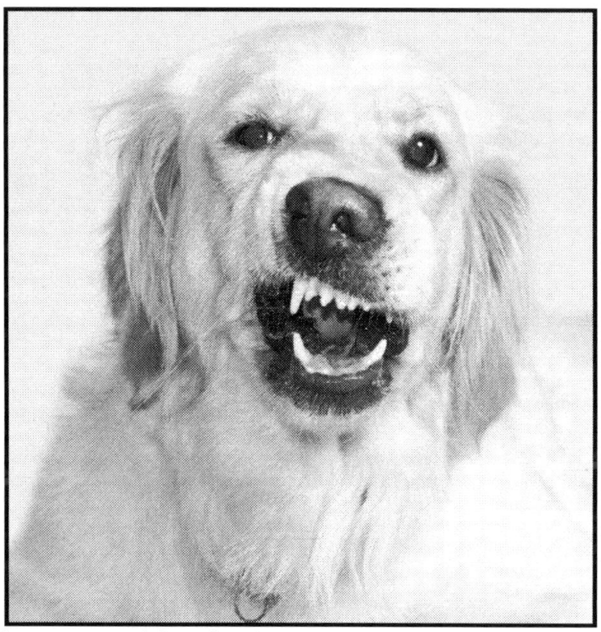

When your golden retriever is displaying dominance aggression it is usually for one of two reasons. Firstly, it might be trying to establish authority over another dog. Secondly, dominance aggression can be displayed to demonstrate your dog is in charge of you and that no other dog should come close.

Whatever the reason for your dog's dominance aggression, the most likely explanation for them developing this unwanted behaviour is because your puppy's training didn't start soon enough or wasn't firm enough, and they have learnt to be their own boss. Correcting this type of behaviour can take some time. To gain control of the situation, you must increase your command energy and be more dominant than your golden retriever.

If you have been too soft on your dog or have not yet begun teaching basic commands or establishing any house rules and boundaries, you may not have a relationship of trust and respect between you. Should this be the case, your golden might believe they are in charge. The following steps will help to turn this situation around:

- Teach them basic '***Come***', '***Sit***', and '***Stay***', commands (see details in Chapter 11).
- Establish house rules and boundaries.
- Firmly tell them '***No***' when they display aggressive tendencies.
- When they greet politely, reward them with a treat.

When you begin to teach commands, rules and boundaries, this will strongly influence your golden retriever's actions. This change in energy will usually 'tell' them you are now in charge, and they no longer need to react with dominance.

Territorial Aggression

All dogs, no matter their size, are naturally territorial to some extent. When you consider their evolutionary history, it makes sense for a dog to want to protect resources—food, water, shelter—from those who might steal them.

FACT ***Territorial or protective aggression might be displayed towards people or other animals who approach your golden's property. Unfamiliar or unusual people and other animals are the most likely targets for territorial aggression.***

Protective territorial displays can range in aggressiveness from growling and barking to lunging, chasing, snapping, or biting. They may exhibit this behaviour at windows, doors, behind fences, or in the car. When out, some dogs have been known to claim territory and show similar behaviour at picnic areas, park benches, etc.

Dogs who are frustrated by being physically restricted with a barricade or lead from gaining access to the stimulus might suffer from heightened aggression. They could also develop displacement behaviour—spinning, circling, self-mutilation—or redirected behaviour where they turn their aggression towards you when you attempt to reach for or grab your retriever.

Even when the cause of their behaviour has entered the territory or home, your dog might continue their aggression, which could result in biting and severe injury. Due to the high arousal level of the dog, in some cases, an element of frustration might present itself and lead to redirected behaviour towards objects, other animals, or people.

There are techniques to help eradicate this type of aggression:

- Give a solid foundation of obedience training, as this teaches your dog to control excited energy and listen to your directions.
- Teach the '***Leave it***' command (see how to teach this command in Chapter 11) to distract their attention, so they leave what is exciting them.
- Reward them for calm behaviour.
- Burn off excess energy with plenty of daily exercise, as they will be less likely to spend their time being mega watchful.
- Close the curtains to restrict their view of the window to stop them from barking at anyone walking by.
- Go outside and stand between your dog and the fence, door, or gate they are patrolling, and firmly tell them, '***Go***' as you point away.
- If they bark at people walking past, let them know you do not want them to by firmly telling them '***No***' and making them sit.
- Exercise their brain by teaching your golden tricks or canine sports, as this will tire them out
- Always remember to reward good behaviour, for example, when they remain calm when seeing a person walking by but do not react to them.

While it is difficult to completely eliminate a strong, territorial instinct, when you take the time to interrupt any unwanted behaviour and teach your dog what is acceptable through positive reinforcement, it is certainly possible to effectively manage the situation.

Possessive Aggression

When your golden is being possessive, their instinct is to growl, bare their teeth, snap, or furiously bark to tell another dog, animal, or person not to get too close. Guarding resources is an instinct for dogs. Depending on the dog and what they are being possessive about, this instinct can vary in intensity. In your dog's evolutionary history, survival meant learning how to fend for themselves in the wild, so possessive behaviour is perfectly natural.

Some dogs only display aggressive tendencies over a particularly prized object, such as a favourite toy or their dinner bowl. Others guard anything they find around the house, such as a rubber bone, a pair of shoes, or a tissue they rescued from the rubbish bin. Furthermore, some dogs can display possessive outbursts over a favourite person. Some goldens have issues with resource guarding and show control-dominant behaviour. In other words, the intensity of possession aggression will depend on the dog and the value they place on each object they are being possessive about. Signs to be aware of include:

- Lowered head and intense stare.
- Curling their lip.
- Low growling.
- Baring teeth.
- Snapping or biting.
- Protecting an item by drawing it near.
- Running away with an item.

As well as the guarding instinct, there are several other reasons why your dog might display possessive aggression, including:

- Competition from other dogs or family members.
- The introduction of another dog to the home.
- Prolonged time in a shelter with limited resources.
- Learned behaviour from their mother or littermates.

FACT ***Possessive aggression, also known as resource guarding, simply means your golden retriever is being possessive of their toys, food bowl, treats, or other objects they value.***

When your dog is guarding an object, young children should be kept away as your golden may bite. Rather than making them give up their prized possession, they need to understand that giving them up voluntarily results in them receiving something better. They need to learn to trust people when they are around their treasured objects. The following steps can help:

- Reinforce the '***Leave it***' command, so they will drop the object of their own volition.
- Offer them something perceived to be of higher value than whatever they are guarding, such as a special treat or toy.
- After they receive the higher value reward, give them back the item they were guarding, so they understand there was no need to protect it.
- If they are seriously trying to bite and the above steps are not helping, it might be time to seek help from a trainer or behaviourist.

Patience and a careful approach, plus the above behavioural modification exercises, are very effective in teaching your golden retriever there's no need to guard their resources.

Frustration Aggression

Frustration aggression occurs when your golden is constantly restrained or prevented from getting what they want. For some dogs living in a human-controlled environment, this can be a large part of their day. Frustration aggression is more common in higher-energy dogs. Here are some reasons why your golden retriever might feel frustrated:

- They are always held back when they are on their lead.
- They are locked in their crate for too long.
- They are shut in a room inside the home.

- They have been left inside a closed vehicle.
- They saw an animal through the window but were unable to chase after it.
- They are tied up in the back garden.
- There is a dog outside, but the fence stops them from visiting.

Depending on your dog, their circumstances, and the level of frustration, if your dog has not learnt how to safely deal with it, frustration can escalate into destructive behaviour. This could include ripping the furniture, destroying their crate, or even snapping at their owner. It might help your golden retriever improve their impulse control and frustration tolerance if you can teach them patience. This includes instructing them to sit and wait at a door before entering/exiting or before they are given their food.

Instead of immediately giving in when they whine or cry, only give your dog what they want after they stop making a fuss.

Illness or Pain Aggression

Since, for the most part, your golden is unable to tell you when they are ill or in pain, if your normally friendly puppy suddenly starts to act aggressively by growling, biting, or snapping when you move them or pick them up, they might be telling you something is medically wrong. There are many signs to be aware of that can indicate your dog is sick or experiencing pain, such as:

- Sudden change in habits.
- Refusing to go on a walk.
- Lethargy.
- Avoiding other dogs.
- Not wanting to play.
- Declining to eat.
- Being unusually clingy.
- Yelping, whining, growling, flinching, pulling away when touched.

TIP ***Pain can be a common cause of aggression, and a careful approach is needed with a sick or injured dog to avoid being bitten. Usually, if your dog bites because something is hurting them, it is not because they want to harm you but because they are simply reacting to pain.***

If your golden retriever has been injured or is ill, they need to be taken to the vet, where a professional can determine the best course of action. If moving them makes them aggressive, wear gloves to protect your hands, be as gentle as possible, use a soothing tone of voice and wrap them in a blanket for easier transport. Being aware of your puppy's usual behaviour can help to identify signs and seek medical assistance before the problem becomes worse.

Rage Syndrome

Also known as sudden onset aggression (SOA) or avalanche of rage syndrome, this syndrome is a serious behavioural issue that has been reported most frequently in the English springer spaniel. It can also affect other dog breeds.

Often, rage syndrome is confused with other forms of aggression and can be misdiagnosed by veterinarians and behaviourists. This condition can be inherited and is believed to be genetic in origin.

Dr Roger A Mugford, an animal behaviour consultant, is attributed with introducing the term rage syndrome. If your golden suffers from rage syndrome, they will suddenly act aggressively toward anyone or anything nearby, but within minutes will go back to normal.

A dog who has rage syndrome does not seem to remember what has taken place and can be friendly towards the person they previously attacked. Unfortunately, these types of attacks will never be controlled through training as the dog cannot consciously control their behaviour due to their condition. These attacks will happen without any cause or apparent reason and often with no warning signs, which makes them all the harder to control.

However, if you observe your golden closely shortly before any attack, you may notice that their eyes will glaze over and go hard. This is followed by your dog becoming exceedingly alert before finally attacking. To an outsider with no prior knowledge of the condition, it will appear to be an exaggerated form of aggression.

During his research, Dr Mugford identified the problem as starting during the adolescent stage, on average at around seven and a half months old. There are a variety of treatments for affected dogs, including antiepileptic tablets, which have been reported to be effective. Sadly, not every treatment works, and in many cases, euthanasia is the only solution.

The Unruly Adolescent

The transition from being a juvenile to becoming an adult occurs in adolescence. With the golden, the 'teen' years start at about 6 months and continue until they are approximately 18 months old. During this time, your golden retriever's brain undergoes a reorganisation, and dramatic hormonal changes happen.

The hormonal changes in adolescent dogs can make them seem less obedient. In reality, their unruly behaviour is more of an increase in motivation for exploring, interacting, and running and a need to interact with the environment and people around them. Adolescent goldens have the energy and drive to do more, just like human teenagers. While they play, explore, and interact with their friends—human and non-human—they do not possess the necessary wisdom and experience to think about and manage their actions and reactions.

FACT ***No matter how friendly, any golden retriever can develop excessive levels of barking, digging, and other undesirable behaviour when bored, untrained, or unsupervised. During adolescence, such behaviour is more prevalent, making your dog a challenge to live with.***

Due to teenage goldens' highly energetic nature, they often feel conflicted when told to calm down or stop what they are doing, even in situations where they were previously obedient. Dog owners often interpret these changes as their dog being stubborn or trying to assert their dominance rather than understanding they are just having difficulty controlling their impulsiveness. During adolescence, you might experience changes in your retriever's personality that you don't like. For example, your young golden might:

- Bark or whine when left alone.
- Be less friendly with strangers.
- Be more aggressive towards other dogs.
- Begin to be possessive of their owner.
- Start to bark at unknown people and dogs.

- Dig up the back garden.
- Become possessive of their toys or food bowl.
- Look for opportunities to chase the neighbour's cat.
- Be more stubborn.
- Ignore their owner when called.
- Display selective deafness.
- Ignore commands they've already learnt.
- Regress with their toilet training.
- Begin to mark.
- Attempt to escape from the back garden.

Welcome to the world of canine adolescence! This is the time when it appears all the previous socialising and training work has flown out the window, and your adorable puppy has turned into some sort of monster.

Too often, golden retriever owners become frustrated and impatient and give up on their dogs when they transform from being a cute, cuddly, and mostly obedient little puppy into a total terror. Nevertheless, with consistency, understanding, endless patience, and perseverance, you and your furry friend can survive this adolescent period and come out with a much stronger bond.

It is important to note that not all dogs go through an intensely crazy adolescent period. For some dogs, the adolescent period can pass unnoticed.

Remember, you have already lived through toilet training, teething, socialising, and basic rules and boundaries with your golden retriever puppy. You should feel proud of all the progress you have made over the last few months. Also, bear in mind that you will eventually be able to enjoy the rewards all these months of diligent puppy training have brought to your relationship. Here are some top tips to help you through the teenage years:

Keep your dog stimulated – Not getting your attention can also be exasperating for your adolescent golden retriever, but predictability is a good way to avoid frustration. Try to include more interactive games in your dog's routine, such as playing with a ball or Frisbee, or hiding something for them to find.

Remember to give cues, so your retriever knows when the play session begins and ends. You can tell your dog '***Playtime***' or show them a toy when you want to start. When it's time to end the fun and games, you can either say, '***Finish***' and throw the toy away from them or remove the toy and give your golden retriever something else to do. This helps minimise their feelings of frustration at the end of a pleasant activity. Additionally, you can scatter some treats or give your dog something to chew on, so they don't feel suddenly deflated.

Do not tell your golden off – If your dog used to play happily with other dogs but is becoming too aggressive or boisterous, telling them off will only worsen the situation. Use a cheerful voice, instead of reprimanding your retriever, to distract them from the situation and to take them out of it.

It could be safer to continue socialising your golden with dogs they are familiar with and minimise their exposure to other dogs to prevent the problem from worsening.

Keep up activity levels – Dogs going through adolescence are energetic. They can benefit from longer walks in quiet environments, plenty of exploration and being allowed to use their nose. During this time, the best way to ride the storm is to be consistent with the rules and continue to be a firm, yet fair leader while increasing training time to keep your golden's body exercised and their mind occupied.

Adolescent dogs can become more panicky and anxious, which might make them ignore your instructions, behave in destructive ways, soil your house, or start barking excessively. If frustration is getting the upper hand, rather than letting things deteriorate, you might want to hire a professional who can provide valuable assistance to help you get through this stage of your golden retriever's development.

Fear Issues

Although there are many reasons why your golden retriever can develop fear issues, the most common cause is inadequate socialisation when they were a puppy. A dog who has not been adequately socialised and learnt to calmly accept many different situations, places, people, dogs, and other animals might become fearful of them.

Goldens, in general, do not tend to be apprehensive dogs, especially with proper early socialisation.

If your dog is frightened, they may react in several ways. For example, they might try to run away or hide, shake, tremble, whine, or bark. If they are very scared, they could even become aggressive. To stop your golden retriever from becoming afraid, use consistent and gentle training methods to obtain the results you are looking for.

It is useful to pinpoint some of the common things that can make your dog feel scared:

- Other dogs.
- Strangers.
- Other animals.
- Young children.
- Being left alone.
- Bath time.
- Visits to the vet.
- Changes in their environment.
- Vehicle travel.
- Air travel.
- Stairs.
- Bridges.
- Water.
- Mirrors.
- Shiny surfaces.
- Loud noises

Helping your nervous or stressed dog learn to overcome their insecurities may require behaviour modification. 'Behaviour modification' is simply a systematic approach designed to change or 'modify' your golden retriever's behaviour to minimise an unwanted habit. In this case, it refers to changing your dog's attitude, emotional response, or reaction to a trigger that causes fear.

Changing your golden's emotional response when they are afraid depends on the level of fear your dog is experiencing. If your dog didn't get extensive socialisation when young, which helps to prevent nervousness and fear responses, several positive steps can improve confidence and reduce fear issues:

- Revisit their basic obedience training (in Chapter 11).
- Be careful not to reinforce fearful behaviour by saying words they associate with stress, such as, '***It's okay.***'
- Be careful not to accidentally reward fearful behaviour by saying, '***Good Boy***' or trying to offer a treat while they're displaying fearful behaviour.

- When your puppy is afraid, remain calm and distract them by asking them to do something they have already learnt.

It is possible to help your golden puppy work through a fear of just about anything if they can focus on your commands. The best approach is to slow the process down and break up training into patient, little steps that are reinforced along the way. Let's say your retriever is afraid to cross a bridge. You could work on this fear by following this process:

- Make sure they are securely on their lead.
- Ask them to 'Sit' and wait until they calm down.
- Do not force them to move closer to the bridge until they are completely calm.
- Quietly wait and let them know you are relaxed and confident about the bridge.
- Ask a friend with a dog who is not afraid of bridges to join you.
- If there are other people and dogs happily crossing the bridge, even better—your retriever will learn by observing and might even decide to follow another dog.
- Give them a treat for staying calm and take one step closer.
- Give a gentle, forward tug on the lead and offer another treat.
- If they take the treat, this means their fear level has decreased.
- Continue steadily moving forwards and rewarding them as they confront their fear.
- If they are beginning to show signs of agitation, end the session and come back the next day.

Depending on your dog, their level of anxiety or fear, the sort of relationship they have with you, and how well they have learnt to trust and follow your lead will affect the time needed to make it across the bridge.

Other Curious Behaviour

Sometimes, our canine companions can seem to have some strange behaviour. While all dogs are unique and act in different ways, the following few pages outline some of these behavioural issues and offer suggestions on why they might occur and what you can do.

Being Clingy

Initially, when your golden puppy is clingy and wants to be with you all the time, this is often simply the result of not yet feeling comfortable in their new surroundings. Once they are used to their living arrangements, depending on the natural confidence level of your dog, this will often subside.

Of course, every puppy is an individual, and how they were raised is different from what their siblings in the litter might have encountered. In other words, their life experiences and how you interact with them will contribute to how clingy your puppy becomes.

FACT ***Many of the more sensitive breeds tend to be naturally clingier compared to others. If they are bored, aren't exercised enough to burn their excess energy, or get away with clingy behaviour, golden retrievers can develop needy and attention-seeking attitudes.***

When your puppy receives constant attention from their human family during their early developmental months, they can grow to feel nervous about being alone. As your puppy becomes used to their new environment and continues to demonstrate clingy behaviour, this is typically a learnt behaviour. Some other reasons why your golden might become clingy are:

- Getting old.
- Loss of hearing or vision.
- Illness.
- Boredom.
- When sensing your stress or anxiety.

Some owners might not mind when their dog follows them from room to room, but if it becomes an undesirable habit, here is what you can do:

- Increase the amount of daily physical exercise. If your dog's tired, they are less likely to follow you everywhere.
- Desensitise them to actions they have learnt to associate with specific results—e.g., pick up your keys but do not go out the door, go to the kitchen but do not get food, go to the bathroom but do not take a shower, etc. All of this will teach them these are boring activities and do not warrant their attention.
- Train them to go to their special, relaxing bed, crate, or place where they have access to their favourite chew toy whenever you need to do something without their company. Say, 'Relax', and when they go to their special bed, reinforce this behaviour by giving them a reward. Ask them to 'Stay', and when you return, if they have stayed, praise them. You can start with just a minute of them 'staying' and increase the length of time you are away over several days and weeks until they always stay in their relaxing space until you return

Shaking

When your dog is visibly shaking, this could simply be because they are afraid of something, such as a loud noise they do not understand. Other reasons why your dog might be trembling include:

- They are excited you've arrived home.
- They have just had a bath, and being wet is making them cold.
- They just came in from a walk in the rain or snow and are wet and cold.
- They want attention. Some dogs learn that shivering elicits a sympathetic response and lots of attention from their owner.
- They are in pain from injury.
- They are ill.
- They are feeling nauseous from motion sickness or eating too much too fast.
- Their muscles might have weakened with age.
- Old age has caused arthritis or joint pain.
- They could have White shaker disease syndrome, also known as generalised tremor syndrome.

If they are startled by a sudden, loud noise, this trembling will soon pass, and even quicker if you can show them the source of the noise. If they are cold, warm them with a hairdryer or wrap them in a warm blanket until the shivering stops.

TIP ***Shivering from excitement or happiness will subside on its own when they have calmed down. If your dog trembles from eating too much too fast, simply feed them smaller portions and buy a slow feeder bowl, so they are unable to consume their food so quickly.***

As your golden enters their senior years, their muscles might start to weaken, or they could suffer from arthritis and joint pain, any of which can make them develop tremors. If there is a medical reason for the trembling, such as generalised tremor syndrome or arthritis, they need to be diagnosed by a qualified veterinarian who will prescribe the proper treatment.

Burying Items & Bones

Burying objects, particularly bones, is a throwback to a time before dogs became domesticated. At that time, they lived in the wild and had to make do with a 'feast or famine' diet. This meant when they were lucky enough to find food, any excess food needed to be protected, hidden, and preserved in a buried stash they could return to in times when food was scarce.

When your golden buries bones and carcasses in the earth, this creates a natural refrigerator that keeps it cool while also hiding it from view and disguising the scent to protect it from other predators who might catch the scent and pilfer their stash.

Even though most domesticated dogs do not need to stress about where their next meal is coming from, some still retain a strong instinct to bury bones or other prized possessions. Also, rather than burying items in the back garden, they may have learnt to use the sofa cushions or the bottom of the laundry basket as prime locations for squirrelling away things to keep them safe.

If your golden is constantly burying or hiding food, treats, toys, or your favourite pair of socks, they're not being naughty. They're following their instincts to preserve their treasured objects in a place where they can find them later. If there are other pets in the home, your dog might also hide their prized items to stop what they view as competition from stealing them. The following points can help reduce this type of behaviour:

- If they are hiding your belongings, keep them out of reach.
- Give them more exercise and teach them interesting tricks, so they are not bored.
- Rather than giving them lots of toys, give them just two at a time and rotate them.

The bottom line is that it's normal for your golden retriever to have the urge to bury things, whether in the back garden or under a convenient blanket or cushion.

Eating Faeces

The one thing you need to know about canine coprophagy—the scientific term for the act of your dog eating their faeces—is it is far more common than you might think. According to studies conducted in 2008 and 2018, 16-49% of all dogs will eat their own poop.

Eating faeces can be down to several factors, such as:

- Your dog is young and will taste everything at least once. The good news is puppies usually grow out of the habit of eating poo.
- Dogs are natural scavengers who seek their food through smell. They think poo smells great.
- Their diet may be lacking in nutrients, minerals, and calories.
- They could have an enzyme deficiency.
- They might have parasites.
- They may have diabetes or thyroid issues, which can make them hungry enough to eat stools.
- Nursing females eat the poo of their young to keep the den clean.
- Your puppy might smell faecal odours on their mother's breath and learn to associate the smell with a food source.
- The poo of other animals may taste good to a dog. Many dogs like goose poo and cat poo.
- Puppy mill dogs are more likely to eat poo because of poor nutrition and stressful, overcrowded living conditions.
- They might be ill.
- They may not be properly absorbing nutrients in their food.
- They might not be getting enough food in their daily diet.
- Attention seeking. If they have learnt that this gets them attention, they may do it more.

If your golden puppy continues to regularly eat poo after they have grown out of the tasting everything stage of their development, here is what you can do to control this unsavoury habit:

- Immediately clean up any poo.
- Keep them away from the cat's litter box.
- Keep them on their lead in areas where they might encounter another dog's poo.
- Feed them a well-balanced, nutritious diet that contains all the required enzymes, minerals, and calories.
- If you're feeding a cooked diet, add digestive enzymes.
- If you suspect a key nutrient is absent from their diet, add supplements.
- Screen them for parasites.
- Keep their body and brain healthy by developing an exercise and mental stimulation routine.

Medically, there is little risk to a dog who eats their faeces. However, if your golden retriever eats the poo of other animals, they can pick up parasites and bacteria that may cause vomiting, diarrhoea, decreased appetite, and tiredness.

Eating Grass

The most common assumption about why dogs eat grass is because they have an upset stomach and want to throw up, but research has proven this isn't necessarily true. Based on statistics, most grass-eating dogs are not previously sick, and fewer than 25% of dogs throw up after eating grass.

A better explanation for this behaviour involves looking back to a time when dogs roamed the wild and ate a balanced diet by consuming what they hunted. Although we often think of dogs as being strictly carnivores—solely meat eaters—this is not entirely true, and they are also not strictly omnivores—meat and plant eaters—either. When dogs had to fend for themselves, they would often eat an entire animal. This involved a balance of meat, bones, and organs, as well as the stomach contents that contained the plants and grass—fibre—consumed by their prey. Back then, dogs were scavengers who consumed anything that would fulfil their dietary requirements. Interestingly, the examination of stool samples taken from wild wolves has shown as many as 47% of wolves eat grass. Therefore, it is likely that the urge to eat grass is a hangover from the past.

In addition to this instinctive behaviour, many puppies and adult dogs today eat grass purely because they like it. Some dogs become grass-eating connoisseurs whose refined tastes only lead them to eat the new, tender grass that emerges during the springtime growing season, while others eat grass all year long.

Being scavengers, dogs navigate their world through scent and touch and are always on the lookout for something to eat. If the grass is healthy and has not been sprayed with toxic chemicals, a little grass eating should not be a concern for your golden retriever.

Eating from the Cat's Litter Box

As disgusting as it may be to us, raiding the cat's litter box is a natural behaviour for dogs who are natural-born scavengers. Many goldens find cat poo especially tasty, as it smells like the cat food they are never allowed to eat. Even though eating cat faeces is not likely to seriously harm your dog, they may ingest parasites and bacteria that can cause vomiting or diarrhoea.

Furthermore, if they eat a large quantity of cat litter, it could create a harmful blockage that leads to difficulty with their bowel movements. If your dog seems to have a problem and you know they were just in the cat's litter box, it is time for a visit to the vet. To prevent your golden retriever from eating cat poo, try the following:

- Keep the cat's litter box well out of reach of your dog. You might like to keep the door to the room closed.
- Put up a baby gate, so they cannot get to the litter box.
- Invest in a closed-top or dog-proof litter box.

If neighbourhood cats are pooing in your back garden and it is hard to keep a close watch on your golden retriever puppy to ensure they do not eat it, you might want to make regular visits to the vet to check for internal parasites.

Licking People

Golden retrievers lick as an instinctive behaviour. It can be soothing and therapeutic as it releases endorphins. Your golden retriever might try to lick other dogs to show dominance. They could lick you because they like the taste of salt on your skin. Furthermore, your golden retriever could be licking people for the following reasons:

- To show submission. Licking shows other dogs they mean no harm.
- As a welcome home greeting.
- As a learnt habit.
- To get your attention.
- For a reward.
- To enjoy the taste since your skin may contain food residue.
- To communicate with you—licking can identify where you have been.

In the wild, a wolf puppy will lick their mother's face to encourage them to regurgitate food. Is this what your golden retriever is hoping for when they lick your face? While the jury is still out concerning any definitive answer about why dogs like to lick people, it would appear this is mostly an affectionate form of self-expression rather than a reason for worry.

Licking and Chewing their Paws

Most dogs occasionally engage in licking and/or chewing their paws. It's a totally natural behaviour. If this licking or chewing is excessive, occurs suddenly, or is accompanied by limping, swelling, redness, or bleeding, this is frequently a sign of injury, pain, or infection requiring diagnosis and treatment at the vet.

TIP ***You can tell if a white or light-coated dog has been persistently licking at their paws as the saliva in their tongue will turn their feet a rusty, pink colour.***

There can be many reasons for your dog licking or chewing their paws:

- A burn or cut.
- Arthritic pain.
- A fur ball between their pads.
- They are under-exercised and bored.
- A puncture wound.
- An allergic reaction or skin disease.
- A broken or fractured claw.
- Their paws are dirty or wet from grooming.
- A cyst or tumour.
- A disease of the pads or nail beds.
- A food allergy.
- A foreign object lodged between their pads—burr, spear grass, splinter, etc

If your golden is licking their paws as part of their grooming regimen, that's fine. Also, if they are licking or chewing simply because they are bored and need more exercise or mental stimulation, this is easily remedied by taking them out more or teaching fun tricks to exercise their brain.

If you think there's a medical reason behind your dog's behaviour, unless you can clearly see what is causing the licking and can remove it—such as something stuck between their pads—it would be wise to seek professional help at the vet's.

Rubbing Their Face

Dogs rub their faces on a wide variety of surfaces, from the grass in the back garden to the cushions on the sofa. Here is why they do it most often:

- It just feels good.

- To relieve an itch they can't reach to scratch—often, a coarse carpet will find that elusive spot.
- Marking territory—rubbing leaves invisible pheromones to signal ownership other dogs can smell.

- They like how it smells.
- To alleviate eye irritation or dental pain.
- To clean or dry their face—many dogs rub their face on a chair, carpet, pillow, or another surface after a meal or drink.
- To relieve collar irritation—say if it's too tight, has a sharp edge, or is making their hair mat and pull on their skin.
- To relieve the itching caused by insect bites.
- Allergies—skin irritation leads to rubbing.

If any of the rubbing sessions are the result of a medical issue, and you can see red, irritated skin, it is wise to take your golden to the vet for a professional analysis and treatment protocol.

Bottom Scooting

Bottom scooting—also known as the bottom crawl—is usually carried out on a nice, plush surface, preferably at a friend's house with pristine, white carpets. Most frequently, it's an attempt to relieve an itchy rear end. The exact reasons why your dog might practise this embarrassing behaviour include:

- Anal gland issues—overfull, infected, or cancer.
- Allergies–a reaction to something in the environment or food.
- Dingleberries—dogs with long hair often get poo stuck in the fur around the anus, which causes irritation.
- Diarrhoea—this prevents the anal glands from emptying and can also irritate the anal skin.
- Parasites—tapeworms can cause anal irritation.
- Attention seeking—if your golden retriever learns this behaviour makes you fuss over them or creates attention of any sort, they may decide to do it more often.

FACT ***Located on either side of your dog's anus, the anal glands are approximately the size of a small grape. Whenever your dog poos, the anal sphincter squeezes against these glands, which then release a super smelly secretion—much more aromatic than the poo itself—specific to each dog. This anal sac secretion leaves a 'message' to other dogs identifying who was there before them.***

It's rare, but some dogs have anal gland issues requiring regular help from a qualified individual who knows how to express them when the glands are overfull, such as a groomer or veterinary technician. Should the glands become infected, impacted, or cancerous, or bottom scooting is an allergic response or the result of a parasitic infestation, these are situations you will need to consult your veterinarian.

If your golden is experiencing bouts of diarrhoea, this will prevent the natural expression of the anal glands. If the situation is chronic, it is important to seek the advice of a qualified veterinarian.

Howling at Sirens

The most popular explanation for why some dogs howl at sirens is that it is simply a throwback to their instinctual, wild wolf-like ancestry when wolves howled to communicate with their pack. Perhaps the reason why some dogs howl and others do not is that the pitch of a siren needs to be within the perfect range to trigger the dog's primal urge to respond. In this case, perhaps they believe the sound of the siren is another dog howling in the distance. The strong connection with howling and working in a breed such as the golden retriever might encourage a strong drive to howl and verbally communicate.

In some cases, howling can also be contagious, just like when one dog starts barking and then another joins in. Often, your golden's howling might kickstart a chorus of wailing neighbourhood dogs. Additionally, some dogs howl like wolves to communicate their misery when their owners leave them alone in the house. Howling is nothing to worry about, as it is a completely natural behaviour and usually does not last long. However, if the howling becomes excessive, here are a few things you can do:

- Distract your golden with a toy or treat when they throw back their head to begin howling.
- Whenever they hear a siren and do not react, praise them and give them a reward.
- Get a recording of a siren that you can play and practise the above steps.

Once your golden learns that not howling will reap the benefits of a reward, they will usually decide against it.

Depression

As golden retrievers are a highly sociable dog breed who love to be with their human companions, insufficient time with their human family can leave them feeling depressed, as can major life changes and events. Signs of depression can mask illness, so if your dog's behaviour changes, consult a vet. Some of the signs indicating your dog is feeling depressed are as follows:

- Sudden changes in mood or behaviour.
- Change in appetite.
- Change in sleeping patterns.
- Antisocial behaviour or hiding.

Depending on how well you know your golden's regular behaviour and facial expressions, you might only need to look at their face to know they are down in the dumps. Some retrievers are more sensitive than others when it comes to triggers for sadness or depression. However, some common events could make your dog depressed, such as:

- Moving house.
- Home renovations.
- A change in their usual daily schedule.
- A new pet or baby in the home.
- Loss of a family member.
- You have gone on holiday.
- They are physically unwell.
- Loss of a close animal companion.
- You are feeling depressed.

If your golden is depressed because they are missing an animal companion, when the time is right, getting another animal will usually help. If you travel for work or are away on holiday and cannot take your retriever with you, it might take a while for them to get used to being cared for by a new person. But your dog will usually settle down within 3 or 4 days.

FACT ***Dogs are very sensitive to human emotions. If you are feeling depressed, your dog might also succumb to a feeling of sadness or depression.***

Thankfully, it is not usually too difficult to reorientate your dog if they are feeling blue. Here's what to do:

- Increase the amount of time you spend with them.
- Take them to different parks, trails, or walks.
- Teach them some fun new tricks.
- Enrol them in an exciting canine sport.
- Take them for a check-up to make sure they are healthy.

If you take the time to engage your golden in new, interesting tasks and adventures, it will usually improve their mood. If all the above suggestions seem to make little difference and there is nothing physically wrong, the vet may suggest a natural remedy or prescription medication to help elevate their mood.

7. Energy and Body Language

'Actually, my dog I think is the only person who consistently loves me all the time.'

~ H. G. Bissinger ~

Good communication between owner and canine is not just about the words you speak. Your human energy and body language are probably even more important than your words when delivering messages to your golden retriever. While your dog can learn many human words, their natural form of communication is much more about feeling the energy and reading the body language of other animals and people around them. For example, when your golden doesn't get confident energy from you to provide them with a feeling of security so they can relax, this uncertainty can create confusion in your dog's mind and may often be the beginning of behavioural issues.

Since dogs are pack animals, they cannot function as well as they might unless they have a leader to follow. When your golden becomes a member of your human family, they need to feel that you are a confident leader who is always in charge for them to be a relaxed and well-behaved family member who follows directions. You might ask, '*What is a confident leader?*' The dictionary definition of 'confident' is '*being certain of your abilities or having trust in people, plans, or the future.*' Therefore, in a dog/owner relationship, a confident leader would feel sure of their success when they interact with their dog.

TIP ***When walking your golden retriever, remember that the second they sense you are no longer completely in control, they will take this as an unspoken 'message' that they are now in charge.***

On the other hand, if you are focused on your dog, clearly in charge of the walk, and aware of your energy and body language, the likelihood of your dog misbehaving or acting in a loud or aggressive manner towards others will usually be very slim.

Your energy matters

Every living creature generates an energy field. Possibly the most profound communication difference between humans and their dogs is that humans do not consciously consider energy when interacting, while dogs sense energy as a central part of how they communicate.

When connecting with our canine counterparts, you need to convey the right energy to them. For example, when you have difficulties getting a message across to your puppy, it may be because the energy level you are giving off is either too mellow or too forceful. Just like the nursery story about Goldilocks and the Three Bears, the human energy needs to be 'just right' for your puppy to learn to trust, respect, and eagerly follow you.

Weak Energy

When your dog senses your energy level is too mellow, gentle, or weak, they might not feel confident in your ability to lead them, and the following may occur:

- Your dog becomes confused.
- They do not follow commands.
- They become nervous or timid.
- They don't know where they fit in the hierarchy of their human family.
- A naturally assertive dog can become more dominant.
- They pull on the lead while walking.
- They become protective and bark at everyone when out and about.
- They are territorial and bark at neighbours.
- They become protective of food, toys, and treats.
- They show aggression towards other dogs and people.

If it appears you can't get your dog to do what you want, you might need to implement some of the following energy exercises when communicating with them:

- Stand up straight.
- Square your shoulders.
- Expand your chest.
- Breathe deeply.
- Hold your head high.
- Make eye contact with your dog.
- Speak in a firm, yet calm voice.
- Be focused and without distractions.
- Recall a time when you felt powerful.
- Check commands do not have a questioning tone—there is a big difference between '***Sit?***' and '***Sit***' when expecting your dog to do as they're told.
- Imagine you are a person who is a confident, no-nonsense leader, real or fictitious.
- Visualise a successful outcome.
- Believe you have what you need.
- Never doubt—just do it.

Forceful Energy

On the other side of the coin, when your golden senses your energy is too forceful or sounds angry or frustrated when communicating with them, this is counterproductive, and the following may occur:

- Your retriever becomes confused.
- They become nervous or afraid.
- A naturally timid dog can become neurotic and unstable.
- They engage in fear peeing.
- They stop listening to commands.
- They hide or run away from you.
- They cower or shake nervously.
- If your golden is very sensitive, they might throw up.
- They shut down completely.
- They start fighting back out of fear.

TIP ***Sometimes, when you interact with your dog during training or ask them to perform specific commands, you might use a tone with an overly forceful energy that almost borders on anger. Typically, almost all dogs respond best to firm but calm energy.***

While some dogs react better to firm energy, more sensitive dogs usually respond better to a softer approach. If firm energy is not getting the desired results, the following exercises will help you tone down overly forceful energy to find the right balance:

- Take a deep, relaxing breath and slow down.
- Do not let your frustration get the better of you.
- Make a conscious change in your mindset. Trying a different approach could produce the desired results
- Ask yourself if you are feeling calm. If not, take a deep breath, relax, and try again.
- Try using a softer tone.
- Notice how your golden is responding to you—when you change something, does this improve your dog's response?

Just the Right Energy

It can take some self-awareness and a little time to discover the right energy balance when communicating with your golden retriever. Since every human and dog is individual, when putting the two together, many different family dynamics come into play.

When you bring your golden puppy home, they could be timid and uncertain as everything is new to them. They will need time to adapt to the energy of their new family while they get used to being away from their mother and siblings.

However, as your new puppy becomes familiar with their home and gains more confidence, their true personality will slowly begin to emerge. By the time they enter adolescence, they will have already worked out many of the house rules and identified who is really in charge.

As your puppy begins to mature, you will see whether the rules are being followed and if your golden listens when given a command. This is the time when paying closer attention to your human energy becomes really important. For instance, if your commands are largely ignored by your puppy, this suggests your energy is not confident enough for your golden retriever to respect or pay attention to you.

Raising the energy in your voice does not mean you need to yell. Rather you need to feel more confident and in command of the situation by implementing some of the suggestions above and be sure to mean it when giving your puppy a command. As the energy in your voice gradually increases, you will know when you've achieved the perfect energy balance because your golden will start to pay attention and do what is asked of them. On the other hand, if you're communicating with energy too forceful for your dog, slowly tone it down until the desired balance has been achieved.

Once you know the right energy to use when asking your puppy to perform various commands, it will quickly become second nature. After a certain point, you will not even realise you are adjusting your energy level to get your message across to your golden.

Canine Sounds

Apart from discovering the perfect level of energy when communicating with your retriever, it is also worth familiarising yourself with basic canine body language and the sounds they make. This includes their body and tail positioning, face, eyes, posture, barking, and growling noises.

Often, people assume gestures or actions mean one thing when the dog is saying the exact opposite. For example, knowing what that wagging tail or barking means can sometimes be the difference between a tummy rub and a bite. Knowing the difference can help prevent an unpleasant encounter during a visit to the local park.

The following are common canine sounds and postures and what they are trying to convey to other dogs and people around them.

Barking

Since the very first canine, dogs have communicated over long distances by barking or howling to one another, and when in closer proximity, barking or growling to warn off other dogs encroaching on what they consider to be their territory. Dogs also bark and whine in excitement or happiness when greeting a returning member of their pack.

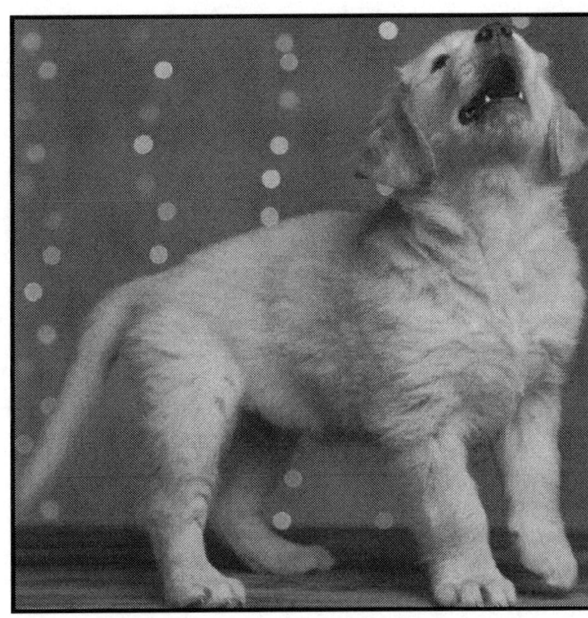

These days, domesticated dogs bark for a wide variety of reasons, such as when they sense danger or are alerting their owners to someone approaching the home. Barking is an effective way to get the attention of their owners, as it is a loud and difficult noise to ignore. While it can usually be easy to interpret what your golden retriever's bark is 'saying', there are some circumstances that might not be so easily understood and require more explanation.

When your dog barks for unknown reasons, the first step is to calmly assess the situation rather than instantly become annoyed or upset with your golden retriever. As your dog's sense of smell, hearing, and sight is usually far more acute than yours, they need you to teach them what they can bark at.

FACT ***While any dog, no matter their size, can learn to be a big barker, how they react to various circumstances largely depends on how they are raised.***

If your golden seems to be too keen on barking at everything, they need to be taught what is acceptable.

Attention – Most dogs bark to get your attention. Some reasons for this attention are:

- You are on the phone or computer.
- You are talking to someone.
- You are watching a movie.
- They want to play a game.

- They want a treat.
- It is dinner time.
- They need to go to the toilet.
- They want to go for a walk.
- Their water bowl is empty.

Danger – Many dogs bark to warn you about visitors or intruders, and part of training your golden puppy includes teaching them the difference between what they perceive as danger and what is truly dangerous. In other words, your puppy might bark because they haven't learned to recognise the noises the neighbour's children make when returning home from school, the sound the washing machine makes during the spin cycle, or the sound of neighbours walking down the hall in shared accommodation. You want your golden to alert you when there is real, imminent danger. If there's an intruder, you want them to bark loudly to try and scare the threat away.

Boredom – Dogs get bored, just like we do. Often, when they have had enough of lazing around the home, playing with their toys or chewing on a bone and want to get outside for a change of scenery and some exercise, they might bark to let you know they need to go out.

Separation Anxiety – Dogs are naturally pack animals, so long periods in isolation can be difficult for them. While dogs would never choose to be left alone, when introduced to it with kindness and compassion, they can learn to quietly accept short periods of solitude.

Unfamiliar Noises – When introducing your puppy to their new home, it can take time before they learn what noises are part of their new daily life and can be ignored. You can help your golden puppy to understand they do not need to bark at unfamiliar sounds by letting them see what caused the noise.

Excitement – Many puppies and dogs bark out of excitement in many circumstances, such as when you arrive home, if they see other dogs at the park, in anticipation of going for a car ride or a walk outside, or when getting wound up during a game. Depending on your living situation, you may not find excitement barking problematic. If, for example, you live in a multi-complex situation, such as a block of flats, you should discourage your dog from loud barking that could potentially disturb the neighbours.

On the other hand, if you live on a farm or smallholding where your nearest neighbour is further away, excitement barking will not be a worrisome or disturbing problem, and the sound of your golden retriever barking could be the type of security system that might discourage unwanted trespassers.

An Interesting Scent – Some dogs are more naturally prone to barking or howling when they smell an interesting scent in the wind.

Food or Toys – Golden puppies and dogs can be understandably excited in anticipation of receiving a treat, their food bowl, or a prized toy. If they have not yet learnt to control their enthusiasm, it can often erupt into a bark. If they bark intensely, simply ask them to '***Sit***' but do not give the treat, food bowl, or toy until they are quiet.

TIP ***If your dog is barking, they are being too demanding. They need to learn to be patient and less insistent before you give them what they want.***

Knocking at the Door or Ringing the Doorbell – Some dogs bark loudly whenever someone knocks at the door or rings the doorbell. Initially, they are simply letting you know someone is at the door, which is acceptable. What might not be acceptable though is persistent barking. It is up to you to firmly tell your golden when to stop barking by saying, '***No***' and asking them to '***Sit***' and be calm.

Fear – A dog will bark when they are afraid, nervous, or uncertain about something. There may be a new object in the neighbour's garden they have not seen before, so they bark at it. Or they might bark if they are uncertain about an unknown dog they encounter when out on a walk or when hearing thunder or a car alarm. If you do not want your dog to bark at something, you must teach them not to bark by saying, '***No***', and slowly approach and let them see it is nothing scary.

Pain – Another reason for your dog barking is if they are in pain. Usually, this bark sounds quite different to normal and is often a combination of a bark and a whine or a yelping noise. This is a bark you will want to pay close attention to, so you can quickly respond and offer the assistance your golden retriever needs.

Territorial – Dogs bark at other dogs and people if they feel the need to protect their property and/or people. Normally, this happens when your dog is not receiving a strong enough lead from you. If you become more confident, your golden will typically decide they no longer need to protect you or be territorial. When this happens, your dog can relax and let you take control, which will stop the barking.

If your golden has learnt to randomly bark at every new person or dog they encounter when out on a walk, they will need you to tell them this behaviour is unacceptable by firmly saying '***No***'.

Manipulation – When your golden retriever learns to become the centre of attention, they won't like it if you're interrupted by other people or various communication devices, such as the telephone. If your dog is used to getting all the attention, they might bark in impatient protest if they feel they are no longer the centre of your world. If this is the case, your golden needs to learn patience, so tell your dog to '***Sit***' or '***Wait***'.

If loud barking worked once, a dog never forgets that success. When a ball or other object they desire appears, they understand they can take charge with just some loud barking. If your dog becomes excited about chasing their ball, they could bark, so rather than immediately throwing it for them, you should say '***No***', tell them to '***Sit***' and '***Wait***', and make eye contact with them before you throw the ball.

Whining

Whining is often a precursor to full-blown barking. The first time you will probably hear your golden retriever puppy whine is when they think they have been left on their own and are feeling the panic of loneliness. Other reasons why your dog might whine include:

- They are unhappy with being confined in their crate.
- They are telling you they want or need something.
- They are hungry or thirsty.
- Being in new surroundings is making them nervous.
- They need to go to the toilet.

During house training, your puppy learns their toilet is in a specific place, such as the back garden. They might whine to get your attention when they need to go outside. When they first come to their new home, your puppy could whine at night when they are expected to sleep in their crate, as this is a lonely routine compared with their previous one of cuddling next to their littermates.

Talking

Some dogs are naturally vocal and seem to be talking to you. If only we could learn to speak 'dog'! Your retriever might do this because they like to make those noises and has learnt that when they make their growling, 'talking' noises, it seems to please you, which usually results in attention being switched to them.

Dogs are very adept at reading their people and quickly learn what sounds get them what they want. When your golden makes a noise that sounds as if they are trying to talk to you, the result can often be that you mimic the sound back to them. Then, if there is also a reward that reinforces your dog making that sound, bingo! They have just learnt how to have a conversation with you. Now, your smart dog can use their voice to ask you to do many things, such as:

- Take them for a walk.
- Give them a treat.
- Fill their water bowl.
- Give them a pet or a scratch behind the ears.
- Play a game.
- Goldens are often quite a vocal breed. When they become excited, they like to 'talk'. When their vocalisation starts, you will have to work on rewarding their quiet times to avoid it becoming an out-of-control habit.

Growling

Growling is just another form of canine communication frequently used when more subtle forms have not had the desired effect. When your golden is upset, afraid, nervous, or aggressive, they sometimes growl. Your dog might growl as a precursor to a full-blown bark.

Also, golden retrievers often growl noisily when play fighting with other dogs or even their owners. In this case, the growling does not mean they are being aggressive unless the play session gets too rough and one dog begins to become more threatening. You can defuse this by paying close attention and stepping in when you notice their play is beginning to get out of hand.

You will not usually have any difficulty recognising the difference between playful growling noises and the much louder and more intense sound that occurs when two dogs are seriously fighting.

Finally, there are other happy growls your golden retriever will use when communicating with you, which usually sound quite different from the rest. These growls are typically a lower sound that your dog affectionately makes when being petted, having a tummy rub or wanting your attention.

Howling

Howling is a deeply ingrained form of primal canine communication. Some breeds are naturally more prone to engage in howling—such as hunting hounds, like the beagle—as this is their way of telling their owners they have found the scent. Depending on the breed and the circumstances, howling can occur for much the same reasons as barking.

TIP ***Whatever the reason for your golden howling, you will not usually need to do any formal training to teach them not to howl, as this noise is likely to be quite infrequent and short-lived. If your dog has an insistent howling problem, the best way to eliminate it is mostly through redirecting their attention and rewarding them when they stop.***

Body Language Messages

The following are other subtle body language messages our furry canine friends use to convey messages to their owners. These may not be as easy to interpret as those already discussed, but with a little practice, they will soon make sense.

Stalking Stance

A stalking stance, often accompanied by raised hackles—hair along the back—is when your golden retriever lowers their head and shoulders, crouches, and slowly creeps forwards with an intense stare. Typically, this happens just before a serious attack.

When your dog approaches with raised hackles, this is an indication they are feeling dominant or aggressive. It may also be an indication they are excited, fearful, startled, nervous, or overly timid.

In any of these circumstances, keep a respectful distance and place your golden behind you until it becomes apparent what is going on because any dog who is nervous, anxious, or fearful can quickly turn into a reactive, biting dog.

Staring

Golden retrievers can stare at you for many reasons, and even more so if you are a confident leader who your dog has learnt to trust, respect, and obediently follow. For example, some of the reasons why your golden might stare at you include:

- Manipulating you to get what they want.
- They need a toilet break.
- They want to go for a walk.
- They want food.
- They need their water bowl filled.
- They are watching you eat, hoping for your leftovers.
- They are guarding something.
- They are waiting for instructions.
- They are reading your energy.
- They find what you are doing fascinating.
- They are expressing affection.

Usually, your clever retriever will have learnt the act of staring at you is a way of communicating that will eventually get them something they want.

Play Stance

Also called the 'play bow', the play stance looks like the 'stalking' stance, and without scrutiny, it can be difficult to identify the difference between the two. Whenever your golden retriever wants to play with you or another dog, they might:

- Bring their chest low to the ground.
- Lean on their front elbows.
- Stretch out their front legs.

This bowing posture is your golden's way of inviting another dog or human to play and is normally accompanied by an excited bark that, in the doggy world, invites you to, '*Come on, let's play*'.

Ear Movements

The many ear movements your golden makes are especially subtle and challenging to interpret. All dog breeds can move their ears forwards and back to display different emotions. When your dog is feeling relaxed, their ears are typically held slightly back or out to the sides. As your golden retriever becomes curious, more alert, or pays closer attention, their ears move farther to the front or towards what has caught their interest.

FACT ***When dogs are feeling afraid, they flatten their ears against their head. They also do this when they feel aggressive while making menacing facial gestures, barking, baring teeth or growling.***

Lip Licking

Of course, some dogs lick their lips in anticipation of a tasty treat or when they are about to be given their dinner. However, when there is no food involved, lip licking can be an indication that your golden is feeling worried or threatened by something going on around them. Dogs also lick their lips as an 'appeasement' or submissive gesture to signal to a more dominant dog they are not interested in fighting.

During training sessions, a confused dog might lick their lips because they're feeling stressed and don't understand what you're asking them to do. Should this happen, ask your golden to perform a simple task they have already learnt, and then offer the reward of a treat to end the session on a high note.

Finally, dogs can lick their lips if they are not feeling well or are experiencing pain as the result of a tooth or mouth problem.

Crotch Sniffing

Dogs sniff the privates of other dogs to try to get to know them. The same is true when a dog rushes in to sniff an unfamiliar person's crotch. It is their way of gathering information about who the person is.

The reason your dog will try to sniff someone's groin is that the groin and armpit areas contain the highest concentrations of apocrine or sweat glands, which produce pheromones. This means sniffing these areas will provide the most social information to your golden.

Head Tilting

There are several different views and hypotheses about why your golden might tilt their head when listening to you, including:

- It makes you smile and often results in praise for your dog.
- It allows your dog to determine the direction of the sound.
- It helps your retriever understand what the noise is.
- A higher-pitched sound might be appealing to your dog's ear.
- It improves or better focuses your dog's vision.
- The word or phrase is familiar to your golden.
- Persistent head tilting is due to an ear infection.

Whether we understand or not why dogs tilt their heads at different sounds, words, or phrases, there is no doubt this head tilting is rather adorable.

Yawning

When your golden yawns, they can be sending various messages, including:

- Indifference.
- They feel stressed and might yawn in rapid succession.
- When a dog encounters a more dominant dog, they might yawn to 'tell' the aggressor they are neither willing to be submissive nor interested in challenging.
- Sometimes, a yawn is a calming signal and a way to avoid conflict. Yawning might be enough to defuse the aggressive approach of another dog.

What is interesting about yawning is just like the 'contagious' aspect of yawning between people, the same thing happens between dogs or humans and dogs who know one another well. Therefore, while a yawn may indicate stress, it can also be a normal part of life and a sign your dog is closely bonded with you.

Tail Vocabulary

Your dog's vocabulary includes an extensive tail language common to all canines. Tail language is an important mechanism to signal the emotional state of your canine companion. For example, the position and speed of your golden retriever's wagging tail function much the same way as a smile or frown on the face of a human when greeting others.

Tail Positions

A well-socialised dog will happily wag their tail when greeting others. However, it can be a mistake to automatically assume if a dog is wagging their tail, they are friendly. It is important to take into consideration all the different messages a dog's tail can convey before interpreting what they're doing. They may be wagging their tail just before they decide to take an aggressive lunge toward a person or another dog.

The height or positioning of their tail is more important in determining the emotional state of most dogs. Here are the possible positions and what each of these can mean.

Stiffly Vertical – A stiffly held tail pointing skywards could mean your dog is feeling aggressive and dominant and about to challenge or threaten another less dominant dog. It might also mean your golden is very excited. Some breeds—such as terriers—naturally hold their tails in a vertical position. A tail held stiffly and slowly sweeping is frequently an aggressive communication.

In-Line with the Back – A tail held parallel to your dog's back usually suggests they are feeling alert and attentive. They're involved in gathering information about what's going on around them with neutral energy and possible interest in exploring their surroundings.

Held Much Lower – When your dog holds their tail much lower than in line with their back, it can mean they are feeling stressed, afraid, submissive, or unwell. If you notice this tail position, keep a close eye on your golden to determine if they were just upset by a particular situation or an unknown dog or if they might be unwell and need to be checked out by their vet.

Tucked Underneath the Body – When your golden tucks their tail under their body between the back legs, this is commonly a submissive sign. They are likely feeling highly stressed, nervous, fearful, or threatened by an older or more dominant dog, person, or unfamiliar situation.

The Speed of the Wag

How quickly your dog's tail is moving also offers an idea of their mental state. The speed of the wag usually signifies how happy or excited your dog is but can also mean they are feeling aggressive.

Slow Low Slightly Swinging Tail – A stiffly held tail that is low and reminiscent of a broom sweeping the floor frequently means your golden is feeling anxious, unsure, or tentative about greeting another dog. This is more of a questioning type of wag that could become aggressive. If accompanied by a raised paw, your dog is questioning.

Fast-Moving Tail – Typically, the faster the wag, the higher your retriever's level of excitement. Also, the stroke of the tail sends different messages. Smaller strokes of the tail can indicate your golden feels nervous or uncertain about a meeting. On the other hand, when the strokes are broader, this can mean your retriever is feeling happier about a situation.

The Circle Wag – This type of tail wag, often also referred to as the '***propeller***' or '***helicopter***' wag, almost always indicates a happy, friendly dog who is overjoyed by a situation.

Tail Wagging to the Left – When your golden wags their tail to the left, it could indicate they are feeling more wary or dominant because they are coming near an unfamiliar dog or person.

Tail Wagging to the Right – When your dog wags their tail to the right, this usually means they are pleased about meeting or greeting someone.

8. Feeding Your Golden

'It's just the most amazing thing to love a dog, isn't it? It makes our relationships with people seem as boring as a bowl of oatmeal.'

~ John Grogan ~

We are what we eat, and the same is true for our dogs. A dog fed a balanced, breed-appropriate diet is a healthy, content, and longer-lived companion.

Mostly, a domestic dog's diet consists of meat, but they also consume grains, fruits, and vegetables. Non-meat foods do more than serve as fillers. They provide a range of essential vitamins, minerals, and fibre. Quality dog food includes meat, vegetables, grains, and fruit. High-quality versions of these ingredients are used in the best dog foods that are safe for your golden's digestive system.

It is important to feed your dog the best quality food you can afford. The problem with choosing lower-priced food is that cheaper dog food is frequently less nutritious. Inexpensive dog food brands can include low-quality fillers such as wheat, corn, soy, and other unnecessary ingredients to add bulk to the product rather than providing any nutritional benefit. It is worth noting that dogs cannot efficiently digest corn or wheat. If you have a farm food shop nearby, you may be able to get working dog food there, which is better quality than many supermarket dog foods but are more affordable.

TIP ***Whilst you might pay a little more for a better-quality diet for your golden retriever, their improved health is well worth it, but there is an additional bonus. You will probably find that you need to visit the vet less often, as your dog's immune system is strong and their general health much better too.***

Canine Teeth and Jaws – All your golden's teeth are sharp and pointed because they are designed to rip, shred, and tear into animal meat and bone. On average, an adult dog has a third more teeth than their human owner.

Adult canines have 42 permanent teeth compared to a human's 32 (excluding wisdom teeth). On average, puppies have 28 baby teeth or 'milk teeth', while human babies have 20 baby teeth.

Puppies begin to lose their sharp, baby teeth at approximately 12 to 16 weeks old. By four months, almost all your golden puppy's milk teeth will have been shed and replaced by their permanent, adult teeth (see picture).

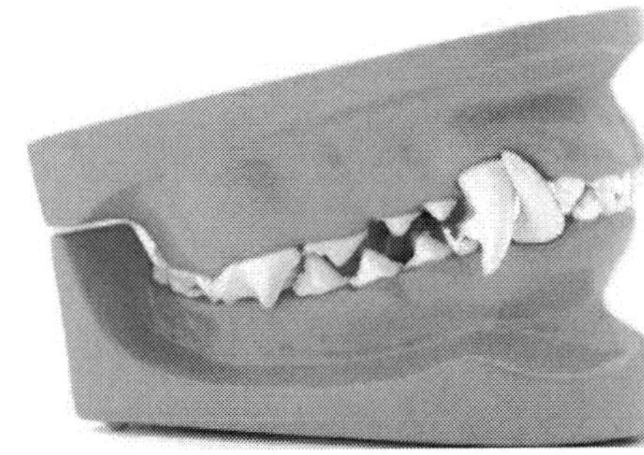

Every dog is born equipped with powerful jaws and neck muscles designed so they can pull down and tear apart their hunted prey. The jaw of every canine opens wide to hold large pieces of meat and bone, while the mechanics of the jaw permit only vertical—up and down—movement designed for crushing.

Getting into the habit of **carefully reading the food labels** can go a long way toward avoiding over-processed foods that contain fillers, such as corn meal or wheat gluten, which are inappropriate for a healthy canine diet.

As your dog grows and ages, their dietary needs change. A puppy's nutritional requirements are different from those of an adult or senior dog. **Most dog food companies offer specifically formulated foods for dogs at various life stages. They are commonly labelled as Puppy, Adult, and Senior.** There are even some companies that have products explicitly for the adolescent phase, identified on the label as 'Junior'. It is important to choose the right food for your golden's stage of life to make sure they are getting the right amount of nutrients.

If you are concerned about what is the best food for your retriever's life stage, consult your veterinarian to determine what is appropriate for your golden.

In the United Kingdom, the Pet label Manufacturers' Association (PFMA) standards state that 'all information given on a pet food label must be truthful and not misleading about the nature and quality of the product'. Also, 'the law requires a statutory statement to be put on every label or package, which must contain certain obligatory declarations.'

These must state:

- Whether the product is complete or complementary.
- What species the product is for.
- Directions for use/feeding instructions.

An ideal nutritional diet for your golden retriever contains protein, carbohydrates, fats, fibre, vitamins, and minerals, so your dog gets all the nourishment they need. Feeding them a healthy, well-balanced diet will not only keep your best friend trim, but it will also help them live a longer, healthier, and happier life.

Emerging (but inconclusive) scientific evidence suggests a dog might cope with a 'plant-based' diet. These studies argue that available meat sources today are often polluted with wheat, chemicals, drugs, and other products that would not be part of a wild dog's natural diet. It is interesting to note that one of the world's longest-living canines was a highly energetic border collie who was fed a clean, organic, plant-based diet and lived to be over 25 years old, even though the average for the breed is 14. Feeding a clean, organic diet to a dog may well increase their lifespan.

28 Tips for Healthy Food Choices

As responsible owners, we should be actively involved in what we are feeding our dogs and look for ways to improve their diet. Hopefully, the following tips will make it easier for you to choose the best food possible for your golden retriever:

1. Carefully examine the ingredients.

HELPFUL TIPS

2. Be careful not to choose food because you like the adverts. Beware of clever marketing simply because it IS very clever.
3. Understand that just because a vet is selling food, this does not mean it is necessarily the best choice for your dog.
4. Avoid feeding food that claims a shelf life of 12 to 24 months. This means it contains preservatives that may not be a healthy choice.
5. Add fresh whole foods to your golden's diet.
6. Puree vegetables and fruits for maximum absorption.
7. Add foods that are high in antioxidants, such as blueberries, blackberries, squash, sweet potatoes, etc., to help reduce inflammation.
8. If you can, choose organic fruits and vegetables.
9. If organic is difficult to source, scrub toxins from fruit and vegetables. You can do this by soaking them in four parts of water, one-part cider vinegar, and gently brushing them with a soft bristle brush.
10. Gluten is generally harmless, but it can create long-lasting and occasionally irreparable damage for the small percentage of dogs suffering from celiac disease or gluten intolerance.

11. Stay away from genetically modified foods (GMO) often found in pet food.
12. Consider giving CBD oil to help improve appetite, reduce anxiety and inflammation, and for pain relief of sore or arthritic joints.
13. Clean dog bowls and dishes daily with white vinegar to disinfect them. Some dogs are allergic or sensitive to commercial soaps and cleaners.
14. Practise a controlled feeding timetable and feed at the same time each day.
15. If your golden seems bored, feed their mind when you feed their body by putting the meals in a food puzzle.
16. Familiarise yourself with what foods are dangerous for dogs (see list in Chapter 15).
17. Discard opened canned or wet food within two days of opening.
18. Dogs are always interested in food. However, just because they are happy to eat does not mean they are hungry or need more food. Constantly giving them food can lead to unwanted behaviour problems, such as begging for food and hyperactivity whenever they see people eating. Dogs are hard-wired to constantly forage and look for food. You can prevent obesity by sticking to your dog's regular feeding schedule and monitoring the amount of food you give them.
19. Choose organic, single-ingredient treats.
20. When your golden begins to show signs of ageing—between 8 and 9 years old—their feeding schedule might need to be adjusted to help them maintain their ideal weight. Some senior goldens prefer to be fed once a day.
21. If a kind person offers to give your dog a treat, politely decline and explain they are on a special diet, so your dog will not be eating treats that might not be a good choice.

22. You can help your golden maintain optimum health throughout their life by keeping an open mind, questioning everything, and always feeding based on their specific nutritional requirements. Remember to consider age, size, and activity level, as this will change over time and is different for every dog.
23. The most important thing to bear in mind when feeding your golden retriever is to ensure they eat a complete and balanced diet.
24. Keep an eye on the condition of your retriever's body and coat. If your dog appears to be thriving and has a glossy coat, plenty of energy, and a fit appearance, their food agrees with them. If your dog has a dull coat and lacks energy, try changing to another kind of food. The way the food has been processed or the ingredients it contains could prevent your golden from absorbing all the needed nutrients.
25. Also, check the back garden for other signs of trouble, such as an excessive amount of faeces, which might indicate a problem with digestibility. If this is the case, reconsider your dog's diet.
26. Assess your golden's activity level. If your golden is active and exercises outdoors, they might need 20% to 40% more food than a more sedentary dog. Working dogs usually need food designed for working or performance dogs. Such foods have a higher fat content to provide extra calories.
27. Serious illness, pregnancy, or nursing can increase your golden's energy requirements. Ask your vet about adjusting the quantity or type of food in these circumstances.
28. The feeding charts on pet food labels are a useful guide. Begin by checking the amount recommended for your dog's weight range. If your golden is on the lower end of the scale, feed the lower recommended amount. Dogs who are on the heavier end could require more food.

Many of the common diseases affecting dogs have a direct correlation with over-feeding and/or feeding poor-quality foods.

Dog Food Types

Dog food has significantly changed since 1785 when the English Sportsman's Dictionary described the best diet for a dog's health in an article entitled 'Dog'. This article indicated that the best food for a dog was something called 'Greaves', described as 'the sediment of melted tallow made into cakes for dogs' food'.

From these meagre beginnings, commercially manufactured dog food has become a massively lucrative business that has only recently evolved beyond feeding our dogs the dregs of human leftovers, a cheap and convenient option. Even today, most dog foods are manufactured to be convenient to store and serve rather than being a nutritionally balanced, healthy food choice for our canine companions.

Thankfully, there is always new research being carried out, and we can help ourselves to be well-informed by talking to experts and reading everything published about canine food. Educating yourself about what is available, plus considering the requirements of your golden retriever, such as their age, energy, and activity levels, are key factors when choosing the appropriate food.

Knowing that dogs also suffer from many of the same life-threatening diseases commonly found in human society, such as heart disease, cancer, diabetes, and obesity, helps us make better food choices.

There is no doubt that choosing the best food for your golden retriever can mean the difference between a shortened lifespan or a long life with few health issues. Unfortunately, there is no simple answer to the 'What should I feed' question due to the endless variety of food products on the market and the uniqueness of every dog. Read on to learn about the different diet choices, how to interpret the food labels and what your golden's nutritional needs are. With this information, you can make educated and healthy food choices for your furry friend.

The Raw Diet

Raw feeding has become increasingly popular over the past few years. You can even find commercially prepared raw food in popular pet stores. However, there are conflicting arguments about raw feeding. It can be hard to know how to do the right thing for your retriever, as you will often find strong arguments for and against raw feeding.

Raw feeding is exactly as it sounds—feeding your retriever raw ingredients instead of the cooked food more commonly found in commercial dog food. A raw diet usually comprises organ meats, muscle meat, whole or ground bone, raw eggs, and dog-safe fresh fruits and vegetables. Raw meals for dogs can be homemade, store-bought, freeze-dried, frozen, or fresh.

Advocates of raw feeding believe it is the best way to give your dog what it would have consumed while hunting or foraging in the wild. It is claimed that raw food contains all the essential nutrients required for a balanced diet. Often, raw-feeding supporters are opposed to feeding their dogs any sort of commercially manufactured dog foods, as they consider them to be poor substitutes. They claim a raw diet has multiple benefits, including:

- Healthier, shiny coats.
- Less shedding.
- Fewer allergies.
- Healthier skin.
- Fresher breath.
- Cleaner teeth.
- Higher energy levels.
- Improved digestion.
- Smaller stools.
- A strengthened immune system.
- Increased mobility in arthritic dogs.
- Overall improved health.

However, critics of the raw diet report the following potential issues:

- There may be large fragments of bone in raw dog food that might be hard for dogs to eat.
- A raw diet could lead to infections and gastrointestinal inflammation.
- Dogs with kidney or liver diseases should not be on a raw food diet as it has high levels of protein that are difficult for dogs to digest.

- Making your dog's meals from scratch is time-consuming. Plus, it is more expensive than the ready-made cooked dog food you can buy in any pet food store.
- Potential bacteria and parasites in raw bones and meat present a significant health hazard. Whilst some of these bacteria are unlikely to negatively affect your dog's health, others can have serious consequences. For example, it is estimated that between 20-44 per cent of commercial raw meat diets are contaminated with salmonella. These harmful bacteria can be particularly concerning for families with children, elderly people or those with a compromised immune system.
- Diarrhoea and bowel constructions can be triggered in dogs by eating raw dog food.
- If not properly prepared, raw dog food—especially homemade—is often nutrient-deficient for dogs and can create health problems. Consult your vet first if you decide to feed homemade raw food to your retriever to make sure the nutritional value of their meal meets their requirements.
- Many experts advise that raw dog food should not be given to dogs suffering from cancer or other such diseases since they are more susceptible to bacteria.

Although raw diets have many benefits, you may decide that the cost in terms of finance, time, and contagion risk is too high. If your golden retriever has certain medical issues or allergies, a raw food diet may improve its condition. However, for most people, a cooked, manufactured dog food diet is a better choice due to its convenience and price.

If shop-bought dog food is giving your golden stomach problems, it is worth trying a homemade, cooked diet before going straight to raw. You also have other options to help your retriever if they have digestive issues. Just switching to a different kind of kibble or protein source could be the solution your dog needs.

Instead of feeding your dog a raw diet, you might like to try adding wet food or supplements, such as fish oil, to your golden's kibble. These adjustments are much easier for most owners and still give many of the benefits associated with a raw diet.

If you do decide to try a raw diet, you'll need to choose good-quality ingredients to give your dog. In the United Kingdom, vets and owners can easily source frozen raw meals readily prepared and formulated to the same European standards as the other pet foods found in our supermarkets and veterinary surgeries.

If you can, always source your raw foods from Defra-registered producers. These products are governed by bacteriological rules more stringent than even human-grade raw meat products. They are supplied in clean, hygienic packaging. A huge variety of frozen raw meals specially formulated to meet canine nutritional needs are available from companies such as Paleo Ridge and Naturaw.

You will need a big freezer to store your retriever's frozen raw food. If you don't already have one, this is an extra expense to add to the cost of the food, and not everyone has the extra space required to install it.

Over the years, several variations of raw diets have been developed. The most popular ones are the Raw meaty bones, the BARF diet, and the Prey model raw. We'll go into these in more depth below.

Raw Meaty Bones

Renowned Australian veterinarian, Dr Tom Lonsdale, advocates this diet, which consists mainly of the following:

- Raw meaty bones or carcasses when available—do not feed cooked bones as they can tear the oesophagus, stomach, or intestinal lining, which can cause internal bleeding or perforation.

- Cooked and raw table scraps, such as vegetables.
- Fresh, clean water must always be available.
- Poultry by-products, including heads, feet, necks, and wings.
- Turkey and chicken carcasses left after the meat has been removed for human consumption.
- Sheep, goat, calf, and deer carcasses sawn into large chunks of meat and bone.
- Whole fish, including their heads.
- Other by-products, including pig's heads, pig's trotters, tail bones, sheep heads, brisket, and rib bones.
- Tripe, liver, lungs, trachea, hearts, and omasums (the stomach of ruminants).

Based on raw, meaty bones, an approximate food consumption guide for the average dog is 15-20 % of body weight in one week or 2-3 per cent per day. That means, if your golden has an average weight of 30 kg, they require up to 6 kg of carcasses or raw meaty bones every week. This is only a rough guide and pertains to adult dogs in a domestic environment.

The raw meaty bones diet cites that fish, birds, and low-fat game animals provide the best source of food for domesticated carnivores. If sourcing meat from farm animals—cattle, sheep, and pigs—avoid excessive fat or any bones too large to be eaten.

Growing puppies and pregnant or lactating females might need more food than adult animals of similar body weight.

You can find further information about this diet on Dr Tom Lonsdale's site: www.rawmeatybones.com.

If you are considering switching your golden to a raw meaty bones diet, it is highly recommended you consult your vet first.

BARF diet

The Bones and Raw Food, or Biologically Appropriate Raw Food (BARF) diet, is the original raw food diet. It was introduced by veterinarian Dr Ian Billinghurst in 1993. Like other raw diets, this diet is designed to mimic what dogs ate before they became domesticated. Although a dog's natural diet would largely comprise hunted animals, they also scavenged for fruits and/or vegetables that were available to them. The BARF diet aims to replicate this and consists of roughly 70% meat, 10% bone, 10% offal—5% liver, 5% any other secreting organs—7% vegetables, and 3% fruit.

Prey Model Raw

A version of the raw diet is the Prey Model Raw (PMR), which is like BARF but without fruits and vegetables. There is a debate raging in the raw dog food world about whether you should give your dog fruits and vegetables and, if so, how many. The guidelines for a PMR diet recommend 75-80% muscle meat, 10% raw edible bone, 5% liver, 5% other secreting organs, and 0-5% animal-based fibre, such as animal segments, including fur or feathers.

The Dehydrated Diet

To preserve essential nutrients, vitamins, and minerals found naturally in the ingredients, dehydrated dog food (see picture) is made using a gentle, low-heat drying method. The drying process mimics the natural process of the sun burning down on a carcass, preserving the ingredients. Drying food is a preservation technique that has been around for millennia, allowing you to keep food safe for longer.

Dehydrated recipes are made from unprocessed, fresh whole foods to create a healthy and nutritionally balanced meal to meet or exceed the daily dietary requirements of a healthy canine.

TIP ***Dehydrated dog food offers all the benefits of a raw diet without the hassle of defrosting. This makes it convenient for travelling or camping since it is lighter and more nutrient-dense than frozen, raw food and does not need refrigeration.***

Preparation is easy. All you need to do is stir warm water into the food. The ratios/amounts are displayed on the feeding guide of the dog food bag, normally on the back of the packaging. Make sure you let it sit for 2-3 minutes so the water fully rehydrates all the ingredients. This guarantees all the nutrients, flavours, and aromas reach their optimum state, so your dog loves the taste and the benefits. If the food is not fully rehydrated, it can swell in your golden's stomach, causing bloating and discomfort.

Once mixed with water, the dehydrated dog food resembles a stodgy form of gran's homemade stew. The chunks of ingredients in the food, such as chicken, barley, potatoes, flaxseed, organic oats, carrots, etc., are clearly visible.

The Freeze-Dried Diet

As with dehydration, freeze-drying is a way to remove water from perishable foods. The process of dehydration uses warm air to eliminate moisture. There are three steps: freezing, primary drying, and secondary drying. By freezing before drying, freeze-dried foods (see picture) contain more nutrients than dehydrated ones because protein, vitamins, and minerals remain intact.

According to American holistic veterinarian Dr Marty Goldstein, your retriever will thrive when you feed them freeze-dried, raw food that contains three essential nutrients:

- Organ meat: a nutrient-rich source of energy for dogs.
- Omega-3 fatty acids: to help maintain brain health, make training easier, reverse ageing, relieve joint pain, relieve allergies, and provide more energy for senior dogs.
- Natural prebiotics: flaxseed, pea flour, carrot, and ginger are prebiotics for good gut bacteria to promote digestion and serotonin production in dogs.

A freeze-dried, mostly raw meat diet with some healthy fats, vegetables, and fruits for good gut bacteria, as well as powerful antioxidant support, help maintain your dog's health. Freeze-dried food is lightweight, easy to store, and simple to prepare. All you do is add a little water and wait three minutes for it to rehydrate. The freeze-drying process preserves all the nutrients destroyed by cooking, so you can feed your golden a healthy meal without losing any of its nutritional value.

The Dry Kibble Diet

Dry dog food, or kibble (see picture), continues to be the most popular choice due to its convenience. There are several reasons why you might choose to feed your dog a dry kibble diet, such as:

- It is generally more affordable.
- It doesn't require refrigeration.
- Hard food exercises your dog's jaws.
- It helps clean your retriever's teeth.

Kibble brands have different ingredients, but all must be balanced and meet the nutritional needs of your golden retriever.

Kibble is prepared by processing raw ingredients together and then cooking them. Typical ingredients include protein sources such as beef, poultry, fish, and eggs, as well as cereals, grains, vitamins, minerals, and antioxidants. Preservatives are necessary for all dry dog foods to stop the fat from going rancid. Some brands have a high carbohydrate content or use low-quality ingredients and added sugar.

TIP ***Always check the label. Make sure the main ingredient in the kibble is a protein, not a grain. In quality kibble, protein dominates over starch, and you can even get grain-free brands. The best kibbles have a single protein source, such as lamb or chicken. Although there are grain-free kibbles, carbohydrates are necessary for energy. However, the choice of grain is important since some dogs suffer from wheat, corn, or soybean allergies.***

The Home-Cooked Diet

It is hard to say whether cooking food for your golden retriever yourself is better than purchasing commercially produced dog food. However, it does have one major advantage: when you prepare your own dog food, you know exactly what your dog is eating. There are several other reasons why you might choose home-cooked food (see picture) for your dog, such as:

- To provide variety for a picky eater.
- To provide fresh food with higher nutritional value.
- To feed organic ingredients.
- To completely control what your dog is eating.
- To avoid the issue of commercial food recalls.
- To avoid food allergy problems.

Although having complete control over what goes into your retriever's dinner bowl can offer peace of mind, there are considerations to take into account, including:

- The meal might not be balanced or contain all the essential nutrients required by your dog.
- You need to make sure you do not use toxic ingredients, such as onions, garlic, etc.
- It is challenging to find healthy and balanced recipes.
- Knowing the amount of home-cooked food to feed your dog can be difficult.
- You will probably need to add a multivitamin to ensure all vitamin and mineral requirements are met.

While a home-cooked diet certainly has its benefits and can be a healthy alternative when done correctly, a lot of research and planning is required to be sure the diet is nutritionally balanced.

The Canned (Wet) Food Diet

Some feel that a canned food diet is better than dry kibble, as it:

- Contains fewer carbohydrates.
- Provides moisture.
- Is more appetising to most dogs.
- Contains no synthetic preservatives.
- Might contain fewer artificial flavours and colours.
- Usually has more meat.
- Comes in air-tight packaging.
- Has a longer shelf life.

Looking at this list, you might think canned dog food is a healthy option. However, there are a few things to consider about this dietary choice, such as:

- Canned food is usually more expensive.
- It cannot be left out for more than 1-2 hours.
- Once exposed to the air, it can easily grow bacteria.
- Opened cans (see picture) must be kept refrigerated.
- It will only stay fresh for 2 to 3 days.

Many people choose to feed their retriever a combination of wet and dry food. This can cut the cost of your golden's food while still giving them some of the health benefits and taste of wet food. If you decide to go down this road, make sure you still feed them the correct number of calories.

Several varieties of semi-moist dog food are available as well. These tend to be loaded with by-products and sugar, making them unhealthy as a primary diet for your dog. If your golden retriever is extremely picky, it is healthier to feed them wet food or mix some wet food into their dry food.

Canine Nutritional Requirements

Before heading off to the pet food store to get the best food for your dog, it is worth taking some time to learn the basics about canine nutritional needs. Most of your dog's nutritional requirements should come from animal sources, including meat, fish, eggs, poultry, and seafood. Dogs also need a balance of protein and fat in their diet, plus healthy carbohydrates to provide energy, fibre, and other essential nutrients.

Protein

The building blocks of protein consist of 23 amino acids, ten of which must come from food. Protein is essential for survival and a strong immune system.

FACT ***Protein is the most important nutrient for your golden retriever and is essential for healthy puppy growth and development. When your puppy is growing, protein helps them maintain lean muscle mass so they do not become overweight or obese. Your puppy needs at least 22% protein in their diet. When they reach adulthood, they only need 18%.***

Fats

The second most important nutrient for your golden is fat. While you might think of fat as a bad thing, it is an essential part of a balanced diet for your dog. Fat provides a concentrated source of energy and helps your dog absorb and utilise fat-soluble vitamins. Fat should come from healthy animal sources, such as chicken fat or salmon oil, and be at least 8% of your young golden retriever's diet. An adult dog requires a minimum of 5%.

Many kibble diets do not provide enough high-quality fats necessary to generate the much-needed energy in your dog's unique metabolism. Fat also helps keep your golden retriever's hair and skin healthy, reduces inflammation, and is essential for the development and normal function of body tissues, muscles, and nerves.

Remember that your dog isn't human. Concerns over a high-fat diet don't apply. You may not have realised, but 90 to 95% of fat is easily metabolised by dogs and fats in their diet yield 2.5 times as much energy as proteins or carbohydrates.

Carbohydrates

Technically, even though your golden does not have a specific need for carbohydrates, they can provide energy as well as fibre and other nutrients. Your dog's body is not adapted to digest and absorb nutrition from plants as much as from animal products, which means carbohydrates in your dog's diet should be limited. They should come from sources such as whole grains, starchy vegetables, beans, or legumes.

TIP ***When your retriever eats a diet with a high amount of carbohydrates, instead of utilising the fat in their diet to fuel their metabolism, they use sugar. Burning sugar for fuel is known to place metabolic stress on your dog's body resulting in an increased risk of serious health problems, such as cancer, obesity, diabetes, and more.***

Many commercially prepared dog foods use cheaper, abundant carbohydrates with a long shelf-life as the dominant ingredient. The percentage of carbs found in a portion of an average off-the-shelf dog food is far higher than a dog would normally eat in the wild. Some statistics say the amount of carbohydrates has increased from 14% of the total ancestral diet to somewhere between 46 and 74% today.

It is important to choose healthy carbohydrate sources from plants and fruits called 'functional' carbohydrates. These contain minerals, vitamins, and phytonutrients that help support your dog's health and offer a wide range of additional health benefits, including:

- The prevention and repair of DNA damage caused by daily exposure to environmental toxins.
- Lower inflammation.
- Protection against heart disease.
- The regulation of hormone metabolism.
- Antioxidant protection of cell damage from free radicals.
- Enhancing your dog's immune system and ability to fight disease.
- Blocking tumour activity.
- Killing cancerous cells.

Carbohydrates that are highly unsuitable for your golden include anything processed with white sugar, salt, or flour. These are empty calories for your retriever and quickly raise blood sugar levels. In moderation, carbohydrates have a place in your dog's diet if they are 'functional' and healthy. The following are good sources of healthy, dog-friendly carbohydrates:

- Unprocessed whole vegetables and legumes—such as broccoli, Brussels sprouts, bok choy, carrots, cauliflower, cabbage, lettuce, parsley, spinach, black-eyed peas, garbanzo beans, kidney beans, lentils, lima beans, pinto beans, pumpkin, sweet potato, winter squash.
- Unprocessed whole fruits—such as apples, bananas, blackberries, blueberries, cantaloupe, pear, raspberries, and watermelon.
- Whole grains—such as amaranth, buckwheat, millet, quinoa, sorghum, teff, and gluten-free oats.

Minerals and Vitamins

Your golden retriever will need to take supplements if they are not receiving all the minerals and vitamins essential for building strong bones and helping the many chemical reactions inside their body. While vitamin and mineral requirements vary depending on your dog's age, all dogs have the following basic requirements:

- Minerals: calcium, chromium, copper, fluorine, iodine, magnesium, manganese, phosphorus, potassium chloride, selenium, sodium, sulphur, and zinc.
- Vitamins: A, B family, C, D, E, K, Choline.

Water

Water accounts for half the weight of your adult golden retriever. It is so important that a loss of just 10% can be fatal. Your golden must always have access to fresh, clean water. Water is the main component of the living cells in your dog's body, and every vital function depends on it. An adequate amount of water:

- Helps digestion.
- Aids the absorption of nutrients.
- Cools the body and maintains normal body temperature.
- Helps eliminate toxins and waste.
- Lubricates and cushions joints.
- Keeps the cells hydrated.

Depending on their size, age, activity level, and the climate they live in, your golden will usually need to drink approximately 30 millilitres (1 ounce) of water for every 0.5 kilograms (1.1 pounds) of body weight each day to maintain their health. As an example, a dog weighing 30 kilograms (66 pounds) will need to drink 1.8 litres (61 ounces) daily.

FACT ***Just like us, dogs can only last about three days without water. If your golden doesn't drink enough, it is highly likely they will become dehydrated, which can lead to kidney failure. Some signs of dehydration include a dry nose, dry eyes and dry, sticky, or light-coloured gums.***

If you're unsure whether your dog is suffering from dehydration, there is a simple test you can do. Grab the skin at the top of the shoulder blades—where a mother dog might pick up a puppy—and lift it. If it falls back into place quickly, your dog is probably fine. However, if the skin slowly descends to its original form, this could be an indication of dehydration. If your dog is suffering from an extended bout of diarrhoea, they may also quickly show signs of dehydration.

Reading Labels & Choosing Food

Learning how to correctly interpret commercial dog food product labels can be challenging. Familiarise yourself with the manufacturer's lingo, so you can be confident you're feeding a quality product to your retriever.

The Law Versus the Lingo

Legally, pet food manufacturers must list out food ingredients by weight.

However, what you may not be aware of is that the weight is determined before the food is processed, including the moisture content.

You need to be careful to avoid being tricked by clever wording. Whilst 'deboned chicken' might sound good, it is full of weight-adding moisture. When the food is extruded and turned into kibble, all this moisture evaporates, and the chicken content is greatly reduced.

Since the meat content is so important, you'd expect it to be the first ingredient listed, right? It might make sense, but often the most misunderstood ingredient listed on pet food labels is 'meal'. Frequently, you'll see 'meat meals' listed in the ingredients for kibble because meal contains a higher protein content when compared to fresh meat. This sounds good, but is it really?

FACT ***While the law states that a 'meal' must contain bone and meat, there can be other unnamed sources in the meal, including feathers, blood, dead animal carcasses, inedible meat scraps, hide, hooves, internal organs, fat, and bone. In other words, the meal could be almost exclusively comprised of leftover animal parts unfit for human consumption.***

When a meal product is listed, the protein count is increased, tricking consumers into believing they are choosing a healthy product. The truth is high protein might not necessarily mean a high-quality product, as there may be very little beef, chicken, or other meat in the meal.

Of course, you're probably now wondering, 'Should I buy dog food that lists 'meal' as an ingredient?' There is no simple answer to this. Making an informed decision requires discovering where the meal came from and exactly what is in it. You'd need to contact the manufacturer and ask them to provide a written guarantee as to what is in the meal they list on their product. By the time you get a definitive answer, they might have changed their ingredients.

The Rules

In the United States, the FDA enforces rules to regulate how a dog food label is written:

The 95% Rule – In food with few ingredients, at least 95% must be named, excluding condiments and any water added for processing. If the water content is included, the named ingredients must comprise 70% of the product. If, for example, a product is called 'Lamb Dog Food', the product weight, excluding water and condiments, must be 95% lamb. Ingredients added for nutritional purposes, such as minerals, vitamins, and small amounts of other ingredients required to formulate the product, make up the remaining 5%. As ingredients are listed in order of weight, 'lamb' should be the first ingredient listed on the label. It will then usually be followed by water, vitamins, and minerals. However, ingredients are listed by weight *before* being cooked. Beef will weigh a lot more pre-cooked. In the case of a mixed recipe like chicken and rice, 95% should be comprised of chicken and rice, not including water; when you factor in water, the chicken and rice should make up at least 70%.

The 25% Rule – This applies to products often labelled as 'Dinner', 'Entrée', 'Platter' or 'Chow', such as 'Pedigree Chopped Ground Dinner with Beef'. To meet the 25% rule, the named ingredient must make up at least 10% of the total weight and at least 25% of the product weight, excluding water. With food that lists more than one ingredient in the name, like 'Beef with Vegetables & Potatoes', none of those named ingredients can be less than 3% of the total weight.

The With (or 3%) Rule – This rule applies to food labels such as 'Honest Jack's Dog Food with Chicken', and states that this type of food must contain at least 3% of chicken in the total weight. This means that any named ingredient must equal at least 3%. For instance, 'Rover's Dog Food with Beef and Rice' must contain at least 3% beef and 3% rice.

The Flavour Rule – If the label says, 'Beef Flavour Dog Food,' then a specific percentage of the beef is not required, but the product needs to contain an amount sufficient to be detected. In this instance, the word 'Flavour' must appear on the product label in the same size, style, and colour as the word 'Beef.'

Unfortunately, without being personally involved in the manufacturing process or having access to someone who can vouch for the efficacy of the food, there is no way to determine the true quality of manufactured dog food just by reading the ingredients list. Furthermore, many dog food labels try to sell their products based on clever advertising ploys portraying healthy dogs playing or running with wild abandon over grassy fields and looking literally the 'picture' of health.

Be part of a drive for more transparent pet food labelling by taking a more active role. Get involved by calling the number on the food label and asking for product information that may not be as forthcoming as conscientious owners would like.

When shopping for dog food, always take the time to carefully read the information on the package, so you can determine the product quality. If you are going to make comparisons between different products, there are three specific things to look for on the label, as detailed in the next Section.

Choosing a High-Quality Dog Food Brand

Analytical Constituents

In the United Kingdom, the next thing to look for is the Analytical Constituents—called Guaranteed Analysis in the U.S. This tells you the percentages of protein, fat, fibre, and moisture in the product. You can use the analytical constituents to make a direct comparison between products, bearing in mind the minimum values from the previous section. Because your golden will have difficulty digesting too much fibre, look for products with a fibre content of less than 5%.

> **Composition:** cereals, meat and animal derivatives (20%, including 4% chicken in the brown kibbles), oils and fats (including 0.5% sunflower oil), derivatives of vegetable origin (including 2% dried beet pulp), minerals (including 0.7% sodium tripolyphosphate an active ingredient in the brown kibbles), vegetables (4% carrots in the orange kibbles, 4% peas in the green kibbles), vegetable protein extracts. **Analytical constituents (%):** protein: 22; fat content: 13; inorganic matter: 8; crude fibres: 1.9; omega 6 fatty acids: 2.2; iron: 126 mg/kg. **Additives per kg:** Antioxidants; Colourants from natural origin; Nutritional additives: Vitamin A: 15300 IU, Vitamin B_1: 7.3 mg, Vitamin B_2: 12.5 mg, Vitamin B_6: 3.3 mg, Vitamin D_3: 1688 IU, Vitamin E: 150 mg, Cupric sulphate pentahydrate: 28 mg, Manganous sulphate monohydrate: 113 mg, Potassium iodide: 2.3 mg, Sodium selenite: 0.65 mg, Zinc sulphate monohydrate: 300 mg. **For more information on all ingredients, visit**

These are the ingredients you should look for in healthy dog food options, especially if they are organically sourced:

- Meat listed as the first or second ingredient.
- Carbohydrates—brown rice, whole oats, pearled barley, sweet potato, whole grains.
- Vegetables—sweet potatoes, peas, carrots.
- Fruits—apples, blueberries, blackberries.
- Healthy fats—omega-3, omega-6, olive oil.
- Vitamins—B, A, and E.
- Minerals and amino acids—zinc, potassium, calcium, manganese, L-Carnitine, DL-Methionine.
- No cheap fillers such as corn meal or wheat gluten.
- No artificial preservatives (Chemicals to make the food last longer).

Composition List

GUARANTEED ANALYSIS	COMPOSITION:
Protein 36% Fat Content 16% Crude Fibre 4% Crude Ash 9% Omega-6 Fatty Acids 2,2% Omega-3 Fatty Acids 1,1% Glucosamine 900 mg/kg Chondroitin Sulphate 1200 mg/kg	Turkey 32% (Fresh Turkey 16%, Dehydrated Turkey 16%), Chicken 30% (Dehydrated Chicken 16%, Chicken Fat 8%, Chicken Gravy 6%), Peas 20%, Potato Protein, Beet Pulp 4%, Linseed 3%, Dried Potatoes, Salmon Oil 1%, Lignocellulose, Carrots, Apples, Yeast Extract (source of mannan — oligosaccharides) 0,5%, Dried Chicory Root (source of Fructo-oligo-saccharides and Inulin) 0,5%, Broccoli, Spinach, Tomatoes, Blueberries, Cranberries 0,01%, Dried Peppermint, D-Glucosamine Hydrochloride 100 mg/kg, Chondroitin Sulphate 100 mg/kg, Yucca Schidigera.

The final place to look is the Composition List, called Ingredients in the U.S. The composition list is written in descending order by volume. The ingredients at the top of the list are used in the highest quantity, just as on the packages of food you eat.

You'll want to see healthy, high-quality ingredients at the beginning of the list, starting with a source of animal protein. Remember, your golden retriever's body is better at digesting and absorbing nutrition from animal sources.

AAFCO Statement of Nutritional Adequacy (if you are in the U.S.)

First, look for the Association of American Feed Control Officials (AAFCO) statement of nutritional adequacy. This is an organisation that sets and upholds standards for pet food and animal feed.

Before a product lands on the shelf, this organisation checks it to ensure it meets the minimum nutritional requirements for the intended animal, in this case, your golden retriever. If the product is nutritionally balanced for your dog, you will see a statement like this somewhere on the label:

'[Product Name] is formulated to meet the nutritional levels established by the AAFCO Dog Food Nutrient Profiles.'

If you see this on the package, you know it will meet your dog's minimum nutritional needs. However, the AAFCO statement does not guarantee quality. You will still need to read the ingredients list noted on the package to determine whether it is a nutritious choice for your dog.

Choosing the Right Bowls

There are many different types and categories of food and water bowls for dogs, and it is important to choose one appropriately sized for your golden.

The various water and food bowls in the market are:

Long Ear Bowl – This bowl (see picture) is designed with long-eared dogs in mind, such as cocker spaniels. It is narrower at the top, allowing the dog to put their head in it without getting their ears dirty or wet. Long-eared dogs are very prone to ear infections, and this type of bowl will help avoid them. You shouldn't need one of these for your golden unless you have other long-eared dogs in your household.

Elevated Bowls or Dining Tables – These bowls (see picture) provide easier access to food and water and a more comfortable drinking and eating experience as your dog is not bending down to floor level. For dogs who are messy eaters, elevated dog bowls are perfect, and according to some veterinarians, they are a healthier way for dogs to feed. Older dogs with stiff necks or backs may also find these feeders more comfortable.

Ceramic or Stoneware Bowls – The stylish ceramic or stoneware bowl is another good choice for your retriever. Though they can be broken if they are dropped onto a hard surface, they are easy to clean and available in many attractive shapes, colours, and styles or with cute pictures or wording. As they are heavier than other bowls, they shouldn't slide across the floor as the dog eats. Dispose of the bowl if it becomes chipped, cracked, or broken. When the surface is damaged, it can harbour harmful bacteria.

Travel Bowls – Travel bowls are lightweight, often collapsible and can be a useful addition to your golden's travel essentials. These bowls can be attached to your dog's lead. They can be a lifesaver when out with your thirsty dog on a hot day.

Stainless Steel No Skid, No Tip Bowls – This type of bowl (see picture) is almost indestructible, easy to clean, and, since the bottom is wider, won't tip over. Also, the rubberised base prevents it from skidding across the floor. This kind of bowl can also be used as a slow feeder simply by turning it upside down.

Travel Water Containers – Your dog can be trained to drink water from a bottle, or you could carry a collapsible bowl and water bottle. Additionally, there are many travel containers designed for active dogs who need to quench their thirst. Whatever travelling water system you choose, it is always a good idea to get your puppy used to drinking from it when they are still young. Otherwise, they may refuse to drink from anything other than their usual bowl.

Slow Feeder Bowls – If your dog gulps their food too quickly, consider using a slow feeder bowl (see picture) to slow the speed at which they eat. Anti-gulp and slow dog feeders are a great way to ensure your golden takes time to eat properly, so they don't suffer from stomach pains, discomfort after eating, or life-threatening bloat. Their specially designed rivets prevent dogs from eating the complete bowl in just a few mouthfuls.

Gravity Water Container – Your golden retriever needs to drink a lot of water every day to stay healthy, and sometimes, you might not notice if their water bowl is empty. Choosing a larger water gravity container or an automatic watering fountain is a good way to ensure your retriever always has access to the water they need.

When your golden retriever is a puppy, choose smaller bowls and as they grow, adjust the bowl, so it is compatible with their size.

How much food

This is a common question posed by owners. Unfortunately, there is no simple answer. Depending on the breed, age, weight, lifestyle, activity level, and metabolic rate, a dog's needs vary. **Even two same-age golden retrievers might have totally different caloric requirements, as one could be super energetic and the other a couch potato.**

There's an adage which says: 'Watch the dog, not the dish'. Portion sizes should be determined by your dog's body condition, not by how much is eaten or left in the bowl. The size of your golden's appetite depends on their metabolism and body type. Nutritional needs vary from one dog to another. Do not worry if your puppy occasionally skips meals or picks at food. You may have given them too much and need to reduce the quantity served, or they may simply have had enough.

Follow the advice of your vet and check the feeding instructions on the dog food manufacturer's labels to manage your dog's weight. Bear in mind the recommended portion size is often more than required. Label recommendations should only serve as a guide. Dogs' metabolisms vary just as humans' do, so adjust the amount of food offered as they gain or lose weight.

A practical way to check your dog's weight is to apply slight pressure to the sides of their chest. If you can feel their ribs without being able to see them, their weight is okay.

To help owners understand their dog's daily food requirements, there are many online dog calorie calculators, such as the Pet Food Manufacturers Association (PFMA) calculator:

www.pfma.org.uk/dog-calorie-calculator-nrc-method

Enter your golden's weight, activity level and your chosen dog food % constituents, and the calculator will give you the recommended daily feeding amount. Again, these are still just generic recommendations and each dog, and their energy requirements, are different.

Feeding Puppies

Proper feeding is vital when it comes to puppies. Since goldens grow so quickly during their first few months, they need a nutrient-dense, high-calorie diet to grow into healthy, strong adults. They should be fed a high-quality puppy food brand.

If you feed your puppy regular adult dog food, they may not develop properly. Consult your veterinarian for specific recommendations, but as a guide, the best puppy foods are high in protein, calcium, and calories.

How Often – Unlike adult dogs, puppies need to be fed small amounts regularly throughout the day to avoid overstretching their stomachs. This also keeps their energy levels high all day long. Here is a typical retriever puppy feeding schedule:

- After weaning—around 8 weeks old—and up to 4 months old: **4 meals per day**.
- Between 4 and 6 months: **3 meals per day**.
- Over the age of 6 months and for the rest of their life: **2 meals each day**, morning and evening.

Note, when feeding twice a day, it is recommended you give one-third in the morning and the rest at night, but not too late.

Your golden retriever puppy should have their meals evenly spaced. For example, when they're on four meals a day, if you feed them at 7:00 am, their next meals should be at 11:00 am, 3:00 pm, and 7:00 pm. You can change the times to fit your schedule but make sure you leave plenty of time between their last meal and bedtime to allow them to digest their food.

Always ensure your puppy is eating and drinking enough throughout the day. The smaller the puppy, the more important this is.

When you bring your puppy home, the breeder might give you a small bag of puppy food with instructions about their feeding schedule. It is recommended you continue feeding this to your golden retriever as the food will be specifically formulated for your pup's growth and development during their early months. Their delicate stomach and digestive system are used to this brand, so keeping continuity will help avoid any tummy upsets.

Transitioning to Adult Feeding – Once your golden puppy reaches adulthood, they won't need as many calories. Unless they are highly active, continuing to give rich puppy food to your adult retriever can quickly lead to excessive weight gain, so it is important to transition to adult food.

Typically, most puppies successfully transition to eating adult dog food by the time they are six to eight months old. They should definitely be on adult food by the time they're a year old. When it is time to switch, select a dog food labelled '***Adult***'.

Here are a few puppy-feeding tips that might come in handy:

- Let your puppy eat in peace. If you take their bowl away while they are eating, it can make them anxious, which could lead to food aggression. To make sure your retriever feels comfortable when you approach them at mealtimes, add a small amount of food to the bowl while they are eating so they see you as an ally, not a threat.
- Never feed your puppy before travelling in the car, as this can cause carsickness.
- Avoid feeding your puppy an hour before or after exercise, as this could contribute to stomach dilation and torsion, also known as bloat. This is a life-threatening condition requiring immediate veterinary intervention.
- Growth-and-weight charts are available both in print and online. Weigh your puppy every week and record their progress, comparing them to breed-appropriate weight charts. Adjust their food intake to achieve an average rate of growth.
- Before implementing any major change in your retriever puppy's diet, consult your vet and, if possible, the breeder. Once you have a formula that works, stick with it. Any sudden changes in food can cause digestive problems.
- To ensure your retriever puppy's nutritional needs are met, choose a puppy food specially designed for them and buy the best you can afford.

Feeding Senior Dogs

Just like people, as dogs become older, their metabolism slows down, and they become less active. Continuing to feed the same amount of food when your dog is exercising less results in fat being stored, which could add excess weight. The last thing you want for an older retriever with weakened joints is for them to have to carry around extra kilos.

TIP ***If your senior golden retriever is gaining weight, cutting back on their food—20% fewer calories as a rule of thumb—will usually keep them trim.***

Conversely, some ageing dogs start to lose weight because their muscle mass diminishes. If this happens to your dog, you will need to increase their caloric intake and add more protein to help maintain muscle mass.

Occasionally, an older dog suffering from kidney disease will urinate more often. In addition, some medications have a diuretic effect, making them more prone to becoming dehydrated. Always provide a fresh, cool source of clean water because drinking enough water is even more important as your dog ages.

As dogs enter their senior years, their joints might not perform as well as they once did, and they could become stiff or feel pain from arthritis. In this case, your vet might recommend a dog food with added glucosamine, which many senior dog foods (see picture) have. This can help reduce pain and allow your dog to get around easier. You can also buy glucosamine supplements and/or a natural pain reliever, such as CBD drops, to keep your dog active and pain-free.

As your golden ages, they might begin to lose fur or develop strange skin issues. Your vet might recommend dog food with a higher fat content—specifically omega-3 and omega-6. These beneficial fats can be found in widely available fish oil supplements, which most dogs love.

If your golden retriever suffers from dental issues, you might want to stop feeding dry kibble. You could try softer dog food, such as wet canned dog food or freshly delivered dog food, both of which have a lot more moisture. This will allow your dog to eat comfortably, even with missing teeth or sensitive gums.

Many dog food companies manufacture dog foods with 'Senior' in the name or labelled for the 'Senior' dog. You might be surprised to learn there are no standards for what makes a 'Senior' dog food. In the U.S., the Association for American Feed Control Officials (AAFCO) has no 'Senior' life stage guidance for dog food nutrients. This means manufacturers can create any formula they want and market it as senior dog food.

While senior dog food might be marketed as a better diet for older dogs, there are no agreed-upon standards to ensure that's really the case. Given this, don't feel you need to feed your retriever senior dog food. You don't need to move on from adult dog food as they get older purely because of their age. Most golden retrievers don't need special senior dog food to live a healthy life. If you have been feeding your dog a certain kind of dog food for years, there is no reason to change unless there are valid medical reasons to necessitate a switch.

If you decide to switch to senior dog food, it is important to make the transition to their new food gradually. Ideally, just as when you transitioned your puppy to adult food, this should be done slowly over 7-10 days or more, completing the process within 14 days. If your retriever is prone to digestive problems, you might want to take longer to introduce the new food. If your golden experiences digestive upset with the new food—vomiting, diarrhoea, or not eating—it would be best to stop serving it and contact your vet.

If you are feeding your older golden retriever food that has been stored in the fridge, you will need to take it out up to two hours before mealtime to get it to the right temperature. If that is not possible, you can briefly microwave wet foods to warm them, but be careful to ensure it doesn't get too hot, or it could burn your golden's sensitive mouth!

When it comes to mealtimes, try to feed your senior dog in a quiet place where they can enjoy their meal in peace without being interrupted. If you have more dogs, feed them separately but at the same time so one doesn't bully or snatch food from the other.

Treats

Most pet shops and grocery stores have shelves filled with an array of dog treats (see picture), which can make it an overwhelming task to choose wisely unless you keep one simple rule in mind: **Choose treats that contain either one ingredient or very few ingredients.**

Whatever you give them, if you treat your golden too often during the day, they can become overweight. Treats are usually very flavourful and appealing to your dog's palate. Too many tasty treats throughout the day can create a picky eater. Your retriever isn't stupid. They know if they wait long enough, treats will soon be coming their way, so they might be less excited about consuming their dinner.

Your puppy will probably consume more treats or snacks during training when you use them as incentives. However, it is still suggested you feed no more than 10% of your dog's recommended daily caloric intake when giving treats or snacks. This is called the 90/10 rule.

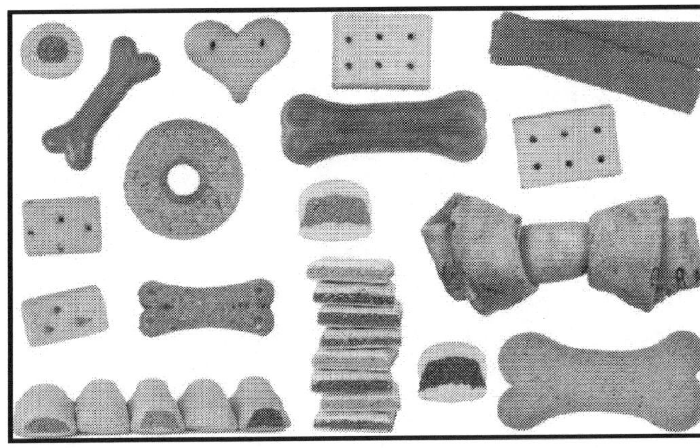

FACT ***Researchers in Sweden have discovered that dogs were happier when they had to earn their treats as a reward for completing a task, rather than being given one just because. Like humans who have that happy 'eureka' moment when finally solving a problem, the same is true for dogs.***

Dangerous Treats

It is important to carefully read labels and take note of where treats are manufactured because not all countries have high manufacturing standards. You should also be aware that there are some treats you absolutely should NOT give to your golden, which are the following:

Rawhide – Rawhide is made from the inner layer of horsehides or cowhides. During manufacturing, rawhide is soaked in an ash/lye solution to remove every particle of meat, fat, and hair, then soaked again in bleach to remove any lingering traces of the ash/lye solution. After this process is complete, technically, the product is no longer food, so it does not have to comply with food regulations.

The wet rawhide is shaped into chews. When dry, it shrinks to approximately 25% of its original size. Then, arsenic-based products are used as preservatives. Antibiotics and insecticides are added to kill bacteria. Some rawhide treats include beef, chicken, or liver flavourings to make them more appealing to dogs.

While rawhide chews are tough and long-lasting, gnawing on them means your golden is ingesting many harsh chemicals. In addition, when your dog swallows a piece of rawhide, it can swell to four times its size inside their stomach, which can cause anything from mild to severe gastric blockages. This can be life-threatening and require emergency surgery.

As convenient as it might be to give your golden a treat to keep them occupied for ages, find something else. Avoid rawhide at all costs.

Pig's Ears – Pig's ears are exactly that—the dehydrated ear of a pig, specifically the flap of the ear called the pinna. This part of the ear is comprised of skin and cartilage, with barely any muscle, making them more flexible for dogs to munch.

These are very attractive to dogs and most eagerly devour them. And owners love them because they're 'natural', so what could be wrong? They might be natural, but they're also thin, crispy, and very high in fat, which can cause stomach upsets, vomiting, and diarrhoea. Also, sharp pieces can break off and become stuck in your dog's throat or perforate the mouth, throat, or digestive tract.

Pig's ears are often processed and preserved with unhealthy chemicals. As a discerning dog owner, you will NOT want to feed them to your golden.

Hoof Treats – These are cow, bison, horse, and pig hooves that are cleaned, shaved and dried. They are marketed as healthy and 'natural' treat choices for dogs. However, the truth is, after processing with harsh chemicals and preservatives, hooves retain little, if any, of their 'natural' qualities.

What's more, hooves are very hard and can chip or break your golden retriever's teeth as well as perforate their mouth, throat, or intestinal tract, or create blockages in their intestines. Another downside of giving hooves to your dog is the smell, which gets worse as they are chewed. The stench can linger on the carpet for days or even weeks.

Healthy Treats

With so many healthy treat choices available, there is no excuse for feeding your golden retriever unhealthy, toxic, nutrient-deficient, or dangerous treats.

Examples of healthy treats include:

Hard (Crunchy) Treats or Dog Biscuits – These come in a range of shapes, sizes, and flavours and are designed to help keep your golden's teeth clean. These are a great choice as an everyday reward for your dog.

Soft Treats – Soft, chewy treats are available in endless varieties and flavours. Due to their pleasant taste and soft texture, small pieces are especially useful during training for instant gratification. Since your retriever can quickly devour the treat, they'll know this is a reward.

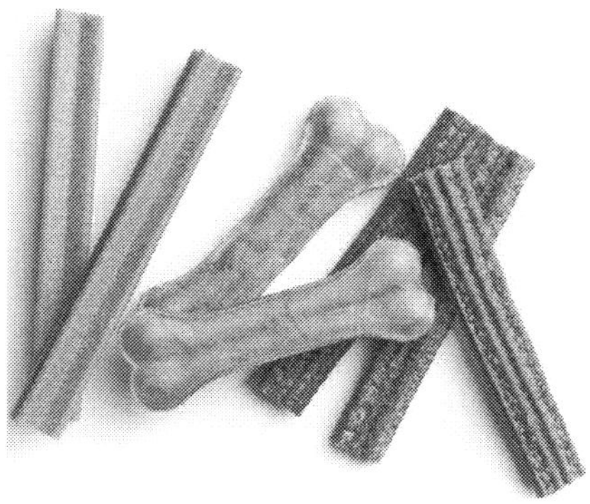

Dental Treats or Chews (see picture) – Dental treats are designed specifically to help your retriever maintain healthy teeth and gums by exercising their jaws and massaging their gums while removing plaque build-up near the gum line.

The best way to care for your golden's oral hygiene is to brush their teeth every day. However, dog dental chews can be an excellent top-up between brushing or for dogs who won't let you get anywhere near their teeth without a struggle.

Dental chews come in edible and non-edible varieties. Many goldens love these tasty treats. Non-edible chews are a bit like toys for dogs and satisfy their natural urge to chew while helping clean their teeth at the same time.

Freeze-Dried and Jerky Treats (see picture) – These treats offer a tasty morsel most dogs find irresistible since they are usually made of simple, meaty ingredients, like liver, poultry, and seafood. Be careful to choose quality jerky treats, as they are often processed with too much salt.

Since they are so flavourful, many dog owners find these treats highly valuable when training. It is important to find a reputable manufacturer of jerky treats. Alternatively, if you have a food dehydrator, you can make your own meat jerky for your dog.

TIP ***Always check labels for quality. Make sure you choose treats that are the right size for your golden retriever, and try to find treats with just one ingredient or minimal ingredients.***

Supplements

Most commercial pet foods are formulated to meet all the nutritional requirements your dog needs to thrive. However, not all foods are created equal, and neither are all dogs. Better pet food companies create their foods based on monitored feeding trials. Not all companies go to such lengths and simply develop, package, market and sell a formula that might have never been fed to a dog before it hit the store shelves.

Just as with humans, supplemental vitamins and minerals can improve your golden's health, as they help protect the immune system and ensure your retriever's nutritional needs are met. It might be helpful to discuss this with your vet, who will be well-versed in optimal diet requirements for golden retrievers.

These are the most frequently recommended supplements for dogs:

- Glucosamine.
- Fish Oil.
- Antioxidants.
- Probiotics.
- CBD oil.
- Chondroitin sulphate.
- Multi-vitamins.

Glucosamine – This is the most popular supplement for dogs. Glucosamine is an amino sugar found naturally in the fluid around the joints and helps build cartilage. It is derived from the shells of shellfish but can also be made in a laboratory. Many dog owners and vets believe glucosamine is effective in treating arthritis in dogs. In older dogs, it can relieve joint pain and improve mobility. It comes in several forms, including pills, powders, and treats, so you can use the supplement which your dog is most likely to accept.

Fish Oil – The second most common supplement given to dogs is fish oil (see picture). It contains omega-3 fatty acids believed to ease skin allergies and improve coat quality and shine. A study in the American Journal of Veterinary Research showed that fish oils can also reduce inflammation.

Even if your retriever doesn't display any symptoms indicating an omega-3 deficiency, you should keep an eye out for a few signs. A dull or dry coat, hair loss, obesity, eye problems, poor wound healing, or muscle weakness could all indicate your dog could benefit from some fish oil. Before giving your golden a fish oil supplement, discuss it with your vet. They will be happy to put your dog's need for omega-3 in context by customising their diet and daily intake of supplements.

FACT ***Omega-3 might also influence your golden retriever puppy's mental development. Studies have shown that an omega-3-rich diet in a dog's infancy can improve cognitive functions, memory, and learning ability as they grow.***

Antioxidants – Antioxidant supplements (see picture) help slow and/or counteract the effects of the ageing process by fighting 'free radicals', which are part of the normal metabolic process in both dogs and humans. These are cells that are missing a molecule. When this happens, the cell tries to repair itself by stealing molecules from other healthy cells. This process then damages your golden retriever's DNA, which in turn makes them more prone to disease.

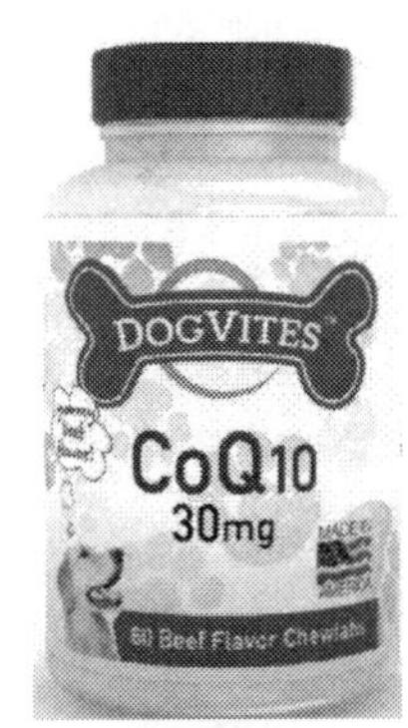

When your dog's body's natural defences against free radical damage are hindered, the result is chronic disease and increased ageing that often includes cancer, heart/kidney/liver disease, damage to the joints, and brain dysfunction. The antioxidants' function is to strengthen the body's natural defences against this damage. Although antioxidants are naturally found in foods containing vitamins C and E, such as apples, blueberries, pumpkins, and strawberries, the introduction of Coenzyme Q10 (CoQ10), a powerful and natural antioxidant, can easily be added to your golden's diet.

CBD Oil – Cannabidiol (CBD) oil is extracted from the flowers, leaves, and stems of the cannabis plant. It does NOT contain the chemical 'tetrahydrocannabinol' (THC) that gives the well-known 'high' people get from smoking cannabis. Research is still in its infancy for any long-term effects when giving your golden CBD oil (see picture). However, many human studies have shown it can relieve chronic pain, anxiety, seizures, aggression, muscle spasms, and even neurological disorders. Since both people and dogs have an 'endocannabinoid' or complex cell-signalling system, it stands to reason that both species can benefit from the use of CBD oil.

There is a great deal of anecdotal evidence to support this from doting dog owners who strongly believe adding CBD oil or treats to their retriever's diet provides many benefits and relief from chronic conditions.

N.B. When considering a CBD additive for your golden's diet, choose a product as pure and organic as possible and discuss it with a professional since there can often be a trial-and-error period before identifying correct dosage amounts.

Probiotics – As humans have increasingly turned to probiotics to support gut health, it is hardly surprising that probiotics for dogs (see picture) have also become popular. Probiotics live naturally within the body in the form of live bacteria and yeasts that aid digestion and intestinal health. As supplements, they are used to treat diarrhoea and other digestive problems. Probiotics come in several forms, including yoghurts, capsules, chews, powders, and dog food formulations. You can choose the one which most appeals to your dog.

Chondroitin Sulphate – This joint supplement is often used alongside glucosamine as it is a healthy building block of cartilage. The School of Medicine and Health Sciences at the University of North Dakota carried out a study of the benefits of combining chondroitin with glucosamine and found that this combination can repair and even reverse cartilage damage.

Chondroitin sulphate is a chemical that is part of a protein molecule found in both human and animal cartilage. This protein supports the retention of water to provide elasticity in the cartilage. This is important for the proper nourishment of the tissues to ensure shock absorption during movement.

Supplements containing chondroitin and glucosamine are regularly used for dogs with joint stiffness and reduced mobility. The right supplement could help support your dog's mobility and joint structure. Discuss with your veterinarian before adding to your golden's diet.

Multivitamins – Using a multivitamin can help ensure your golden gets all the vitamins and minerals they need in their daily diet. The best choice is a tasty chew that appeals to canine taste buds. They contain minerals and vitamins that support many different aspects of your dog's body, including the coat, digestion, heart, joints, skin, and immune system. There are specially formulated products available for retrievers of all ages and sizes.

The Canine Fitness Centre in the United Kingdom stated: 'The International Centre for Nutritional Excellence, an independent laboratory specialising in nutraceutical analysis, surveyed label claims of human joint supplements and found 6 out of 10 failed to meet label claims.' Their advice is, 'consumers need to be very careful when purchasing such supplements, be it for themselves or their pets'.

The healthiest choice with multivitamins would be to look for one without artificial flavourings, preservatives, corn, and soy. However, you should discuss your golden's current diet with a specialist to ensure that adding a supplement will not result in a harmful excess of vitamins.

Anxiety supplements

Loud, booming noises can unsettle some dogs and make them nervous. Choosing an anti-anxiety or calming supplement might help your golden retriever relax.

Many dogs suffer from anxiety-related stress. Whether it comes from the fear of being left at home alone, the stress of a loud home environment, or anxious pacing during celebrations when fireworks are exploding, there are natural supplements that can help—known as 'canine chill pills'—as they contain ingredients promoting relaxation. These are the most common active ingredients found in anti-anxiety supplements, often given as a tasty treat or chew:

- CBD Oil – See above.
- L-theanine – Increases dopamine in the brain to ease anxiety.
- L-tryptophan – Raises serotonin levels in the brain, which can reduce aggression and hyperactivity.
- Melatonin – This hormone promotes relaxation, especially for dogs suffering from hyperactivity.
- Valerian Root (see picture) – Not suitable for all dogs, especially those on medication. There are no conclusive studies on the effects of valerian root on dogs, although it is thought that it can have multiple benefits. If your golden is particularly fearful of specific scenarios, such as a trip to the vet's, visitors, or thunderstorms, it may be helpful.

Synthetic supplements are not as good for your dog as natural sources such as fresh fruits and vegetables for the same nutrients. When it comes to mineral supplements, chelated minerals are ideal. These are minerals that have been bound to protein molecules, making them easier for your golden's body to metabolise. If you see 'dried fermentation products' on the list, do not be alarmed – these are probiotics that can support your dog's digestion.

20 Tips for a Happy Feeding Routine

Apart from purchasing the best quality food you can afford for your golden retriever, here are some tips to ensure a pleasant, enjoyable feeding experience for your dog:

1. Observe how fast your golden eats their food. Eating too quickly can cause health issues that can be prevented by choosing a slow feeder bowl.
2. Get your puppy used to things happening around them during feeding time so they don't become food possessive and get into the habit of growling when anyone comes near. Put a small amount of food in their bowl, wait until they have eaten it, and then give them more, so they associate people approaching their bowl with a positive experience.
3. Your golden puppy needs to know you are in charge of the food source, and they must be respectful and patiently wait for dinner. Tell them to 'Sit/Stay' and wait for their food bowl to be offered before they are allowed to eat.
4. If you use a scoop or measuring device to put food into your dog's bowl, you could be missing an opportunity to 'tell' them you are in control of their food supply. Instead, mix the food with your hands, so your scent is on their food, letting them know you are their leader. This mimics what happens when a pack of wild dogs is out hunting since the leader always eats first, leaving their scent on the food, while the rest patiently wait their turn to eat the leftovers.
5. Some adult golden retrievers prefer a single meal each day. If your golden seems to have little interest in a morning meal, they may be better off having one evening feed.
6. If your golden is a picky eater, they need to understand there is only a 'window of opportunity' for eating. Give them 20 minutes, and if they do not eat, take away what's left and make them wait until the next feeding time.
7. If your retriever is a fussy eater, they might be more enthusiastic about eating more flavourful food, such as canned or home-cooked meals, rather than dried kibble.
8. It is never a good idea to let your golden eat cat food, as it usually has more protein than a dog needs and can cause diarrhoea, vomiting, or hair loss.

9. Regularly weigh your golden, especially if their longer hair hides any extra kilos. Occasionally, it can be difficult to notice them gaining weight until they're already obese.
10. Get into the habit of cleaning your dog's bowl daily. While it might look clean, it will have a film of saliva and food residue all over it, where unhealthy bacteria will quickly grow.
11. Not feeding your dog immediately after an energetic play session or a large drink of water will help prevent stomach upsets or bloat. Wait until your retriever is relaxed and calm enough to eat slowly.
12. It might seem distasteful, but monitoring your golden's poo habits can help you discover potential health problems. For instance, if they have diarrhoea for longer than a couple of days, they might have a gastrointestinal problem requiring a visit to the vet.
13. Waiting at least an hour after they have eaten before taking them out in the car will ensure their stomach contents have settled. Some dogs are more prone to motion sickness, and if they throw up in the car, they may associate vehicle outings with something unpleasant.

14. Avoid taking away your puppy's food bowl while they are still eating. This can create anxiety or food aggression, especially in a dog with a healthy appetite, as they will think someone is stealing their food.
15. When feeding more than one dog, give each of them their own space. Feed them at least two metres (six feet) apart, so they do not feel threatened or worried the other dog might try to take their food.
16. Always avoid feeding your golden any foods high in salt or sugar, as this can lead to obesity, diabetes, and dental problems.
17. If your dog is a fussy eater, adding a little unsalted chicken or beef broth, grated parmesan, or a highly-flavoured topping can encourage them to eat.
18. Instead of just giving your golden their meal, use mealtime as an opportunity to reinforce training and patience. Practise the '**Sit/Stay**' command, and work on the '**Okay**' release command, so they learn to sit and wait patiently until they hear the '**Okay**' command that allows them to eat their food.
19. If your dog's activity levels change during certain seasons, feed less when they are less active and more when they are highly active to avoid weight gain.
20. Highly intelligent dogs, like the golden retriever, are easily bored and appreciate being fed via a food puzzle. This type of toy dispenses food while simultaneously exercising memory and manipulation skills.

Weight Control

Goldens are renowned for being prone to weight gain because they love their food so much. No matter what the time of day, they are always ready to eat and so easily pile on the pounds. Conscientious dog owners who want the best for their furry friends need to control their dog's weight. This will help avoid serious future health problems that could dangerously affect their dog's life. Packing on the kilos will soon create a pudgy pup who could suffer from many health problems, including:

- Diabetes.
- Heart disease.
- Respiratory ailments.
- Stress to the joints and skeleton

However, don't feel you're doing your dog a favour by underfeeding them. An underweight dog can also suffer from health problems, such as:

- Reduced bone density.
- Muscle loss.
- Weakened immune system.
- Increased risk of infections.
- Lethargy and lower physical stamina.
- Skin and coat problems, including hair loss.

While being overweight is far more common than being underweight, both conditions warrant immediate attention. You may need professional intervention to get your golden retriever's weight under control.

Sometimes, a medical condition, such as Cushing's disease or hypothyroidism, makes a dog gain weight. Another risk factor is advancing age when metabolism naturally slows and your dog is not as active.

Helping Lose Weight – The first step towards helping an overweight golden retriever lose weight is to get your vet to assess their weight. They will then tell you how many kilograms your dog needs to lose to be within healthy limits. Next, based on their age, activity level, and how overweight they are, it's likely your vet will ask what they are being fed and how much.

TIP ***Depending on the size of your dog, simply switching from feeding a heaped cup to a level one could have a significant effect on their weight. In cases where your dog needs to lose more than 2 kilograms (5 pounds), once they have been checked for possible hormonal conditions and excluding other health issues, the vet might suggest an increase in exercise in combination with reduced daily calorie intake.***

Sometimes, all you need to do is cut back on the amount you are feeding your dog, keep track of how many extra treats are given, and increase their daily exercise.

Helping Gain Weight – Being underweight occurs less often in well-cared-for canine companions. If your golden cannot maintain an ideal weight, this is a cause for concern and should be discussed with your veterinarian. If there is no underlying medical condition, there are several steps you can take to help an underweight dog put on some needed kilograms, including:

- Feed a higher calorie diet—more protein and fat.
- Feed a larger meal at night to encourage fat storage.
- Supplement main meals with snacks throughout the day.
- Make a dry diet more enticing by adding fresh or wet foods.
- Boost fat and fibre by adding canned pumpkin or sweet potato.
- If your dog is a picky eater, try switching up what you feed them.
- Feed organic peanut butter treats before bed.

- Get more exercise to build muscle.

Dogs and Human Food

Many golden retriever owners have questions about what human foods are suitable for feeding their furry friends. Many human foods are a definite no-no (see Chapter 15). However, there are also many other foods you can safely give your dog. Below are some of the most frequent questions asked about dogs and human food.

What Fruits Can My Dog Eat?

Fruits are higher in natural sugars than vegetables and should be given in controlled quantities, especially for overweight retrievers. The following fruits are safe to feed and have helpful vitamins and antioxidants:

- Apples.
- Bananas.
- Blackberries.
- Blueberries.
- Cantaloupe.
- Cranberries.
- Kiwi.
- Oranges.
- Pears.
- Pineapple.
- Pumpkin.
- Raspberries.
- Strawberries.
- Watermelon.

Fruit should comprise no more than 10% of your golden's daily diet. Do not forget to include these extra calories in their daily calorie count.

What Vegetables Can My Dog Eat?

Retrievers can understandably get bored with eating the same meat-based food every day and appreciate a little variety. There are many benefits to be gained from offering vegetables, as they are rich in enzymes, minerals, phytonutrients, and vitamins.

Pureeing gives optimum digestibility from the following dog-friendly vegetables:

- Asparagus.
- Beets.
- Broccoli.
- Butternut squash.
- Carrots.
- Celery.
- Cucumber.
- Green beans.
- Kale.
- Mushrooms.
- Parsley.
- Peas.
- Spinach.
- Sweet Potatoes.
- Courgette

Although a purely vegetable-based diet does not make for a well-balanced canine meal, supplementing meat with a few vegetables enhances health and will prolong your dog's life.

What Meats Are Safe for my Retriever?

The following list contains meats that are safe to feed your golden retriever:

- Beef.
- Bison.
- Chicken.
- Duck.
- Goat.
- Lamb.
- Ostrich.
- Pheasant.
- Pork.
- Quail.
- Rabbit.
- Tilapia.

- Turkey.
- Venison.

The safest meat sources are grass-fed, organic, free-range, or wild-caught. The protein and fat content will vary depending on the meat source you choose.

Can My Dog Eat Ice Cream?

You may be tempted to share this refreshing treat with your furry friend. Most retrievers will certainly devour one with much gusto given the opportunity. However, there are several good reasons to avoid giving a dog ice cream, including:

- Their digestive system is not set up to digest milk after weaning.
- They may be lactose intolerant.
- They might be allergic to milk and dairy products.
- It may make them throw up or give them diarrhoea.
- They might develop itchy, red skin.
- Sugar can contribute to obesity and other health issues.
- 'Sugarless' ice cream often contains xylitol, which is toxic to dogs.
- Some flavours are toxic to dogs.

Rather than giving your dog ice cream, choose an alternative wholesome dog snack that is good for their health instead.

Can I Feed My Dog Porridge?

There are some health benefits associated with eating porridge. It contains a host of nutrients, antioxidants, and minerals that help keep your golden looking and feeling their best. However, there are some considerations to bear in mind:

- Always feed bland, plain porridge with no added sugar.
- Make it with water, not milk.
- Do not use fancy, flavoured packets with unnecessary added ingredients.
- Do not use instant porridge as it may contain artificial sweeteners.
- Read the label and make sure your porridge is 100% whole, rolled oats.
- If possible, only buy organic.
- Be aware that 200 grams of cooked porridge have 150 calories.
- Do not give more than one tablespoon of porridge for every 9 kilograms of your golden's weight.

Feeding porridge should be considered a treat or a supplement to a well-balanced main meal and not a replacement. As healthy as porridge may be, it still lacks many of the minerals and vitamins necessary for a healthy golden.

What Grains Are Safe for My Golden Retriever?

Grains (see picture) contain valuable nutrients and provide carbohydrates, fat, and antioxidants. Grains can be part of a healthy canine diet. However, not all dogs can easily digest some grains, especially wheat and corn, particularly those who already have digestive problems.

Some dogs might experience unpleasant and painful symptoms such as stomachache and constipation if they consume grains. Golden retrievers with digestive issues benefit from a grain-free diet that provides carbohydrates via fruits and vegetables.

In addition, some dogs develop allergies to certain grains. If your regular dog food triggers allergic symptoms, you may need to switch to grain-free foods.

Here are some common, ancient grains you can try adding to your dog's diet:

- Amaranth.
- Brown rice.
- Chia.
- Corn (only non-GMO).
- Einkorn.
- Emmer.
- Kamut.
- Millet.
- Porridge—Oatmeal.
- Quinoa.
- Sorghum.
- Spelt.
- Teff.
- Wild rice.

Other Human Foods Safe for Dogs

Some other human foods can be given in small amounts as a treat and will not usually be harmful to your dog:

- Eggs—free range.
- Cashews—no added salt.
- Cheese—in small quantities.
- Honey—pollen helps with allergies.
- Yoghurt—plain.
- Peanut butter.
- Pineapple.
- Popcorn—nothing added.

When deciding whether to feed treats that are high in fat, such as peanut butter, consider your golden's weight.

Dogs can eat peanut butter but never give them one containing xylitol, as this is toxic to dogs. Never feed dairy products as a treat if your retriever is intolerant to lactose.

Common Eating Issues

While there can certainly be as many eating issues as there are dogs, some of the more usual ones are noted below.

Eating Too Quickly

Eating food too quickly is also called 'wolfing', 'scoffing', 'bolting', 'gulping', 'inhaling' or 'hoovering'. This habit can result in an upset stomach, burping, passing wind, throwing up immediately after eating, or suffering from the serious, life-threatening condition called 'bloat'—gastric dilatation volvulus. No matter what the reason for your golden bolting their food down in record time, it is important to slow them to a healthier pace. Here are some techniques for this:

- Hand-feed.
- Put their food in a slow feeder bowl.
- Place their food in a puzzle feeder.
- Turn a stainless-steel bowl upside down to reduce its size.
- Place a fist-sized rock in the centre of their stainless-steel bowl.
- Feed smaller meals more frequently.
- Make sure their food contains the nutrients they need.

- Feed on a regular timetable.

Picky Eaters

Although many dogs become fussy eaters, it is often smaller and less-active breeds that tend to be picky about their food. There are some dogs who live to eat and others who eat to live. Some of your dog's eating habits may simply be the result of their breed's genetics.

FACT ***Golden retrievers are known to have quite robust appetites and are generally not picky eaters. However, there's always an exception to the rule.***

Occasionally, your dog will 'tell' you that they simply do not like the food being offered. A surefire way of getting this message across is refusing to eat. If you're feeding kibble, it might be wise to check the ingredients to make sure it contains all the nutrients your golden needs. If the kibble is well-balanced, they may need a stronger flavour to entice them, such as adding some wet food.

When your dog has sore gums from teething or dental disease, or loose or broken teeth, they may refuse to eat hard kibble food because it hurts to chew. Adding warm water to soften the food or changing to a softer canned or home-cooked meal could be the answer. If their kibble diet has very large pieces of kibble and their jaws are smaller, they may also have difficulty chewing the large pieces and simply refuse to eat. If size is the problem, a simple solution is to break the large kibbles into smaller, more easily chewed pieces. Next time buy one with smaller pieces.

Your golden could refuse to eat their main meals because they've had plenty of treats or snacks and aren't hungry. Cutting back on treats and snacks between meals helps a fussy eater to feel hungrier at mealtimes.

All dogs thrive on adequate daily exercise. A dog who is not exercised enough will not use up enough energy to feel hungry. It might make a huge difference to mealtimes if they are first taken out for a walk and some fun exercise. Once back home, after they have had 10 or 15 minutes to settle down, give them their meal.

Stress is caused by any number of underlying sources—conflict between family members, a new carpet, a new baby or pet, moving home, painting a wall, unidentified noises, etc.—and can make your dog go off their food. If there has been a significant change in your golden retriever's usual environment, this could be the problem. Usually, once some time has passed, and they have become used to the changes, normal eating habits will resume. If your dog is very sensitive and needs a calmer environment, eliminating the source of their stress will re-establish peace and tranquillity.

Finally, your golden retriever can become a fussy eater if they suffer from an underlying medical condition. If all other possible causes have been eliminated, and they are still refusing to eat for more than 24 hours, it could be time to consult your vet.

Pica

Pica is a health condition characterised by the compulsive eating of non-food items. This may include cardboard, wood, paper, cloth, or plastic. A golden puppy may eat things simply because no one has told them not to, or they are exploring their new world and increasing their sensory bank by tasting everything. While annoying, this is not down to pica.

Most golden retriever puppies will grow out of putting everything in their mouth by the time they are six months to a year old. However, some may have come to like the taste of fermented grass clumps or worms that surfaced after rain, and it can take a considerable time to discourage them from this activity.

The root cause of pica is either behavioural or medical. If the habit is behavioural, it could derive from issues not addressed during puppyhood. These include anxiety, boredom, or stress making your golden act destructively by ripping up bedding and items of clothing or chewing the wooden legs of your coffee table.

Several symptoms will show if your puppy has been swallowing non-food items, such as:

- Lack of appetite.
- Tiredness or inactivity.
- Diarrhoea.
- Vomiting.

FACT ***While chewing up the occasional tissue might not be worrisome, pica may become a problem when an older retriever continues to chew and swallow non-food items such as plastic, which can cause perforations of the intestines or stomach or blockages that require surgery.***

Behavioural pica can be eliminated by providing your dog with a more interesting and engaging lifestyle—more fun, vigorous exercise, mental stimulation, trick training, socialising, off-lead playtime—and appropriate alternative items to chew. It also helps if you keep their preferred non-food items safely out of reach. When trying to work out what triggers could be making your retriever ingest these things, look at their environment to identify any obvious stressors that might be causing this unwanted behaviour, such as:

- Other pets in the home.
- Teasing children.
- Too much time alone.
- Inadequate exercise.
- No interesting toys to play with.
- Not enough mental stimulation.
- High-pitched noises.
- Loud neighbours with aggressive dogs.

If pica is the result of a medical condition or a nutritional deficiency, once your vet has identified the problem and devised a treatment plan, the condition should resolve itself. For instance, if there is a nutritional deficiency, a different type or amount of food, adding a supplement or experimenting with a different feeding schedule could be all you need to stop your dog from eating things they should not.

9. Golden Care and Grooming

'If you are a dog and your owner suggests that you wear a sweater, suggest that he wears a tail.'

~ Fran Lebowitz ~

Golden retriever grooming is more than just brushing and bathing your dog. The process also involves checking their ears, eyes, claws, and teeth, which are vital for their health. The best time to establish simple, healthy habits that will be routine for the rest of their life is when you bring your puppy home. This chapter explains how to take care of your golden retriever's coat, teeth, nails, ears, and paws.

Coat Care

The golden retriever has a double coat, which means they have two layers of fur, an outer coat and an undercoat. The outer coat is long and smooth, while the undercoat is soft and fuzzy.

FACT ***Undercoats are short, soft and dense, acting as insulation, so your retriever doesn't become too hot or too cold. This is ideal for working dogs such as the golden retriever but can increase shedding and grooming time.***

Goldens need to be brushed frequently because of how much shedding their protective, double-layered coat does. Without regular brushing, their fur may develop matting, knots, and tangles. They shed all year round but during spring, be prepared to be vacuuming up a lot of fur as your golden will shed their thick, winter coat ready for summer and again when the temperature falls, leaving them with a new, warmer coat ready for winter.

Keep shedding in your golden under control by setting up a strict, regular grooming and cleaning schedule. Bathe your golden occasionally and groom them at least once a week. After grooming, you will need to vacuum any hairs around your house. Do not forget to regularly wash their bed and any soft toys they use.

Goldens do not need a full haircut but would benefit from a trim around the ears, feet, neck and tail to keep them looking tidy. Doing this will neaten up your pup's appearance but not drastically change how they look. If you live somewhere hot, you may worry that your golden can't be cool under all that fur.

However, most of their double coat will thin out before the hottest time of year, and their thinner summer coat will protect their skin from sunlight.

During winter, your golden's coat will get thicker to keep them warm. This is very important, regardless of whether they're a family pet or a working dog. Without this dense, thick coat, they could get too cold during exercise and walks, and they may struggle to warm up again once their body heat has dropped.

If you cut or shave all your golden's fur to cool them down, this will increase their chances of suffering sunburn or skin damage. What's more, the fur will be itchy when it grows back and scratching excessively could damage the newly exposed skin.

The main reason people are tempted to give their goldens short haircuts or shave them is to prevent shedding. However, this won't solve the problem. The fur that grows back will be shorter, and ironically, when it sheds, it will be harder to clean it up. Many owners find these shorter hairs are not picked up by a vacuum and just stay on the carpet.

Hair Brushing

A thorough brushing once a week is ideal for goldens, as it removes shedding fur and helps stimulate and spread their natural oils to give a clean, shiny, healthy appearance.

Taking a few minutes to brush their coat will make your dog feel good while allowing you to check for lumps, scrapes, hot spots, bugs, and dry skin or hair. Here are a couple of brushing tips:

- Don't use a bristle brush because this won't get through dense golden fur. Instead, use a pin brush (see picture) to remove dirt, debris, and dead hair while distributing natural oils to keep the coat looking healthy and shiny. You might like to first spray the coat with water or use a coat conditioner to make brushing easier
- Start at the base of the neck and work your way down the back and sides, always brushing in the direction of hair growth.
- Next, brush down each leg.
- Finally, have your golden roll over so you can brush their underside and finish with the tail.

An effective home brushing regimen includes not just surface brushing but also getting to all those sensitive areas easily missed around the ears, collar, armpit, stomach, back end and tail.

FACT ***Many goldens develop heightened sensitivity, especially about having their legs and feet held, ears inspected, teeth brushed, or nails clipped. They will do anything they can to avoid these necessary maintenance procedures.***

Try getting your golden used to a grooming routine early on, rewarding them for calm behaviour with a tasty treat. Maintain a habit of carrying out regular sessions so grooming can be a pleasant experience for both you and your dog.

Removing Tangled Hair – While tangles can be removed with a brush, you may find a comb to be more effective. When choosing a stainless-steel comb, look for one with rotating teeth (see picture), as this will tug less, reducing any discomfort from having their hair pulled. Comb slowly and carefully when removing tangles, following this process:

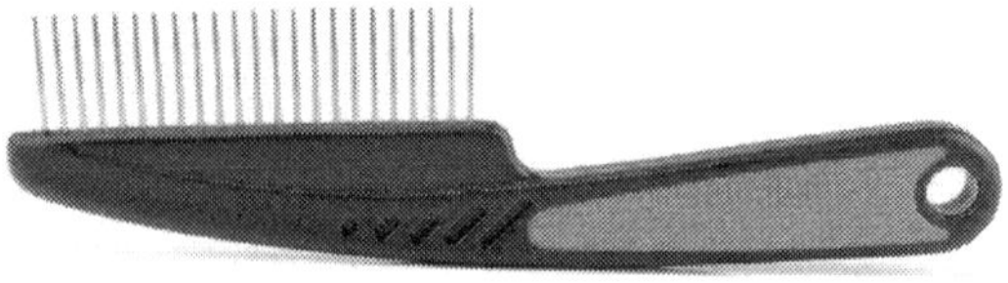

- Hold their hair close to the skin.
- Gently brush the tangles with a pin brush.
- Separate persistent tangles with a stainless-steel comb before brushing.

Removing Matted Hair – When hair becomes tightly matted, it will pull on your retriever's skin—especially if it is wet—which can be irritating and painful. In this case, a special, sharp mat-splitting tool is needed (see picture). Here's how to remove mats from your golden retriever's coat:

- Hold their hair close to the skin.
- Slowly and carefully comb through the matted hair with the splitter.
- Once the mat is broken up, you can comb it out.
- If the mat is very tight and behind their ears or between their foot pads, it is probably best to carefully cut it out with scissors.

In an extreme situation where your dog has not been regularly brushed or properly groomed for a long time, their entire coat should be closely clipped by a professional groomer rather than having your golden retriever suffer the pain of a lengthy session to remove countless mats.

Bathing

Introducing your Puppy to Bathing – Everyone has stories about how their golden retriever hates having a bath, how they run away, hide underneath the bed, or do anything to avoid it. If you introduce your puppy to the bathtub in a fun and rewarding way, you can prevent trauma, and your dog will be happy to get into the tub on their own.

TIP ***When introducing your puppy to bathing, it is far better to do it when they are young. The procedure should be initiated slowly, in small steps that include tasty treats over several weeks, so the puppy learns to trust and accepts the routine.***

The following steps will help your retriever learn to love bath time:

1. Put your golden in the tub without water and give them a treat. Do this several times during the session.
2. The next day, put your dog in the tub, give them a treat and wet their feet. Praise them for getting their feet wet, give them another treat, dry their feet with a towel and end the session. Repeat this step for a couple of days.
3. Put your retriever in the tub, give them a treat and wet their whole legs. Praise them for getting their legs wet, give them another treat, dry them off with a towel and end the session.
4. Continue gradually getting your puppy a little wetter every day until they are entirely wet. Dry them with a towel and give them a treat.
5. Once you can get your golden totally wet, it's time to get them used to shampooing. Work a small amount of shampoo into their fur and shower it off before drying and giving your dog a treat.
6. The final step is to have your puppy wait a little longer after shampooing, so you can condition their coat before drying them and giving them a treat.

If you follow this process, your puppy should be calm and patient at bath time, and instead of running to hide, they will happily jump into the bath whenever you ask.

Equipment and Products – Before putting your dog in a bath, ensure you have all the necessary bath products close at hand, such as:

- Canine Shampoo (see picture below).
- Canine Conditioner.
- Sponge.

- Non-slip mat for the sink or bathtub.
- Plenty of towels.
- Hairdryer.

When it comes down to how often you should bathe your retriever, the answer is: it depends, and opinions vary. Since they are water dogs, their fur is strong and more than capable of getting wet on a regular basis. **Regular care of your golden retriever's coat should typically include bathing them every 4-8 weeks**. You can increase the frequency if they regularly get dirty running in muddy fields or splashing about in dirty water. However, overbathing your dog can dry out their skin and cause itching and flaking, as it depletes the skin's natural oils.

Canine Shampoo – It is important to know that shampoo designed for people can harm your golden's coat and skin. It usually contains strong detergents that strip the natural oils from your dog's coat, leaving them with dry, itchy skin. Here's a list of the many kinds of canine shampoos, some designed for a specific purpose:

- Anti-bacterial/anti-fungal—to eliminate bacteria or fungus.
- Anti-itch—with anti-irritation and anti-inflammation properties.
- Brightening and whitening—often used on white coats.
- Deodorising—for a dog who just rolled in something smelly.
- Flea and Tick—to eliminate unwanted parasites.
- Hypoallergenic—for allergies or fragrance sensitivity.
- Natural—containing gentle, natural ingredients.
- No more tears—gentle shampoo for puppies.
- Organic—100% natural and non-toxic ingredients.
- Waterless—for spot cleaning between baths.

Whatever type of canine shampoo you choose, make sure it has a pH of between 7.0 and 7.52. When picking a shampoo, unless you need one for a specific purpose, it is always best to go for an organic, 100% natural shampoo free of any toxic ingredients.

Canine Conditioner (see picture) – After a bath, it is a good idea to take extra time to condition your golden's coat. Doing so will not only make them look and feel better, but it also has many additional benefits, such as:

- Preventing the loss of natural oils and moisture.
- Keeping their coat cleaner for a longer time.
- Repairing a dull, damaged, or dry coat.
- Restoring a soft, silky feel to their coat.
- Helping their coat dry quicker.
- Protecting from the heat of the dryer and hair breakage.

Those extra two minutes spent conditioning your retriever's coat will make a huge difference. Your retriever will have healthy, moisturised skin and a coat with a smooth feel and natural shine.

Bathing Step-By-Step – Before you start your golden retriever's bath, be sure to give them a good brush to remove any debris, dead hair, mats or tangles from their coat. This will make bathing easier and faster, as well as avoid clogging up your drains with dead hair. Follow these steps to give your retriever a good bath:

1. Lay down a rubber bathmat to give your dog a more secure footing and prevent them from scratching the tub.
2. Have everything you need for their bath ready next to you, so you do not have to search for them once your golden is wet. Place cotton balls in your dog's ears to prevent accidental splashes from entering the ear canal, as this could cause an infection.
3. Fill the tub with 10-15 cm (4-6 in) of lukewarm water—not too hot, as dogs are more sensitive to hot water than people. Place your dog in the water. Thoroughly wet your golden's coat down to the skin by using a detachable showerhead. If a spray attachment is not available, a cup or jug is an acceptable alternative.

4. Apply a line of shampoo along your dog's back and work down the sides, under the body, and down the legs and tail. Wet the sponge, add shampoo and scrub it around the head area. Be careful not to get shampoo in their eyes, nose, mouth, or ears. Once your dog is completely lathered up, comb the shampoo lather through their coat with your fingers, making sure you do not miss the areas under their legs and tail. No dog enjoys having water poured over their head and into their eyes, so use a wet sponge or flannel to wet, lather, and rinse their head.
5. After leaving the shampoo on your retriever's coat for a couple of minutes, thoroughly rinse it away with clean, lukewarm water using the spray attachment. Comb through their coat with your fingers to ensure all shampoo residue is totally rinsed away. If you don't completely remove the shampoo, the residue may cause irritation and itching. While rinsing, be especially thorough in their armpits and underneath the tail area. Finish by using your hands to gently squeeze their body and legs to help remove excess water.
6. Apply a line of conditioner starting at the top of the head and moving down the back to the tail. Thoroughly work it through the coat. Leave the conditioner in your retriever's coat for two minutes, then rinse again with plenty of lukewarm water. (Unless the conditioner is a leave-in, no-rinse formula.) Your dog is now ready to be dried (see below).

TIP ***Dogs who live in warmer climates may benefit from a brand of conditioner containing sunscreen to protect them from ultraviolet radiation when they're outside on sunny days.***

Drying Step-By-Step – Have dry towels close at hand and on the floor where your golden is being bathed, and then:

1. Close the shower/bath curtain (if there is one) and let your dog shake off excess water by themselves.
2. Place them on a towel on the floor, wrap them in another clean, dry towel and gently squeeze out excess water.
3. Wrap them in another clean, dry towel so they don't get cold and shiver.
4. Remove the cotton balls from their ears.
5. Unless it is a warm day, dry them straight away with a hairdryer.
6. Place them on a dry towel and begin to blow-dry their coat on a warm setting. Place your hand between the dryer and the coat, so the hot air does not get too close to their skin.

7. Use your hand or a soft brush/comb to lift and fluff the hair to help it dry faster. Never blast hot air directly into your golden's face or ears.
8. Give your dog a delicious treat as a reward for good behaviour.

15 Tips for a Healthy Coat

There are many things you can do to ensure your dog has a beautiful, soft, shiny, healthy coat, always looking like they could step out onto the show ring:

1. Include quality protein in their diet. As your retriever's coat is 95% protein, it is essential to give food that contains high-quality animal protein, such as chicken, lamb, and fish. These contain special amino acids that ensure the skin and coat are properly nourished, maintaining a healthy structure and function. Up to 35% of your retriever's daily protein intake is used to keep their coat and skin in good condition.

2. When feeding dry meals, add a teaspoon of organic coconut (see picture) or pumpkin seed oil, as they contain zinc. Often, a rough or dry coat or red/dry skin is the result of insufficient zinc in their diet. Adding this mineral helps improve the condition of the skin and coat.
3. Feed single-ingredient, organic treats. These have no unnecessary added ingredients, sugars, salts, or preservatives that can cause itchy skin and dull coat.
4. Include eggs in your golden retriever's diet. These are rich in protein and are a good source of linoleic acid and fat-soluble vitamins, such as vitamin A, which is perfect for your dog's skin and coat.
5. Feed herbal horsetail and spirulina to enhance coat quality. Horsetail contains silica, which is an important ingredient in maintaining healthy skin, bones, and coat. Spirulina contains vitamin B and carotenoids that nourish the skin and coat.

6. Provide a clean water source to keep your golden well-hydrated. Proper hydration keeps their skin and coat healthy while removing any toxins like chlorine that may cause tear staining and damage to your dog's skin.
7. Add omega-3 to your golden's diet. Small, freeze-dried oily fish treats, such as herring, mackerel, and sardines or oil derived from these fish, are rich in fatty acids, essential for healthy skin and coat.
8. Adding a vitamin B supplement (see picture) can improve the quality of your dog's coat. The deficiency of this vitamin can make the skin dry and crusty, leading to a brittle and dull-coloured coat.
9. Use a leave-in conditioner during sunny weather. This helps hydrate your retriever's skin and coat, improves hair elasticity to prevent breakage and protects from the sun's harsh rays during warm, dry weather.

10. Brush your golden retriever's coat thoroughly and frequently (see Hair Brushing section for recommended frequency) to distribute natural oils. This also removes dead hair and lubricates growing hairs so they flow in the same direction to improve skin protection and retain heat. Have a regular grooming schedule of brushing and combing your retriever and taking them to the groomer. This will keep their coat at a manageable length and prevent uncomfortable mats.
11. Apply sunscreen (see picture) or put your retriever in protective clothing during hot, sunny weather. Sunscreen reduces the risk of certain skin cancers. Just like shampoo and conditioner, you must only use sunscreen formulated for dogs on

your golden retriever and make sure they do not lick it off. Alternatively, protective clothing such as a light-coloured T-shirt will provide even higher UPF protection.

12. Rinse off salt or chlorine picked up from the sea or swimming pool. The salt that dries on your dog's skin after a swim in the sea can cause itching and scratching. Dogs who swim in pools will also get dry skin and a brittle, dull coat from the chlorine in the water. Chlorine can even bleach their coat or turn it green.
13. Keep on top of fleas and ticks. Keeping your golden's coat clean helps prevent infestation since it's easier for parasites to take up residence in a poor-condition coat.
14. Make a DIY coat treatment with aloe vera and coconut oil. This mixture helps soothe irritated skin while restoring moisture and elasticity to your retriever's coat. Before covering their coat and skin with this concoction, first test on a small area to ensure there is no allergic reaction.
15. Rub their coat with a dry, leather chamois to make it shine. This buffs and polishes the hairs and helps them fall in the same direction.

Choosing a groomer

Under the Animal Welfare Act 2006, in the United Kingdom, a dog groomer is responsible for meeting the dog's needs whilst in their care. Sadly, there have been cases that have highlighted the need for owners to think carefully when choosing a groomer. If a groomer has used faulty equipment or left animals unsupervised whilst being dried, dogs have suffered severe burns or even fatalities.

If you decide to have your golden groomed by a professional, it is extremely important to leave them in the care of a responsible and reputable adult who will meet all your retriever's needs. When choosing a groomer, be certain to:

- Consult your vet—they might be able to recommend a reputable groomer. Alternatively, ask friends and family for recommendations.
- Before booking with them, meet the groomer. You need to know they will care for your dog properly and that they will get on well with your retriever. The grooming visit should be an enjoyable experience for your dog, and you need to be confident the groomer will meet your dog's physical and behavioural needs while with them.
- Check the facilities are clean and secure. It is important the establishment is suitable for your retriever, and they will not be at risk while there. You should be comfortable leaving your dog there.
- There must be enough staff to look after the needs of all animals in their care. A groomer who works on an appointment-only basis is more likely to give your dog an appropriate amount of time so the job is done properly. Appointments also mean fewer dogs are groomed at any one time.
- If your dog has any special needs, such as sensitive skin, then make sure you are satisfied that the groomer can cater for them. Your golden might also be nervous or not like certain parts of their body being touched. If you still want to use a groomer, reassure yourself they know how to recognise signs of anxiety in your dog and will respond accordingly.
- A good groomer might be willing to show you how to groom properly at home using the correct techniques and the right tools. This will enable you to maintain their good work between visits.

- Be realistic about the price. Though £10 might sound like a bargain for a grooming session, it may also reflect the quality of the service being provided.

Teeth Care

As your golden's teeth do a lot of work, they need to be properly cared for if you want to avoid dental problems. Dogs use their teeth and mouths for more than just eating, including playing, exploring, and tasting much of their surroundings. You know how miserable a toothache can be. Imagine what it would be like for your poor dog, who cannot tell you how miserable they feel.

How Often and When?

Teeth brushing is important for every healthy dog. Establishing a strict teeth brushing routine for your dog can prevent dental problems. Get into the habit of brushing your golden's teeth at least two to three times a week. **Once a day would be even better**. Ideally, you should aim to brush before bedtime and after all their meals and snacks are finished, although most dogs (and owners!) would probably feel this is excessive.

When brushing your dog's teeth, it is important you can see what you are doing. Put your golden up on a table or worktop padded with a non-slip surface. Alternatively, one person could pick up your dog and hold them at chest level while another person brushes their teeth. Wherever you brush your retriever's teeth, make sure your dog is comfortable and has a secure footing.

Keeping your golden's teeth healthy is a much easier task if a brushing routine is introduced soon after your new puppy is brought home. Getting your pup used to having their mouth handled and fingers rubbing their teeth and gums is beneficial as they grow older.

TIP ***Reward your dog with a treat before brushing begins—not after—so there are no food particles left behind to cause plaque build-up in the mouth overnight.***

When adopting an older golden retriever who has never had their teeth brushed before, getting them used to it is the same as with a young puppy. Go slowly and gently. Give treats to reward calm behaviour but do not rush the process.

Step-By-Step Teeth Brushing

Here are the steps to brushing your retriever puppy's teeth to get them used to it:

1. Check your puppy's teeth and gums often to identify what's normal so you can spot any issues or problems.
2. When your golden pup is stress-free and feeling sleepy, lift their lip and rub the gums with your finger several times every day for a week.
3. When they are comfortable and relaxed, gently stroke the outside of their cheeks with your finger for 1-2 minutes.
4. Next, get some toothpaste specially formulated for dogs (see picture below) and apply this to your puppy's teeth with your finger several times a day for a week.

5. Get a finger cap toothbrush (see Tips below for definition) and use it to rub your golden's gums and teeth several times every day for another week.
6. Next, move to a soft-bristled toothbrush. Add a little doggy toothpaste and slowly brush their teeth for a few seconds, several times a day for a week. Don't press too hard, as their gums may bleed.

7. If you wish, you can switch to an electric brush once your puppy has their adult teeth. Before making the change, it is a good idea to get your puppy used to it while they still have their milk teeth. Show it to them, turn it on, and let them feel the buzzing while you are manually brushing. Do not rush brushing with an electric toothbrush.
8. Once your puppy has their adult teeth, let them feel the buzzing sensation on their body while moving the electric toothbrush slowly towards the head and muzzle.
9. When your retriever puppy allows you to touch their muzzle with the brush turned on, lift their lip and quickly brush a couple of teeth at a time until they get used to having them all brushed at the same time.
10. While brushing, angle the bristles, so they extend below the gums to help prevent plaque build-up.
11. If you take things slowly, your retriever pup will become familiar with the buzzing and vibrating of the electric brush. This will clean their teeth and remove plaque faster than a manual toothbrush. All you need to do is hold the brush against the teeth.
12. Always praise your golden puppy for letting you brush their teeth, especially when they are first introduced to the practice.

Teeth Scaling – Scaling is cleaning the areas of their teeth just below the gum line with an ultrasonic or handheld instrument. Using this tool helps remove stubborn tartar build-up that might be lurking beneath the gums. Most accumulation is found on the outside of the teeth and the back molars near the gum line. Scaling is usually done by a professional while your golden is anaesthetised. They have all the right tools and can polish the teeth afterwards to remove any scratches and prevent further accumulation.

Top 20 Teeth Care Tips

1. Hydrogen peroxide is effective for killing germs, whitening, and cleaning your dog's teeth. It is far less expensive than canine toothpaste. As you use so little on the brush, you do not need to worry about your golden swallowing it. Simply dip the toothbrush in a capful of hydrogen peroxide, shake off any excess, and brush their teeth. You can use it at full strength or combine 3% food-grade hydrogen peroxide with aloe vera juice (1:1) and a pinch of baking soda.
2. Giving your dog bones at least once a month helps prevent tooth plaque, bad breath, and tartar build-up. Bone munching will also polish and whiten your golden's teeth.
3. Choose only large bones, so there is no danger of swallowing. Do NOT boil the bones first, as this softens them, defeating the purpose of removing plaque. It also makes the bones splinter into smaller pieces that could create a choking or puncturing hazard for your retriever.
4. Feeding a daily dental chew or hard biscuit can help remove tartar while exercising their jaws and massaging their gums. Some dental chews contain natural, breath-freshening cinnamon, cloves, or chlorophyll.
5. Coconut oil can eliminate bad breath while boosting your golden's digestive, immune, and metabolic functions. Most dogs love the taste. Simply add ¼ teaspoon to their dinner.

6. Remember, frequent teeth brushing is an essential part of your dog's health routine. Once a day after dinner is perfect.
7. The many canine kinds of toothpaste on the market are usually flavoured with beef or chicken to appeal to your dog's taste buds. Some others are infused with mint or other breath-freshening ingredients.
8. Some canine toothpastes are formulated with active enzymes designed to work chemically by breaking down tartar or plaque to keep build-up at bay. These do not need to be washed off your golden's teeth and are safe for them to swallow. Whether they remain on their teeth long enough to do any good is debatable.

9. Another usual ingredient in toothpaste is baking soda. This is the same mild abrasive found in many human toothpastes and is designed to gently scrub your dog's teeth. Again, the issue is how much your retriever will tolerate brushing before they have had enough, as it might not be enough to deliver results.
10. Water dental additives, such as Arm & Hammer Fresh Coconut Water Additive (see picture), can be added to the water in your retriever's drinking bowl. They use chemicals (natural or manmade), some of which could be anti-bacterial or antiseptic. These products are designed to break down minerals and plaque in your dog's mouth when they drink. They also help rid the drinking bowl of bacteria and keep your golden's mouth cleaner.
11. Feed your retriever Himalayan Yak Cheese treats. These high-protein, natural, hard cheese treats make excellent chews that last a long time for even the most aggressive chewer while helping to scrape and clean their teeth.
12. Antimicrobial dental wipes are usually formulated with chlorhexidine gluconate—a disinfectant and antiseptic. This chemical works with your dog's saliva to remove plaque and bacteria while also freshening their breath. Simply wipe over your golden's teeth and gums.
13. Hard rubber or nylon toys with bumps help exercise your golden retriever's jaws and clean their teeth.
14. There are many dental sprays and gels available to help remove plaque and tartar from your dog's teeth. These products are useful to keep plaque at bay between regular brushing sessions.
15. Performing a weekly check of your dog's gums will flag up possible problems. If your golden has a healthy mouth, their gums should be pink. Any other colour could indicate dental disease.
16. A finger cap toothbrush is the easiest way to get your golden puppy used to having their teeth brushed. As the name suggests, this is a soft silicone cap that fits over your finger and has small, raised bristles on the end. While they are too soft to clean an adult dog's teeth effectively, they are a great way to begin desensitising your puppy to the idea of regular dental care. 'Waggletooth' is a finger cap brush with bristles all around designed by a dentist to be stronger for adult dog teeth.

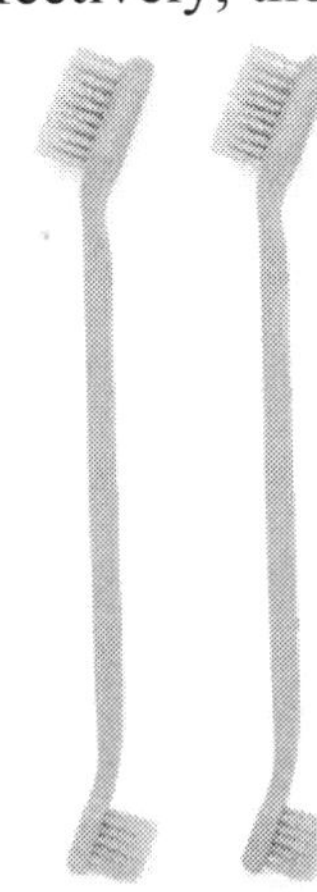

17. Most manual toothbrushes designed for dogs have a long handle. Some have a larger brush on one end and a smaller brush on the other, such as 'Enzadent Dual-Ended Toothbrush' (see picture) for getting to your golden's difficult-to-reach back teeth. When choosing a manual toothbrush, make sure it has soft bristles and is the right size for your retriever's mouth.
18. The three-sided manual toothbrush—Espree Oral Care—is designed to reach their teeth and stimulate your golden's gums at the same time. This toothbrush cleans teeth in fewer strokes, which is convenient for both you and your dog.

19. The easiest and most effective way to keep your dog's teeth clean and their gums in healthy condition is with an electric toothbrush, such as the rotary 'Oral-B'. A child's size is perfect for your dog. This brush does all the work for you, and there is less concern over potentially brushing too hard and making your golden retriever's gums bleed.
20. It is helpful while brushing their teeth to give your dog a piece of a hard material—rubber or leather—to bite down on, so they can relax without fully closing their mouth.

Nail Care

Letting your dog have long, untrimmed nails can result in various issues, including infections or an irregular, uncomfortable gait that can damage their skeleton.

Although most retrievers do not particularly enjoy having their nails trimmed, regular trimming is a crucial grooming practice that should never be neglected. If your dog gets used to having their nails trimmed while young, they will learn to tolerate the process for the rest of their life.

How often your retriever needs their nails trimmed varies considerably. Several factors dictate the frequency, including:

- The consistency of the nails—soft, medium, or hard.
- How quickly their nails grow.
- Your golden's age and activity level.
- The different surfaces they walk on.

TIP ***As a rule, you should trim your retriever's nails once a month. It is time to clip them if they click when your dog walks on hard flooring. You can also tell by examining them. Nails must not extend beyond the pad or scratch on the ground when they stand upright.***

Dewclaws – These are the claws located on the side of the foot that never touch the ground but continue to grow. Some puppies have their dewclaws removed when very young by a veterinarian, so growing dewclaws will never be a problem.

Dewclaws on adult dogs can be more difficult to clip, but it is very important to do this regularly. If they are not trimmed, they can grow so long they curl into a circle, which may grow back into your golden retriever's leg, causing excruciating pain.

Clippers, Scissors – Toenail scissors (see picture) are a good choice for trimming the curved tip of your puppy's softer nails.

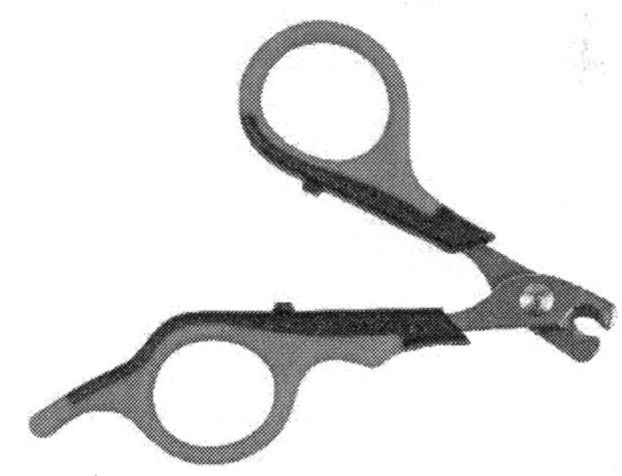

There are also 'guillotine' nail clippers that have a hole where your retriever's nail is inserted. This type of trimmer is not recommended as: (1) it is difficult to get the nail into the hole at the right depth; (2) it is hard to see how much of the nail is going to be sliced off; and (3) the chances of cutting into the quick and causing your dog pain and blood loss is much higher.

Introducing a Puppy to Nail Clipping

Many dogs develop an aversion to having their feet held, which then makes it difficult to trim their nails. The only way to avoid this problem is to get your golden puppy used to having their feet touched and toes inspected as soon as they come home from the breeder.

When your golden puppy is relaxed and tired after a walk, have them sit beside you as you hold each paw—one after the other—and separate their toes while inspecting their nails. If your pup does not try to pull their foot away, give them a treat and move on to the next foot. If they object, simply hold the same foot again and before they can pull it away, give a treat. If you perform this foot holding and inspection exercise every day and reward them with treats, your retriever puppy will soon learn to accept it as a regular part of their day.

Nail Scissors – Once your pup is happy to have you handle their feet, it is time to introduce the nail scissors. Let your puppy see and sniff them and give them a treat. Hold one paw, separate the toenail, and snip off just the curved tip. Give them a treat for not making a fuss. It is okay if you just get one paw snipped each day instead of doing too much at once and possibly upsetting your golden pup. Make the procedure as pleasant as possible and stop before they start fussing.

Once your puppy is approximately six months old, their nails will have grown stronger, thicker, and tougher. This is when you should switch from nail scissors to a rotary trimmer/grinder or plier clippers (see picture).

Plier-type Nail Clipping

You probably already know leaving your dog's nails too long can lead to many problems later in life, such as sore feet, painful joints, back pain, and difficulty walking. Therefore, to take good care of your golden, you need to learn how and when to perform this essential task.

Step-by-Step Instructions – When trimming your retriever's nails, be sure to only snip the tip. You do not want to accidentally cut into the vein, as this is painful and will make your golden's nail bleed. Here is how to trim your dog's nails using the plier-type clippers:

- Hold your dog's paw firmly but gently.
- Trim the nail below the quick—where the dead nail begins—at a 45° angle, removing small slices at a time.
- Continue until you reach the white inside the nail—this is dead nail—with a small, black dot at the centre. If you cannot see the dot yet, and the nail is completely white, you can trim off a little more.

Rotary Nail Trimming

Trimming your retriever's nails with a rotary device MUST be done with a tool designed especially for dogs (see picture below). Otherwise, the tool's speed might be too high, which will burn your dog's nails. Some retrievers prefer having their nails trimmed with a rotary device that grinds away any excess nail.

If you plan to use a rotary trimmer, it is important to introduce it to your retriever when they are young so they learn to calmly accept the noise and vibration. Here's how:

- Show the grinder to your golden puppy.
- Let them sniff it and turn it on so they get used to the sound and vibration.
- Hold it against their feet one at a time so they learn not to fear the vibration.
- When they do not object, give them a treat.

Once your golden is familiar with a rotary trimmer, this type of tool is all you'll ever need. Plus, your dog's nails will always be smooth and round, with none of the sharp edges left behind when a plier-type clipper is used.

There are several benefits to using this tool to trim your dog's nails:

- There is less chance of cutting into the vein.
- It is easier to keep their nails short.
- Many dogs prefer it because there is no squeezing sensation or clicking sound.

- A rotary trimmer is usually faster than plier-type clippers.
- If you use this tool, you don't have to clip their nails, which is typically more difficult.

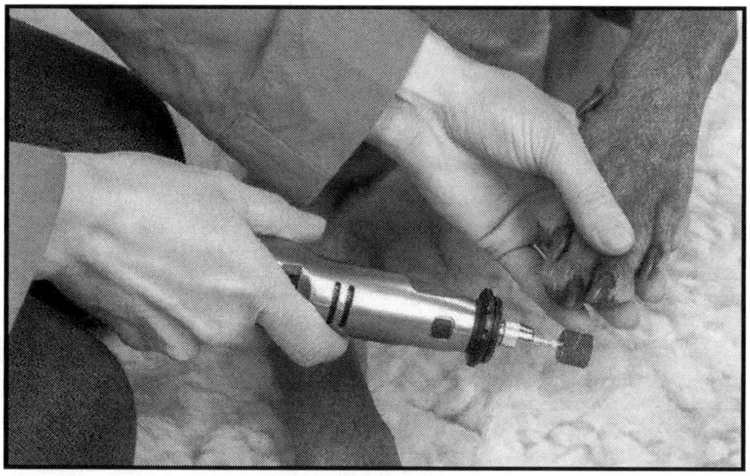

Rotary Trimming Step-by-Step - This is the step-by-step process for trimming your golden retriever's nails with a rotary trimmer:

1. Trim their nails when your dog is relaxed, say, after a walk or play session.
2. Have your retriever lie beside you on the sofa or floor.
3. Have some favourite treats to hand.
4. Turn on the trimmer and pick up one paw.
5. While holding the paw in one hand, separate a toe and firmly hold the nail you are going to trim between your thumb and forefinger.
6. Hold the sanding disc lightly against the end of the nail until you see how your golden reacts. This also helps you figure out how much pressure to apply.
7. Move the sanding disc around the end of the nail until the dead part has been ground off and it is smooth with a rounded shape. Stop before the disc cuts into the vein.
8. You may also need to sand underneath the nail to remove sharp edges.
9. Repeat the process on all four feet (16 nails). If your dog has dew claws, trim those as well.
10. Check online videos that show how to use a rotary trimmer.
11. The first few times you use the rotary trimmer, go very slowly, and give a treat after just one nail. Once your retriever realises the trimmer won't hurt them, and they are rewarded with a treat, you can trim the rest of their nails.
12. Make sure you have good natural or artificial light when trimming your dog's nails, so you can clearly see what you are doing.

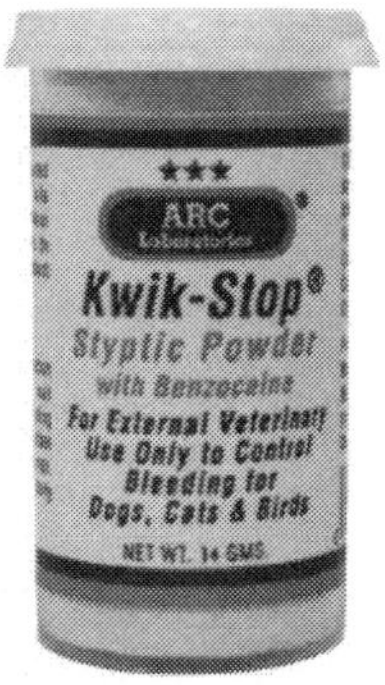

Accidents – Of course, you always want to avoid causing pain when trimming your golden retriever's toenails. You don't want to destroy their trust in you when performing this essential task. However, with the best will in the world, sometimes accidents do happen. If you clip the nail too short and inadvertently cut into the vein, your dog will be in pain, and it will bleed.

Keep some styptic powder (see picture)—often called 'Kwik Stop'—in your grooming kit in case of an accident. This yellow powder is quick and easy to use. Hopefully, you will never need it, but it will give you peace of mind knowing you have it in case. Dip your moistened finger into the powder and apply it with a little pressure to the end of the bleeding nail. This will stop the bleeding in a few seconds.

Ear Care

Golden retrievers often suffer from painful ear infections. Being familiar with your dog's habits and noting if they change will help you spot if they've got an infection. Keeping their ears clean and dry can help prevent this health issue. If your dog is scratching at their ears, moaning, crying, or constantly shaking their head, it is time for a trip to the vet, as they may have an infection.

Check your dog's ears at least once a week to maintain good ear health and catch or prevent problems early on.

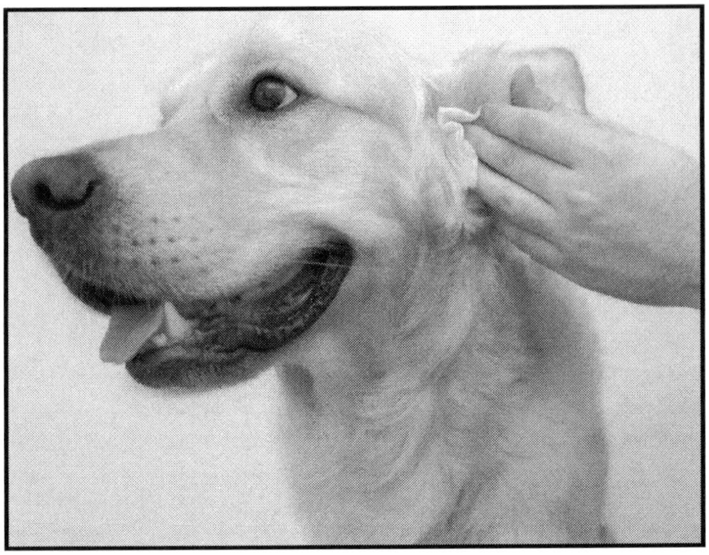

Get your retriever to stand, sit or lie down comfortably. Start by gently stroking their head and giving them a treat to distract them. Lift the ear flap and have a look into the ear canal.

Clean your golden's ears when they look a bit grubby. If the ear appears to have a bit of dirt build-up or the wax is looking thicker or darker than normal, it is time for a cleaning. **Aim to clean your retriever's ears monthly, regardless of condition.**

It is a good idea to keep ear powders and cleaning solutions in your dog's grooming kit. Proper preventative care will minimise the chances of irritating, painful ear issues.

Ear Powders – These can be bought at any pet store and are designed to keep your golden's ears dry while preventing the build-up of bacteria that can lead to infections. Ear powders are also used when removing excess hair growth from inside your dog's ear canal, making it easier to grip the hair.

Ear Cleaning Solutions – All pet stores offer a wide variety of ear-cleaning creams, drops, oils, rinses, or wipes specially formulated for cleaning canine ears.

Your golden's ears are very sensitive. It is always important to read the labels before purchasing products and avoid anything that lists alcohol as the main ingredient.

Ear Cleaning Step-By-Step

1. Lift your retriever's ear, holding it between your thumb and forefinger to get a good look inside.
2. Gently wipe around the entrance of the ear canal with damp cotton wool, removing dirt or excess wax.
3. Insert the tip of the bottle containing the ear cleaning solution into the ear canal. Make sure not to push it in too far, then gently squeeze to release the cleaner.
4. Massage the base of the ear to help the cleaner pass inside the ear canal and wipe away any excess with damp cotton wool.
5. Repeat the process for the other ear.
6. If there is an infection and your vet has prescribed drops, apply them right after your retriever's ears have been cleaned. This will ensure the medicine enters the ear, where it can be absorbed without being blocked by excess wax.

Top 10 Ear Care Tips

1. Establish a regular, healthy ear care programme early on that includes cleaning and inspection for foreign objects and foul smells. Also, remember that scratching or rubbing their ears and tilting or shaking their head often indicates your dog has an infection that needs immediate treatment by a vet.

2. Check inside your retriever's ears for redness. When the inside of the ear appears red and irritated, this is often the first sign of a problem.
3. Look for excess hair growth in their ears. Some dogs grow hair inside their ears, and if not removed, it can cause itching and hearing loss.
4. Regularly check inside your golden's ears for any discharge or odour. If they smell bad, your dog might have a highly itchy yeast infection. This smells like beer or bread baking. Time for a vet visit.
5. A gentle ear cleaner formulated for dogs, such as 'Ear Pro' (see picture), will remove debris, eliminate excess wax, and relieve inflammation.

6. Frequently inspect ears for bacterial infections. Depending on the type of bacteria, your golden might be scratching at their ears or whining. Their ears might smell like bad breath or rotten chicken or sweeter, like caramel or grapes. If you notice any of these signs, it is time to go to the vet.
7. Regularly check for parasites. If your retriever is shaking and tilting their head, it might indicate tiny mites in the ear canal. These are extremely itchy, very irritating, and usually smell like rotten rubbish. Mites are often difficult to spot until there are a lot of them, when they start to resemble coffee grounds. Veterinary attention will be necessary.
8. Ear wipes, such as 'Vet's Best' (see picture), could help between ear cleaning sessions, as they freshen the outer areas of the ear and help reduce odours.

9. Many home remedies can clean your golden's ears just as efficiently as shop-bought products without the high price tag. Witch hazel is one possibility, or a 50:50 solution of organic cider vinegar and purified water. Another option is a 50:50 solution of hydrogen peroxide and purified water.
10. After swimming, always check your golden retriever's ear canals are dry. If salt water has gotten inside their ears, rinse thoroughly with fresh water and completely dry them to prevent infection.

Paw Care

It is important to regularly check your golden's paws to ensure they are in good condition and identify potential problems before they become serious.

TIP ***Anyone living in a wet climate where your retriever could come home with muddy feet after each walk should consider purchasing a 'MudBuster' portable dog paw cleaner. These are simple to use and will keep the mud out of your home. Just add warm water, put your dog's foot in, give a twist, and like magic, the soft, silicone blades will remove any mud.***

Since dogs do not usually wear shoes, their feet get into everything. It's only natural they sometimes pick up burrs, spear grass, or even chewing gum. After a walk, take a minute to check between the pads to make certain they haven't picked up any foreign objects that could cause discomfort.

Top 15 Paw Care Tips

1. Your retriever's nails shouldn't touch the ground when walking. If you hear them clicking or scratching as they walk, it's time for a trimming.
2. After running or jogging with your dog, always check their paws for injury.
3. When visiting the beach, always check your golden's paws afterwards. There may have been sharp barnacles at the beach that can cut or injure their paws.

4. Hot pavements, sand, or road surfaces can burn your dog's paws. Bear that in mind on hot days and walk your golden in shady areas or on grass which is cooler than concrete pavements, roads, or sand-covered areas. Avoid walking during the midday sun when the heat is at its height.
5. Check for spear grass when visiting a park or wooded area. Many varieties of dangerous spear grass flourish during the summer months. These invasive grasses easily cause great discomfort and can lead to emergency surgery. Some of these grasses have a Velcro-like surface and a needle-like point that can easily pierce any part of your golden's skin. Always examine between their toes and all over your dog's body after visiting an area where spear grass is growing.

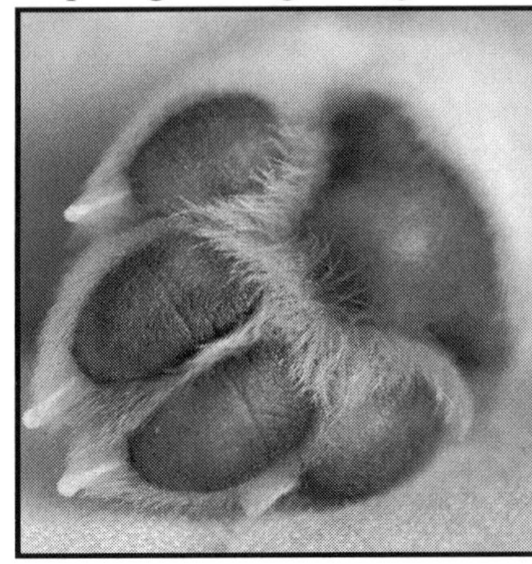

6. Some golden retrievers grow excessive amounts of hair between their paw pads. If this hair is not regularly clipped away, it can form mats between the pads that feel like tiny rocks and make walking painful.
7. Dogs walk on all sorts of debris. They can pick up anything on their feet, from chewing gum to sticky plant leaves and sap from trees. Checking for foreign objects and removing them after a walk helps to keep your dog's feet healthy.
8. Consider dog booties for walking your golden in cold weather. If you start using them when they are a pup, your dog will readily accept wearing booties when walking on snow or ice-covered ground that could have been sprayed with salt.

9. Try 'Musher's Secret Paw Protection Wax' (see picture) during the cold winter months. This product creates an invisible boot around your dog's paws to protect their pads from salt, snow, and ice.
10. If your retriever doesn't go out very often, the rough ground could cause an injury because their paws are unused to it. Take them outside for short periods, gradually increasing play or walk time, so their paws become accustomed to the environment, making them more hard-wearing.

11. Use a long-lasting moisturiser, such as 'Bag Balm' (see picture). It will treat cracked and damaged noses and paw pads. Your dog will not only love you for giving their paws the equivalent of a spa day, but they will also feel better since moisturised paws are softer and less prone to injury or cracking. To improve circulation to your retriever's paws, massage them by gently rubbing between their paw pads and in a circular motion on the back of their paw.
12. Don't use toxic floor cleaning products your dog might walk on. Toxins can enter their body through the pads of the feet.
13. Do not use pesticides or herbicides in your garden. When your dog walks on the grass, these products will enter their bloodstream through their paw pads.
14. When you're walking your dog, avoid any oil or petrol spills on the road so the toxins will not get stuck on their paws.
15. Be careful not to walk your golden through building sites or areas with falling and abandoned buildings where they might step on a nail or other sharp object.

If your dog continually licks or chews their paws, it could be a sign of injury or irritant. Check their paws and remove any debris before wiping them with antimicrobial hydrogel. This will soothe any irritation and support healing. If your retriever continues to lick or chew, contact your vet for advice.

If their paws are cut or cracked, rinse the affected area with a wound care solution to clean away any irritants. Then, apply an antimicrobial hydrogel to soothe and heal the injury. To prevent further damage to the paw, wrap it in a bandage.

Paw care needs to be part of your regular dog care routine in the same way exercise and grooming are.

Removing Parasites

Removing Fleas – Fleas (see picture) are the bane of every dog. For more information about fleas, please refer to *Skin Issues and Parasites* in Chapter 14.

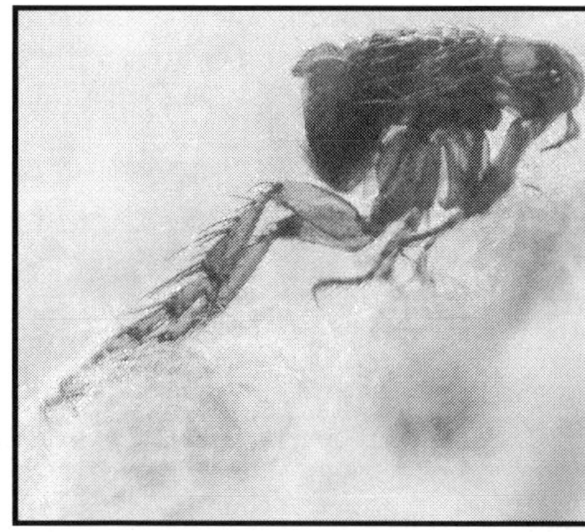

Get a flea comb specifically designed to remove tiny mites or fleas from your dog's coat. These combs are usually small for manoeuvring in tight spots and often have a plastic handle with metal teeth spaced closely together to trap and remove tiny, hiding pests.

TIP ***You'll usually discover a flea infestation when brushing your golden retriever. Unless the infestation is too large to handle at home and requires the intervention of a vet, you should immediately start eliminating these annoying pests yourself.***

Most vets recommend a monthly spot-on or pill flea treatment. If you prefer a more natural approach without harsh chemicals, there are many alternative products and shampoos designed to eliminate fleas, such as:

- Shampoos containing pyrethrum—a botanical extract found in small, white daisies—or citrus, cedar, or tea tree oil.
- 'Cedarcide' shampoo and spray—100% safe for all the family, non-toxic, and highly effective in killing biting and crawling creatures on contact. You can bathe your dog with the shampoo and spray carpets, beds, or even yourself.

While you can simply use a flea comb (see picture) to pick off fleas, depending on the length and density of your golden's coat, this can be an arduous task.

Although you can never be 100% certain you've removed all of the fleas, the following steps will help:

1. First, bathe your dog with a shampoo (see picture) designed to kill fleas and then add plenty of conditioner—it is easier to comb through a clean, conditioned, and dry coat.
2. Fill a container with hot water and a squirt of washing-up liquid.
3. Begin combing at the head, and work towards the back, slowly going through small sections.
4. As the comb fills with dead hair, flea eggs, dirt, and fleas, push down on the teeth of the comb and dump them into the soapy mixture.
5. Work down the chest and sides and then the stomach.
6. Finish by combing your golden's legs and tail.
7. Since fleas scurry around, a second pass may get any which were missed the first time.
8. Focus under the chin, tummy, and tail areas where fleas tend to congregate.

9. Let the soapy water stand for at least 10 minutes before discarding it to drown any surviving fleas.

Although using a flea comb is time-consuming, it is a safe, effective, and inexpensive way to remove these pests. Remember to wash all bedding, or spray with a treatment designed to kill them, so all fleas, eggs, or larvae are removed from your retriever's environment.

Removing Ticks – Before learning how to remove these nasty pests, find out more about ticks in *Skin Issues and Parasites* in Chapter 14.

Since ticks (see picture) are larger than fleas, ranging in size from tiny larvae to the size of a human fingertip, they are usually easier to spot. The following tips will help you find ticks on your golden retriever:

1. Start at the head and run your hands over the body to feel for new lumps or bumps.
2. When checking around the neck, do not forget to feel underneath the collar and inside their ears.
3. Search the rest of your golden's body, inside the groin area, underneath the tail, and between the toes.

Several tools can be used to remove ticks. While you can use the tweezers you have in your medicine cabinet, having a tool purpose-built for easy and complete removal of an embedded tick is always better:

- A fine-tipped pair of tweezers, such as 'Tick Ease', has a V-shaped slot that will remove the entire tick.
- Tick Twister is a simple device for painlessly, easily, and quickly removing ticks embedded in your retriever's skin.

There are many natural and chemical-based tick repellents designed to prevent or kill ticks—and other creepy crawlies—including oral tablets, shampoos, tick collars, sprays, and spot-on treatments.

FACT ***There are hundreds of kinds of ticks. They carry many diseases harmful to both animals and humans. The deer tick is more worrisome than some others, as it infects both dogs and humans with Lyme disease. However, it takes several hours for an attached tick to pass on disease, which is why looking for ticks after each walk and immediately removing them is crucial.***

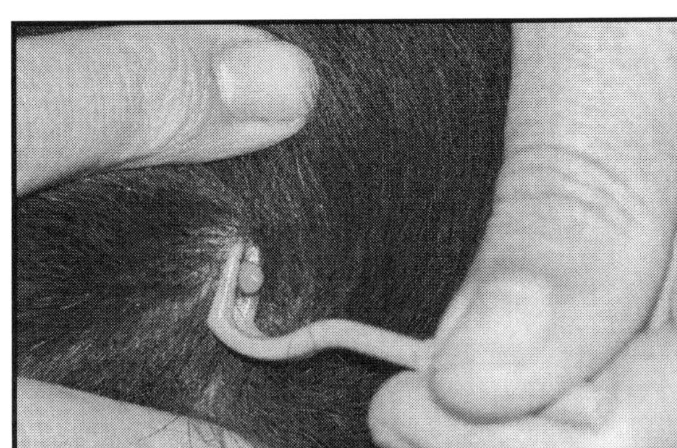

The best type of tick prevention for your retriever depends on where you live, where your dog spends most of their recreation time, and how prevalent ticks are in the area. Choosing effective tools and repellents, plus taking precautions by evading areas known to be infested with ticks, will help to avoid these blood-sucking parasites. If your dog does pick up ticks, here is how to remove or kill them:

- Tick Twister (see picture) – Hold close to the skin and engage the tick from the side so it is securely in the narrowest part of the V-shaped hook. Lift very lightly and twist the hook two or three times until the tick is detached from your retriever's skin. Disinfect with alcohol.
- Tweezers – Spread the fur, grasp the tick as close to your golden's skin as possible and pull it out in a steady, slow, straight upward motion to prevent the mouth from breaking off and remaining embedded in your dog's skin. Disinfect the area afterwards with rubbing alcohol.

- Cedarcide spray – Lightly mist your retriever's coat or apply with your hands. Massage into their coat and cover their legs, underbelly, and around the ears and tail. Apply to your dog's face with your hands, avoiding their mouth and eyes.

Summer & Winter Care

Unless you live in a part of the world where the day-to-day climate remains constant, you will probably need to consider care items to keep your dog comfortable in all weather.

Summer Care

While summertime usually means more outdoor adventures, it can also bring biting ticks and flea season, burnt paw pads, or heatstroke that can seriously injure your retriever.

The ideal temperature for fleas and ticks is between 21-29º C (70-85º F), which is why these pests are more prevalent during summertime. Make sure you are vigilant about your tick and flea prevention/treatment routine (as described in the section above) during those hot summer months.

Your golden should never be left alone in a parked vehicle, even on mild days, as they can develop heatstroke within a few minutes. Even though your car might be parked in the shade and have the windows open, this has little effect on how hot the vehicle gets. It can become considerably hotter inside the car compared to the outside temperature in a matter of minutes. **The best rule is to never leave your retriever alone in a vehicle.**

When walking your dog outside during the heat of summer, bear in mind that hot tarmac, car parks, and pavements can cause burns and blistering to your retriever's foot pads very quickly. For example, when the air temperature is 30°C (86°F), the road surface can reach 57°C (135°F), which is far too hot for your golden's feet to deal with. Also, your dog's body will be heated both from below—radiating up from the surface—and from the sun's rays beating down from above, which increases the possibility of heatstroke. Always test the surface temperature with your hand before setting out with your dog. If it is too hot, choose to walk in shady or grassy areas or walk during cooler times of the day.

Anyone who has ever been to the beach on a hot summer day will know all about hot sand, making it almost impossible to walk without burning your feet. If the sand is hot enough to scorch your feet, it will be just as damaging to your golden retriever's feet.

Just like people, dogs are at risk of burning in the sun if they are not protected, especially lightly coloured or thinly coated dogs. The good news is most pet shops stock specially formulated sun cream for your golden retriever. Ask your vet if you are unsure whether your dog needs sun cream.

It is important to help your dog stay fit and healthy all year round. Regular clipping and/or grooming will keep your retriever's coat clean and free from knots. This is particularly important in the summertime, as matting traps heat and makes your retriever feel extremely hot.

It is especially important to support your pooch in maintaining a healthy weight during warm weather. Your dog will probably want to be less active when it is hot, and any walks or playtime should be taken at cooler parts of the day with plenty of breaks. Giving them time in the shade can be a good idea. Adjust the amount of food you give to reflect how much energy they are using.

FACT ***Dogs do not sweat the way people do and regulate their temperature by panting. They need constant access to drinking water during hot weather. Never forget to take water with you when you go out walking on sunny days.***

You can buy evaporative cooling vests that will keep your dog cool when the weather is hot. You soak them in water before putting them on your golden. Another simple way to help your dog stay cooler when the sun is shining is to put them in a T-shirt or vest a lighter colour than their coat.

If your golden is panting excessively and feeling uncomfortably hot, here's how to make them feel better:

- Have them rest in the shade.
- Get them to stand in cool water.
- Use a wet towel.
- Give them a cooling bath and let them air dry.
- Spray your golden with the garden hose.
- Fill an appropriately sized paddling pool with water.
- Give retriever access to a fan.
- Add some ice cubes to their water bowl.

Winter Care

Since your golden has a fur coat, many people mistakenly believe they can tolerate the cold better than we do. Unfortunately, this is not always the case. Like us, our fur-coated friends are used to the warmth of an indoor shelter, so cold weather is as hard on them as it is on us. You should be aware that our beloved dogs need a little extra care during the winter months. Here are some tips to think about as you explore the winter landscape with your golden retriever:

Watch the signs – If it is too cold for you to stand at the door without your coat, it will probably be too cold for your dog. Pay attention to their behaviour when they are outdoors. If your golden retriever is whining, shivering, acting anxious, or they stop playing and start looking for places to burrow, they're cold and it's time to bring them in.

Coat – Your dog might need to wear a coat or jumper during winter walks. A cosy coat should reach from your golden's neck to the base of their tail and protect the stomach. Remember, coats do not prevent frostbite on the ears or feet, so never keep your retriever out too long in freezing temperatures.

Walk timing – If your golden is sensitive to the cold, try walking them in the late morning or early afternoon when temperatures are a little higher, avoiding early morning or late evening walks. If it is sunny, spend time playing outdoors. The added benefit of sunshine is that it gives both you and your dog vitamin D.

Limit outdoor time – Take your retriever out for frequent walks, exercise, and play. However, when the temperature drops, do not leave them outdoors for long. A good rule is to go out with them. When you are ready to come in, they will be too.

Warm bedding – The right bedding is vital to keep your dog warm. Warm blankets create a snug environment. Heated dog beds can help keep the stiffness out of ageing joints. Place your golden's bed in a favourite spot to sleep so the area does not feel unfamiliar.

Heating sources – Goldens often seek heat during cold winter weather by snuggling close to heating sources. It's important to avoid space heaters, so your pet doesn't get burnt. Fireplaces can also pose a threat, so make sure you have a dog-proof system to keep your heat-seeking retriever out of harm's way.

Grooming – Your golden retriever needs a clean, well-groomed coat to keep them fully insulated. This is especially important if they spend a lot of time outdoors. If they need a bath, thoroughly dry them afterwards, especially if you are going to allow them outside again.

Moisturise their skin – Cold and dry weather can adversely affect your golden's skin. To prevent dry, flaky skin, add a skin and coat supplement to their food. Coconut oil is an excellent natural moisturiser that will help keep your dog's skin and coat healthy.

No overfeeding – Although your golden might need an additional layer in winter, make sure it is provided by a coat and not fat. Cold temperatures often encourage lazy behaviour and the need for fewer calories. Be attuned to your dog's activity level and adjust their calorie intake accordingly.

Antifreeze – With winter comes antifreeze. This toxic chemical tastes sweet, and your retriever will readily lick or drink it. A small amount can prove fatal. Keep your golden out of the garage and off the driveway, where they could encounter antifreeze or other harmful chemicals.

Do not leave your retriever in the car – In the same way as cars get dangerously hot in summer, cold winter temperatures are equally dangerous for your dog. Leaving your car running brings additional risks that include possible carbon monoxide poisoning if your car is parked in the garage. Leave your retriever at home when you go out to run errands.

Special care for seniors – Cold weather often aggravates existing medical conditions in dogs, particularly arthritis. It is essential to maintain an exercise regimen for your arthritic dog but be careful of slippery surfaces and also make sure your dog has a warm, soft place to recover after any activity. If you do not give your senior golden a natural joint supplement to lubricate their joints and ease the discomfort of arthritis, you might want to consider doing so in the winter months. Just like people, your golden retriever is more susceptible to other illnesses during winter weather.

Snow in their paws – Inspect your dog's paws and dry them thoroughly after they have been out in the garden. Snow can compact between their toes and turn into ice balls, which can be very painful. Always trim any hair between your golden retriever's toes to help avoid this.

Recall command – There can be reduced visibility in foggy or snowy conditions. If you are letting your retriever off their lead, be certain they have a good recall to avoid losing them. As always, make sure their microchip details are up-to-date with your correct contact information.

Conspicuousness – As the nights draw in and the sun begins to rise later, attach a small light to your retriever's collar so they can be seen when walking in reduced visibility.

Watch where they play – Although your golden is probably having a great time outdoors, bring them indoors frequently for water and to warm up. Remember not to stay out too long. If you are walking or playing in an area unfamiliar to your dog, keep them close. It would be easy for them to venture onto unsafe surfaces like frozen ponds or lakes. These could be covered in snow and not easily visible.

Holiday times – During Easter, Halloween, and Christmas, toxic foods are more likely to be within reach, such as chocolate or other sweet treats. In addition, holidays like Halloween and New Year's Eve often mean fireworks displays that can be exceedingly unsettling for our furry friends. Remember to leave them indoors where they are in familiar surroundings. Disguise disturbing noises with soft, soothing music.

10. Socialisation

'No one appreciates the very special genius of your conversation as much as the dog does.'

~ Christopher Morley ~

What is socialisation? It is the learning process your retriever puppy must go through to learn key life skills to ensure they are secure and content in their environment and can communicate effectively within their social group. You achieve this by introducing your puppy to everyday sights, sounds, and situations to get them used to their surroundings. This should be done in a positive, non-threatening way.

Socialising your golden retriever puppy is one of the most important steps towards guaranteeing they will live a happy, stress-free life with their new family. If you don't properly socialise your puppy, you may have to deal with unwanted behavioural issues later.

A dog acting aggressively towards a person or other animal can be so severe that they may need a muzzle every time they go out in public. Severe aggression may mean you have no choice but to put your dog to sleep. The good news is that since they're such a docile breed, any sort of aggressive tendencies your golden might display are usually avoidable if thorough socialisation steps are taken. While early socialisation of your puppy is critical, it is also important you continue socialising them throughout their lifetime.

Every dog needs a leader to guide them. If your golden is not properly socialised, trained and taught to respect your word as their owner, they could feel forced to take over the family 'pack' and make their own decisions. This can lead to all sorts of problems, especially if your dog decides to act aggressively towards other dogs or people. Aggression is a huge stress for both dog and owner, and as most people are aware, stress can shorten your life and make it hard for you to feel happy.

Socialising Puppies

Socialising your new retriever puppy can be a fun and entertaining time for both of you. It is one of the most important aspects of raising a well-behaved companion who is a joy to be around.

TIP ***It is far easier to socialise a puppy than an adult dog. When bringing your new retriever puppy into your home, you should take advantage of the critical socialisation period, which lasts up to 16 weeks of age.***

Though this is the age when your puppy is more accepting of being introduced to new things, it is never too late to get started. Just because this important period in your puppy's life is over does not mean socialisation is at an end.

Before embarking on your socialisation journey, it can be useful to think about what your plans might be over the next 10 to 15 years and then imagine how you would like your golden to react in those circumstances. For instance, if you intend to fly often to visit relatives, you will want your dog to be content staying in a travel crate and not be freaked out by the noise of the plane.

Perhaps you might want to spend your leisure time enjoying open-air concerts. In this case, getting your puppy used to large crowds and loud music is essential. Note that it is never a good idea to take your retriever to any event involving fireworks.

Maybe you like to go kayaking, paddle boarding, or surfing. It is easy to teach puppies not to fear these fun water sports when they are young.

When you think about your daily life, what you enjoy, and the places you want to go, it makes sense to begin socialising your golden puppy in those areas.

Additionally, taking your puppy to places they do not normally visit or doing things they wouldn't ordinarily be exposed to also helps them feel more confident and comfortable as they grow. When socialising your retriever puppy, the following checklist for their exposure will help you start:

People

- Babies, toddlers, and children of all ages.
- Men and women of all ages and ethnicities.
- Men with beards.
- People wearing masks, hats, and backpacks.
- People carrying boxes or using a walking stick.
- People lying down or limping.
- People jogging, riding bicycles, and skateboarding.
- People on crutches, in wheelchairs, or on scooters.

Dogs

- Small dogs.
- Large dogs.
- Young dogs.
- Old dogs.
- Energetic dogs.
- Calm dogs.

- Aggressive dogs.
- Dogs with short muzzles.
- Dogs with no tails.
- Dogs with cropped ears.

Vehicles

- Motorcycles.
- Cars.
- Trucks.
- Buses.
- Ambulances.
- Fire engines.
- Planes.
- Trains.

Sounds

- Babies crying.
- Beeping noises.
- Children screaming.
- Doorbells.
- Door knocking.
- Sirens.
- Smoke Alarms.
- Noisy traffic.
- Planes landing and taking off.
- Children playing in a schoolyard.
- Animal and bird noises.
- Loud music.
- Hoovers.
- Cars backfiring.

Surfaces

- Smooth floors.
- Tiled floors.
- Gravel.
- Stairs.
- Bridges.
- Grates.
- Metal surfaces.
- Mirrors.

Situations

- Busy pavements.
- Quiet lakeside walks.
- City parks.
- The vet's.
- Riding in a lift.
- Long car rides in a crate.
- Inside a Sherpa bag or crate on a plane.
- Inside dog-friendly stores.
- Visiting a friend's house.

You should always let your retriever puppy know when they are doing well during socialisation sessions. Reward them with praise and a favourite treat when they react calmly in any of the above situations and look to you for direction. Never force your puppy into a new situation. If they appear nervous or frightened in any way, move away from the cause of stress and try again another time. Successful socialisation involves ensuring every new experience is a pleasant one.

Socialising Adult Dogs

The same puppy checklist above also applies when socialising an adult dog, which will often be a much more time-consuming task. As long as you are patient and do not force issues too quickly, anything is possible. The process typically takes longer as an older dog is more apt to react with fear aggression when exposed to sounds, people, animals, and situations they have not experienced before.

TIP ***All dogs are curious about their environment and will want to check it out. The best way to start socialising an older dog is to take them for frequent walks. This will expose them to many new social situations and provide plenty of opportunities to practise proper behaviour.***

If your golden retriever growls, barks, or appears fearful when seeing a person or dog approaching, stay calm and confident. Remember, this is all new for them. Simply move away from the stressful situation by turning in another direction to give them space so they can calm down.

By socialising your older dog slowly and remaining composed, they will feel your energy and soon become more confident and less concerned about new situations. Every time they stay calm and look to you for direction, reward them with a treat and loving praise. Soon, your dog will realise going out to socialise is a rewarding experience they look forward to having.

If your adult retriever has never had the opportunity to socialise with other dogs, it is important not to force this but let them observe from a distance while out and about. When they are relaxed, gradually move a little closer and carefully watch their reaction. Should they respond with fear or aggression, move farther away until they calm down. Slowly introduce your retriever to the park and reward their good behaviour. By doing this, your dog will soon want to move closer for a sniff with the other dogs. Before you know it, they will be eager to visit their new friends every day.

Socialising with Unknown Dogs

Despite their naturally friendly personality, any retriever who is not regularly socialised can become shy, nervous, afraid, suspicious, or overly bossy around unfamiliar dogs. Daily on-lead walks are the perfect opportunity for your golden to see and possibly meet other dogs, as well as practise proper behaviour.

Always take things slowly and never put your retriever in an uncomfortable situation where they feel forced into being around other canines who might unsettle them. Whether a puppy or an adult dog, your golden should always be given the option to walk away to create space.

Below are some tips to help your retriever quickly make friends:

1. When walking on a loose lead, encourage your golden to stay focused on you. When they do, reward them, and keep practising until they calmly walk on the lead.
2. Walk at a distance from other dogs. Make sure your golden's attention stays on you and stay far enough away from other dogs to avoid getting them excited or agitated. Be sure to have some treats on you so you can reward their calm behaviour.
3. Gradually reduce the distance between your golden and other dogs.
4. Once they are accustomed to seeing other dogs, arrange a walk with a friend who has a dog. That way, your retriever will learn to walk alongside them. At first, keep both dogs on a lead.
5. If both dogs are relaxed, let them greet each other on a lead. Once they have said hello and had a sniff, you can start walking.
6. When they have got to know each other and are relaxed, you can let them off their leads to play together. Just be sure your retriever knows to come back when you call them.

Always remember to go at your retriever's pace. If they seem overwhelmed or unsure at any point, go back to the previous stage where they were calm, before continuing at a slower pace.

When you start to socialise your golden puppy or adult dog, it is best to introduce them first to calmer and friendlier dogs rather than overly boisterous or less friendly dogs. Any sort of negative experience can result in teaching your dog to be afraid or feel they need to act aggressively.

Be vigilant when visiting the park, where there could be dogs with unknown personalities and play styles. Matching dog sizes is a good idea, as your retriever puppy needs to be protected from playing with a significantly larger dog. The moment any dog is playing too roughly or causing your golden to yelp or feel afraid, you need to step in and immediately stop the play.

Socialisation with Senior Dogs

When your puppy has had all their vaccinations and can visit the park to meet and greet fellow canines of all shapes, sizes, and ages, an important interaction is with a senior dog. While it is vital to carefully supervise any interaction between any dog and your excited, bouncing golden puppy who has not yet learnt to control their enthusiasm, it is even more crucial around a senior dog.

Some senior dogs are extremely tolerant and will put up with crazy puppy energy, while others will not. Close supervision is key around an older dog who might not appreciate being pounced on or having their ears pulled or tail bitten by razor-sharp puppy teeth. Here are a few steps to keep your puppy under control while teaching them to be respectful during play:

- Take your golden puppy for a walk to tire them out before visiting the park.
- Lift your puppy and let the senior dog sniff their bottom.
- If the senior dog is agreeable, let your puppy sniff their bottom.
- If all seems fine, let your puppy play with them under close supervision.
- The second your retriever seems to be aggravating the senior dog, step in and end the play session.

Depending on the age of your puppy, a play session with a willing, elderly dog may not last long before both have had enough, and it is time to head home. A senior dog may have aches and pains and not want to play for long. If the elderly dog has had enough, they might decide to give your puppy a nip. While a good-natured senior dog will probably not harm your golden, it is always best to avoid any situation that has the potential to frighten your puppy enough to make them scared of other dogs.

Socialising with Unknown People

Proper socialisation also means taking your golden retriever to many different places and introducing them to different people of all ages, sizes, and ethnicities (see the People checklist at the beginning of the chapter), so they can learn what is normal, acceptable behaviour in their daily life.

First Meeting Introductions – When a new person or child is approaching for the first meeting with your golden, ask them to do the following:

- Approach calmly and slowly.
- Hold out the back of their hand rather than trying to pat your golden's head.
- Let your dog sniff their hand and approach at their own speed.
- Never force your dog to get closer.

Introducing your dog to your children

You should introduce your new golden retriever to your children sooner rather than later. This will help them get accustomed to one another. Start slowly, and do not rush things as they might not hit it off immediately. Brief, frequent encounters are the best way to gradually let them interact together.

When children want to play with your dog, always supervise, so no one becomes nervous or overwhelmed.

An older dog will usually have more stamina for long play sessions. They will also be stronger, so when playing too vigorously with very young children, they could unintentionally bowl them over or scratch them.

Your golden puppy will easily get tired, so keep play sessions short. Be especially careful when allowing young children to play with your small puppy, who might accidentally get hurt. You do not want your puppy to become fearful of children, as this could lead to fear or aggression issues later.

When introducing your child to your golden retriever, the 'sniff test' is normally the best place to start. Hold your child's hand out to allow your dog to learn their smell. This is important before your child tries to stroke them. If your golden appears uncertain after sniffing, they might not be willing to be touched. Instead, encourage your child to speak softly to your dog to soothe their nerves and wait for your dog to approach them.

If you are adopting a golden retriever, involving your child in the selection and adoption process is a good way to teach them about the responsibility that comes with a dog. It will also start the bonding process between them. Your child needs to learn that there are certain times when they should not approach the dog. These include when they are eating, playing with a toy, going to the toilet or asleep. Special care should be taken if your dog is blind or deaf as they can easily take fright.

Playing together – One of the mutual benefits of dogs and children playing together is the exercise and stimulation they get from their interaction. However, young children are often overly enthusiastic and loud when playing. This could frighten or over-excite your retriever, so you need to teach your child to play calmly and quietly with the dog. Rough, aggressive games could encourage corresponding aggressive behaviour in your dog.

TIP ***To help children and dogs form a strong bond, have them play together with your golden's favourite toys, such as a pull rope, or let them run together. Teach your child how to recognise when a dog is scared or anxious—tail tucked in, ears flattened, or hiding—and get them to back off straight away.***

Never allow your golden and child to play unattended, particularly if either is young, as your dog could easily misinterpret the situation and become overly excited. Discourage your dog from jumping up, as they might knock over an infant. Teach your child to keep dog toys away from their face.

If your retriever appears unhappy or too boisterous, be ready to intervene to stop them from biting or scratching. If your dog shows signs of tiredness or over-stimulation, it is time for a nap in a quiet and safe place away where they will not be bothered.

It is vital to remind your child to handle their pet gently and respectfully, as children can think of pets as cuddly toys. Also, some dogs do not like being picked up, and smaller breeds are often quite delicate. Teach your child to be patient with their golden and let them come to them in their own time. Discourage your child from getting too close, as some dogs dislike face-to-face contact. Teach your child to treat their retriever as they would another child. They should not climb on them, pull their ears or tail, or play roughly.

Other tips – Often, puppies steal, chew, and swallow children's toys and clothes, so teach your child to keep them safe by tidying up after themselves and storing their toys out of paw's reach.

Most children love nothing better than sharing their food under the table, without realising it could be unhealthy for their golden. Keep a watchful eye on your dog if they are sniffing around for titbits, or better still, put them in a different room at mealtimes.

Sometimes, nervous dogs cope better around children when they know there is somewhere to escape if things get too much. Crate training your retriever offers a safe place filled with their favourite blanket or toy away from loud or excitable children. Be sure your child knows that the dog crate is off-limits.

If they're old enough, it is a good idea to get your child involved in the pet care routine. They can learn valuable lessons about the constant care and attention pets need to live happy, healthy lives through filling their water or food bowls, walking your golden, or cleaning their toys and bedding.

TIP ***When it comes to protecting themselves from small children who might not understand to respect a dog's space, golden retrievers are usually gentle and patient. Still, bear in mind that any dog who is pushed too far may feel the need to protect themselves from a child invading their space, getting too close to their toys or food bowl, or treating them roughly.***

Fear of Loud Noises

Many goldens show extreme fear of loud noises. Piercing sounds can be very painful for their sensitive ears. The best way to prevent or eliminate this fear is to take the time to desensitise your dog to these noises when they are little. However, it is still entirely possible to achieve it with an older dog. Once your dog learns that these sounds are not to be feared, it is far less stressful for them when they hear them.

Desensitisation Devices – There are several devices you can use to desensitise your golden, so they are not traumatised by high-pitched alarms or loud popping or banging noises, such as the following:

- CDs (see picture) – Purchase CDs with a collection of unusual sounds, such as vacuum cleaners, aeroplanes, sirens, smoke alarms, fireworks, guns firing, people clapping, children playing, and more. Play them while pottering about in the kitchen or chilling in the living room. If you show your dog that everything is normal while listening to the CDs, the next time your puppy hears these sounds in real life, they will not become upset, as they will have already learnt to ignore them.

- Bubble Wrap – There is a simple way to desensitise your retriever if they are fearful of unexpected popping sounds. Show them the bubble wrap, pop a few of the cells and if they do not run away, give them a treat. Begin with bubble wrap with small, quieter cells, and then graduate your puppy with the louder, larger-celled bubble wrap.
- You can also take things even further by blowing up some small paper bags or balloons and loudly popping them in front of your golden puppy or taking them to a rifle range. When you

reward them with a nice treat for not showing fear or running away, they will soon associate these sounds with receiving something pleasant.

- Relaxation Collars – There are two kinds of collars designed to help relax or calm an upset puppy. One uses scent or calming pheromones, while the other plays music at an appropriate decibel level to calm a fearful or stressed dog.
- TV or Radio – Sometimes, all you need to calm a golden puppy stressed by loud noises is to turn on a TV or radio station playing relaxing music. Play it louder than you might normally to help disguise exterior noises.
- Thundershirts (see picture) – Some retrievers respond well to wearing a 'Thundershirt'. This is a vest designed to reduce anxiety or trauma from loud, rumbling, popping, or banging noises. The idea behind it is that the gentle pressure it creates is like a hug, which has a calming effect.

FACT ***Some dogs do things that make no logical sense when they hear loud popping or screeching noises. They start trembling, running, or trying to hide and will not listen to you at all.***

Make certain your retriever cannot hurt themselves trying to escape from these noises. If possible, calmly hold them until they start to relax. Always act appropriately when your dog is under this kind of stress by not panicking or having sorry, angry or frustrated energy around them. This tends to make things worse.

When you are the person who is your dog's support system, and you are also feeling weak or acting unstable, your golden will have nowhere to turn for help. Even if you're feeling nervous, it's best to pretend nothing is wrong and talk to your retriever in a soothing yet assertive and reassuring tone.

11. Training Your Golden

'Intelligent dogs rarely want to please people whom they do not respect.'

~ WR Koehler ~

As soon as your gorgeous retriever puppy arrives at their new home, they learn who is really in charge and where they fit in the family hierarchy. While we might like to believe all people are created equal, this is not the case in the dog world. For our beloved canine companions, there is a pecking order regardless of whether you are an animal or a person. As the owner, if you are not quick to demonstrate to your puppy that you are higher up the totem pole than they are and aren't consistent with the rules, your retriever puppy will soon begin to push the boundaries. You can establish authority by being a strong leader during training sessions and your daily encounters with your dog.

This does not mean you should be harsh, loud, or mean. It simply involves you finding the right energy within yourself (see details in Chapter 7) that your dog responds to best. For example, when teaching your dog to '***Sit***' on command, if your voice sounds weak or questioning rather than commanding, your puppy will probably ignore you. Dogs need to have a dominant leader who they trust and respect, so they can learn to obediently follow commands and understand the rules and boundaries.

Basic Rules and Boundaries

You can prevent many future issues when you take the time to teach your golden retriever basic rules and boundaries. All you need to effectively teach your puppy these basics is a composed, consistent, and firm approach, along with endless patience.

Basic rules and boundaries include things such as:

- No barking at every little sound.
- No dogs in the kitchen when preparing food.
- No begging at the dinner table.
- People through the door first.
- No sleeping on a human's bed.
- No raiding the rubbish bin.

- No jumping up on tables or worktops.
- No jumping on people.
- No chasing the neighbour's cat.
- No digging in the flowerbed.

When teaching a rule or establishing a boundary, you need to tell your puppy when they have done something wrong. The way to do this is through tone of voice, so your puppy removes themselves from the unwanted activity.

For example, if your retriever barks excessively every time someone knocks on the door or rings the doorbell, you must take control and tell your dog to stop barking and move away from the front door. The following simple steps can help:

- Walk to the front door.
- Stand between the door and your retriever.
- Make eye contact with your dog while pointing away from the door and firmly saying, '***Go!***'
- If your retriever does not move away, walk towards them so they must back up.
- Keep pointing and forcing them to back away.
- Firmly say, '***Go!***' again.
- Once your dog has backed away at least three metres, keep an eye on them while returning to the door to let your guest in.
- If your golden immediately rushes to the door when it opens, step between them and your guest again while firmly saying, '***Go!***' and pointing away.
- Walk to the front door.
- Repeat as necessary.

Every situation is unique, and every dog is different, which means it might only take one or two times to teach your golden to desist from this unwanted behaviour. Alternatively, it may take considerably longer. Persistence and consistency are key. The same steps outlined above can be very effective when teaching a range of rules and boundaries.

TIP ***To establish boundaries, it is useful to have a 'Discipline Sound'. You can use it to redirect your puppy when they engage in unwanted behaviour. They will quickly learn what they can or cannot do.***

The best discipline sounds are short and sharp, so they immediately get the attention of your puppy. You can use them to interrupt or redirect your pup before they make a mistake. It doesn't matter what the sound is if it gets your dog's attention and everyone in the family is consistent with it. In most cases, a simple 'Uh!' said sharply and with emphasis is very effective. Most dogs respond immediately to this, and if caught doing something they are not supposed to be doing, they will quickly stop and give their attention to you.

Enrol your golden in a training class

If you are a new owner, it is advisable to book your puppy on a puppy training course. It is a good way to socialise your golden with other dogs whilst they learn basic obedience and commands. Your puppy can then implement what they have learnt when meeting other dogs at the park or on walks.

With an expert on hand to guide you and your retriever, taking your dog to a professional training class is an excellent way to build your relationship in a safe and structured way. If possible, attend a class rather than just training at home, even if you've trained a pup before. A professional trainer can give you tips to help you effectively teach your dog and can offer advice on subjects you may not have considered.

Before booking, try to go along and watch a class without your dog to get a feel for what's involved. Good classes have:

- An approachable trainer who positively helps dogs and their owners.
- A calm atmosphere with no overly excited dogs or lots of barking, which can be a sign of stress. Both dogs and owners should be relaxed.
- The dogs should not be playing uncontrollably.
- The ratio of trainers to dogs should be sufficient to handle the number of dogs in the class.
- There should be positive and reward-based training methods. If dogs are punished, or equipment such as choke or electric collars are recommended, do not enrol.

It is worth noting that there are no regulations for dog training classes, so quality can differ greatly. Blue Cross only recommends training classes where the trainer uses modern, science-backed training methods. These focus on rewarding your dog with praise, food, and play for doing well rather than punishing them when they get it wrong. If you make it clear your retriever has done well, they are far more likely to repeat their clever work. Positive training is an effective way to build their confidence in themselves and trust in you.

Avoid trainers who advise aversive training equipment, such as choke or pinch collars, or punitive methods, such as physically forcing a dog into a sit or yanking them into position. These training techniques can be stressful for your dog and may even cause them pain.

TIP

Search the Association of Pet Dog Trainers or Puppy School websites to find a trainer local to you. Also, the Kennel Club in the United Kingdom—and the AKC in the U.S.A.—offer training classes, as do other dog trusts and funds, which can be online or in person. Additionally, many veterinary clinics provide dog training classes.

The largest dog training programme in the U.K. is The Kennel Club Good Citizen Dog Scheme. It is open to all dogs, young or old, pedigree or mutt. Your dog does not need to be registered with The Kennel Club to take part. This scheme aims at promoting responsible dog ownership by teaching guardians to train their dogs for everyday life situations. It has four award levels: Puppy Foundation, Bronze, Silver, and Gold.

Top 20 Training Tips

1. It's never too early to begin training. Start as soon as your golden puppy arrives home. Puppies are much more susceptible to learning new things when they are very young.
2. Always train with an upbeat attitude and positive energy. Dogs learn quicker when they don't feel stressed or pressured by their owner. If you are not in a friendly and positive mood when training, your dog might get confused. When training sessions are fun and filled with plenty of food rewards, your retriever will be a content, attentive student who trusts and respects you and looks forward to learning new commands, tricks, and routines.
3. Use positive reinforcement for good behaviour—toys, treats, play, games, love, walks, and happy praise. Give treats or other rewards to your puppy the moment they complete the desired behaviour. The faster you confirm the behaviour you want, the easier it is for your puppy to understand what you are trying to teach.

4. Train your puppy often and for brief periods—5 to 10 minutes. Puppies have short attention spans, so if training sessions are too long, they will zone out, and you'll be wasting your time.
5. Do not train your puppy when they are hot, tired, or in the middle of playing. You want them focused and eager to train.
6. Eliminate distractions during training. Choose a quiet place away from noise, children, or other pets. When puppies are young, they are easily distracted and will have a more difficult time concentrating on training if there are other things to get their attention.
7. Be consistent when teaching and always follow the same routine. Changing the way you are teaching a certain command/trick or using a different approach will only confuse your retriever and make it more difficult for them to learn.
8. Resist using too many confusing words—one-word commands work best. For instance, when teaching your dog to lie down on command, rather than saying, '***Hey boy, lie down***', simply say, '***Down***'.
9. When teaching commands, use a hand signal and the command word at the same time. Once your dog has learnt the hand signals for the commands, you won't need to say the words.
10. Never become short-tempered, frustrated, or impatient during training, as your dog will pick up on this negative energy and get confused. If you feel you are about to lose your cool, end the session and try again later. Yelling at your retriever could make them nervous, and they will stop paying attention to you. If they fear training, they might decide following directions is not a good idea.
11. Say a command word, such as '***Sit***' or '***Down***' once. Dogs are smart, so they can follow a command the first time. Repeating the cue word multiple times will not help your pup sharpen their listening skills, and like a teenager, they will tune you out. Moreover, you'll teach them they don't need to obey you until you've repeated yourself a few times.

12. Schedule training sessions before mealtimes. This way, they might pay closer attention to the instructions so they can earn a yummy treat.
13. When several family members are involved in training, everyone needs to use the same command words and hand signals to avoid confusing your dog.
14. Use what your dog loves best as a reward for learning commands or routines. This can be a toy, treat, playtime, or a walk. Some dogs desperately want a food treat for learning, while others prefer a toy or a game of fetch as a reward after a training session.
15. Have realistic expectations of your puppy's mental and physical limitations. Do not expect too much too soon with a very young puppy. Be patient and do not give up on your golden retriever puppy if they take longer than you would like to learn what you are teaching them.
16. Dogs learn quicker when they receive a reward for good behaviour. For instance, if your dog is barking at the postman, calmly correct them and give them a treat when they stop barking.
17. Dogs live in the moment. Two minutes after they have done something, they have already forgotten about it. So, when your golden pup is doing something bad, use your chosen 'Discipline Sound' immediately so they can make the association between the behaviour and the correction. Consistent repetition will reinforce the lesson.

18. Avoid using punishment such as lead corrections or yelling. Punishment can make your retriever confused and unsure about what is being asked of them.
19. Always finish a training session on a high note, with plenty of loving praise, scratches, tummy rubs, a toy, a treat, a walk, or a game. If your puppy has trouble learning a new behaviour, end the session by getting them to do something they have already learnt. Then give them plenty of praise and a reward for their success. We always want our dogs to look forward to their next training session, and the best way to ensure that is through positive reinforcement.
20. It is also a great idea to record your puppy's progress so you know exactly where you left off at any given time. You can film the training sessions or just take notes.

Basic Obedience Training

A puppy needs to learn the basic obedience commands to ensure that they remain safe in almost every situation. For example, when your puppy correctly learns the '***Come***' command, you can quickly call them back if danger is approaching. Also, when teaching these commands, you are further reinforcing your leadership role. If your golden understands that you are the boss, they will be a safe and obedient follower. If it is fun, your puppy will look forward to their next session.

TIP ***It is important to use the hand signals accompanying verbal commands while training your golden retriever. These hand signals can be particularly helpful during the senior years of your dog's life when their hearing might be compromised.***

When you take the time to teach your golden hand signals for all basic commands, you are communicating with them at a level they instinctively understand. In addition, you are helping them to become a focused follower because they need to watch you to understand what you want.

The Three Ds

Sometimes, you can think you have trained your dog to do something, only for them to act as if they haven't got a clue what you mean when you give them a command. Perhaps your retriever stayed beautifully when they were next to you in your quiet kitchen. But when you ask them to '***Stay***' from 10 metres away in the park, they ignore you. This is a powerful demonstration of the importance of the three Ds of dog training.

The three Ds are duration, distance, and distraction. They affect almost every command. Dogs are not good at generalising. If they learn to stay in front of you, they do not automatically understand that '***Stay***' has the same meaning when you are on the other side of the room. As each D increases, it is harder for your golden to know how to successfully perform your command. If all three are in effect at any given time, if you haven't individually trained your dog for each D, the chances of them doing what you want are slim.

Duration is the length of time your dog can hold a command. Some commands, such as shaking hands or jumping over an obstacle, have no specific duration. With other commands, such as '***Sit***' or '***Down***', you need your dog to maintain a position for a certain amount of time. The longer they must hold it, the more difficult the task becomes.

Whenever you teach a new command, start with a very short duration, such as a second. Then incrementally increase the amount of time, trying not to expect more from your dog than they're capable of doing. If your retriever gets it wrong, reduce the duration to something you know they can handle and start building one second at a time from there.

Distance is how far away you can get from your dog before they ignore the command. The farther away you are, the less reliable your dog will become. As with duration, when you are training distance, start close and move away slowly. Ensure your retriever can handle a relatively long distance with you in front of them before you move to their side or behind them. Keep leaving the room for last. Your dog knows when you cannot see them, so turning your back or walking out of sight is really challenging for them.

Distraction involves everything going on around your dog when they perform a command, from a squirrel running across the garden to the sound of the doorbell. Anything your dog finds exciting or disrupting is a distraction. Some dogs even find treats distracting. Make sure your dog has mastered duration and distance before you work on distractions. Start by training new commands in a familiar, quiet environment where you are the most interesting thing in the room.

When training your golden retriever, focus on one D at a time. You should only combine the Ds once your dog has mastered each D on its own. So, when working on distance, shorten the duration and keep distractions to a minimum. Set your golden up for success by not rushing them.

If you see your dog struggling to perform a command you thought they knew, think about the three Ds. The chances are something is too difficult for them to handle. Incorporating duration, distance, and distraction into your training will ensure your retriever understands what you are asking no matter what.

Come

The first and most important command to teach your golden is the '***Come***' or '***Recall***' command.

- Start in a larger room in your home, such as the living room or hallway.
- Put your puppy in front of you and attach their lead to their collar. Back away a couple of metres.
- Say '***Come***' in an excited, upbeat voice and stretch your arms out wide.
- If your golden does not immediately move toward you, gently tug on the lead so they understand what they are supposed to do.
- When they come to you, enthusiastically praise them, and give them a treat.

Once your puppy can obey the '***Come***' command almost every time inside the home, they can be taken to a nearby park or quiet outside space to work on their recall where there are many more distractions. The goal of the '***Come***' command is to keep you and your dog safe. Successful implementation of this cue is when your golden retriever always comes to you when asked, despite distractions.

A helpful tool when working on the '***Come***' command is an extra-long, lightweight line of 6-12 metres (25-50 feet). You can use this to attach the puppy to you and encourage them in the right direction should they become distracted by noises, scents, and other dogs.

When first working on the '***Come***' command outside, choose a time of day when there are fewer distractions. For example, if you know there are going to be lots of children or dogs running around at the local park at certain times, it's best to avoid these distractions when working on recall. Instead, try to go out when the park is quiet, such as early in the morning.

TIP ***The most important thing to remember is that coming on command must always be a pleasant experience for your retriever. If you ask your dog to 'Come' when you are annoyed so you can discipline them, your dog will soon learn to ignore this important command. You should always give positive praise and/or a treat when your retriever comes when called.***

Once your dog always comes happily running to you when called, you don't always have to say '***Come***'. Instead, you can simply show them the signal. The best thing about the arms wide open gesture is that it can be seen from afar. A well-trained puppy will come running to your open arms, even if they are on the other side of the park.

However, it's important to remember that even if your dog has good recall, sometimes they can still be distracted by an interesting scent or fast-moving object or creature. Keep your young golden on lead in an area where they can easily run off in pursuit of any distraction.

Sit

The '***Sit***' command is another important one which helps keep your puppy safe. For example, if you teach your dog to sit at kerbs, it will make crossing roads safer. Asking your dog to sit when they greet people means they are less likely to jump up.

- Have a treat in your hand as you ask your retriever to '***Sit***'. Put the treat in front of their nose and lift it above their head. They will naturally sit as they follow the treat with their nose.
- Do NOT just push them down into a sit, as this can cause damage to their back or joints.

- The moment they sit, give them a treat and praise them.
- When saying the word '***Sit***', at the same time, show the hand signal for this command.
- The universal hand signal for '***Sit***' is a right arm—palm open facing upward—parallel to the floor, and then raising your arm while bending at the elbow towards the right shoulder.
- Once your dog is reliably sitting on command, remove the verbal '***Sit***' and replace it with just the hand signal.

Every time you take your retriever out for a walk—which is a really exciting time!—get into the habit of asking them to sit quietly and patiently at every opportunity, including:

- When putting on your puppy's lead.
- While you are putting on your shoes or jacket.
- Before you open the door.
- When you are on the other side of the door.
- While you lock the door.
- Every time you arrive at a road junction.
- Every time you stop during your walk to speak to a neighbour, greet a friend, admire the view, etc.

TIP ***If you consistently take advantage of the many opportunities during a walk to ask your retriever puppy to 'Sit', it will become automatic for them to calmly sit every time you stop walking. Congratulations! This is called an 'automatic' sit.***

When asking your golden retriever to '***Sit***', you are actually teaching them multiple things. You are telling them they need to stay still while paying attention to you. You are showing them you are their boss. As such, they must look to you for direction and respect you as their leader.

Remember, a sitting puppy is easier to control than one bounding about, ready to bolt out the door or jump up on someone. As an added bonus, the action of sitting helps to calm the mind of an excited puppy. Teaching this command can enhance their daily interactions with family members, friends, and even strangers.

Stay

When your golden can reliably '***Sit***', it is time to introduce the '***Stay***' command. This command tells your retriever to remain in place until they are released. Using this command in conjunction with a movement command such as '***Sit***' helps your retriever to understand what is expected of them.

The biggest mistake people make when teaching '***Stay***' is undermining the command by encouraging their dog to break the position rather than hold it. For example, if you ask your dog to '***Stay***', walk away, then call them to you, you are teaching them to break the position you just asked them to hold. Smart dogs will anticipate your release, and their '***Stay***' will become unreliable.

- Place your dog in a '***Sit***' and say the word '***Stay***' with authority in your voice. Hold your arm outstretched, and your palm open towards your retriever's head as you back away a few steps.
- If they try to follow, calmly say, '***No***' and put them back into '***Sit***'.
- Give them a treat and then repeat, '***Stay***' with the hand signal and back away a few steps.

- Do not let your dog break the '***Stay***' until you return to them. Give them a treat and say something appropriate like 'Off you go.'

Down

Another basic command every dog should know is the '***Down***' command. This instructs them to lie down. This is very useful to get your dog to settle on the floor, either at home or when you are out and about in shops, restaurants, etc.

- Start with your dog in the '***Sit***' position, then hold a treat about 15 centimetres in front of their nose.
- Slowly lower the treat to the floor in front of them, moving your hand farther away as you lower it.
- Simultaneously say, '***Down***' in a firm but encouraging voice.
- You want your dog to stretch forwards and slide down, following the treat.
- Once their tummy hits the floor, give them the treat and plenty of praise.
- With patience, consistency, repetition, and copious treats, this is a command most dogs learn very quickly. Practise often and in different places. Once your golden is happily lying down on command in your home, continue training in more distracting environments, such as the garden or your local park.

Leave It

As an owner, you'll sometimes need to take things away from your golden retriever, for example, if they have picked up something dangerous or are playing with your favourite shoe instead of a toy. Getting your dog to '***Leave it***' teaches them it is all right to have something taken away from them because they'll get a treat instead. Follow these basic steps:

- Offer your dog a delicious treat and encourage them to take it in a cheerful, friendly voice.
- Hold another treat in your hand with your fist closed around it. Your golden is likely to nudge and lick your hand to get the treat out. Ignore their attempts.
- Wait patiently and say nothing until your dog backs off from your hand, even if only momentarily. As soon as they do, when there is a small gap between your hand and your retriever's nose, open your hand, release the treat, and shower them with praise.
- Repeat these three steps until they consistently choose to move away from the treat.
- Once your dog always moves away from the treat, you can start adding in the cue words '***Leave it***'. Say this in a gentle tone as they back off, and then open your hand to give them the treat and praise them.
- Once your retriever has made the association between the words '***Leave it***' and backing off from the treat, you can start making it more challenging. Place a treat on your open palm, so your dog can see and smell it. Instruct your dog to leave it by saying '***Leave it***'.
- If your dog does not touch the treat, reward them with lots of praise and a treat from your other hand. If your golden goes to take the treat from your open palm, simply close your hand and wait for them to back away.

Practise the above basic commands everywhere at any opportunity and use them as frequently as possible to ensure their success. As your puppy matures and their attention span increases, you can train them for longer periods and introduce more complicated routines.

Teaching Tricks

Many people only think about basic dog training commands as being the essentials of dog training. Although those are important, do not underestimate the benefits of training your dog to do tricks. They are a great way of giving your golden retriever some much-needed mental stimulation. Several tricks build on the basic commands, reinforcing them. Also, it can be a lot of fun teaching your dog some cool tricks to show off to friends!

Shake a Paw

Who doesn't love a well-trained dog who knows how to give a handshake? This is one of the easiest tricks to teach your dog.

- Stand or sit in front of your retriever.
- Place them in the sitting position.
- Say the command '***Shake***' while putting your right hand behind their left or right paw. At the same time, pull the paw gently towards you until you are holding their paw in your right hand. Most dogs are naturally either right or left-pawed. If you know which paw your dog favours, ask them to shake that one.
- Immediately praise them and give them their favourite treat.
- Most dogs learn this trick quite quickly. If won't be long before you can put out your hand, and your golden will immediately lift their paw to meet it without assistance or verbal cues.

Practise every day until they are completely reliable with this trick. Then it's time to add another one to their repertoire.

Roll Over

You will find that just as your retriever is either naturally right or left-pawed, they will also prefer to roll either onto their right or left side. Take advantage of this by asking your dog to roll to the side they naturally favour.

- Sit with your dog on the floor and put them in a lie-down position.
- Hold a treat in your hand and place it close to their nose without allowing them to grab it.
- While they are in the lying position, move the treat to the right or left side of their head—their nose will follow the treat—so they must roll over to get to it.
- You will very quickly see which side they want to naturally roll to. Once you've identified it, move the treat to that side.
- When they roll over to that side, immediately give them the treat and praise them.
- Say the verbal cue '***Over***' while you demonstrate the hand signal—turning your right hand in a circular motion—or move the treat from one side of their head to the other with a half-circle motion.
- With enough practice, your retriever will roll over when they see just the hand signal.

Sit Pretty

'***Sit pretty***' or '***Beg***' is a cute trick. Your golden retriever starts in the sit position and then raises their front legs until they are sitting on their back legs with the front legs curled and held in front of them. This trick is a little more advanced, so always exercise patience.

- Sit or stand in front of your dog and ask them to '***Sit***'.
- Have a treat nearby. When they sit, use both hands to lift their front paws into the sitting pretty position while saying the command, '***Sit pretty***'.
- Help them balance in this position while you praise them and give them a treat.
- Repeat these steps until your retriever can perform the balancing part of the trick without your help.
- Sit or stand in front of them while holding the treat above their head level with their nose and tell them to '***Sit pretty***'.
- If they attempt to stand on their back legs to get the treat, you may be holding it too high, which will encourage them to stand on their back legs to reach it. Return to the first step and put them back into the '***Sit***' position, and again lift their paws with their backside on the floor.
- After they learn to do the trick on verbal command, try saying the verbal cue while performing the hand signal. Holding your arm straight, fully extend it over your golden's head with your fist closed.

- Practise a few times every day until they can '***Sit pretty***' with just the hand signal command every time you ask.

Collar, Harness, and Lead Training

Adjusting the collar/harness

Whether you decide to have your puppy in a collar or a harness, make sure they fit properly before teaching them to walk beside you on a lead.

TIP ***When fitting your retriever's collar, it shouldn't be so tight it almost chokes them, but also it shouldn't be too loose as your puppy could pull their head out of it. As a rough guide, a flat collar should be approximately five centimetres larger than your puppy's neck.***

When adjusting a Martingale collar, the two outside rings should never be touching when the lead is attached and there is tension on the lead.

If using a harness, it should be snug around the broadest part of your golden's chest, so they can't slip out of it, but not so tight that they can't move freely.

Putting on the collar/harness

It is always a good idea to introduce your retriever puppy to their collar or harness shortly after you bring them home from the breeder so they get used to wearing one before you start using a lead. Below are the steps for putting on their collar. The process is the same for putting on a harness:

- Ask your puppy to come to you and calmly sit.

- Let them see and sniff the collar and then put it on them. Have plenty of treats to hand so you can distract them if the sensation of the collar causes them to act as if they are being tortured.
- If your puppy fights having their collar put on, offer a treat or play a game to distract them. Only remove their collar when they stop fretting. Give them another treat for being so good.
- Soon, they will learn that when the collar goes on, they get a nice treat.

Attaching the lead

Once your retriever puppy is used to the feel of the collar or harness, it is time to introduce the lead.

Some new dog owners experience a frustrating situation when first introducing a lead to their puppy. Instead of sitting quietly while their lead is attached, the pup decides that now's the best time to play catch me if you can.. This type of game is very entertaining for your puppy, so every time they see you pick up their lead, the chase is on. You can avoid this type of situation by following these steps every time you attach their lead:

- First, stand or sit in front of your puppy and show them the lead.
- The moment your golden shows any interest in it, immediately give them a treat.
- Put the lead behind your back for a few seconds and then show it to them again, and instantly give them a treat. Now your puppy is learning to associate their lead with something positive.
- Next, attach the lead to your puppy's collar and again follow with a treat.
- Take their lead off and put it away. Repeat this process several times during the day until your retriever regularly sits calmly while their lead is attached.

Practise all this before going out for your first on-lead walk. Once your puppy learns to associate their lead with a fun outdoor adventure, they will not need a treat for sitting quietly while you attach it.

Walking on a lead

Before your golden's first outside lead walk, attach the lead to their collar—or harness—and practise a few short walks inside. This will help them get used to the feeling of being attached to the lead. If they refuse to walk with you and there is tension on the lead because your puppy lies down, keep some forward tension on the lead and encourage them to walk towards you. When they do, give them a treat. Continue short indoor lead walks until your puppy feels more comfortable.

Now you can set out for the great outdoors with your puppy on a lead. A young retriever puppy who has not yet explored their new neighbourhood will be distracted by all the sights, sounds, and smells. Depending on the puppy, their first lead outing could be the source of much excitement and darting everywhere, or it might be scary and overwhelming.

Whatever type of puppy you have, you should be patient and take the time to show them lead walking is not an exercise in tug-of-war but is about walking together with no tension or lead pulling.

There are two important habits you want your golden to grasp early on in their lead training: looking to you for direction and never moving forwards when there is tension on the lead.

Habit 1: When your puppy looks to you for direction, they recognise they are not walking alone but walking with you. Forming this habit begins with the very first on-lead walk:

- As you walk, cheerfully say your puppy's name, and the second they look at you, reward them with a treat or happy praise.
- Repeat, repeat, repeat, and soon your golden puppy will regularly look to you for direction when out on a walk.

Habit 2: At the same time, you want your retriever puppy to form the habit of stopping when there is any tension felt on the lead. Some people call this exercise 'Red Light/Green Light' or 'Stop/Go'. Whether you call it a game or an exercise, all it means is your puppy can only move forwards if they are NOT pulling on the lead. Be prepared to be patient. You may well find there are many outdoor walks that are short and sweet. That is okay because if you practise the following steps, after a while, on-lead walks become a breeze:

- Start walking slowly with your retriever by your side.
- The second your puppy begins to tug on their lead, simply stop moving—Red light.
- Wait for them to look at you.
- Encourage them to come closer—with praise or a treat—which will release the tension on the lead.
- Start walking again and keep going as long as there is no tension on the lead—Green light.

Practising these two habits every time you take your puppy outside on-lead will soon result in a comfortable walk with no pulling and an attentive dog who always checks in with you.

Leads

Leads (see picture) come in many types, materials, and lengths. When choosing a lead for your dog, consider the following:

- The size of your dog—larger dogs need a stronger lead.
- The strength of the lead—a lighter lead for a smaller dog.
- The width of the lead—a wide lead might be uncomfortable to hold.
- The size of the clip at the collar end—a large and heavy clip will not be suitable for a small dog.
- The length of the lead—1.5 to 2 metres (5 to 6.5 feet) is suitable for any sized dog.

FACT ***In the U.K., according to the Countryside and Rights of Way Act 2000, dog owners must keep their dogs on short, fixed-length leads—two metres or less—in some circumstances. However, many councils have decided to reduce this to 1.5 metres, and in Devon, one council has reduced this even further to 1 metre.***

As there are so many styles and designs of dog leads to choose from, it can be difficult to decide which one you need. Your best option is to choose one that is functional and fits your lifestyle. These are the main lead types:

Standard Lead – These leads are for basic training and everyday use. They have a loop handle at one end and a metal clip at the other end to attach to your golden's collar. Typically, they are 1.2 to 2.4 metres (4 to 8 feet). The 1.8-metre (6-foot) length is ideal for most dogs. These leads are made from leather, nylon, cotton web, or rope and can be flat or round. Flat leads come in a variety of widths. Usually, the thicker and wider ones are for larger and stronger dogs. Leather leads are more durable, and some owners feel they are more stylish. Normally, rope leads are round instead of flat and extremely tough.

Hands-Free Lead – As the name would suggest, these leads keep your hands free because they attach around your waist or over your shoulder like a sash. This is a good option if you need to carry things during your walk or if you want to go on a jog with your retriever.

Double Lead – The double lead is convenient for walking two dogs at the same time because it has two leads attached to one handle. This type of lead works best with two similarly sized dogs since it requires the dogs to move in tandem.

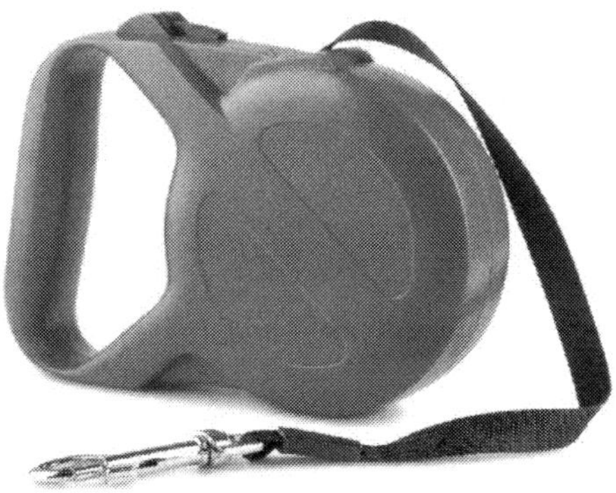

City Lead – A city lead—also known as a 'traffic lead'—is a short lead of less than 1.2 metres (4 feet) used to keep better control of your dog. It is useful when walking on busy pavements or heavily crowded areas where you need to keep your dog's head close by your side.

Flexi-Lead – A flexi, retractable or extendable lead (see picture) is usually spring-loaded and very long—up to 8 metres (26 feet). A thin cord winds up inside a plastic compartment with a handle and a button to control how much lead is extended. These leads are controversial for several reasons, including:

- They can be dangerous for both humans and dogs. Do not let your dog out of your sight when on these leads, especially at longer lengths. It could become tangled, or your dog might get into a hazardous situation. These leads are also serious tripping hazards that can cause broken bones and rope burns.
- Your retriever can get in the wrong walking position. These leads should only be introduced after your dog has been trained to walk by your side on a regular lead. Otherwise, your dog will learn to pull on the lead, an extremely bad habit.
- The large plastic handles are heavy, clumsy, and hard to grip securely. If your retriever suddenly lunges or changes direction, the chances of losing your grip are quite high.
- They are prone to accidentally breaking. Be sure to regularly check along the entire length of your retractable lead for frayed, worn, or damaged areas, as this is quite common.

TIP ***If you just want one lead for your golden retriever, it is recommended that you get a standard 1.2 metre (4-foot) lead. This provides better control, improved training, and safety, and will make your life easier in most circumstances.***

Some dog owners choose to use different types of dog leads for different purposes. One lead could be for daily walks and another for hiking with your golden in the mountains or bike rides. You might choose a certain type of lead specifically for dog training.

Collars

It is vital to choose the right kind of collar for your retriever. There is an ever-increasing array of tempting colours, materials, and styles to choose from. This makes it easy to become distracted by appearances and forget about choosing what is most appropriate for your dog. Here are the most common collar types:

Flat Collars – The most important feature of a collar is its ability to keep your golden safe and secure. Flat collars (see picture) can be relatively easy for most dogs to get out of unless they are so tight that they almost cut off your dog's air supply. Even with a firm grip on the lead, your retriever could back away, wiggle, twist and contort themselves in an instant, flip their head, and the collar is off—bye, bye doggy!

Martingale Collars – While the Martingale collar is considered a 'training' collar, there is no reason why it cannot be your retriever's everyday collar, as it is very comfortable. There are several reasons why this type of dog collar (see picture) is considered better than a flat collar:

- It is comfortable for your dog to wear all day.
- They are strong and safe, and your dog cannot wriggle out of them.
- They are the best training collar.

The Martingale collar looks much the same as a flat collar, with one very important difference—it has a triangular piece of chain in the middle. This chain is attached to the collar—the red loop in the picture—with two rings and a third ring in the middle of the chain for attaching the lead.

When there is no tension from the dog pulling on the lead, the collar hangs comfortably loose. However, when there is tension on the collar, the chain tightens so your golden cannot escape the collar. The chain also makes a slight noise when you sharply tug or jiggle it, sending a message to your dog that you want their attention on you. This is considered one of the best collars for teaching your dog to walk calmly by your side.

Some Martingale collars have a plastic clip attachment. However, these are not as strong as the ones that fit over the head.

When buying one of these collars, take your golden with you because it needs to be the correct size to fit over the widest part of the head. Then, once you have the right size for your retriever, you need to learn the correct way to adjust the collar for maximum effect and safety. Adjust the length so that when the lead is attached to the outside ring and pulled tight, and the two inside rings come together, there is still a gap between the two rings of approximately two finger widths so your dog won't be choked. The two inside rings should never touch.

Bark Collars – There are three different types of bark collars. Some vibrate, others release a strong-smelling citronella spray, while others emit a high-pitched sound only audible to your dog. All these methods are designed to stop barking but may or may not be effective.

FACT ***This negative training tool can incite fearful, anxious, or aggressive behaviour in your dog, especially if you don't understand how to use them properly.***

Choke Chain Collars – Also known as a '*slip chain*', this type of collar can be painful and uncomfortable. This is a negative way to teach your golden retriever not to pull when lead walking.

There is a great deal of controversy about these collars among dog owners because, as the name suggests, when your dog pulls against the lead, they feel a choking sensation. While this type of collar can help train larger dogs when used correctly, there are better ways to teach a dog to walk beside you without making them uncomfortable.

Halti (Head) Collars – This type of collar is known by several different names, including '*gentle leader*', '*Halti*', '*head collar*' or '*head halter*'. It is designed like a halter on a horse to provide better control of your dog's head and prevent them from pulling when out lead walking.

Depending on your dog and how early you introduce them to this type of collar, it might be an appropriate training tool. However, some people think the Halti is a muzzle and will avoid you because they think your retriever could be dangerous. Furthermore, some dogs will fight this type of collar and do everything to remove it, while others can become overly subdued.

Prong or Pinch Collars – This type of aggressive-looking collar has inward-facing prongs. When your dog pulls on their lead, these twist and pinch the skin of your dog's neck and scruff, hurting them. The idea behind the collar is to prevent a large, powerful dog from pulling on the lead. It is never a good idea to use pain as a deterrent, as this can backfire and create other problems, especially when there are so many other positive ways of teaching proper lead walking.

Relaxation Collars – There are two types of collars designed to help relax or calm an upset retriever. One uses scent or calming pheromones, while the other uses species-specific music at an appropriate volume to calm your fearful or stressed dog.

Harnesses

There are many different types, styles, and colours of harnesses. Some have D-rings in multiple locations, reflective stripes for safety in low lighting, pockets for carrying gear, or handles for lifting your dog.

Even if your dog doesn't pull, harnesses are comfortable and offer excellent control of your dog.

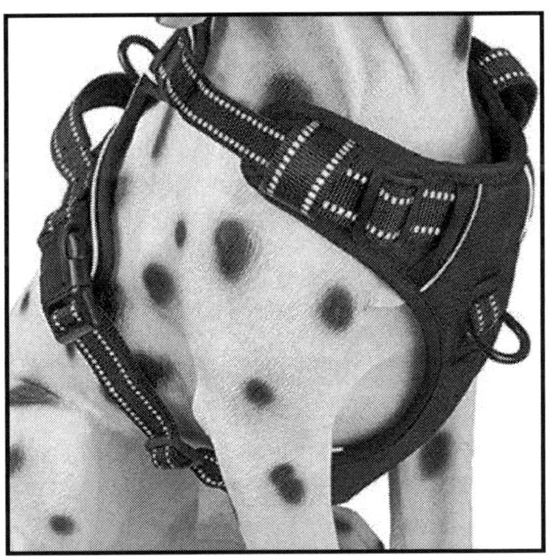

Vest – The vest harness is a good choice for dogs who do not pull. The advantage of this type of harness is that they fit comfortably like a piece of clothing and are less likely to chafe under your retriever's armpits.

You need to consider all your options when choosing the harness that works best for you and your dog. Take into consideration your golden's weight and personality when determining the best size and type of dog harness. The various styles of harnesses fit differently.

Measure around your retriever's rib cage to ensure you are buying the right size. If the harness is too tight, it will be painful for your dog, but if it is too loose, your dog might easily slip out of it.

It should not be possible to pull the harness over your retriever's head, but you should be able to fit two fingers under all the straps that attach it to your dog. To test the dog harness, have your dog walk around your home with it on so you can be certain the harness does not shift about their body or rub uncomfortably against their skin.

Consider how much or how hard your dog pulls when choosing a harness. Buying the wrong harness can make it easier for your dog to pull you around. Get an 'anti-pull' harness if your retriever pulls.

FACT ***Harnesses work by distributing the weight and pressure of the lead away from your golden's collar and neck and onto their shoulders, chest, and back. This will significantly reduce the risk of neck strain or choking.***

Back Clip – One of the most basic yet versatile harnesses is the back clip. The harness has a metal D-loop sewn into the fabric at about the middle of your dog's back to attach the lead. This type of harness might encourage a puller to pull even more.

Front Clip – This is also known as an 'anti-pull' harness and is like the back clip, but in these harnesses, the clip is placed in front of your dog's chest. These can help teach your golden retriever not to pull and tug on their lead.

Side Clip – This type of harness is also considered an 'anti-pull' type, as it has the D-ring at the side, so when your dog begins to pull on their lead, they are directed back towards you.

Training Methods

There are many different types and combinations of dog training methods. For most dogs, the most effective training method is positive reinforcement. One form of positive reinforcement is clicker training using a clicker.

Positive Reinforcement (Training with Rewards)

As the name implies, this positive reinforcement involves teaching your golden commands, routines, tricks, or sports by rewarding them for wanted behaviour. The reward could be anything your dog likes, including treats, toys, praise, being groomed, going off lead during walks, playing in the water, or travelling in the car. Every dog is different, so they naturally find different things rewarding. However, almost every dog enjoys food, toys, and attention.

Reward training is all about teaching your golden retriever that good things happen when they make the right choice. If your dog receives a reward, they will associate it with whatever they just did, which will make it more likely for them to repeat it next time.

The best way to encourage your dog to behave the way you want them to—such as learning to settle down when you are busy—is to train them with rewards for the following reasons:

- Science tells us that reward-based training is the best way for dogs to learn.
- Training with rewards is fun and helps build a positive bond between dog and owner.
- Owners who train using rewards report fewer behavioural problems with their dogs.
- Reward-based training can help build confidence and encourage dogs to think for themselves.

All the training instructions for the various commands, tricks, and routines presented in this chapter are reward-based for positive reinforcement.

Reward your puppy whenever you notice them doing something good instead of telling them off for doing something wrong. Make sure it is a reward your golden really likes. It could be a gentle fuss, stroking them, or simply speaking softly to your dog when they are behaving calmly, so the reward does not excite them. By contrast, if they are doing something active, such as running over to you as soon as you call them, rewarding this behaviour with an active and energetic game is the perfect prize.

When you start teaching your retriever a new skill, it is important to reward them every time they do what you want. You can change the type of reward once they have learnt the new behaviour and can repeat it consistently in several different environments. This means you won't have to give them a treat for obeying the '***Sit***' command for the rest of their life. Instead, you can say, '***good dog***' and randomly give them a treat as an unexpected bonus.

For example, if you use food to teach your retriever a new behaviour, to begin with, you'll want to reward them every time they follow a command until they understand what you want them to do. As soon as they reliably obey, reward them every other time, then every third time. Then alternate giving a food reward and just giving verbal praise or making a fuss of them. This will keep your retriever engaged because they will not know when to expect their favourite type of reward.

It is a good idea to have a specific signal to let your retriever know when they are doing something you are happy about. The signal tells your dog, '*Great job! You did what I wanted, and I am about to give you a reward.*' It is essential to reward your dog immediately after the marker to reinforce the message that your dog has done what you required.

Some owners use a short, punchy word, such as '***Yes***' or '***Nice***', but you might prefer to use a clicker or simply give them a thumbs up. Whatever signal you choose, make sure everyone involved in training your dog uses it, so your retriever never becomes confused, no matter who is training them. When teaching a new behaviour, use the signal at the precise moment your dog is doing what you want. That will tell your retriever their reward is on its way, and they will have learnt exactly what to do again to get another reward.

You might need to offer different rewards at different times and places. There could be moments when your dog requires an extra or different reward. Sometimes, what was easy for your dog in the comfort and calm of home can become much harder when the environment is busier and more distracting. What was rewarding at home might not be as exciting for them outside. If there are distractions that make it hard for your golden to react, you might need to use something extra tempting in that location. It could be a favourite treat, game, or toy.

One of the best rewards you can give your golden retriever is your attention. Often, we underestimate how important it is. Most dogs feel good any time we look at, touch, or talk to them. It isn't only treats or toys which can persuade your dog to do something. We constantly influence their behaviour with our attention. Make sure your dog receives positive attention for the good choices they make, not just negative attention when they do something you don't want.

The Effect of Punitive Training on Emotion

Dogs who are trained using duress and force, using fear or pain to get them to do what you want, suffer much higher stress and anxiety levels than those trained using positive reward methods. Studies show that if your dog is punished by being pinned down on their back or side in an 'alpha roll' for example, this triggers the release of cortisol. Cortisol is a stress hormone produced by an activated amygdala—the part of the brain primarily involved in the processing of emotions and memories associated with fear—and primes the body for danger. If high levels of cortisol are released, the brain becomes overwhelmed, and the resulting state overrides rational thought. An owner might think their golden is being submissive or calm while they are being held down, but in fact, it's the opposite.

Stress from threats makes your retriever 'shut down,' effectively freezing them until the threat disappears. In this state of anxiety, your dog will stop learning and become insecure, frightened, and/or angry. If your dog cannot get away, the only option left is to bite, which is why so many trainers and owners who use this method of punishment are bitten. Most dogs get up and shake themselves after they experience an 'alpha roll'. This is called the 'shake-off' and is an effective way for them to relieve stress after a negative experience.

Clicker Training

Clicker training is a form of positive reinforcement training using a clicker. A clicker is a small, mechanical device that makes a clicking sound when you press a button.

The value of the clicker (see picture) is that it tells your dog exactly which behaviour you are rewarding so there is no confusion. By clicking at the appropriate time, you can 'mark' the moment your golden does what you want. Rather than having to guess what you wanted them to do, the click tells your dog exactly what they did right.

The clear and loud sound of the click also eliminates the different tones that come from your mood when voice training your golden retriever. The precise sound of the clicker helps your dog focus by removing some of the confusion that may occur with verbal commands.

The most important aspect of clicker training is timing. You must click at the exact moment your dog exhibits the desired behaviour and then immediately offer a treat. This encourages your puppy to work out exactly what they did to receive a reward. Most puppies learn to associate the click sound with the requested action very quickly, and they will be eager to do what you ask to get another treat.

If you decide to use a clicker, you need to teach your retriever what the click sound means. Sometimes referred to as 'loading the clicker,' you must pair the sound with a reward. Hold the clicker in your hand with treats at the ready. Place your dog in front of you, click the clicker and immediately give them a treat. Repeat this several times until your retriever realises that the sound of the click means they get a treat. Now, you can move on to using the clicker to teach some basic commands:

'***Come***' command with a clicker – Use the hand signal to ask your golden to '***Come***' (see Commands Training section above). The second your dog comes to you, CLICK the clicker and give them a treat.

'***Sit***' command with a clicker – Have your dog in the same room and use the hand signal for '***Sit***'. The second your dog's bottom touches the floor, CLICK the clicker, and give them a treat.

'***Stay***' command with a clicker – Have your dog sit in front of you and give the hand signal for '***Stay***' while you back away a metre or two. When your retriever remains sitting, immediately CLICK the clicker, and return to give your dog a treat.

You can use this training method for acknowledging good behaviour too. If your retriever is lying quietly on the mat instead of begging at the dining table, click then reward their behaviour. Likewise, if the doorbell rings and your dog keeps all four paws on the floor instead of jumping on your guests, click that moment.

TIP ***A clicker is a tool that can be used to increase the efficiency of positive reinforcement training. After the clicker has been repeatedly associated with a treat or reward, it will become a conditioned reinforcer. Note that this type of training method might not be very effective for a dog who is not particularly food motivated.***

Whilst you can use your marker with lure-and-reward training—using a reward to lure your dog into the behaviour you are looking for—it is also useful when shaping their behaviour. Shaping entails building complex behaviour by taking baby steps. For example, you can train your golden retriever to put all their toys back in the toy box. With patience and repetition, your retriever will soon learn to identify their toys, pick them up, take them to their toy box and drop them in it with just one word. For full details on how to train your golden retriever to perform this task, see *Top 15 Mental Stimulation Tips* in Chapter 12.

12. Golden Retriever Exercise

'The dog lives for the day, the hour, even the moment.'

~ Robert Falcon Scott ~

Golden retrievers are generally energetic dogs with plenty of stamina due to their hunting background. They have a lively and playful temperament, love to chase and romp, and are happiest and content when given a task to do. Depending on your interests, your retriever could make for a great hunting companion or a blue-ribbon performer in many different canine sports.

Supervision during play exercises with other dogs is always important with a young retriever puppy who has not yet learnt the rules and boundaries and is excited to see other dogs. You need to be fully in control to stop potential squabbles and be willing to quickly intervene to shut down any problematic situation, such as dogs exhibiting dominance.

Golden Exercise Requirements

Bear in mind that how active you are will impact the energy level and exercise tolerance of your dog. Maintaining your retriever's fitness through regular exercise goes beyond keeping them in shape. Here are some of the benefits of exercise for your dog:

- It burns excess calories to combat obesity.
- It keeps them well-behaved. Being active means they do not have to find other ways to entertain themselves, such as chewing on furniture or barking.
- It keeps their brain active, especially if you include mental stimulation games and puzzles in their exercise routine.
- Exercising with your golden is a good stress reliever for both of you.
- It reduces the risk of health problems such as arthritis, hip dysplasia, and obesity-related diseases such as diabetes and heart disease.
- When you spend time having fun out and about, it strengthens the bond between you.

Puppies

When golden retriever puppies are very young, you should avoid taking them on excessively long walks. It is more important to focus on short walks as part of their toilet training, complete their vaccination schedule, and let them get their exercise through indoor play sessions.

As a rule, young puppies should not be exercised beyond a few short walks a day as part of training them to go to the toilet outside. Puppies need a lot of time for napping and growing, which means that during the day, walks should be interspersed with play sessions, napping, and feeding.

Another consideration will be your puppy's vaccination schedule. Your puppy should not be taken out of the home or garden until approximately two weeks after their final vaccinations are complete.

TIP ***Vigorous exercise or long walks should only be considered once your puppy is at least six to eight months old. This gives your golden puppy plenty of rest and time to grow without harming young bones and muscles.***

Young puppies love entertaining games involving retrieving toys or balls, but they also need mental stimulation to grow their minds. Teaching simple tricks and basic commands can start as soon as you bring them home. Introducing your puppy to food puzzles, how to walk on lead or playing hide-and-seek will tire them out faster than a physical walk. Taking the time for regular play sessions with your new puppy will also make them happy and build a positive relationship between the two of you. Try to set aside times during the day when you have a break from your chores and engage your golden retriever puppy in fun games for 5 or 10 minutes.

By the time they are six months old, their bone structure will have developed enough that they can go for longer walks. Do not let them become exhausted, but gradually increase their exercise routine.

Adults

Adult golden retrievers need a decent amount of exercise every day to keep them active and healthy and stop them from getting bored. They are more than happy to walk with you a few times a day and love any opportunity to play with you. Be aware that if you've chosen a golden retriever puppy from working stock, they may need more time to run around than the average golden retriever.

Ideally, your golden retriever will need two hours of exercise every day. Most adult goldens will be content having a brisk walk for about an hour morning and evening with plenty of opportunities for a good sniff around. They will also need off-lead exercise in a secure area—such as your back garden—so they can run off any excess energy. They need lots of playtime with you and enjoy training sessions and games to challenge them (see Mental Stimulation section for games), although these can count towards their exercise time.

FACT ***The golden retriever is a quick and agile dog which loves to please their owner, so it's no surprise that they're one of the most popular breeds among agility fans. Look online to find a local place to train your dog in agility games. They also like to play with a ball or Frisbee. This is a great way to burn off energy. In most cases, they will be happy to walk for considerable distances, so you can take them for long country walks.***

Seniors

When your dog reaches their senior years, even if it's had a high-activity lifestyle, it will begin to slow down and prefer shorter walks, more sedate play sessions with other dogs, and less vigorous daily exercise schedules. Pay attention to how quickly your golden seems to get tired or to be less interested in the energetic pursuits they used to adore and adjust their lifestyle accordingly.

Dogs thrive on routine, which means exercise still needs to be regular and consistent as they get older. Exercise is beneficial for the senior dog too, because it keeps joints and muscles moving and the mind active, which can extend their lifespan.

While your senior golden may need more sleep, shorter walks and ball retrieval games, and be less interested in play sessions with younger dogs, they will still enjoy walks and activities that do not wear them out too much.

When your dog reaches middle age, they are more likely to develop joint problems, physical conditions, and other medical issues. For 7 to 9-year-old retrievers, replace high-impact sports with shorter sessions of moderate exercise. Swimming, walking, or other joint-friendly activities are ideal for keeping them in shape without any risk.

16 Top Exercise Tips

Here are the top tips to remember when training your golden retriever:

1. If your dog is unaccustomed to regular exercise, but you want to take them for long walks, start gently to let your dog build up stamina. Start your dog's exercise routine with short periods of activity at slow speeds, gradually increasing the time, speed, and distance until your golden is getting the requisite amount of exercise.
2. Avoid exercising your dog immediately before or after meals, as walking or running on a full stomach can upset their system. Also, make sure your dog has enough water at mealtimes so they stay hydrated and ready for exercise.
3. Remember, your puppy's physical abilities are limited. Their bones are still growing and more susceptible to injuries. As a rule, puppies should have no more than five minutes of exercise for each month of age, twice a day.
4. Dog exercises should not just be long, boring treks. Keep things interesting by varying your walking routine. Dogs become bored just as much as their owners if they do the same thing every day. When you switch things up, you will both be happier to exercise. Plan several different dog walks you can do regularly, and make sure to include games in your routine.
5. Give your golden retriever the chance to release all their pent-up energy, but do not push them too hard. Be aware of how long they can run around before becoming tired, and make sure they have the energy to get back home.
6. If your golden has a history of medical problems, consider consulting your vet to plan a suitable exercise programme for their specific needs.
7. Remember that your dog loves to spend time with you, so make walks special rather than just plodding around the same old park every day. Meeting new dogs is all part of the fun.

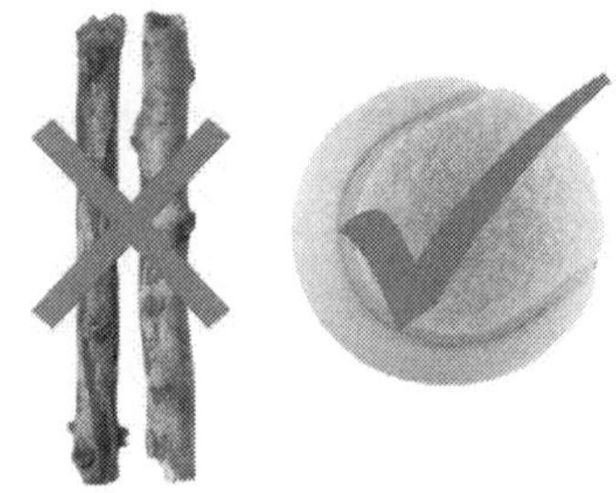

8. Do not throw sticks for your dog to chase. They can splinter and injure your golden's mouth and throat. If you throw a ball, make sure it is not too small, or your dog might swallow it.
9. Always allow your dog to have a good sniff around. This is important for their mental health.
10. 'Varied walking' can be good for you and your dog. This is where you speed walk for about 30 seconds, walk at a normal pace for about a minute, speed up, walk normally, etc. It is a good exercise for both of you and something you can do randomly throughout your walk.
11. Just like people, not all dogs enjoy exercise. Each dog has different exercise needs. You can often find dogs of the same breed who are completely different, with one being high energy and the other much more laid back.
12. Exercise as much as necessary. If your dog is not getting tired or is still full of energy when you get home, you might need to go on longer walks or play more games. If your retriever is struggling or refuses to go at all, you could need to cut back. Just follow their cues.

13. Most goldens love the water. Swimming is a great activity for dogs with joint problems, as it provides low-impact exercise. It also improves circulation and boosts metabolism. For an optimum cardio workout, a life jacket can help your dog stay in the water longer.
14. Fetch does not have to be boring. Shake up a game of fetch by making your dog run uphill to retrieve a ball or toss it into the water. Alternate between balls, Frisbees, and other prized toys to keep your dog on their toes.
15. If you are looking for a great dog exercise for your retriever, you might consider a treadmill. With careful training, your dog may love their treadmill workouts. While they cannot replace a walk or a run outside, treadmills build endurance and do not rely on good weather.
16. Climbing stairs is the perfect way to build leg muscles. Place your dog on their lead and walk up and down your stairs. Be sure to vary it by adding some high steps and side steps to work various muscle groups.

Visiting the Park

Visiting the local park with your retriever can be the highlight of their day if you are aware of proper etiquette, how to keep them safe, what to bring and when to avoid.

For many dog owners, the first visit to their local park is after their puppy has finished their vaccination schedule, and they want to get busy socialising. While this is a great idea, you will have a much easier transition into this new world if you keep a little basic etiquette in mind.

For instance, being new to the park, your golden puppy might become overexcited about meeting and greeting other canines. However, an extremely rambunctious puppy can be too much for older dogs to tolerate, and they might react by growling or snapping.

TIP ***Before going to the park, take your puppy for a disciplined, on-lead walk to burn off some energy first so they will be more sedate when first meeting the new canine crowd.***

Once at the park, keep your puppy on a lead until you are certain they will react politely and not simply jump at every other dog with wild abandon. Carefully observe your golden retriever's reaction to their exciting new world and be aware of other dogs they meet to make sure no one becomes overwhelmed or obnoxious.

Keeping your puppy safe when visiting the park requires you to be vigilant about the following:

- The size of other dogs.
- The behaviour of your puppy and other dogs.
- The intensity and length of play.
- Your retriever's hydration level.

While it is entertaining watching dogs having fun in the park, sometimes they play too vigorously or do not know when to stop. You should always pay attention and make sure your dog is not playing too hard for too long and getting overtired, overheated, or dehydrated.

Allowing your retriever puppy to play enthusiastically with a dog who significantly outweighs them can lead to accidental injury. While the larger dog might have no ill will, your puppy can easily be injured during boisterous play. Do not let your golden pup interact with large breeds.

In general, dogs prefer to play with their own breed or dogs of comparable size. However, sometimes your feisty little puppy will be excited and have no concept of size and no fear when up against a much larger dog during a play session. This is when you need to step in to prevent any accidents.

Observing the behaviour of other dogs in the park will also help keep your puppy safe. If the other dogs are playing and it seems quite intense with lots of shoulder checking, body slamming, nipping, and pouncing on one another, this is the time to keep your retriever on their lead and just watch from a safe distance.

Other times when it might be a good idea to **simply avoid the park** with your dog include when:

- There are many dogs in a small space.
- Your dog seems nervous.
- The dogs are being overly dominant with one another.
- Play is becoming aggressive or out of control.
- Other owners do not seem to be paying attention.
- It is a hot day, and there is no shade.
- You don't know the other dogs.
- There are unpredictable strong breeds around.
- Someone arrives with a dog they cannot control.

Things to Bring – There are at least three things you will never want to be without when you take your retriever to the park, as well as a few optional extras to play with:

- Lead (always).

- At least three poo bags (always).
- Water (always).
- Treats (optional).
- Ball (optional).
- A vest for your dog to reflect the sun (optional).
- Frisbee (optional).

Responsible dog walking

Going for a walk is an important part of your golden retriever's day. The countryside can be the perfect place to do this. Follow these simple tips for a safe countryside dog walk to keep you, your dog, and other animals safe:

Crops – Follow designated footpaths, always close gates behind you, and never wander into fields. Crops can be easily damaged by dogs and people walking on them when they're in the early and later stages of growth.

Litter and dog poo – Wildlife and farm animals can suffer serious harm if they try to eat discarded litter and poo bags. Always dispose of rubbish and dog poo in a bin or take it home with you.

As a dog walker, you can play a key role in keeping the countryside safe and clean for everyone by picking up any litter you see, even if it isn't yours.

Wildlife – No matter where you are in the countryside, you'll always be surrounded by wildlife, even if you can't see it. They may be hiding in bushes or hedgerows, but your golden retriever can still sniff them out thanks to their fantastic sense of smell. You may encounter young wild animals waiting for their parents to return or adults keeping their young safe, such as ground-nesting birds sitting on their eggs. Be aware of places where wildlife might hide, and make sure your dog does not disturb them, as they might chase them and cause significant injury.

You need to keep your golden safe, too, as wild animals often become aggressive when they think they are going to be attacked or if they feel the need to defend their young. This is true all year round, but especially in the spring and summer when most wild animals breed and have vulnerable offspring. If you walk your retriever in an area where deer reside between early May and late June, keep an eye out for new-born deer as they are particularly vulnerable at this time, and many are killed or injured by dogs.

If you walk along beaches or near areas where seals rest, be certain your golden stays on their lead and remains at least 50 metres away from the seals to avoid disturbing them.

Livestock – Most dogs show an interest in livestock. Even if you don't think your golden would harm another animal, accidents happen. Dogs easily frighten animals, especially ewes and lambs. Frightened ewes can abort their unborn lambs, become separated from the herd, or seriously injure themselves. Give livestock adequate space, and never feed them as this might harm them.

Mental Stimulation

All dogs need mental stimulation in their day, and without it, they can decide to create their own entertainment in a way you won't like.

First, let's discuss what 'mental stimulation' means, as the term can be confusing or have different connotations for different people. We've known for a long-time that physical activity is vital to keep your dog healthy, but what about your golden's brain? Mental stimulation simply means finding ways to make your dog think. This exercises their brain, making them smarter and far less likely to spend their time causing mischief because they are bored.

FACT ***Mentally challenging games, tasks, or sports are more tiring than the same amount of time spent on physical activities.***

One of the reasons most dogs get into trouble with their owners is that they don't have any regular thinking tasks. In other words, they are not mentally challenged or stimulated.

You can begin mentally challenging games or tasks for your golden retriever as soon as you bring them home. The sooner your puppy's brain is engaged in solving tasks or learning something new, the better for their mental health.

How much mental stimulation a dog requires depends on their breed and age. A smart, working breed such as the golden needs far more daily mental stimulation to keep them happy and out of mischief than a breed bred solely as a lapdog.

When your retriever is less than six months old, shorter mind games of 5-15 minutes are enough. As your dog matures, start bringing in longer and more challenging tasks that keep their mind occupied, such as an invigorating canine sport.

Top 15 Mental Stimulation Tips

Although every dog is different concerning what sort of mental tasks they find interesting, the following tips will help you keep your golden retriever mentally challenged:

1. Teach your puppy rules and boundaries so they learn what they can and cannot do. For instance, when your puppy knows they are not permitted into the kitchen when you are preparing food, they have learnt a 'rule'. Teach them this by firmly saying, '***Go***' while pointing away from the kitchen. If they do not go, simply walk towards them, forcing them to back away. Giving a treat once they leave when told will help reinforce this rule.
2. Teach basic tricks that require positive reinforcement. Most goldens love to learn tricks, which exercises their brain. You can start by teaching 'Shake-a-paw' (see how in Chapter 11).
3. Take them for walks in locations where there are unfamiliar smells and dogs. When you walk your retriever in the same place every day, it is not as stimulating or mentally exciting for them as the new smells and sights they encounter when they go to a new place.
4. Take your dog to off-lead parks, so they can interact with other dogs. Dogs like to meet, greet, and play with different dogs, and the park is a good place to have this type of interaction. Do not forget park safety rules.

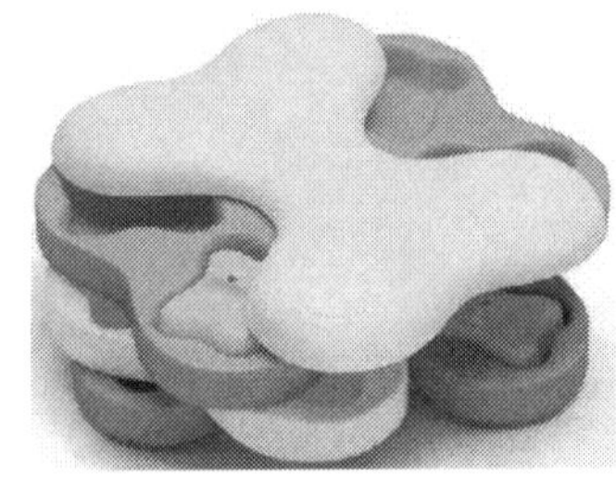

5. Hide treats inside a puzzle toy (see picture), so your dog must use their mind to figure out how to get them out. Your golden's sense of smell will identify a treat they want, and then they must use their brain to figure out what to do to get the puzzle to release the treat.
6. Set up an agility course in the back garden. You can buy agility obstacles online or create your own. Set up a course that involves jumping up onto a box, leaping over a hurdle, weaving through poles, or crawling through a tunnel. The only limit is your imagination.
7. Teach your retriever to swim and fetch a floating object. Start with something simple like a ball tossed near the shoreline, and when your dog brings the ball back, give them a treat to reinforce this behaviour. Slowly introduce greater distances until your golden must swim to grab the floating object and return it to you.
8. Enrolling your dog in an obedience class can be beneficial if you are a first-time owner and you need support in teaching the basics. A beginner class usually includes basic commands (see Chapter 11), whereas an advanced obedience class may focus on off-lead skills, such as Recall when the dog is out of sight.
9. Teach your smart dog to help with daily chores. Goldens love to have interesting tasks that are part of their daily routine to keep their mind active. There are many tasks your dog can help with around the house. Begin with something simple, like collecting the post from the doormat. Once your dog has accomplished this daily chore, think of other tasks they could learn.

10. Play the 'Cupcake Tin' game. Get a cake tin, place treats in some of the cups and cover them with dog-approved tennis balls. Then, your retriever must sniff for treats and figure out which balls to remove to get to them.
11. Teach your golden the names of their toys and get them to fetch each one by name. This takes patience and repetition. When the toys have short names, it is easier for your dog to remember them. For instance, if they have a stuffed cat toy, call it '***Cat***', or if they have a ball toy, call it '***Ball***' and so on. Begin with just two toys—Cat and Ball—and place them in front of your dog. Say the word '***Cat***' and point to the cat toy. When your dog picks up the cat, give them a treat. Repeat this exercise with the ball until your dog picks up the correct toy every time they are asked. Now you can add more toys for more mental stimulation.
12. Get a toy box and teach your dog how to put their toys away. Ask your golden to pick up a toy—or give them one—and say '***Box***', then lead your dog immediately to their toy box and say '***Drop***'. When your dog drops the toy in the box, give them a treat to reinforce this behaviour. This can take some patience and repetition before they understand that when you say '***Box***', it means to put the toys in their toy box.
13. When out on a walk, keep your dog on a lead and encourage them to follow you around trees, and poles, jump up on benches, walk along retaining walls, do a figure of eights or circles, stop and start suddenly and vary walking speeds and directions. Changing speed and direction when walking helps your golden learn the correct walking position—beside your leg—without pulling. It also makes them think, as they can't anticipate which direction you might take next.

14. Teach your golden a freestyle dance routine. Freestyle dance is a canine sport requiring dedication, patience, and many hours of practise. Choreographing and designing a trick training routine for a piece of music is a creative challenge for the owner and a huge mental exercise for any dog. Many organisations provide a good starting point for learning how to dance with your dog, such as the Canine Freestyle GB, the Musical Dog Sport Association, and the World Canine Freestyle Organisation.
15. Join 'Dognition', an online game assessment tool that helps you better understand and connect with your dog. All you do is provide information about your dog in the canine personality questionnaire and then play science-based games with your golden and a friend. Games take around ten minutes and test five dimensions of your dog's cognition: communication, memory, reasoning skills, and how cunning or empathetic they are. The results are analysed in your retriever's profile report.

Playing Games with your Golden Retriever

Indoor Food Games

Kong wobblers, food puzzles and the shell game are interactive games that involve solving puzzles to get the reward of food. The game of search involves finding a treat hidden somewhere inside the home.

FACT ***Most golden retrievers are highly food motivated, which is why indoor games that involve finding food treats are almost always a winner.***

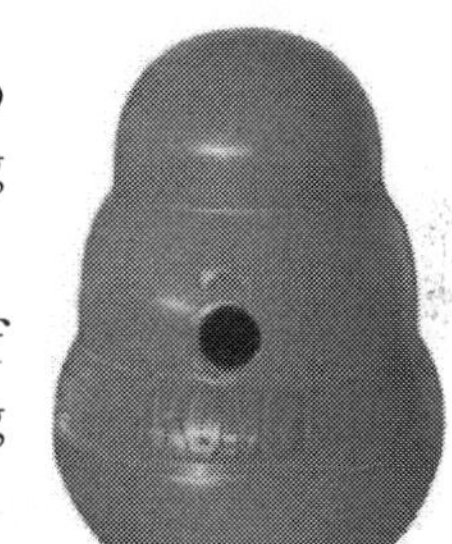

Kong Wobblers/Feeder Balls – These fun toys (see picture) make your dog work to get their treats, as they dispense the treats while your golden is playing and pushing the toy around.

Food Puzzles – There are many different types, sizes, and difficulty levels of interactive food puzzles that involve moving levers, pulling out drawers, toppling cones, flipping cups, sliding compartments, and rotating discs to get to a treat.

The Shell Game – This is a simple, beginner-level game you can play indoors with your golden. All you need are three cups and one treat. Have your golden sit and stay while they watch you place three cups upside down on the floor. Place a treat under one cup, change the position of the cups, and then release your dog to find the cup that hides the treat. This is a game any dog will quickly figure out because their nose will tell them which cup the treat is hidden under. Once they have found the right cup, they must figure out they have to overturn it to get the prize.

Search – This game is easy to teach to any dog who has mastered the sit/stay commands. First, ask your retriever to sit/stay while you slowly back away and place a treat where they can still see it. Return to where your dog remains in a sit/stay and say, 'Okay! Search' while pointing to where the treat was placed. Each time this game is played, you can make it increasingly more difficult by placing the treat farther and farther away and then finally out of your dog's sight before they are released to search.

Scatter Feeding – Scatter feeding is one of the easiest games to play. It encourages your golden retriever to search for their food and helps them display their natural foraging behaviour.

Essentially, scatter feeding is what it sounds like. Instead of placing your golden's food in their bowl, scatter it on the floor around the house or in the garden. If you're playing this game indoors, it's a good idea to use a hard, easy-to-clean surface. As your dog's ability to use their nose to find the food improves, scatter it over a larger area or uneven surface, such as grass.

You can start hiding small pieces of food for your dog to find after they've mastered this skill. Choose places you don't mind them rummaging around in and where there is no danger of anything getting damaged. As their confidence grows, make the hiding places more challenging, or even conceal the food beneath something such as a flowerpot.

If your retriever finds it too hard to find the food and becomes frustrated, you can help them by moving them closer to the food.

Other Indoor Games

Hide and Seek – This is a simple game that exercises both mind and body and is fun for dogs - and people - of all ages, especially on cold or rainy days when nobody wants an outdoor adventure.

When first teaching your puppy to play Hide and Seek, have a family member or friend hold your retriever while someone takes a treat and hides with your dog watching. The person hiding calls out '***Find me***', and the assistant releases the dog. As soon as your dog runs to the hiding place, give them a treat or toy.

Once your puppy grasps the concept of this game, you can increase the difficulty by hiding farther away in more complex locations, so your retriever must search and use their nose to find the person hiding. Make the first few times easy on your puppy, and give them a treat when they find you.

iDig – This interactive game provides a safe and rewarding way for dogs to exercise their natural desire to dig. It comes with three different digging flap challenges you fill with toys or treats to provide mental stimulation while your dog hunts for treasure.

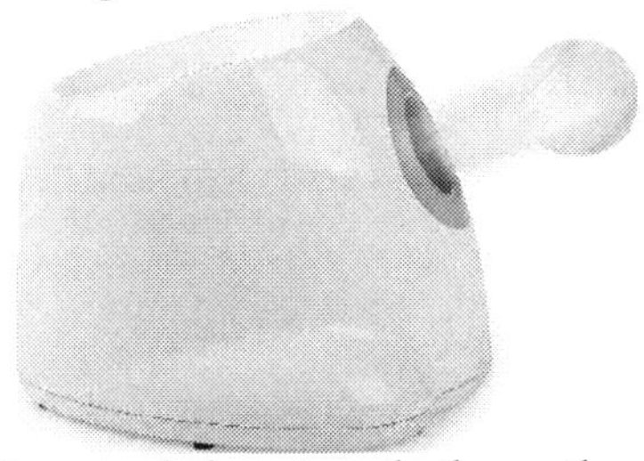

iFetch – This automatic ball launcher (see picture) has three distance settings. Your golden will be mentally challenged as they figure out where to drop the ball so it can be launched from the machine. They are rewarded with the chance to chase and bring it back again.

Obstacle Course – It is easy to set up an indoor obstacle course for your dog and then teach them the routine—sort of like your own indoor agility course. You can get the whole family involved in creating obstacles by using whatever is close at hand.

For example, make a tunnel out of a couple of chairs and a blanket or a large box, use a step stool as an obstacle to jump onto or over, a coffee table to crawl under, or arrange boxes so your dog must weave their way through. You'll be amazed at how much fun you can have when you put together an indoor obstacle course for your retriever.

Tug-of-War – In this game, you and your golden pull at opposite sides of a rope tug toy (see picture) until one of you gets the toy. This is both an indoor and outdoor game that also teaches basic impulse control. Dogs who enjoy this game become quite excited and can get their teeth too close to your fingers. If this happens, it is time to stop the game.

Impulse control comes into play when teaching your dog to '***Leave it***' when it is time to end the game. This is easy to do with a tasty treat as a reward. Simply stop pulling, and while still holding the end of the tug, firmly say '***Leave it***' and offer a treat. You must end the game as the one holding the toy. Otherwise, your dog may start to believe that they are in control.

Outdoor Games

Though it is certainly possible to play all your favourite indoor games outdoors, some games are much better suited to an outdoor arena, such as fetching balls or Frisbees.

Search – This game, where the dog gets to eat a treat once they find it, can also be played in a grassy back garden. Simply take some favourite treats and place them in random locations in the grass, so your golden must use their nose to find them.

TIP ***While it is fun to create an indoor obstacle course, if you have a back garden, you can easily set up an agility course for your golden. Creating a digging pit for your dog is also a fun activity because you can bury their favourite toys and your retriever can dig for them.***

In addition, there are many organised activities and canine sports that are mentally challenging for our canine friends:

Agility – This is an organised obstacle course (see picture) involving navigating various jumps, tunnels, balancing boards, and walkways in a specific order, with direction from their owner.

Barn Hunt – A relatively new canine sport, barn hunt is inspired by the traditional role that many breeds were developed for - eliminating destructive vermin from barns, storage areas, and homes. This sport is open to any breed or crossbreed that can fit through a 45-centimetre (18-inch) tunnel in a straw maze. The rats used in this sport are carefully protected inside aerated tubes so no harm comes to them.

Canicross – This sport is cross-country running with dogs. Your dog wears a harness connected to a bungee attached to you on a belt around your waist. Originally designed to exercise sled dogs during the off-season, many dogs run in front, although beside is also acceptable.

Conformation – Also known as 'a dog show', this is simply the best of the best strutting their stuff around a ring in front of judges who decide which dog best conforms to the ideal characteristics of their breed.

Disc Dog – Dog and owner, or handler teams are judged in disc-throwing routines involving distance/accuracy, chasing speed and catching ability of the dog.

Lure Coursing – This is a very fast-paced, timed sporting event that appeals to breeds with a strong chasing instinct. The dogs compete for the best time as they chase an artificial lure across an open field.

Dock Diving or Jumping – As the name implies, this sport involves water-loving dogs jumping off a dock into a body of water to retrieve a toy or ball thrown by the owner. The object is to get the dog to jump the longest distance possible.

Field Trials – In this competitive event, dogs are judged on how well they retrieve out in the field over a long distance.

Flyball – This is a time-recorded relay race involving teams of four dogs. The first dog runs down a course jumping hurdles along the way before pressing a panel to release a ball, which they grab and bring back to their owner before the next dog sets off.

Herding Trials – Many dogs enjoy learning how to herd, even those not specifically bred to herd. Those with a natural herding instinct who don't live on a farm can satisfy their instincts with these trials.

Mushing – This competitive category includes bikejoring, carting skijoring, scootering, and sledging and simply refers to one or more dogs pulling a person on a bike, cart, skis, scooter, or sledge, either on dry land or snow.

Nose Work – This sport is designed to mimic what detection dogs are trained to do - locate a specific odour and alert their owner or handler when they find it.

Rally Obedience – This is a type of obedience course open to all breeds to compete for championships and titles. The course is made up of specific obedience tasks that must be completed as the dog and handler navigate their way through the course.

Schutzhund – This is a protection dog sport that includes obedience and tracking. These dogs are highly intelligent and display a strong desire to work. They are tested for traits that are found in a wide variety of working or service tasks, such as police work or search and rescue.

Tracking – This is a type of test using your dog's strongest sense—smell. Following a scent trail imitates what search and rescue dogs are trained to do. If they get good at it, perhaps they'll have a part-time job!

Weight Pulling – While some criticise this sport, many breeds were traditionally used to pull carts to market or sledges across miles of snow. In a weight-pulling contest, the dog is attached to a loaded cart or sledge by a special harness to minimise injury. They then need to pull the weight across carpet, dirt, grass, or snow.

13. Golden Retriever Health

'Dogs die. But dogs live, too. Right up until they die, they live. They live brave, beautiful lives. They protect their families. And love us, and make our lives a little brighter, and they don't waste time being afraid of tomorrow.'

~ Dan Gemeinhart ~

The last thing you wish to worry about as a golden retriever owner is whether your dog might develop any health issues in their lifetime. However, part of being a responsible dog owner is learning about the conditions that commonly affect retrievers and making sure you have easy access to a veterinarian. Some conditions can be hard to detect, and you should never leave it until it is too late. In this chapter, we're going to look at some of the most common health issues affecting retrievers and what clinical signs to watch for to ensure the optimal health and quality of life for your dog.

Please do not panic reading these pages. Remember, golden retrievers are typically healthy dogs and will probably not suffer from any of these issues, especially if you follow the health tips outlined below. Key to protecting your dog's health is looking for these health problems, doing everything possible to prevent them, knowing what to do if an accident occurs, and having regular vet check-ups.

Diet – The cornerstone of health

Note that there are three ingredients found in almost all manufactured dog food —including organic food—that are compromising our dogs' health and shortening their lives:

- Preservatives, such as BHA and propylene glycol, which can create poor digestion, skin and coat issues, weight gain, and more.
- Fillers, which are contributing to the rising rate of canine cancers. These can be anything the food company puts into the food that does nothing for your dog's health, such as heavy grains, including barley, flour, oatmeal, soy, wheat, and white rice.
- Meat by-products, often called 'meat meal' or 'bone meal'. These are slaughterhouse waste that may contain beaks, brains, feathers, feet, intestines, and other items inedible to humans.

Many health problems can be attributed to bad breeding practices. It is certainly true that some breeds are more prone to specific health concerns. However, the number one health destroyer for dogs is their diet, something most owners are unaware of.

A wholesome, balanced diet is the cornerstone of keeping your golden in tiptop condition. Firstly, research companies that use high-quality ingredients and create nutrient-rich, balanced foods. Next, choose a quality diet your dog enjoys.

TIP ***Many companies offer samples you can try before you spend money on a case or bag. Some other brands offer money-back guarantees if your dog does not like the food. Discuss your options with your vet if you think you might like to provide a homemade diet.***

Be aware that numerous studies have shown that most recipes provided in books or on the internet are not nutritionally balanced or complete.

Make small batches until you are sure your golden likes it, and schedule regular vet visits to ensure your dog is receiving all the nutrients they need.

During the first few weeks after you find an appetising diet, observe how your retriever responds. Symptoms such as low energy, gastrointestinal problems, and a dull coat might indicate a change of diet. If you do change your retriever's food, do it gradually by mixing some of the old food with the new to avoid gastrointestinal upsets or food aversions. Your vet can also provide nutritional advice, especially if you have noticed changes in your dog's health. Water is also essential to keep your dog healthy, so make sure they always have access to fresh, clean water.

Apart from diet, many other factors can influence your golden's lifespan, both positively and negatively. Dogs are like small children whose health can be put at risk when exposed to only small amounts of toxic products, fumes, and foods.

There are many little things you could do that may seem insignificant, but combined can add up to a positive health effect over the years, increasing your golden's lifespan. We've covered these factors in detail in other sections of the book, but as a reminder, they include:

- Not overfeeding.
- Sufficient daily exercise.
- Playing games that exercise the mind.
- Providing a calm, safe, and stress-free environment.
- Early socialisation with other dogs and people.
- Removing toxic products and cleaners from home.
- Not using pesticides and fertilisers in the garden.
- Removing toxic plants.
- Keeping harmful foods and liquids away from your dog.
- Regular vet check-ups.
- Regular bathing and grooming sessions.
- Having pet insurance.
- Having access to a securely fenced back garden.
- Training basic commands to minimise accidents.

- Becoming familiar with canine body language.
- Keep your dog on a lead when in high-traffic areas.
- Not exposing them to toxic fumes or smoke such as car exhaust or cigarettes.

Signs of a Healthy Golden Retriever

We all want our retrievers to look, feel, and be healthy inside and out with a sound body and mind. The following are the most important indicators of health:

Skin

Healthy skin is soft, smooth, and free of scabs, growths, white flakes, or red areas. Check your dog for fleas, ticks, lice, and other external parasites. You can do this by blowing gently on your retriever's stomach or brushing the hair back in a few places to see if any specks, fleas, or ticks are attached to the skin. Black 'powder' on your dog's skin or bedding could signify a flea infestation.

Coat

A healthy coat is glossy and pliable, free from dandruff, bald spots, and excessive oil. It should smell fresh and feel smooth. The appearance and texture of your retriever's coat can be affected by illness or stress, which may cause excessive shedding. A dull, lacklustre coat can be a sign of hormonal imbalances, parasites, digestive disorders, or even cancer.

Ears

Ensure that the skin inside your golden's ears is clean and light pink. Some yellow or brownish wax is normal, but if there's an excessive amount, get them checked out. Your dog should not scratch their ears or shake their head excessively. There should not be any redness or swelling inside the ear. A dog with floppy ears, such as the golden, requires extra attention to keep their ears dry and clean. Golden retrievers are prone to ear infections, so it's important to regularly care for them.

Mouth, Teeth, and Gums

Healthy gums are pink, black, or spotted, just like the skin of your golden. Young dogs have white teeth that may darken with age. Adult dogs typically have 42 permanent teeth, while puppies have 23 baby teeth. Baby teeth will fall out as permanent teeth grow in.

If you want to inspect your dog's mouth, try talking to them gently, then put your hand over their muzzle and lift the sides of their mouth. Ensure that adult teeth are coming in properly and are not crowded by baby teeth. Check the gums are healthy and their breath does not smell foul. Look for soft, white matter and hard, white, yellow, or brown matter. This is plaque or tartar and needs to be brushed away by a professional. An infection in your retriever's mouth can lead to serious problems in the gums and other parts of the body, including the heart, so it is important to take care of your dog's teeth and mouth.

Eyes

Healthy eyes are shiny and bright. The presence of mucus and watery tears is normal but should be minimal and clear. Eyelids should have a pink lining that is not inflamed, swollen, or discoloured. At the inside corner of your retriever's eye, you can sometimes see their third eyelid, a thin, transparent membrane. During sleep, this may slowly cover the eye. The whites of your dog's eyes should not have a yellow tinge. Their eyelashes should not rub against the eye.

Nose

Your dog's nose should be cool and moist. Depending on the breed, it may be black, pink, or self-coloured—the same colour as the coat. There should be no yellowish, thick, bubbly, or foul-smelling nasal discharge. Dogs with cool, wet noses are not always healthy, and those with dry, warm noses are not necessarily ill. Taking their temperature is a more reliable health indicator.

Breath

Your dog's breath should smell bad, despite what many people think. Obviously, it won't smell minty fresh unless you've brushed its teeth, but there should not be any offensive smell either. If your golden has bad breath, it could be the result of bacteria build-up that may cause gingivitis and periodontal disease. Some specific odours may indicate illness. For instance, if your retriever's breath smells like ammonia or urine, it could be due to kidney disease.

Elimination

Your retriever's urine colour is an indicator of health. It should be clear yellow. On average, adult dogs will have one or two bowel movements each day. Stools should be brown and firm. Symptoms such as bloody, runny, or watery stools, excess urination, and straining require veterinary attention.

Heartbeat and Pulse

Dogs' heartbeats vary depending on their size. In a resting dog, a normal heart beats between 50 and 130 times per minute. Puppies and small dogs have faster heartbeats, while large dogs in good condition have slower ones. You can check your golden's heart rate by placing your fingers over the left side of their chest and feeling the strongest beat. When testing the pulse, which is the same rate as the heartbeat, press gently on the inside of the top of the hind leg. An artery runs through that area and the skin is thin, so it is easy to feel their pulse.

Weight

A healthy dog's weight will be determined by their diet and exercise level. If they are eating right and exercising regularly but still seem over- or underweight, they might have a health problem. Avoid giving your golden too many treats between meals; obese dogs typically develop serious health problems. You can tell whether your dog is overweight by feeling their rib cage. Ribs should be easy to feel under the surface of the skin without much padding.

Alertness and attitude

You can tell when your golden retriever is happy by their body language. Your dog should be eager to engage with you, aware of their surroundings, and lively. Instead of showing signs of nervousness or anxiety, they should seem happy and content. They should be enthusiastic about life and full of energy. Their posture should be relaxed and confident.

Top Illness Indicators

Your dog cannot tell you how they feel with words. However, their body language is highly expressive. In the early stages of an illness, your dog will instinctively hide that something is wrong. Knowing your golden retriever well, you might be able to recognise subtle changes in their behaviour and personality. Typically, these changes indicate a health issue. You can help your dog recover quickly by recognising there is a problem as soon as possible. A few warning signs that your dog might be ill and need veterinary treatment include:

Vomiting or Diarrhoea

The most common reason to seek veterinary care is vomiting or diarrhoea. While these are usually transient and mild, they can be life-threatening. They may be down to a change in diet, ingestion of nondigestible objects, viral or bacterial infections, or getting into the rubbish.

Temperature

The normal temperature for a canine is between 38.3 to 39.2 °C (101 to 102.5 °F). As your dog's body temperature is naturally higher than a human's, feeling warmer than you is not automatically a cause for concern.

FACT ***A dog with a temperature of 39.5 °C (103 °F) or higher is considered to have a fever. In this case, call your veterinarian.***

Loss of Appetite

It is common for dogs to have their own eating habits and to eat varying amounts of food from day to day. However, an ongoing loss of appetite is often a sign of underlying problems. These can range from mild to serious. Anorexia can indicate dental disease if accompanied by bad breath. It might help to offer your dog their favourite treats. A vet should be consulted if your dog doesn't eat for more than a day or the lack of interest in food is associated with other symptoms such as lethargy, vomiting, and weakness.

Changes in Personality

When dogs are in pain or feeling unwell, they display changes in behaviour, such as decreased energy levels and lethargy. Dogs who are normally social might start to withdraw when they are sick. A loving and energetic dog may show signs of snippiness or aggression. Notice if your golden growls whenever you go near a specific place on their body. Be aware that not all sick dogs display negative behaviour. Some might become clingy or show signs of increased neediness.

Coughing, Wheezing, or Trouble Breathing

Coughing, wheezing, nasal discharge, and trouble breathing indicate respiratory problems. They can be down to something as simple as a cold, to more severe conditions such as canine influenza, kennel cough, or heart failure. Honking noises can be an indication of a condition known as tracheal collapse, which is common in small breeds. It is an emergency if your retriever has difficulty breathing or their tongue or gums appear blue. Coughs should be closely monitored, and if they do not go away or there are other symptoms, take your dog to the vet.

Joint and Spine Issues

Golden retrievers can suffer from several musculoskeletal problems. Even though it may seem overwhelming when you first find out your dog has an issue, every condition can be diagnosed and treated to prevent unnecessarily painful outcomes. If you are aware of your dog's behaviour at home and know about any conditions that could affect their bones, joints, or muscles, you can provide them with the required care throughout their life.

Hip Dysplasia

Hip dysplasia is a hip deformity that occurs during growth. The hip joint is a ball and socket joint. During growth, both the ball—the head of the femur or thighbone—and the socket in the pelvis—acetabulum—need to grow at equal rates. In hip dysplasia, there's no uniform growth during puppyhood. This results in a looseness of the joint, which leads to degenerative joint disease (DJD) or osteoarthritis (OA), which is the body's attempt to stabilise the loose hip joint. In other words, the head of the dog's femur does not fit properly in the socket of the hip joint (see picture).

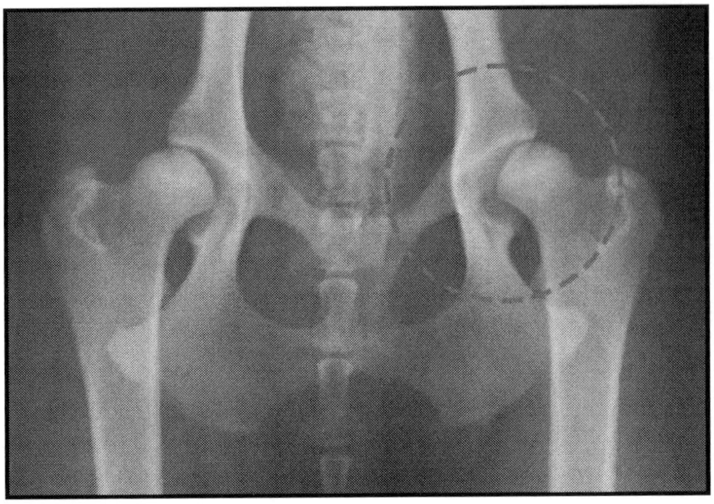

Clinical signs of hip dysplasia include weakness and pain in the hind legs. The affected dog appears wobbly and avoids getting up from a sitting or lying position. Many dogs limp or are reluctant to climb stairs. The signs can be noticed in puppies as young as a few months old, but they are most common in dogs between one and two years of age. Dogs with mild hip dysplasia can develop minimal arthritis without showing clinical signs until they are older. Even though hip dysplasia typically starts in puppies, most dogs do not show any clinical signs until they are an adult. It often takes years of progressive bone degeneration for a dog to exhibit symptoms.

FACT ***Hip dysplasia is a genetic condition influenced by factors including diet, environment, exercise, growth rate, muscle mass, and hormones. The disease is most often seen in breeds of large dogs, but it can be seen in smaller breeds as well. According to a study from the Orthopaedic Foundation of Animals (OFA) in the U.S., on average, 19.8% of golden retrievers suffer from the condition.***

Diagnosis – Your vet can diagnose hip dysplasia by taking an x-ray of the hip.

Treatment – Clinical signs and your dog's level of discomfort will determine the appropriate treatment. Non-steroidal anti-inflammatory drugs (NSAIDs), such as Meloxicam, will give excellent pain relief. There is no universal approach when it comes to finding the right medications, and various drugs might be tried before finding the most effective one.

In most cases, dogs with hip dysplasia should be given glucosamine, chondroitin sulphate, and omega-3 fatty acid nutritional supplements. Many dogs suffering from painful hip dysplasia also benefit from regular injections of polysulfated glycosaminoglycan. A moderate amount of exercise, avoiding high-impact exercises such as jumping, might help an affected dog to stay mobile.

In addition to other treatments, physiotherapy has been proved to significantly improve the quality of life for affected dogs. Weight loss is strongly recommended for overweight dogs, as excess weight puts undue stress on the hip joints.

Surgery is an alternative to NSAIDs and medical therapy. A variety of surgical procedures are available to treat hip dysplasia. Total hip replacement and femoral head osteotomy are the two most common surgical treatments. Your dog's age, health condition, and lifestyle will dictate the type of surgery required. The best recommendation for your retriever will be provided by your vet.

Hip Dysplasia Screening Scheme – In the United Kingdom, the British Veterinary Association (BVA)—the OFA in the U.S.—reviews x-rays for abnormalities in dogs' hip joints. Each x-ray is graded by a panel of experts. Your vet can arrange for your golden retriever's x-rays to be scored and relay the results to you.

Scrutineers of the BVA evaluate each hip joint based on nine different aspects. A score for each hip indicates how severely your retriever has been affected by hip dysplasia. Scores range from 0 to 106—0 to 53 for every hip—with a score of 0 representing the least and a score of 53 representing the most severe degree of hip dysplasia. Over the last 15 years, the average hip scope for golden retrievers has been 11, so you may like to use that as your benchmark.

Patellar Luxation

Patellar luxation is when your golden's kneecap—the patella—slips out of place (see picture).

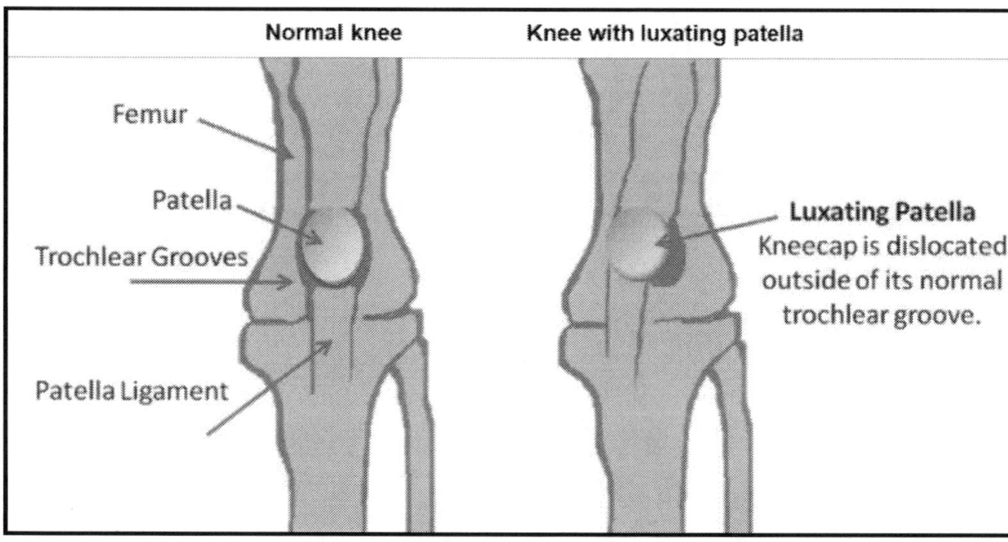

During a run, you might notice that your dog picks up a back leg or skips and hops for a few steps. Then, they may kick their leg out sideways, a natural instinct to pop their kneecap back into place. Both are common symptoms of patellar luxation. This condition used to be most common among toy and miniature breeds such as chihuahuas, Pomeranians, and Pekinese. However, it is starting to be increasingly seen in larger dogs, with the golden retriever being one of the more susceptible.

When a healthy knee bends, then the kneecap slides up and down a groove in the thighbone. Kneecaps should not slip out of this groove. If they do, it is referred to as a luxating patella—dislocating kneecap. When the kneecap dislocates, it prevents the knee from bending, causes a limp, and rubs against the bone as it slips, which can result in pain and arthritis over time.

One or both knees can be affected by patellar luxation, which ranges from Grade 1 to Grade 4:

Grade 1 – The kneecap is loose but stays in place when your dog moves. If forced by your vet, it will dislocate but returns instantly after release. Frequently, grade 1 patellar luxation is not much of a problem.

Grade 2 – The kneecap dislocates occasionally when your dog moves but usually returns of its own accord. The severity of grade 2 symptoms depends on how frequently the kneecap dislocates.

Grade 3 – The kneecap is permanently dislocated. It can be pushed back into place by the vet, but it slips straight out again if the vet lets go.

Grade 4 – The kneecap is permanently dislocated and cannot be put back in its original position.

Diagnosis – To check the stability of your golden's kneecap, your vet will carefully feel it and perform a few different tests. They will also look at your dog's cruciate ligaments because cruciate disease is very common in dogs with patellar luxation. For a full diagnosis, some dogs require a general anaesthetic and x-rays, especially if their knee is very painful.

TIP ***If your dog only limps occasionally—every few weeks—physiotherapy and controlled exercise might be all you need to manage their patellar luxation. However, if your retriever is in pain or regularly limps, surgery might be the best solution.***

Treatment – The type of treatment your dog needs is dependent on the grade of their patellar luxation and their symptoms.

The mildest cases of patellar luxation—grades 1 & 2—can be treated without surgery. Physiotherapy and controlled exercise are used to strengthen the leg muscles and stop kneecaps from slipping further. Dogs with severe cases—grades 3 & 4—may need surgery. You can choose from a few different surgical options, and your vet will help you pick the best one for your retriever. You should be aware that all surgeries come with pros and cons. Some of the more complex ones can only be performed by a specialist veterinarian at a referral centre.

Most dogs with patellar luxation—except some grade 1s—experience pain at some point during their lives. Your vet can prescribe NSAIDs to relieve pain as required. The higher the grade of luxation, the more complicated and expensive treatment will be. Specialist knee surgery tends to be the most expensive procedure. Discuss your budget with your vet as well while determining what is best for your dog.

Intervertebral Disc Disease

Intervertebral Disc Disease (IVDD) is a very serious and common disease affecting thousands of dogs every year. It is one of the most common neurologic disorders seen in dogs. Most older dogs will have some degeneration of their intervertebral discs, which can result in a condition known as spondylosis. In most instances, this won't cause pain or weakness and doesn't progress to become intervertebral disc disease.

There are two main forms of IVDD which affect domestic dogs – Hansen Type I and Hansen Type II. Hansen Type I IVDD is an acute hernation of the disc which suddenly occurs and usually affects dogs which have breed-specific, acceptable skeletal deformities. This includes breeds like dachshunds, shih-tzus, beagles, corgies and dogs with genetic dwarfism. Hansen Type II IVDD develops more gradually and affects non-chondrodystrophic breeds like German shepherds, Doberman pinschers – and golden retrievers.

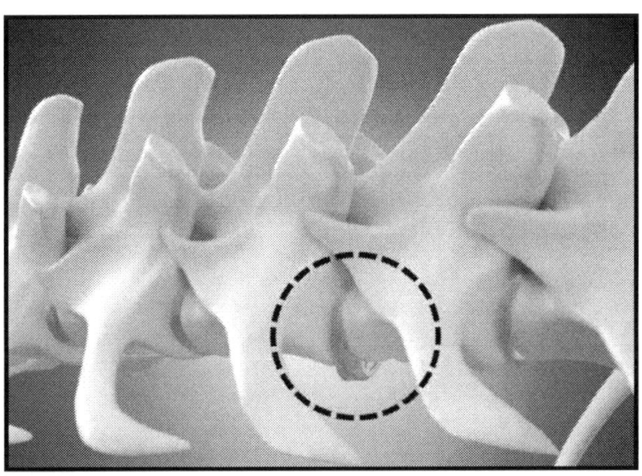

Your dog's intervertebral discs act as little cushions between each vertebra in the spine. These pads act as shock absorbers and provide support to your retriever as they move. IVDD causes the intervertebral discs to gradually lose their elasticity, become hard and fragile, and potentially slip out of place (see picture). A slipped disc presses on the spinal cord, causing pain, weakness in the legs, and even paralysis and incontinence.

IVDD symptoms can occur gradually or rapidly and include back pain, wobbliness, weak legs, falling, tripping, and difficulty getting up.

Diagnosis – When your vet examines your dog, they might suspect IVDD, but further tests are typically needed to confirm the diagnosis. These tests might include the following:

- An MRI scan is the best way to diagnose IVDD since it provides a detailed view of the spine, nerves, bones, and discs. An MRI scanner is a very large, expensive piece of equipment, so they are often only available at specialised veterinary hospitals.
- An x-ray will show some of the changes caused by IVDD and a slipped disc, but not all because nerves and the spinal cord are not visible on an x-ray.
- Other tests might be required for your dog, depending on your vet's findings, such as blood tests, spinal taps, or CT scans.

Treatment – If your retriever only exhibits mild symptoms of a slipped disc, you might want to treat them conservatively. In this instance, your dog will be given pain medication, rest, and physical therapy. They will also need assistance going to the toilet if they cannot urinate or poo. In most cases of IVDD, strict rest is essential for several weeks. The dog needs to be kept in a crate or a small space and only be let out to relieve themselves, during which time they should be restrained on a lead.

While your dog is recovering from a slipped disc, make sure they don't jump, run, or climb stairs. They should be given regular pain relief. A tablet or liquid can usually be given at home, but if that is not enough, your dog could require stronger injections or even be hospitalised for pain control.

In severe cases, such as excruciating pain or an inability to walk, surgery may be required. In many cases, this will be successful if done within a few days of the onset of symptoms. However, spinal surgery is a major procedure, so talk to your vet about the possible risks, recovery time, and costs before proceeding. Unfortunately, some dogs are so badly affected that putting them to sleep is the kindest choice.

IVDD treatment costs vary widely depending on what's required. If your dog needs specialist treatment or spinal surgery, this could amount to several thousand pounds.

Dental Issues

Unfortunately, most dogs suffer dental issues at some point in their life. Studies have revealed that 80% of dogs suffer from dental disease by the time they are five years old. This is a sad statistic as dental issues are completely preventable. The only reason so many dogs suffer from teeth problems is that owners don't establish a dental routine that includes daily brushing.

It is important to commit to a healthy teeth routine early on with your retriever puppy and never put off making sure they have their teeth brushed at least once every day. After every meal would be even better.

While they don't generally suffer from overcrowding or under/overbites, golden retrievers tend to have more dental problems than other breeds. This can start with tartar build-up on the teeth and progress to infection of the gums and roots of the teeth.

Read on to learn about the most common canine dental issues.

Dental Disease

When bacteria in the mouth combine with fluids, food, and saliva, they create a sticky, clear or pale-yellow biofilm called plaque, which settles between the teeth and along the gum line. Within just 4 to 12 hours after their teeth have been brushed, plaque starts forming in your dog's mouth and sticking to every tooth surface. This constantly forming film is the root cause of many dental problems, and the major reason why brushing your golden's teeth is so important.

When plaque is not removed with brushing, it mineralises into hard, cement-like tartar—within 24 to 36 hours of eating—that builds up along the gum line, pushing the gums away from the teeth and causing dental disease. Effectively removing plaque once it builds up requires scrubbing.

The bacteria in the plaque attack the tooth enamel. Enamel loss causes cavities, infection, pain, inflamed, swollen gums that bleed easily, and gingivitis—gum disease. The latter causes bad breath, loose teeth, and eventual tooth loss. The only scientifically proven way to fight plaque and tartar build-up is the same for dogs and humans—daily brushing combined with routine removal of any accumulated hard tartar deposits by a health professional.

FACT ***Vigilant care of your golden retriever's teeth throughout their lifetime will add at least 2 to 5 years to their life.***

Gingival Hyperplasia (Gum Disease)

This refers to a medical condition in which your retriever's gums or gingival tissue become inflamed, swollen and enlarged due to irritation from dental plaque or other bacterial growth along the gum line. Over time, more of the tooth is revealed as the gums recede and the connection to the socket is loosened. In almost all cases, this painful condition can be prevented with good oral hygiene habits. When a dog is suffering from gum disease, they are more likely to be affected by other serious health issues, including cancer, diabetes, and heart disease.

Loose Teeth

The only time your dog should have loose or wobbly teeth is when they are very young and their milk teeth are being replaced by their adult set of teeth. When an adult dog has a loose tooth, it is usually because of an underlying gum problem resulting from poor dental hygiene.

Malocclusions

An abnormal tooth alignment is known as malocclusion. There are two types, skeletal and dental. Skeletal malocclusion is when the jaw length is abnormal, creating a misalignment of the teeth. A dental malocclusion, or malposition, happens if the upper and lower jaw lengths are normal, but one or more teeth are out of normal alignment.

If a dental or skeletal malocclusion causes trauma to the oral soft tissues or other teeth, the condition is called non-functional or traumatic, and treatment is needed. This may include:

- Extraction.
- Moving the offending or affected tooth/teeth.
- Surgically creating additional space for the mispositioned tooth to occupy.

Retained Milk Teeth

Usually, puppies lose their 28 puppy—or milk—teeth without intervention. However, sometimes they do not all naturally fall out. If your puppy has not lost all their baby teeth on their own (see picture below), any remaining ones need to be pulled by the vet to make space for their adult teeth to grow in properly.

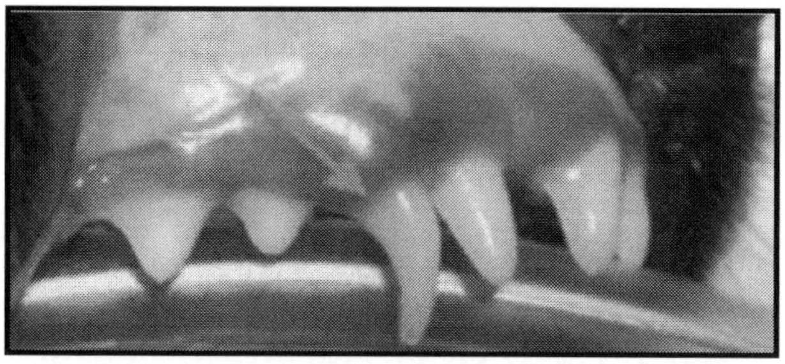

Keep a close watch on your puppy's teeth around the age of 4-6 months to ensure all their baby teeth have fallen out, and their adult teeth have room to grow.

Periodontal Disease

This disease begins with inflammation caused by an infection of the tissue that surrounds the tooth—the periodontium—called gingivitis. As the disease progresses, the covering of the root surface—the cementum—is affected, and then so are the ligaments that attach the tooth root to the bone—the periodontal ligament. When left untreated, this infection spreads into the tooth socket, destroying the bone. At this stage, the tooth loosens and can eventually fall out.

If you've ever had a toothache, you can imagine how painful this must be. Unfortunately, your golden retriever cannot tell you when their teeth are painful. The only indication of a problem will probably be a disgruntled dog who refuses to eat or have anyone touch their face. You can prevent this from happening simply by practising good dental hygiene.

Worn Down Teeth

It is natural for your golden's teeth to show some signs of wear as they age. After all, your dog tends to be always chewing on something. However, severe tooth wear, known as attrition—the loss of the protective layer of dentin—can be the result of chewing inappropriate items, such as tennis balls, rocks, antlers, or other hard objects.

TIP ***Some dogs will fetch anything, including stones and hard rocks. You should not toss rocks for your dog because these can crack, chip, and eventually wear down their teeth. Once your dog has developed the habit of picking up rocks, this can be a difficult behaviour to break.***

Also, never allow your dog to play with tennis balls. These contain fibreglass and are very corrosive, so they can wear down their teeth.

Bad Breath

A healthy dog should not have bad breath unless they have just raided the cat's litter box. If your dog has bad breath, this could be the first sign of an unhealthy mouth and gum disease caused by plaque build-up on their teeth. Beyond poor oral hygiene, the most common cause of bad breath, there may be other contributing factors, such as:

- Diabetes.
- Too many bad bacteria in the gut microbiome.
- Gastrointestinal issues.
- Airway infections in the lungs, sinuses, or windpipe.
- Bowel obstruction.
- Kidney disease.
- Liver disease.

Excessive drooling could also be a symptom of dental disease. Drooling can mean the salivary glands are reacting to inflammation from excessive bacteria in the mouth. If you notice your dog drooling—and it's not because they are anticipating the steak grilling on the BBQ—you should have them professionally checked by your vet.

How to Check the Teeth

Knowing how to check your retriever's teeth can help minimise teeth issues by alerting you to potential situations before they become serious.

Checking your dog's teeth is best done while carrying out their daily teeth brushing. If this routine has not been established, start with your dog sitting quietly beside you or up on a worktop where there is a good light source. Lift their lip so you can see your dog's teeth and look for the following:

- Brown colour—teeth should be white.
- Tartar and plaque build-up—the precursor to serious disease.
- Red and swollen gums—the beginning of periodontal disease.
- Bleeding gums—usually the result of plaque beneath the gum line.
- Lumps or growths on the gums.
- Teeth that are chipped, cracked, broken, or worn.
- Loose or wobbly teeth—might need to be removed.
- Smelly breath—can indicate gum disease.

If you notice any of the above, you should immediately get your retriever checked by a vet. The most likely treatment is a professional cleaning of your golden's teeth to remove all plaque, reduce gum swelling and get the teeth and gums back in good health.

What Should the Gums Look Like?

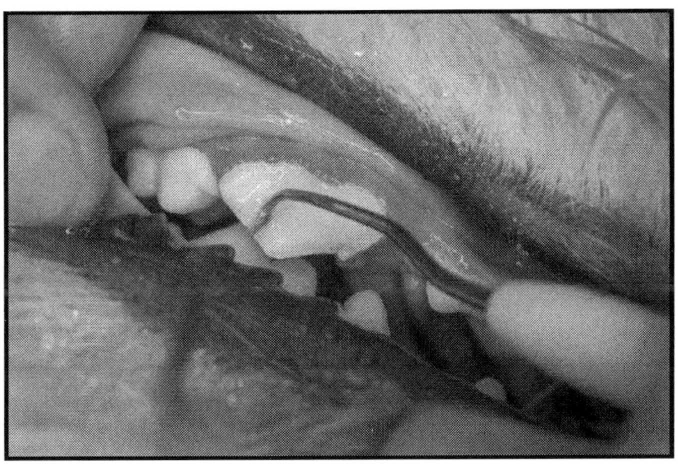

Pale Pink or White Gums are usually an indication of anaemia or low blood count. This can be a warning of a serious problem needing immediate attention from your vet.

Bright Red Gums can indicate that your golden is overheated, suffering from heat stroke or infected inflamed gums—gingivitis—that bleed easily.

Blue Gums are usually an indication your dog's blood supply isn't getting enough oxygen. This may be caused by breathing problems, heart disease, or pneumonia and requires immediate intervention by your vet.

TIP ***The colour of the gums can alert you to the health of your golden retriever. Healthy gums should be wet or smooth and slippery and have a powdery pink colour. This colour should fade to pale pink or white when pressed with your finger and return to a deeper pink within two seconds of removing your finger.***

Growths or Tumours found on the gums may be benign and disappear on their own, a contagious viral problem, or cancerous. The appearance of growths on the gums needs to be checked by your vet.

Healthy Chewing Toys

There are many popular chew toys and objects available that can be dangerous for canine teeth and their health overall. It is important to always keep the following in mind when selecting toys:

- They are vet-approved.
- They are softer than your dog's teeth—otherwise, they might damage them.
- They are size appropriate, so your dog cannot swallow them.
- They are designed for the level of chewing force of your dog.
- They do not contain any toxins.

- They engage your retriever's mind and keep them occupied.
- Avoid soft or plush toys if your golden likes to rip things apart.
- Only buy balls that are designed especially for dogs' teeth.

Eye Issues

Many dogs are born with eye issues or develop them over time as part of the ageing process. The following are the most common eye issues that could affect your golden retriever throughout their life.

Cataracts

Goldens are prone to cataracts (see picture), a major cause of blindness. Cataracts are cloudy spots that develop on the clear lens of the eye which focuses light on the retina located at the back of the eye. Eventually, these spots grow to completely block the light from reaching the retina. As the lens becomes cloudier, it dims the light reaching the retina to the point where it causes blindness. Even though cataracts are not painful, they increase the risk of injury, especially if your dog is in an unfamiliar environment.

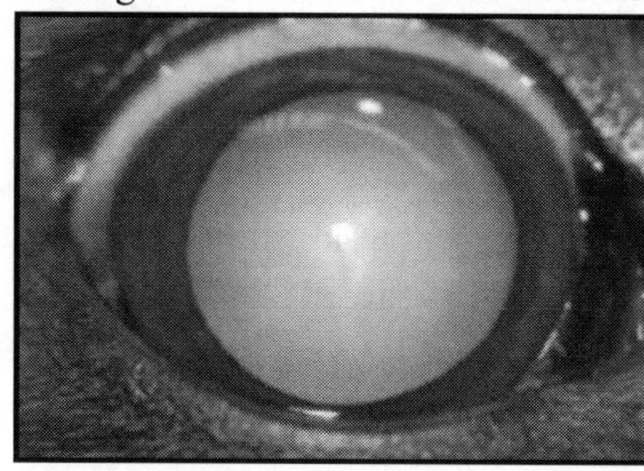

Since cataracts are often hereditary, their progression differs from breed to breed. In some breeds, cataracts develop relatively early, whilst in others, the first signs are detected at an older age and progress is slow, so the dog enjoys reasonable vision well into old age.

At least 70 breeds are affected by hereditary cataracts, including golden retrievers. Despite this fact, little is known about their genetic cause. There are breed-specific characteristics associated with cataracts, such as their appearance, age at onset, rate of progression, and whether they occur bilaterally in both eyes.

Golden retrievers are affected by degenerative cataracts. Dogs with these cataracts are born with normal lenses, which degenerate over time. Degenerative cataracts can develop at anywhere between 8 weeks and 7-8 years of age, depending on the type of cataract and the breed of dog involved. Goldens suffer from anterior and posterior subcapsular cataracts, which typically become apparent between 1 to 3 years of age.

FACT ***Statistics show that 7.4% of golden retrievers examined had some form of cataract. Even though this number includes cataracts from non-hereditary causes, it is significantly higher than the 1.6% of mixed-breed dogs with cataracts.***

It is rare for cataracts to cause diminished vision if they obscure less than 30% of the eye's lens or if only one lens is affected. Visual impairment is usually evident when opacity covers about 60% of the lens. A dog will become blind in the affected eye if this opacity advances to 100%. Cataract progression or stability depends on the type, breed, and other risk factors.

At present, there are no topical medications which can slow the progress of genetic cataracts. However, topical aldose reductase inhibitors have been shown to be effective in treating cataracts generated by diabetes. A veterinary ophthalmologist can surgically remove cataracts and restore your golden's vision. Most dogs recover quickly from surgery and are soon back to their regular self, running and playing within a few days.

Glaucoma

The golden is one of the breeds that are susceptible to glaucoma (see picture below). This is a condition in which aqueous fluid builds up inside the eye and results in pressure build-up.

The pressure of the eye, which is called intraocular pressure (IOP), increases when too much fluid is made or not enough is drained, damaging the retina and optic nerve. This is problematic because the retina converts images into nerve signals and the optic nerve sends these signals to the brain to create an image of the surroundings. An increase in intraocular pressure almost always leads to blindness in the affected eye due to damage to the retina or optic nerve.

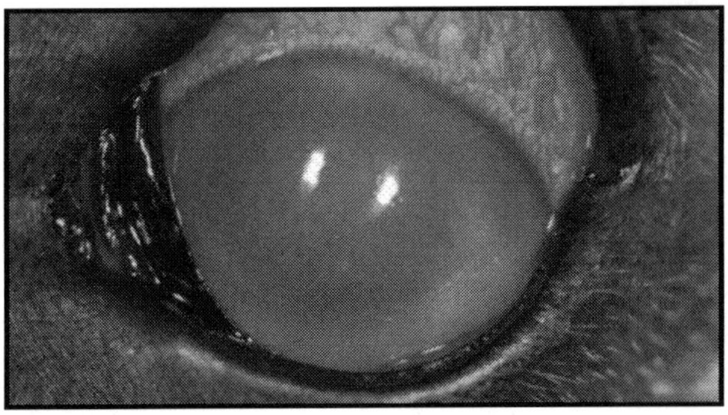

Glaucoma is classified as either primary or secondary. In primary glaucoma, the flow rate of fluid into or out of the eye is abnormal, resulting in increased pressure. The condition is often inherited due to a genetic predisposition within certain breeds, including golden retrievers. Unlike secondary glaucoma, it is not the result of an underlying disease. Primary glaucoma can occur at any age, but most dogs are diagnosed in their middle or late years, between the ages of 3 to 7.

Secondary glaucoma occurs due to another concurrent eye condition. There can be bleeding, swelling, or inflammation; scar tissue may form; the ability for the fluid to drain away may be restricted or completely blocked. Secondary glaucoma is more common in dogs than primary glaucoma. Triggers include infection, advanced cataracts, and inflammation.

As a dog ages, the clinical signs of glaucoma could first manifest in one eye and then the other. The signs are rarely experienced simultaneously or equally in both eyes. It may take years for the second eye to be affected. Check your golden for glaucoma if you notice any signs and symptoms. Time is of the essence with this condition. It is not only painful, but it can also lead to irreversible blindness if left untreated.

Dogs with glaucoma suffer more severe pain than humans. Some of the symptoms to look out for are:

- Eye pain, indicated by rubbing their eye against the floor, an object or with their paw.
- Eye redness.
- Squinting.
- Watery eyes.
- Avoiding light.
- Having a weakened blink response.
- Fluttering eyelids.
- Different-sized pupils.
- Vessels in the white of the eye.
- Swollen, bulging eye.
- Vision problems, which make your dog bump into objects, struggle to find items or be cautious when walking.

Your vet will measure the intraocular pressure of your golden retriever's eye with a tonometer, a device that measures the amount of pressure the eye's fluid exerts.

Glaucoma treatment depends on the severity of the disorder, as well as any underlying contributing conditions. Those issues must be addressed to prevent a recurrence. Treatment options are medications, cyclocryotherapy—cold temperatures are used to kill the cells producing intraocular fluid—and surgery.

If glaucoma goes undetected for a long time, the optical nerve can be damaged beyond repair, which unfortunately means surgery, which could result in the removal of the eye.

Cherry Eye

A cherry eye (see picture below) can affect golden retrievers, although the breeds with the highest risk include Neapolitan mastiff, English bulldog, Lhasa apso, American cocker spaniel, Puggle, Great Dane, Saint Bernard and Pug.

Cherry eye is a genetic eye problem where the gland of the third eyelid prolapses or slips in the corner of the eye because of the weakness of the connective tissue surrounding the gland. This causes a pink, fleshy protrusion to extend or bulge over the edge of your dog's eyelid due to a prolapse of the third eyelid gland. The condition is named because this growth resembles a cherry. It can be large and cover a considerable portion of the cornea, or it might be small and appear only occasionally. Veterinary attention must be sought as soon as possible in the event of cherry eye.

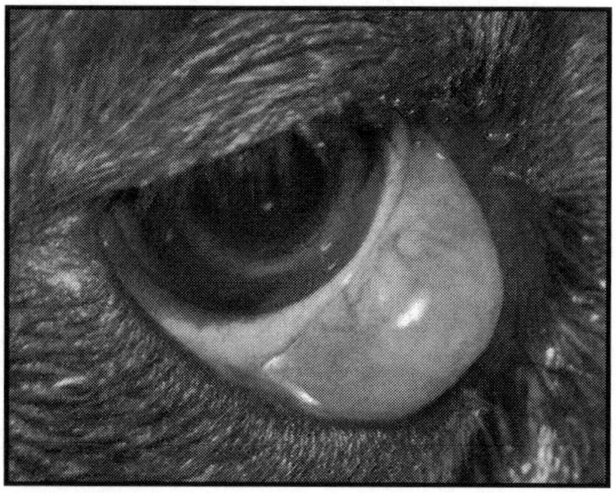

Treatment involves surgically replacing the third eyelid gland. It is essential to treat the condition quickly to minimise the risk of permanent damage to the eye. This is vital as the three eyelid glands produce about 50% of the watery—aqueous—part of the tear film. In the absence of sufficient tear production, your golden is far more likely to suffer from dry eye, which can severely impede their vision. Your vet will assess your dog's condition and decide which surgical technique is best for them.

After surgery, the gland normally returns to regular function in a few weeks. There is a possibility of a re-prolapse of the third eyelid gland in about 5 - 20% of cases. Many dogs with a prolapsed eye will eventually experience the same prolapse in the other eye.

Retinal Dysplasia

Retinal dysplasia in dogs is the formation of clumps known as 'rosettes' or 'folds' in the eye retinal tissue. There are many causes of retinal dysplasia, but the most common is genetics, with several different dog breeds particularly prone to the condition. Labradors, cavaliers, golden retrievers, and springer spaniels are the breeds most at risk of inheriting retinal dysplasia. While this condition can affect your dog's vision, it is not painful or progressive.

Normally, the retina is comprised of two layers that form and develop together. In retinal dysplasia, folds, or creases, form between the two layers when they haven't properly developed. In addition to genetic factors, other causes of retinal dysplasia include vitamin deficiencies, damage to the eye, and viral infections.

The condition cannot be observed with the naked eye, so the first sign that something's wrong is more often the concern that your golden's vision might not be 100%, say, if they seem particularly clumsy or always bump into things.

A veterinary ophthalmologist needs to examine your golden with an otoscope or carry out a more complex examination to positively identify the condition.

Currently, it is not possible to treat retinal dysplasia. A dog who develops the condition will have it for life. This issue is hereditary, so do not breed from a dog with any form of retinal dysplasia.

The associated vision loss from retinal dysplasia may be entirely manageable, depending on its severity. Dogs with retinal dysplasia can live healthy and happy lives with very few problems. After retinal dysplasia is diagnosed, it will not worsen over time since it is not progressive. However, as your dog ages, they may develop additional eye problems, or their sight might fail.

Progressive Retinal Atrophy (PRA)

An inherited disease in dogs, progressive retinal atrophy engenders blindness slowly over several months or years. It is also called generalised progressive retinal atrophy or GPRA. The condition can occur in nearly any breed. However, it is most common in miniature and toy poodles, Labrador retrievers and cocker spaniels.

This is an inherited autosomal recessive disorder that causes the retinal cells in your golden's eye to degenerate and die. As light enters the eyes, retinal (rod and cone) cells transmit information to the brain, where it is translated into vision. The rod cells, which function in low light, are the first to degenerate, causing night blindness. Next, the cone cells, which work in bright light or during the daytime, begin to deteriorate, leading to total blindness over time.

Symptoms usually appear when a dog is around 3-5 years old, and blindness can occur in older dogs. The back of the eye is examined with an ophthalmoscope for characteristic signs of retinal degeneration to diagnose PRA. This is performed by a veterinarian who specialises in ophthalmology. In cases where the retina cannot be examined, such as if there are cataracts, an anaesthetic may be required to carry out an ERG—electroretinogram. This measures the electrical activity and function of the retina.

FACT ***There are DNA tests available for golden retrievers. A DNA test can detect whether your dog has the potential to develop PRA or pass it on to its puppies.***

Sadly, there is currently no effective treatment for PRA, and affected dogs are likely to go blind. There have been suggestions that antioxidant therapy could delay vision loss caused by PRA, but there is still no solid evidence for its effectiveness. Although gene therapy research may hold hope for the future, treatment is still a long way off.

Since PRA is an inherited issue, dogs with the disease must not be bred. In general, many dogs adapt well to vision loss, especially if the condition develops gradually, as with PRA.

Ear Issues

Ear Infections

Golden retrievers are more prone to ear infections than other breeds. Knowing the anatomy of your golden retriever's ear will help you understand why they are susceptible to ear infections:

- They have floppy ears. Unlike dogs with pointed ears that allow air to flow, those cute golden ears enclose the canal and keep moisture locked in. An ear canal that has reduced airflow has a moist, warm, and humid environment. Yeast and bacteria thrive in these conditions.
- They have sensitivities and allergies to food and the environment. Infections and inflammation of the ear can occur even without symptoms in other parts of the body.
- Some retrievers with narrow or very hairy ear canals (that prevent airflow) are also particularly susceptible to ear infections.
- Goldens can suffer from thyroid problems. Hypothyroidism, or low thyroid (T4) function, can predispose your dog to chronic ear infections.

Golden retrievers with their floppy, hanging ears are susceptible to ear infections. Infections in the ear are caused by a build-up of bacteria or yeast in the ear canal. These infections tend to be caused by underlying conditions such as ear mites, a skin issue, or excessive earwax and are the most common ear condition in golden retrievers.

When your golden's ears are damp after swimming, bathing, or walking in the rain, moisture becomes trapped, creating an ideal breeding ground for ear infections. You can prevent this problem by keeping your dog's ears dry.

Ear infections symptoms in dogs include head shaking, itchiness that causes scratching, rubbing their ear on the floor, red and swollen ear canals, whining due to pain, a dark-coloured discharge, odour, and crusts in the ears. More serious ear infections can make dogs lose their balance, walk in circles, have unusual eye movements, or appear to suffer hearing loss. When your golden's head tilts or they lose balance, the infection has spread deeper into the ear. Consult your vet if you suspect your dog has an ear infection. The faster your dog is treated, the faster they will recover.

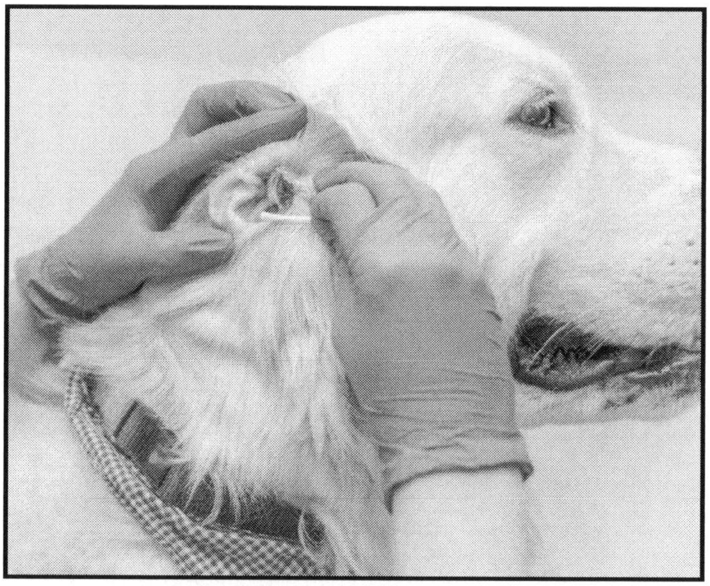

Usually, your vet will examine your golden's ears using an otoscope to determine the pain level and then swab the ears to collect a sample. They usually use a medicated cleanser first, then recommend some of the following:

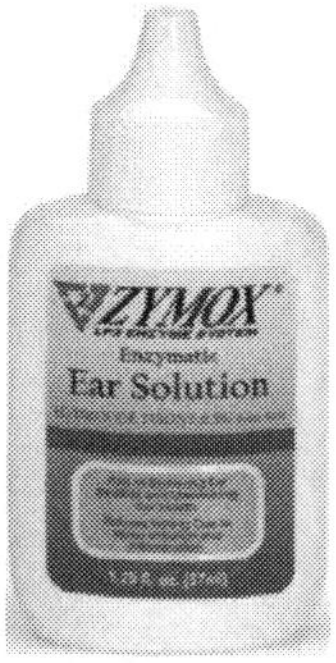

Eardrops – The use of medical ear drops (see picture) containing antibiotics, antifungals and anti-inflammatories can alleviate swelling and pain. Make sure your dog completes the full course of drops, even if it appears that their ears are improving.

Ear cleaning – As your retriever heals, you need to keep the inside of their ears clean. Ask your vet how to do this and what product to use. Do not use cotton buds.

Anti-inflammatory pain relief – If your dog is in a lot of pain, your vet might prescribe anti-inflammatory pain medication.

Antibiotic tablets – A very severe infection could require your dog to be given antibiotic pills as well as eardrops.

Treating the underlying problem – Most ear infections are the result of an underlying condition, such as an allergic reaction. Treatment of the underlying cause is just as important as treating the actual infection; if the cause is left untreated, infections will probably recur.

If your golden's ear infection is detected and treated early, it will most likely clear up quickly. Your dog will need a follow-up check to ensure the issue has been resolved. If your retriever's ear does not improve, your vet might decide to examine or treat it under anaesthetic. Some ear infections take several weeks to clear. Some cases of severe infection require surgery because the infection goes on for so long that the ear becomes misshapen.

Dogs who suffer from ear infections, or are particularly prone to them, such as the golden retriever, need ongoing ear care:

Ear checks – Regularly check your dog's ears for problems. The smell is usually the most obvious sign. As you become familiar with how your dog's ears smell when they're healthy, you will notice when an infected sour/pungent smell develops.

Cleaning – Your golden might need help keeping their ears clean if they are susceptible to infection. Your vet will be happy to show you how to check and clean your dog's ears at home (also check the *Ear Care* section in Chapter 9), so don't be afraid to ask for advice on cleaning them regularly. An effective ear cleanser for goldens is Zymox. It is a non-irritating cleanser designed for long-term use on non-infected dry ears. Zymox products contain LP3 enzymes, which can be safely used by dogs of all ages.

Hairy ears – Often, hairy ears are very warm and moist, making them a perfect breeding ground for bacteria and yeasts. By plucking or trimming the hair, air can be introduced into the ear.

Foreign Objects in the Ear

Occasionally, a foreign object can become lodged in your golden retriever's ear canal. If your dog scratches at their ears without apparent reason, it could be due to spear grass or another foreign object irritating their ear.

Grass seeds are a common foreign object that causes ear problems in dogs. The issue occurs most frequently during the summer months after playing in long grass. The sharp tip of the seed creates irritation by piercing the skin and getting lodged. The grass seeds can burrow into and through the skin, and they may even travel elsewhere on the body. When this happens, they can be difficult to locate. Symptoms of grass seeds include:

- Frequent ear scratching.
- Head shaking.
- An accumulation of seeds in or around the ear.
- Inflammation of the ear or its surrounding area.
- You may also notice some blood in your golden retriever's ear if the seed has become inflamed.

Your vet will first remove the grass seed (see picture) or whatever foreign object is causing the problem. This may necessitate anaesthesia or sedation, depending on where it is and the temperament of your dog. A long pair of tweezers (called crocodile forceps) will often be used. Locating the seed is frequently the hardest part of this procedure. You can't use an X-ray because they won't pick up grass seeds. Sometimes, they can be detected by ultrasound. After the seed has been removed, the infection will likely result in an abscess requiring medication to treat it. It could be necessary for your golden to wear a buster collar and/or bandage.

Mites

Another common ear problem seen in golden retrievers is ear mites, also known as otodectes cynotis. These tiny parasites generate intense itchiness in the ears and are picked up from another dog. Mites cause a mild parasitic infection that is highly contagious and commonly irritates the outer ear canal. You might notice some or all of the following symptoms if your golden retriever has ear mites:

- Head shaking.
- Scratching excessively around the ears and head.
- Brown particles that resemble coffee grains inside the ears.
- Waxy black or brown secretion.
- Further complications might result in blood pooling since blood vessels in the ear can rupture when scratched and shaken.

Mites are microscopic, infectious organisms that resemble tiny, white dots which can barely be seen by the naked eye. A microscope is usually required to detect them.

- Ear mites feed off ear wax and skin oils and live on the skin of the ear canal. Adult mites live for approximately two months. They multiply quickly. Their eggs take four days to hatch and a further three weeks to mature into adult mites ready to breed.

- Irritation in your golden's ear is often caused by allergies, leading to infections other than ear mites. If your dog seems to have an ear problem, it is crucial to get your dog properly diagnosed. Without visiting the vet, many canine owners incorrectly assume their dog has ear mites when they are actually suffering from a bacterial or yeast ear infection. Misdiagnosis can lead to weeks of inappropriate treatment and make the condition get worse.
- Ear mites are contagious. Other dogs and cats in the household can easily catch them from an infected animal. Even if your other pets are showing no symptoms of ear mites, it is imperative you treat them at the same time. Due to their lifestyle, cats are the most prone to catching ear mites. In extremely rare cases, dog owners have developed skin rashes when their pet has ear mites. However, the ear mites that infect dogs are not the same as the parasite that affects humans.

- Several spot-on flea treatments also treat and prevent ear mites. This is the easiest way to protect your dog from these parasites. Usually, this treatment requires only one or two applications to eliminate mites and is less stressful for you and your golden than ear drops.
- Some ear drops require at least three weeks of treatment because the medication won't kill the parasite's eggs. If using ear drops, you must administer them as prescribed for the recommended period. Other stronger topical treatments only need to be used for 10 to 14 days. These kill both eggs and adult mites and include medication to tackle the parasitic infection
- Always consult your vet about the best and most appropriate treatment to use.

Heart Disease

Just like us, our four-legged friends can suffer from heart disease. This might sound scary, but keeping the health of your golden's heart in mind will enable you to recognise the symptoms of heart disease—or worse, congestive heart failure—so you can seek out appropriate treatment if needed.

Here is what you need to know about heart disease in dogs, how to spot the signs and the best ways to prevent the condition for your dog to live a long, healthy life.

Facts – The heart (see picture below) is split into different parts to pump blood through the body. The right side of the heart, which comprises the right atrium and ventricle, pumps blood to the lungs so the blood cells can collect oxygen, which is then delivered back to the heart. On the left side, the left atrium and ventricle pump newly oxygenated blood throughout the body via the circulatory system.

If your golden retriever develops heart disease, their heart will have to adapt so it can continue to function efficiently and deliver oxygen to the rest of the body. In most cases, these changes occur slowly over time—often over years—causing the heart to enlarge. This stage is known as preclinical heart disease since dogs show no obvious signs that they're suffering from the condition.

Heart disease can develop into heart failure over time. This is called the clinical stage because signs of heart failure begin to show—including weakness or fainting after exercise, coughing or difficulty breathing, or fluid build-up. In essence, heart failure—including congestive heart failure—involves a backup of blood in the lungs or other organs, which negatively impacts the heart's function.

Although dogs can be born with heart disease, it can also develop as they age. The most common form of the condition in dogs, comprising 75% of all cases, results from degeneration of the mitral valve—the valve between the left atrium and the left ventricle. This creates a leaky valve, enlarging the dog's heart chambers. This condition is called mitral valve disease (MVD) and can eventually lead to heart failure. It can also lead to a heart murmur your vet can detect.

The second most common form of heart disease is called dilated cardiomyopathy (DCM), which is when the heart becomes so large, thin, and weak that it can no longer pump blood efficiently. Golden retrievers are particularly susceptible to this life-threatening condition.

FACT ***Heart disease is rare in dogs younger than five years old but becomes more common as dogs age.***

Symptoms – The symptoms of heart disease in dogs can go undetected for years. The most prevalent cause of heart disease, mitral valve disease, has a long, preclinical stage during which your dog will be asymptomatic. This means the early signs of heart disease are likely to go unnoticed by owners, although your vet may pick them up.

Even though not all dogs suffering from heart disease will develop heart failure, there are several clinical signs of heart failure to watch out for, including:

- Breathing too fast—more than 30 breaths per minute—when your dog is resting or sleeping.
- Increased effort required to breathe.
- Having trouble sleeping; moving around a lot and changing positions.
- Gagging or coughing.
- Depressed attitude, quiet, and not interactive.
- Weakness.
- Fainting or collapsing.
- Decrease in appetite.
- Losing weight.
- Distended stomach.

Contact your vet if your golden retriever exhibits any of these signs. Diagnosis usually involves x-rays, an electrocardiogram, and an echocardiogram.

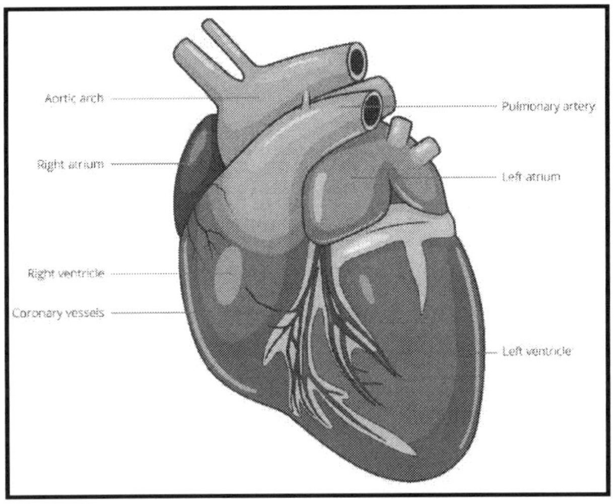

Treatment – For dogs diagnosed with dilated cardiomyopathy, several drugs are available. However, there are no guarantees. DCM is a serious disease that requires accurate diagnosis and aggressive treatment. While some dogs with DCM can benefit from treatment for some time, others will never be able to live a normal life. On average, dogs who respond well to treatment live between 6-24 months after diagnosis.

A vet cannot predict how long a dog will live if the condition is mitral valve disease. All cases are different and life expectancy depends heavily on the severity of the symptoms, the progression of their MVD, and their response to medication.

While some dogs with MVD live don't suffer symptoms for years—sometimes their whole lives—some require medication and respond well, while others suffer from more severe MVD that does not respond to medication. Unfortunately, in severe cases of MVD that do not respond to medication, life expectancy may be weeks or even days.

Heart Murmurs

Dogs often have heart murmurs. This is an abnormal heart sound, usually heard when listening to the dog's heart with a stethoscope. Heart murmurs are typically caused by turbulent blood flow in the heart. Murmurs may be deemed 'innocent' or 'physiologic', but they can also be pathologic or caused by disease. Pathologic heart murmurs can be due to structural heart issues—cardiac disease—or problems outside the heart—extracardiac problems.

The loudness of a murmur is connected to the amount of blood flow turbulence within the heart and does not always indicate the severity of the illness. The intensity of murmurs is usually measured on a scale of 1-6. Grade 1 murmurs are very soft or quiet, intermittent, and may often only be heard on one side of the chest. Grade 6 murmurs are very loud, detectable everywhere you can hear the heart, and can be felt if you place your hand on your retriever's chest in the heart area.

Your vet will be able to detect a heart murmur by listening to your retriever's heart with a stethoscope.

The prognosis can range from excellent to grave depending on the cause of the murmur. If the murmur is physiologic, no treatment is necessary, and the prognosis is usually good to excellent.

Where the murmur is caused by an extracardiac disease—i.e., not heart disease—or a functional issue that can be treated, it might resolve itself over time.

If your golden has a murmur caused by heart disease, the long-term prognosis varies wildly depending on the specific type of defect. Usually, dogs with mitral valve disease can have their condition managed with long-term medications. The prognosis for a dog suffering from dilated cardiomyopathy varies, but if there are signs of heart failure, the outlook is not great.

Depending on the result of diagnostic tests, your vet will decide on the prognosis and treatment options for your retriever. It will be necessary to monitor your dog's condition on an ongoing basis and conduct periodic diagnostic tests throughout their life.

FACT ***A physiologic or innocent heart murmur is one that does not affect your dog's health. Puppies, especially large breed puppies, are prone to developing an innocent heart murmur because they grow rapidly. Innocent heart murmurs typically become apparent at 6-8 weeks of age, and your puppy will outgrow them by about 4-5 months of age. These murmurs are benign.***

Other Common Health Conditions

There are other common health conditions which can affect a golden retriever's quality of life. While a well-cared-for and healthy dog will probably never suffer from any of these, it is always a good idea to be aware of the possibility.

Diabetes

Diabetes is a chronic disease that affects humans, dogs, cats, and other animals, including pigs, horses, and apes. Dogs can develop diabetes from as young as 18 months old, although the condition is most often diagnosed between the ages of 7 to 10 years old. Even breeds that do not have a genetic predisposition to diabetes can develop the condition in later life due to obesity or a poor long-term diet.

An interesting statistic is that about 70% of dogs with diabetes are females. The disease can affect any breed, but Labrador retrievers, cocker spaniels, golden retrievers, Pomeranians, terriers, and toy poodles are at a higher risk.

Mechanism – During digestion, some nutrients are broken down into glucose, a type of sugar that provides energy to the cells and organs. Glucose is absorbed into the bloodstream through the intestines, which then transports it to every cell in the body. In addition, the pancreas secretes insulin into the body. The insulin acts as a 'gatekeeper', telling cells to pull glucose and other nutrients out of the bloodstream and use them as fuel. However, in diabetics, the glucose-insulin connection does not function correctly. There are two forms of diabetes in dogs:

Insulin-Deficient Diabetes – This happens when a dog's body does not produce enough insulin because the pancreas is damaged or malfunctioning. For dogs with this type of diabetes, daily shots are necessary to replace the missing insulin. This is the most common form of diabetes in dogs.

Insulin-Resistant Diabetes – This happens when a dog's pancreas is producing some insulin, but their body is not using it properly. The cells do not respond to the insulin's 'message' and cannot absorb glucose from the blood. Diabetes of this type is commonly seen in old, obese dogs. Female dogs can also develop insulin resistance during pregnancy or while in heat.

Regardless of the type of diabetes, the effects on the body are the same. There is an excess of sugar in the dog's bloodstream, and yet cells in the body cannot access it. As a result, diabetes causes two adverse effects on your dog's body:

- The cells are starved of vital 'fuel'. Cells in muscles and certain organs are deprived of glucose, essential for energy. As a response, the body breaks down fats and proteins to use as fuel instead.
- Many organs are damaged by high blood sugar levels. In the absence of insulin—or in insulin-resistant cases—high levels of glucose build up in the bloodstream. As a result, this abnormal blood chemistry acts as a poison and eventually damages organs, most frequently kidneys, eyes, heart, blood vessels, or nerves.

Symptoms – Usually, the first signs of diabetes will be increased consumption of water, followed by weight loss, even though a dog might be consuming normal amounts of food and seem hungry all the time. This is because the cells in the body are not receiving the glucose they need to function properly.

As the disease progresses, the dog might show signs of depression, lose interest in their food, lack energy, and vomit. If the signs are not detected and a treatment protocol is not put in place, there can be other serious consequences, including cloudy eyes leading to cataracts, enlarged liver, kidney failure, ketoacidosis, seizures, and urinary tract infections.

Risk factors – Even though diabetes can occur in any dog, some factors increase the possibility of the condition developing:

Age – Middle-aged to senior dogs are most likely to develop diabetes. Noticing any changes in eating or drinking habits in a dog older than five can help detect the early signs of the disease.

Chronic Pancreatitis – When the inflammation of the pancreas is a repeated or chronic occurrence, this can damage the pancreas, which can result in diabetes.

Cushing's Disease – This condition makes the dog's body over-produce internal cortisol steroids, which can become diabetes.

Genetics – While diabetes can affect any dog, purebred or hybrid, it is believed that genetics could predispose certain breeds to the condition.

Gender – A female dog who has not been spayed is 50% more likely to suffer from diabetes than a male dog. Simply having your female dog spayed will help prevent diabetes.

Obesity – Too many of our canine counterparts are overweight, which contributes to a higher incidence of insulin resistance, pancreatitis, and diabetes. Making sure your golden receives enough daily exercise and is not overfed can go a long way towards preventing diabetes and other weight-related health issues.

Steroid Medications – The long-term use of steroid medications can cause diabetes. If your retriever needs steroids, discuss this possibility with your vet.

Treatment – Diabetes is very treatable. Most diabetic dogs require daily insulin injections (see picture) to maintain their blood sugar at an acceptable level. You will need to learn how to give insulin injections, which is not as hard as it sounds.

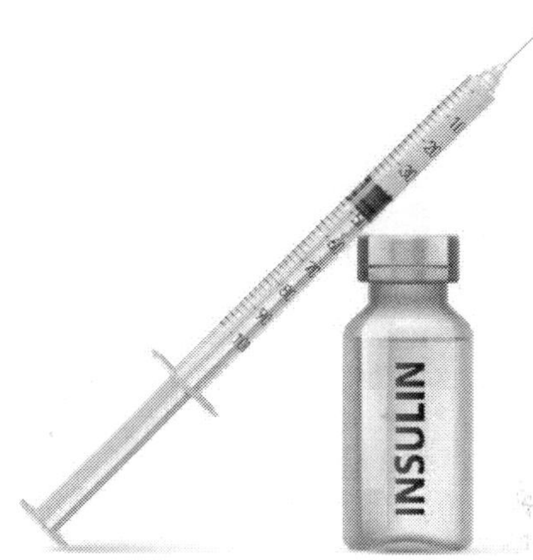

Regular blood and urine testing are needed to ensure normal blood sugar levels. You may need to carry out in-home urine glucose level checks.

Your dog's vet will emphasise the importance of maintaining proper insulin and feeding schedules. A dog receiving insulin therapy needs to maintain a normal consumption of food. Your golden needs to eat regular meals to balance the effect of the insulin injection that removes the excess sugars from the bloodstream. Diabetic dogs must maintain a moderate but consistent exercise routine to prevent sudden spikes or drops in glucose levels.

Some signs that indicate whether your dog is receiving too much or too little insulin include loss of appetite, excessive urination, weakness, tremors, or seizures. If you notice any of these symptoms, immediately take your retriever to the vet or an emergency clinic for examination and possible changes in dosage or frequency of their insulin injections.

With early detection and proper management, including ongoing veterinary care, a diabetic dog can live a long and healthy life.

Cancer

Our canine friends develop similar varieties of cancer at roughly the same rate as their human counterparts. According to studies, dogs have the highest rate of cancer of any mammal on Earth, with the most affected areas being the skin, the digestive system, and the mammary glands of females.

Cancer used to be associated with old age but has now started affecting younger dogs (and people). While some breeds are more susceptible to certain kinds of cancer, it is estimated that overall, 1 in 3 dogs will develop and eventually succumb to cancer, making it the leading cause of canine death over the age of 10. Golden retrievers have one of the highest rates of cancer, with roughly 60% of goldens developing cancer.

In addition, the American Veterinary Medical Association warns that as our pets get older, there is an increased risk of cancer, with almost half of ageing dogs suffering at some point in their life.

FACT ***Cancer is the unrestrained division and growth of cells. Usually, cell division is tightly controlled. If a cell undergoes a series of genetic mutations, cell division becomes unregulated, resulting in a tumour.***

The following are the most common cancer types in dogs:

Mast Cell Tumours – Mast cell tumours are a type of skin cancer. Mast cells reside in the connective tissues, especially the nerves and vessels near the external surface of the dog—skin, lungs, nose, and mouth. The grading of mast cell tumours is based on their location on the skin, how inflamed they are, and how well they are differentiated.

Melanoma – Melanoma is the most common malignant tumour in a dog's mouth. Skin tumours are among the most frequently occurring tumours in dogs, many of which are benign.

Lymphoma – Lymphoma is a cancer of the lymphocyte blood cells and lymphoid tissues. Lymphoid tissue is present in many parts of the body, including the lymph nodes, spleen, gastrointestinal tract, liver, and bone marrow.

Bone Cancer (Osteosarcoma) – Osteosarcoma is the most common bone tumour found in dogs. Whilst it is most often found in larger breeds, bone cancer can affect any breed of dog.

Hemangiosarcoma – This cancer is highly malignant and can spread rapidly, causing tumours to grow almost anywhere in the body. It is often found in a dog's heart and spleen. Frequently, it is already in an advanced stage before diagnosis.

Diagnosis – Since cancer can occur in any part of a dog's body, symptoms are extremely varied. Many of the symptoms overlap with an extensive range of diseases, meaning a diagnosis cannot be made on symptoms alone.

If you have discovered a bump or lump on the surface of your golden's skin, you should certainly visit the vet, but don't stress too soon. Not all surface lumps are cancerous. However, a sore that does not heal should be investigated. Other signs of tumours affecting internal organs—benign or cancerous—include:

- Changes in eating habits.
- Discoloured areas of skin.
- Laboured breathing.
- Swelling of the abdomen.
- Sudden weight loss.
- Diarrhoea or vomiting lasting longer than 1 or 2 days.
- Bleeding from the mouth, nose, or another orifice.
- Heat, pain, or lameness that cannot be explained.

Typically, the vet will take blood samples and x-rays to diagnose cancer. They might also suggest an ultrasound or MRI scan. These tests can help determine whether cancer has spread to other areas of the dog's body—a process vets call 'staging'. They can give the vet an indication of the condition of the dog's health. This affects their ability to cope with treatment.

A biopsy—examining a small sample under a microscope—can help identify a tumour and confirm whether it is cancerous. Making a definite diagnosis can be difficult. For example, biopsies do not always provide enough good quality material even when examined under a microscope.

Treatment – There are various types of tumours, and treatment is available for most of them. Surgery might be the cure for an isolated lump that has not spread in the body, although it depends on where the tumour is growing. In hard-to-reach areas such as a golden's brain, tumours are difficult to remove. If cancer is spreading inwards, the opportunities for treatment depend on the type of cancer and how far it has spread. Quality of life is important and if a dog is in extreme pain that cannot be relieved, the vet will probably encourage the owner to opt for euthanasia.

There are three main types of cancer treatment—surgery, radiotherapy, and chemotherapy. Several other new therapies may also be offered, such as photodynamic therapy or immunotherapy. Certain treatments require frequent visits to the vet or specialists, and it can be important for treatment to be given at specific intervals.

Often, surgery is used on tumours of the skin or distinct internal growths. The lump removed at surgery normally needs to be analysed to find out whether it is likely to have spread. Surgery can sometimes relieve the symptoms caused by internal growths in cases where the size of the tumour is giving rise to illness, although the risk of recurrence remains.

FACT ***Several types of cancer respond well to chemotherapy. Since the doses used are smaller than those for humans, veterinary chemotherapy generally has few or no side effects. Unfortunately, chemo does not normally cure cancer. Its aim is to reduce the symptoms and slow down the disease.***

If removing the whole tumour has not been possible, sometimes, chemotherapy is performed after surgery to try to slow down recurrence. It is also used in widespread cancers such as those involving the white blood cells—leukaemia—that cannot be surgically removed. The vet may be able to provide some types of chemotherapy, but others require specialists.

If your dog has cancer, you'll usually need to make regular visits to the vet for treatment, and sedation could be required. There are several possible side effects from chemotherapy, which include reduced appetite, vomiting, or diarrhoea. Occasionally, the drugs cause the white blood cell count to drop. This can increase the risk of infections, so blood tests are commonly taken to check for this during treatment.

Only a few specialist centres provide radiotherapy treatment. Again, this does not normally cure cancer, and regular visits are frequently required for an extended period. Since the dog needs to be perfectly still for the treatment, a general anaesthetic is given during each treatment.

It is not possible to predict life expectancy with any certainty following a cancer diagnosis. The kind of cancer and how far it has advanced will offer some indication of potential life expectancy. For certain cancers, there are more specialised tests that help with the prognosis. Nevertheless, as with all illnesses, cancers do not necessarily follow a set course. Regrettably, sudden deteriorations can sometimes occur.

The vet will be aware of the importance of keeping your dog pain-free. Current painkillers are highly effective. Unfortunately, any dog with incurable cancer will eventually come to a point when they are suffering too much and have lost their quality of life. The owner should work closely with the vet to recognise when this happens to choose euthanasia at the best time. However, all vets agree that a healthy, happy animal does not have to be euthanised, even if their condition is incurable.

Hypothyroidism

Your golden retriever may have hypothyroidism if they have been extremely tired recently or have issues with their skin or hair. Fortunately, thyroid problems are easy to diagnose and manage.

In both dogs and humans, the thyroid is a butterfly-shaped gland in the neck, situated next to the windpipe. Being part of the endocrine system, the thyroid gland produces hormones needed for cells to function normally. The thyroid affects your dog's metabolism.

Your retriever can develop signs of hyperthyroidism, including diarrhoea, increased heart rate, anxiety, and hyperactivity, if they produce too much thyroid hormone. If the thyroid gland does not secrete enough thyroid hormone, the exact opposite occurs. Hypothyroidism is the most common thyroid problem for dogs.

Hypothyroidism is most frequently diagnosed in dogs between 4 and 10 years old. Mostly, the autoimmune disorder shrinks or inflames the thyroid tissue causing hypothyroidism. The genetic causes are unknown. However, medium to large breeds are at greater risk than toy and miniature breeds, according to the American Kennel Club. The cocker spaniel, dachshund, miniature schnauzer, Doberman pinscher, golden retriever, Airedale terrier, and Irish setter are among those more likely to contract the disease.

Although uncommon, cancer of the thyroid gland can also cause hypothyroidism in dogs. There is an apparent increase in the risk for spayed and neutered dogs. However, the potential risk of hypothyroidism may be outweighed by the many benefits of spaying and neutering.

Signs – In dogs, hypothyroidism affects every system in the body, including the nervous system, the gastrointestinal system, and the circulatory system. If your golden retriever has not been spayed or neutered, hypothyroidism could also affect their reproductive system.

The most prevalent signs of low thyroid problems in dogs include:

- Excessive tiredness.
- Depression or low mood.
- Weight gain.
- Infections of the skin.
- Intolerance to cold.
- Skin and coat changes, such as excessive shedding, hair loss, excessive dandruff, a dry or dull coat, and hyperpigmented skin.
- Long heat cycles for female dogs who have not been spayed.
- Generalised weakness and other neuromuscular problems.
- Walking stiffly or breathing loudly due to laryngeal paralysis—the loss of normal function of the larynx.

Diagnosis – Unlike human thyroid problems, thyroid problems in goldens are usually easy to diagnose and manage. If you think your retriever might be suffering from thyroid issues, make an appointment with your vet. They will ask questions, examine your dog, and probably run some tests—normally blood work and urine testing.

A common indicator of hypothyroidism in dogs is high blood cholesterol. Most clinics can test for thyroid hormone levels in dogs with a simple blood test.

Treatment – Should your golden retriever be diagnosed with hypothyroidism, don't panic. Although hypothyroidism in dogs is incurable, it is usually easy and relatively inexpensive to manage the condition with an oral thyroid supplement. This supplement mimics the effect of thyroid hormone on the body. If successful, your golden will regain their energy, lose weight, stop shedding hair, and have a brighter attitude.

When treating thyroid problems in dogs, the most important thing to remember is to maintain balance. If your golden takes too much thyroid supplement, they can develop symptoms of an overactive thyroid, the opposite of what you want. If your vet prescribes a thyroid supplement for your dog, it is important to follow the instructions regarding the dose. Talk to your vet before changing the dosage.

Once your retriever has started on a thyroid supplement, your vet will probably ask you to come back in a couple of weeks for a follow-up blood test to ensure your dog's thyroid hormone levels are correct. Once they have stabilised, your vet will most likely want to check them every six or twelve months.

Epilepsy

Epilepsy is one of the most reported canine neurological problems. It is estimated to affect 0.6-0.7% of all dog breeds in the U.K.—around 1 in 130 dogs.

Most frequently, epilepsy is a lifelong disease. While not painful, it is still a traumatic experience for the owner. Any breed can be affected by the condition.

Epileptic seizures are the result of abnormal neuron activity in the cerebral cortex area of the dog's brain. The neurons inside the brain communicate with each other via neurotransmitters that either inhibit or excite other neurons.

FACT ***When there is a healthy balance of neurotransmitter activity, everything's fine. However, when there is an imbalance that increases the firing of excitation neurons, this can cause a seizure.***

There are several types of seizures and how they manifest depends on what percentage of your dog's cerebral cortex is firing abnormally. The different types include:

Partial (Focal seizure)

This can be hard to recognise because only one part of the cerebral cortex is involved, with little spreading to other areas of the brain. There are two types of partial seizures that can be either simple or complex, lasting a couple of minutes.

Grand Mal (Generalised tonic-clonic seizure)

This type of seizure occurs when both hemispheres of the cerebral cortex are activated at the same time. It is the most common and easily recognised, typically lasting anything from a few seconds to a few minutes.

Your dog may lose consciousness and fall to the side with rhythmic muscle contraction displayed as chewing jaw movements, paddling motions, or jerking of the limbs. During a grand mal seizure, your dog might also drool and lose bladder or bowel control.

Simple Seizure (Focal motor)

When neurons are only firing in the motor area, a dog may remain conscious, with involuntary muscle movements of the face or jerking of the limbs.

Complex Partial Seizure (Psychomotor)

This is the hardest to recognise because while consciousness may be impaired, this type of seizure may just seem like momentary strange behaviour. For instance, a dog may appear to be biting at invisible flies, stare in the distance or suddenly act out with aggression.

Causes – There are many different causes behind a seizure, including exposure to toxins, kidney or liver disease, anaemia, cancer, inflammation or infection of the brain, head injury or genetics.

'Symptomatic' epilepsy means that there is an identifiable cause or reason for the seizure.

'Idiopathic' epilepsy means a seizure with no known cause. These types of seizures most often occur between the ages of 6 months and 6 years.

How to Help – If you suspect your dog may be suffering from seizures, it is important to have them immediately diagnosed by the vet.

Since isolated seizures are usually self-limiting and rarely life-threatening, make sure your dog cannot injure themselves during one, say by falling off a chair or down a flight of stairs. Stay calm and keep track of how long the episode lasts, so you can report back to your veterinarian. Also, keep your hands out of the dog's mouth because they will not know what is happening and may accidentally bite you.

Some dogs are born with this neurological condition. Sadly, at the time of writing, there is no known cure. Studies have demonstrated promising results for controlling epilepsy by feeding a special diet rich in MCT (Medium Chain Triglycerides). These fatty acids are derived from plant-based oils like coconut oil and are known to improve brain function.

TIP ***The addition of supplements or herbs (vitamin E, melatonin, taurine) to improve liver function may lower the severity and/or frequency of seizures. Some believe that acupuncture can also help to reduce the frequency of seizures.***

When a seizure doesn't stop on its own (within 5 minutes), or two or more occur within 24 hours, this should be considered a life-threatening emergency necessitating prompt medical intervention.

Treatment with anti-epileptic/anti-convulsive drugs to reduce the frequency, length and severity of seizures is an option:

- It can take a while to find the right dose of medication to bring therapeutic relief from seizures. Regular blood testing will be required. Phenobarbital is usually the first drug prescribed for a dog experiencing seizures. Careful blood monitoring will be required; if the levels of Phenobarbital in the blood are too high, this can result in liver disease.
- Potassium bromide is another drug that can help control seizures. This will also need regular blood testing to ensure stable levels in the bloodstream because this drug is connected with the development of canine pancreatitis.

- Newer seizure medications may be prescribed, including levetiracetam (Keppra) and zonisamide—the latter can be used alone or in combination with other medications. When your golden retriever is having a seizure, short-acting drugs—diazepam or midazolam—may also be given.

While a diagnosis of epilepsy is not something any dog owner wants to hear, it is usually a manageable condition. With a solid treatment plan in place, your golden will usually live a happy, long, and normal life.

von Willebrand Disease

Von Willebrand's disease (vWD) is one of the most common inherited bleeding disorders in both humans and dogs. The condition is caused by a deficiency of a specific protein. This protein helps platelets—blood cells necessary for clotting—to clump together and seal broken vessels, and it is called von Willebrand factor (vWF).

FACT ***There are usually three types of this disease: type I, type II, and type III. A dog with Type III bleeding disorder has an elevated risk of spontaneous bleeding and serious bleeding caused by trauma and surgery. Type I is the mildest form.***

A dog with vWD might suffer nose bleeds, excessive bleeding from the gums, and prolonged bleeding during or after whelping. In some instances, there is prolonged bleeding from the umbilical cord at birth or when the pup sheds its baby teeth. The first sign of this condition in a dog is often excessive bleeding following surgery or trauma. You may also notice blood in the dog's urine or stools. Symptoms can vary wildly. Some dogs bleed profusely, while others do not experience any bleeding at all.

This is an autosomal-recessive condition. This means an abnormal gene must be inherited twice—from both the mother and the father—for your golden's health to be affected. Dogs who inherit only one copy of the abnormal gene—from either their mother or father—won't have any symptoms of the disease but will be carriers who could pass it on to any puppies. Over 50 breeds are affected, though the breeds with the highest prevalence of vWD are Doberman pinschers, German shepherds, poodles, Shetland sheepdogs and golden retrievers.

vWD can be diagnosed by your veterinarian using a buccal mucosal screening test. The presence of prolonged bleeding in the test can suggest the presence of this disease, especially in at-risk breeds. A laboratory test will determine the precise amount of von Willebrand factor in the blood to confirm the diagnosis.

It is common for affected dogs to go their whole lives with no signs of this bleeding problem until they undergo surgery or are injured, which is when the disease is identified. If your golden has von Willebrand disease and is actively bleeding, then the bleeding needs to be stopped and their blood replaced. This procedure involves using clotting sponges or styptic powder, giving a blood transfusion, and sometimes administering Desmopressin, a medication that temporarily increases the amount of von Willebrand factor in the blood. Von Willebrand disease has no known cure at the time of writing.

Canine Obesity

Canine obesity is one of the most common and preventable health issues. The Association for Pet Obesity Prevention has estimated that 56% of dogs in the United States are overweight. That's over 50 million dogs, which means that obesity in the canine population can be regarded as an epidemic. There are serious weight-related health conditions associated with obesity that can shorten your dog's lifespan and seriously impact their quality of life, including arthritis, cancer, diabetes, heart disease, high blood pressure, kidney disease and more. Statistics tell us that being just 10% overweight may cut short a dog's life by as much as one-third.

But just as with human obesity, it's not always a clear-cut case of too much food and not enough exercise. There are some congenital causes of canine obesity. Certain breeds, such as the beagle, Labrador retriever, collie, cocker spaniel, golden retriever, and basset hound, are more prone to obesity than others. Also, if your golden has been spayed or neutered, they can experience a drop in metabolism. This might cause problems if you do not adjust their feeding and exercise routine as they grow older. Hormonal disorders can also result in weight gain. Underactive thyroid glands, a condition called Cushing's disease, are linked with canine obesity. When your golden's adrenal glands produce too much cortisol, fat is disproportionately distributed to the abdomen, resulting in a pot-bellied appearance.

FACT ***Today, people live a more sedentary lifestyle, and when our dogs join us in that, they can suffer from being overweight, too. Golden retrievers are active athletes who need to run and explore their world every day. They also love to eat, but when you don't combat their love of eating with plenty of exercise, they easily become obese.***

Obesity is a serious condition that plagues many breeds of dogs. Researchers at the University of Cambridge have identified a genetic variation known as 'POMC', which may explain why some breeds put on weight more easily than others. However, further research is required as some breeds that have this variation are not known to be prone to obesity.

Most goldens are always hungry and will eat anything that comes their way. If the size of your golden retriever is getting out of control, the following steps will help you get your dog trimmed down:

- Diarise when and what treats they are given.
- Feed only the recommended amount for the size of your dog.
- Stop giving them human table scraps.
- Give treats sparingly.
- Monitor your golden's weight each week.
- Understand the risks of obesity to your dog.

If you are uncertain about the ideal weight for your golden, make an appointment to discuss it with your vet. The following chart will give you an estimate of what your dog's ideal weight should be, so you can keep your golden in the optimal range:

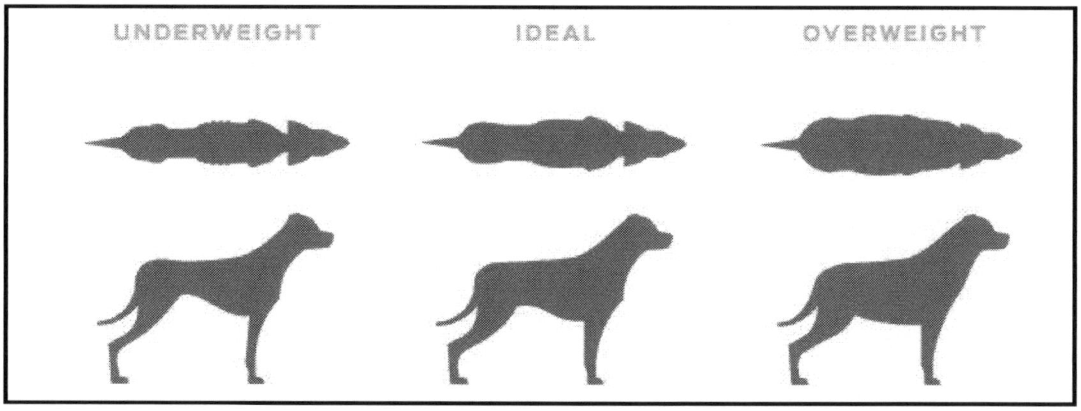

Canine Bloat

While any dog can suffer from bloat, it is seen more often in larger, deep-chested breeds.

Bloat, also known as 'emergency gastrointestinal syndrome' or 'gastric dilatation volvulus', is a common, life-threatening incident. This condition can happen quickly, especially if your dog is fed immediately after vigorous exercise or if they are a very fast eater and gulp in large amounts of air with their food. Their stomach becomes distended with food, wind, and fluid, which can make it twist 180 degrees or more and close. When the stomach is closed off in this way, the food is then trapped inside, where it ferments and makes the stomach bulge. This bulging stomach can in turn create dangerous problems, including:

- Decreased blood flow to the heart.
- Obstruction of blood flow to the veins in the abdomen.
- A tear in the wall of the stomach.
- Low blood pressure.
- Shock and damage to internal organs.

Symptoms can occur very quickly and include:

- Restlessness.
- Drooling.
- Swollen stomach.
- Looking anxious.
- Pacing.
- Attempting to vomit.
- Stretching with the front end down and the back end up.
- Weakness.
- Shortness of breath.
- Rapid heartbeat.
- Pale gums.

FACT ***The reason that bloat is referred to as 'emergency' gastrointestinal syndrome is that it is a serious condition that demands immediate, emergency veterinary intervention. According to statistics, 50% of dogs that develop bloat do not survive.***

While treatment depends on the severity of the condition, it generally involves:

- Placing a tube down the throat to the stomach to release pressure.
- If the stomach is twisted, inserting a large hollow needle through the belly to relieve pressure.
- IV fluids and antibiotics.
- If the x-ray confirms a twisted stomach, emergency surgery is performed to untwist it and return it to the proper position.

While bloat can be a very frightening event requiring immediate intervention, you can take some steps to prevent it from ever occurring, including:

- Not feeding right after energetic play or running.
- Rather than giving one or two larger meals, feed several smaller ones.
- Using a slow feeder bowl to calm down the eating pace.

Useful health tips

Making vet visits easier – Rather than worrying about causing your retriever stress every time they go to the vet, there are several things you can do to prevent 'vet trauma', including:

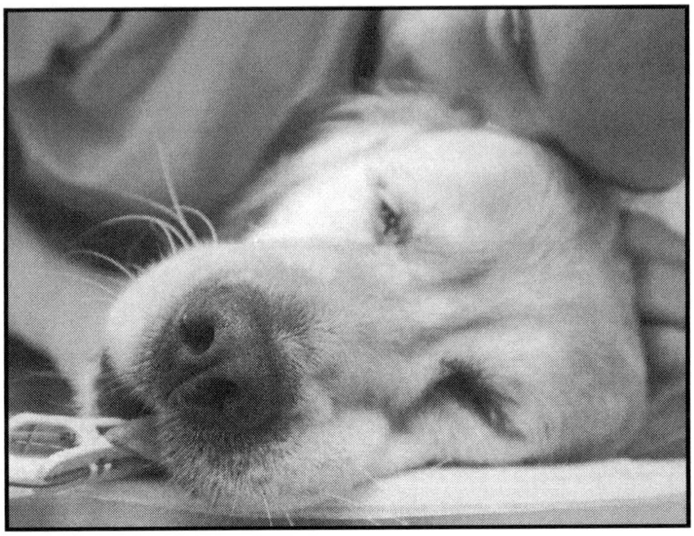

1. Make some social visits before your dog has a health issue, so they can visit the staff, become familiar with the smells, and have a treat for a positive experience.
2. Practise exams at home on a table, so your retriever won't be fearful of the vet's examination table. Look at their eyes and ears, open their mouth, feel their spine, and hold their feet.
3. Take your dog for a walk or play some games before you go to the vet so your golden is more relaxed. A tired dog will feel less anxious.
4. Be aware of your energy. Having a negative 'feeling sorry' energy can make things worse for your golden retriever. Your dog needs you to be confident when being subjected to new smells and procedures, which may make them feel nervous.

TIP ***How often you need to go to the vet will depend on your retriever's stage of life. A young puppy will require more frequent visits for their vaccination schedule and spaying procedure. A healthy adult dog with no problems should only need to visit the vet once a year for a wellness check-up. For a senior dog, increase vet visits to twice yearly to identify any health issues in the early stages and ensure they are maintaining a healthy weight.***

Although a well-cared-for and healthy adult golden retriever will not spend much time in the vet's office, there are times when not a second should be wasted in getting them assessed. For example, when your dog is bleeding, unconscious, shaking with pain, vomiting blood, etc.

Taking your Dog's Temperature – If you suspect your dog might be ill or has a fever, you should check their temperature. There are two ways to do this, depending on the type of thermometer you have in your canine first aid kit.

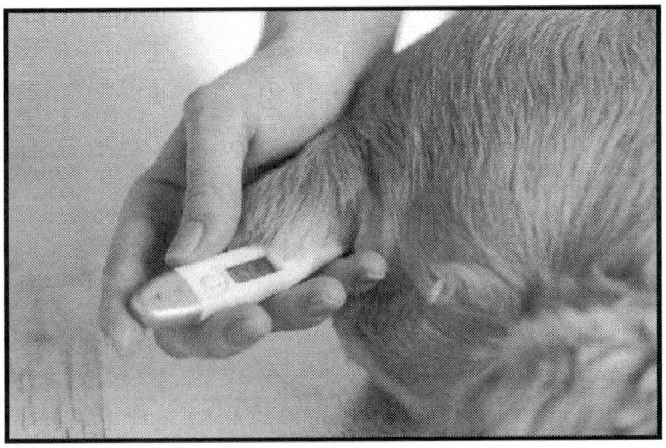

Rectal Thermometer – A rectal thermometer (see picture) is easier to use when you have a friend to help hold your retriever still, by following these steps:

- Have your retriever lie down on their side.
- Shake the mercury down in the thermometer.
- Lubricate the thermometer with petroleum jelly.
- Lift your golden's tail and locate the anus.
- Using a rotating motion, insert the thermometer 2.5 to 7.5 centimetres (1 to 3 inches).

- Talk soothingly to your dog while holding the thermometer in place for two minutes.
- Remove the thermometer and wipe it clean.
- Read the height of the mercury on the gauge.
- A normal rectal temperature is 38 to 38.8 ºC (100.5 to 102 ºF).

Ear Thermometer – When used correctly, an ear thermometer (see picture) is a less invasive and usually more easily tolerated way to take your golden's temperature. The process is as follows:

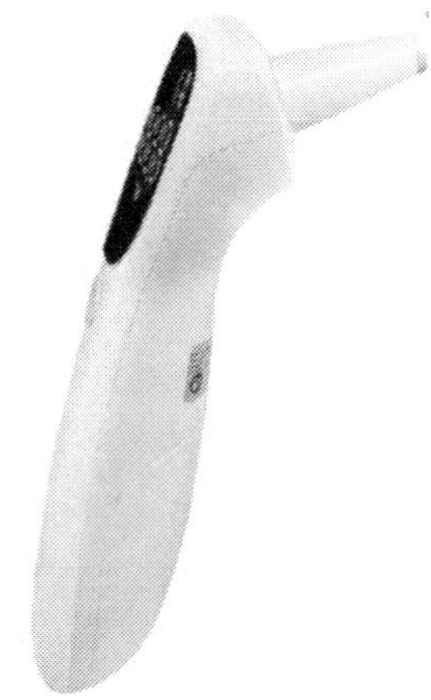

- Have your dog sit or lie down.
- Lift their ear flap.
- Insert the thermometer deep into the ear canal.
- It should only take a few seconds to register their temperature.
- A normal ear temperature is 37.7 to 39.4 ºC (100 to 103 ºF).

If your golden retriever's temperature is outside the normal range—either above or below—it is time to take them to the vet to hopefully determine the reason.

My dog is limping – There are many reasons why your golden retriever might be limping. They may have a foreign body stuck between their toes or a sore muscle from rough play with a heavier dog. They may have a cut on their foot or a broken dewclaw. If they are of advanced years, they might have arthritis in their joints.

When your dog is limping, first find out whether the problem is minor, since your dog may recover quickly on their own. If your dog has been seriously injured, they might need to be taken to the vet. Be aware that most dogs will not attempt to walk on a broken leg. However, if the injury is minor, they might lightly touch their foot on the ground and limp along. If they allow you to examine their leg and foot without biting you—because it is too painful— generally speaking, the injury isn't severe.

TIP ***If there is swelling from a bruise or pulled muscle, rinse it with cool water and apply an ice pack to bring down the swelling. If the limping persists for more than a day, make an appointment with your vet.***

My dog broke a leg – However your golden retriever broke their leg, they will be in severe pain and need to be carefully transported to the vet clinic for immediate assessment and treatment. Ask a friend or family member to drive you, so you can focus on keeping your retriever as calm as possible to minimise pain and further injury to the leg. Once at the vet's, they will stabilise your dog by giving them intravenous fluids, pain medication and possibly antibiotics.

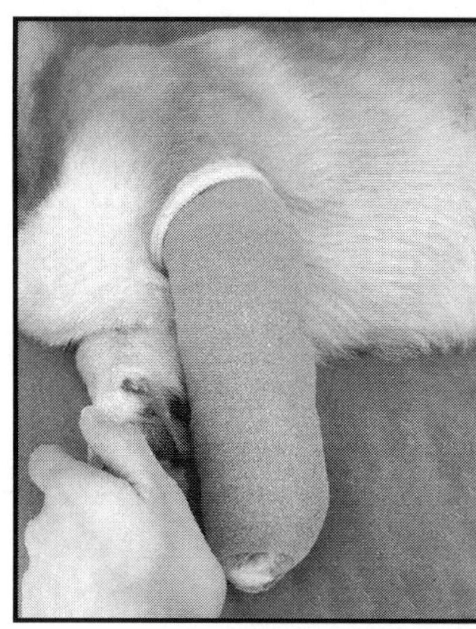

If the broken leg is a simple, closed fracture, all that is needed is to splint or cast the leg (see picture). However, if the leg has been broken in multiple places and is severely damaged, you might be asked to consider amputation in the understanding that dogs can adapt very quickly to getting around on three legs.

Recovery may take between 4 and 12 weeks, depending on the diagnosis, treatment, and age of your retriever. The veterinary team will guide you on how to support your golden retriever and might recommend underwater treadmill therapy or at-home physiotherapy that includes massage, joint flexion exercises, and ice treatments to aid recovery time.

Disclaimer: ***The author of the book is not a veterinarian. This chapter has been compiled to give a broad overview of the medical conditions that might affect your golden retriever, but it is not intended to replace qualified medical advice. Consult your vet or health care professional for a firm diagnosis of any health condition and to devise a treatment plan suitable for your dog.***

14. Golden Allergies and Skin

'My little dog, a heartbeat at my feet.'

~ Edith Wharton ~

Just like with humans, the skin is the largest organ of your dog's body, comprising 12 to 25% of their entire body weight. Their skin regulates temperature while providing a protective barrier against the environment. Without a healthy skin, your golden retriever will not have a shiny and lustrous coat.

Skin consists of the epidermis (outer layer), the dermis (middle layer), and the subcutis—inner layer. In addition, there are other important appendages, including claws, hair, subcutaneous fat, and muscles.

Your golden's skin should be regularly checked for lumps, bumps, redness, insect bites, sores, dandruff, dull coat, and hair loss by brushing and parting their hair to inspect the skin. If their skin and coat do not look healthy, get your dog checked over by the vet before any problems become more serious. Many skin issues can affect your golden's health and the condition of their coat. Allergies are on the rise and are a growing concern for most dog breeds.

Allergy Types

You might have heard from your vet or a friend that perhaps the symptoms your golden has are due to allergies, but what does that mean? An allergy is simply a reaction by your dog's immune system to a substance in the environment, on the coat or skin, or in their food. While different allergies generally require various treatment protocols, symptoms are often similar and may include:

- Red, inflamed skin.
- Hives.
- Swelling of the ears, eyelids, earflaps, and face.
- Itching skin.
- Runny eyes.
- Sneezing.
- Chronic ear infections.
- Itchy ears.
- Constant licking.
- Constant scratching.
- Rubbing their face.

- Unhealthy skin and coat.
- Diarrhoea.
- Vomiting.

Inhalant Allergies (Atopy)

Atopy is one of the most common allergies in dogs. If your golden retriever has an inhalant allergy, their immune system overreacts to an airborne or inhaled allergen. There is a wide variety of allergens that might cause atopy, which are similar to the causes of hay fever in people. When the affected dog inhales pollens, dust, or moulds, an allergic response occurs.

FACT ***The most commonly affected breeds are Labradors, golden retrievers, English setters, German shepherds, boxers, Lhasa Apsos, poodles, West Highland white terriers, Cairn terriers, and Jack Russell terriers, but any breed can develop atopy.***

A dog with an inhalant allergy is usually itchy during certain seasons of the year. However, some atopic dogs can exhibit non-seasonal signs. An affected dog typically chews, licks, and scratches all over, especially the feet and face. Your dog's saliva might stain their light-coloured hairs, resulting in reddish-brown or orange hair. When affected, your golden might also rub and scratch around their eyes and ears, armpits, groin, or the inside of their thighs. Moreover, dogs occasionally display respiratory symptoms in addition to itching. Seasonal allergy and atopy are similar terms that describe the same type of allergic skin condition.

Diagnosis – Diagnosis isn't easy and is done based on the clinical signs and ruling out other causes, such as flea or food allergies. Remember that the clinical signs caused by grass pollen are the same as those caused by dust mites and many moulds. This means your golden retriever might be allergic to several different things, all triggering the same symptoms—excessive scratching and itching. A thorough medical history of your golden will help narrow down the causes. For instance, if itching occurs during spring when certain pollen is present in the air, this narrows the range of possibilities.

Treatment – Once the diagnosis is finalised, it might be possible to desensitise your golden to the offending allergens. A specific allergy serum will be prepared based on the results of the allergy tests and is given in a series of shots to help reduce the allergic reaction in your dog. The principle behind desensitisation with allergy shots is to control the injections by increasing doses of the offending allergens, which will re-adjust your retriever's immune system and reduce their hypersensitivity. On average, these allergy injections result in significantly reduced itching for about 50% of dogs.

Anti-inflammatory drugs, including corticosteroids and antihistamines, as well as other targeted therapies, will often give your dog relief from itching. In addition, omega fatty acids—omega-3—can provide some relief for many dogs with allergic skin disease. Antibiotics might be needed if an allergy causes a secondary bacterial skin infection such as pyoderma.

If infected, you can help your golden retriever by frequently bathing them with specially formulated hypoallergenic shampoos. Research has shown that certain allergens are absorbed through the skin. Regular bathing can help reduce the number of allergens your dog absorbs. Some of these special shampoos also contain omega fatty acids, which can be absorbed by the skin and help reduce itching.

Food Allergies

Food allergy or hypersensitivity is known to affect many breeds, but golden retrievers are at an elevated risk of developing this kind of allergy. If your retriever has a food allergy, they will experience itchiness in their ears and feet and scratch them fervently. Any affected areas will be red, irritated, and swollen. When touching your golden's ears or feet, you might also feel bumps and warmth. Food allergies in some retrievers can impact the gastrointestinal tract, triggering vomiting, diarrhoea, or blood and mucus in the faeces and vomit.

In a dog with a food allergy, the immune system overreacts and produces antibodies against substances that it erroneously perceives as a threat. During an allergic food reaction, antibodies are produced against some part of the food, usually a complex carbohydrate or protein. This type of allergy usually occurs after prolonged exposure to one brand or type of food. Food allergies impact dogs in a different way than humans. While a person may feel nauseous or sick after eating something they are allergic to, your golden is more likely to develop skin problems or throw up what they just ate. Some of the more usual signs indicating your dog is suffering from a food allergy include:

- Shaking their head.
- Scratching their ears.
- Ear inflammation.
- Chronic diarrhoea.
- Wind.
- Stomach upsets/vomiting.
- Itchy, red, and swollen skin.
- Licking or chewing their feet.

FACT ***Proteins are the number one food allergen in dogs, particularly those originating from dairy products, beef, lamb, chicken, chicken eggs, soy, and wheat gluten. An allergic dog eating these substances develops symptoms when the antibodies react with the antigens. In addition to the problems listed above, other more subtle symptoms can develop, such as hyperactivity, loss of energy, and aggression.***

Food allergies are not always simple to diagnose. Discovering the cause of the allergic reaction can take a while—up to 12 weeks—as it involves what is known as an 'elimination diet'. This diet means immediately not giving your retriever their usual diet and then slowly reintroducing previous foods until an allergic reaction occurs to identify the trigger. Furthermore, specialised blood tests can reveal the foods your golden is allergic to. These are called serum IgE tests, and your vet will decide if these could help diagnose your dog's condition.

As soon as the offending food is identified, a diet which doesn't include that ingredient can be given. The good news is that there are several tasty, hypoallergenic diets available on the market that can be fed for the rest of your golden's life. Based on the test results, your vet will recommend the most appropriate treatment options for your dog.

Flea Allergy Dermatitis

Flea allergy dermatitis (FAD) is a major cause of allergic reactions in dogs. In this type of allergy, the body's immune system overreacts or becomes hypersensitive to a substance called an antigen that is normally harmless.

FAD is a frequent cause of itching in dogs. Adult fleas feed off the blood of dogs in order to reproduce. Normally, fleas will not stay on your golden except for the time it takes for them to feed. This means you will usually not see live fleas on your retriever's skin unless there is a severe flea infestation in their close environment. While fleas are feeding, they are injecting a small amount of saliva into the skin. It is the proteins or antigens in the saliva that cause the itchy response in sensitive dogs.

Diagnosis – Clinical signs often give the first clue that your golden retriever may suffer from a flea allergy. Typical symptoms include itching and hair loss in the area from the middle of the back to the base of the tail and down the rear legs—known as the flea triangle. A specialised blood test (IgE test) or an intradermal allergy test—a skin test like those performed on humans—can confirm a flea allergy in your dog.

Treatment – Since it is the injection of flea saliva that causes the allergic response, it is vital to prevent fleas from biting your dog in the first place. This means strict flea control is essential. It is important to continue to maintain rigorous flea treatment and environmental control even if you have not seen fleas on your retriever for a while. Typically, flea infestations are at their worst during warmer seasons, but they can also occur year-round. Monthly oral and topical flea preventive products are an important part of good pet care for your retriever. Do not forget that flea prevention is always better than treatment after the fact.

Contact Dermatitis

There are two types of contact dermatitis, allergic contact dermatitis and irritant contact dermatitis. It is difficult to tell them apart since symptoms look alike. They can both cause irritation, soreness, inflamed patches of skin, thickening of the skin, and fluid discharge from the skin. Both dogs and cats can develop contact dermatitis. This condition can occur at any age and is a direct result of coming into contact with an irritant.

During a flare-up of allergic contact dermatitis, the skin becomes sensitive to a particular substance, which is usually harmless. When the body encounters it, the immune system erroneously thinks it needs to mount a defence, which is what causes the symptoms. For example, if your golden retriever is allergic to a particular soap, they will suffer contact dermatitis whenever they're washed with it.

Irritant contact dermatitis occurs when your dog touches something that aggravates their skin. If your golden has this condition, they will probably suffer from rashes and/or bumps that appear on the skin where it met the substance. So if they walk on something, they will develop symptoms on those parts of the skin that are most likely to contact the ground—the neck, chest, chin, abdomen, groin, anal area, scrotum, tail, and between the toes. These rashes often stop abruptly at the hairline. Other symptoms include swelling, and itching, which is normally overwhelming.

Breeds that are more likely to develop contact dermatitis include Labrador retrievers, cocker spaniels, golden retrievers, poodles (and hybrids), Shih Tzus, and bulldogs. However, any dog breed can develop this allergy.

Diagnosis – Your vet will want to run a few diagnostics to find out what caused the problem:

- A skin scraping (see picture) might be collected to check for a bacterial infection or parasitic infestation. The vet will scrape off a thin layer of your golden's cutaneous skin in a small area. They will take a look at the sample under a microscope to rule out any type of skin mite that could cause the same symptoms.

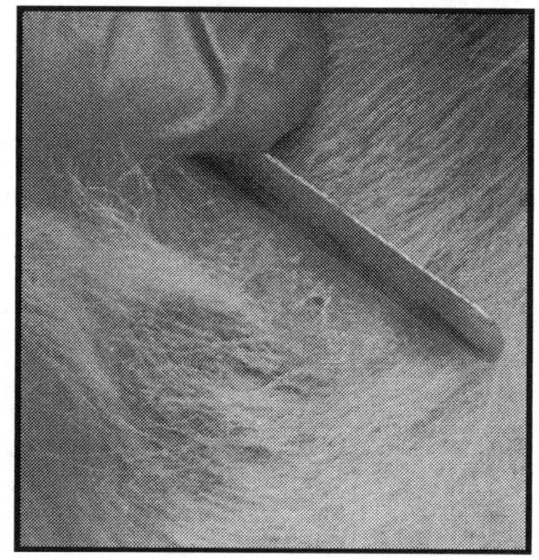

- A patch test may be performed. The suspected substance is placed on a patch, which is taped to the skin for 48 hours. Any reaction is then assessed.
- Your golden is kept away from the offending environment for a while and then returned to the location, monitoring whether it has had any impact one way or the other.
- Bacterial cultures might also be performed. A clip of hair is taken from a patch in an body area which is not affected, applied to a sample of the suspected antigen, and then observed for possible reactions.
- Skin biopsies are also sometimes performed.

Treatment – Medications, such as antihistamines or steroids, will be prescribed to relieve the itching. A soothing cream or ointment might also be prescribed by the vet to apply to the affected areas. If a secondary infection develops, your golden will need antibiotics.

TIP ***You will also need to bathe your retriever multiple times a week with a specially formulated shampoo (see picture). These shampoos have hypoallergenic, antiseptic, antifungal, and antibacterial properties that help heal your golden's skin.***

Firstly, the most important but hardest thing to do is to remove your retriever from the environment which contained the irritant which caused the problem. If the dermatitis is the result of a substance and not an allergy, your dog's recovery will be quick once you've identified the cause. However, if the dermatitis is down to an allergy, it may have taken months or years to develop.

Should your retriever be exposed again, the symptoms will develop three to five days later and could persist for weeks. Once the antigen is identified and removed, your dog's health will probably return to normal within a few weeks. If it is not possible to identify the allergen, there is a chance you will have to treat the symptoms with medicines for the rest of your retriever's life.

Allergy Medications

You might wish to discuss possible allergy medication options with your vet since there are many designed to relieve symptoms, including:

Apoquel – This prescription medicine (see picture) relieves itching by blocking the molecules that transmit the inflammation and itch signal.

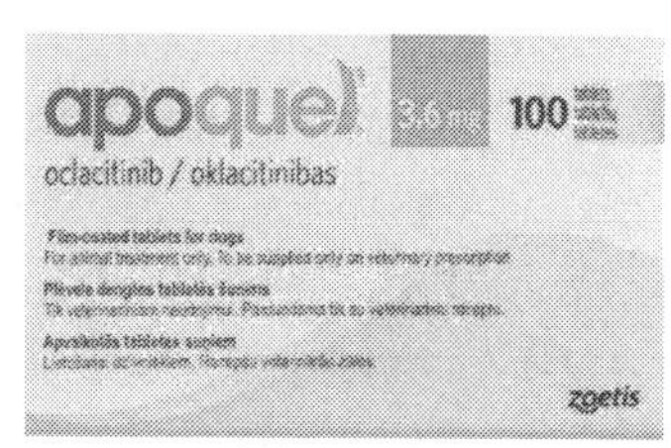

Atopica – This treats skin allergies and other dermatological conditions.

Benadryl – This is an antihistamine used to soothe the reaction to allergens, including environmental substances, parasites, vaccines, or insect stings.

Cytopoint – These injections have proven to be effective for the treatment of dogs with allergic and atopic dermatitis.

Dexamethasone – This is a steroid used for relief from allergies, arthritic pain, or other conditions that can make the immune system overreact.

Malaseb – This is a powerful medicated shampoo used to treat itching skin dermatitis problems, yeast, and fungal—ringworm—infections.

Piriton – This is a sedating antihistamine used to relieve allergic reactions to food, insect bites, or hay fever.

Prednisone – This is a powerful anti-inflammatory steroid that temporarily blocks the symptoms caused by allergic reactions.

Triamcinolone – This is an anti-inflammatory steroid used to relieve itching from allergies as well as acute arthritis.

Zyrtec – This is an antihistamine medication prescribed for dogs with dermatitis or mild to moderate environmental allergies.

Treating Allergies Holistically

Treating allergies with traditional veterinary medications—antibiotics, antihistamines, and steroids—focuses on treating the symptoms. Although these can be highly effective in giving relief to your golden retriever, they might also bring with them unwanted side effects. Taking a holistic approach to allergies focuses on locating the imbalance in your dog's immune system to tackle the cause of the allergic reaction rather than simply dealing with the symptoms.

Allergy symptoms in dogs tend to be dermal. (Skin-related.) Symptoms usually include inflamed, itchy skin that provokes excessive scratching, biting, and licking. Holistic treatments focus on supporting the immune system to regain function while alleviating symptoms, so your retriever is more comfortable. Holistic therapies range from changing the environment to acupuncture, diet, and herbal supplements. There is no one size fits all. Each dog will require different methods or a combination of methods for a successful outcome. Healing allergies holistically is often a case of trial-and-error, and you'll need to be patient before you see results.

Several strategies can be implemented as part of a holistic approach to ensure that your retriever's overall health is maximised and allergic reactions are minimised. These include:

- Adjusting their diet to support their immune system. It is recommended you lower your golden's carbohydrate intake because excessive carbs may impact their immune system. Artificial colours and flavours should be eliminated. Low-carb diets with no additives and raw or cooked meat are recommended for dogs with allergies.
- Offering raw honey can help support the immune system. It is easy to give since dogs can readily eat it as part of their diet. Using local honey can expose your golden to low levels of local pollen and antigens. This trains their immune system not to react negatively to the allergen.
- Making sure parasites such as fleas and ticks are eradicated. Commercial and natural treatments are available.
- Regularly hoovering your home can reduce flea infestations, as can cleaning up your garden where they congregate. Various natural preparations can help prevent infestations.
- Removing toxic cleaning products from home.
- Wiping their feet and coat to remove outdoor allergens.

- Giving skin-soothing baths. This helps remove irritants and biting insects. Baths and medications that soothe irritated skin, such as oatmeal baths, coconut oil, lavender, chamomile, and mullein preparations, can also ease skin lesions. Applied topically, treatments like aloe vera gel, calendula, thyme, chickweed gel, cider vinegar, witch hazel, Epsom salts, and cucumber slices can relieve irritation.
- Using acupuncture which may restore immune system balance.
- Giving your dog herbal supplements—echinacea, ginseng, omega-3, vitamins.
- Feeding your dog natural anti-inflammatories—liquorice root, nettles.
- Offering mushrooms to your retriever. These contain natural antihistamines that can reduce immune system reactions. Consult your vet before using to ensure you give the appropriate dosage and type, and to be certain there are no interactions with any medications.
- Feeding supplements that aid gastrointestinal functioning, such as dandelion root, probiotics, and other herbal preparations.

How effective holistic treatments will be largely depends on your patience and dedication to experimenting. It's a process of trial and error which might take several weeks—or even months—to discover which treatments provide relief from allergic reactions.

Skin Issues and Parasites

Golden retrievers are susceptible to numerous skin conditions that can make their life a misery. While many issues, such as external parasites, are easily treatable at home, other conditions will require the input of a qualified vet. For example, your dog might suffer from rashes on the stomach. This might be caused by an easily treated bacterial infection, or it might have a far more serious underlying cause, such as Cushing's disease, a hormonal imbalance.

Your vet will be able to determine whether the cause is genetic, hormonal, or an allergic reaction. Once the cause has been identified, the next step is to prescribe a treatment plan to relieve the symptoms and potentially cure the condition.

Read on to learn about common skin conditions that can affect golden retrievers.

Interdigital Cysts

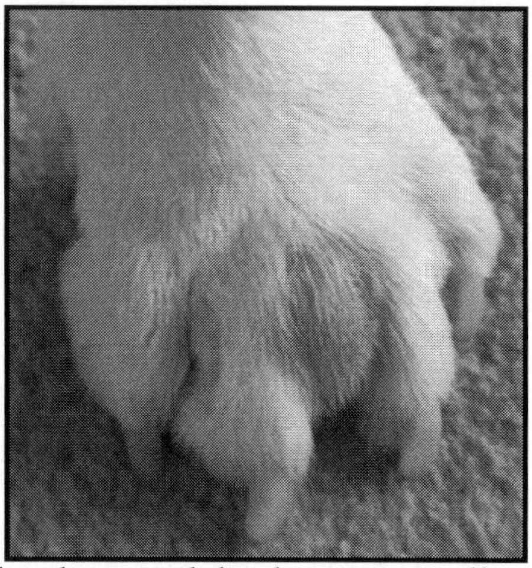

Interdigital cysts are large bumps or nodules between your golden's toes (pictured.) These are extremely painful, making it difficult for them to move or walk. They are also called interdigital furuncles, follicular pododermatitis, or furunculosis. They are filled with blood and/or pus and are most frequently found on the front paws.

Many skin conditions can cause nodules on your golden's paws. These include demodectic mange—from Demodex mites—atopic dermatitis, infections caused by a foreign object stuck between the toes, poor foot conformation, and yeast infections. Any breed can get nodules, including golden retrievers.

Your golden might show signs of lameness on the affected foot an interdigital furuncle is developing. If left untreated, the problem can quickly spread to other areas, causing multiple nodules. Eventually, these nodules become swollen, inflamed, and painful before they burst and exude fluid. They typically develop on the upper side of your dog's paw, but they can also appear on the underside. If your golden suffers from interdigital furuncles, they will usually:

- Limp, especially when walking on uneven surfaces.

- Lick and chew their paws.
- Bite at the lesion on their paws.

Diagnosing the Problem – Your veterinarian may be able to diagnose interdigital cysts based solely on their physical appearance during a routine exam. Further diagnostic testing might be needed to rule out other conditions—such as skin tumours—and to determine the underlying cause of your golden's interdigital cysts.

If your vet suspects the problem is palmar or plantar follicular cysts, they will recommend a skin biopsy.

These tests may be performed for a correct diagnosis:

- Skin scrapings—checks for Demodex mites.
- Impression smears.
- Fine-needle aspirates.

Treatment Options – In most instances, topical antibiotics and antibiotic ointments are enough to treat this condition. However, any type of treatment will depend on how deep the infection has gone, which could necessitate more intensive treatment. For antibiotics to be effective, you must ensure your retriever completes the prescribed course. If the course of antibiotics is not completed or the doses are inaccurate, your golden might develop an interdigital furuncle again. A warm compress or foot soak has been found helpful when treating interdigital furuncles.

FACT ***A corticosteroid or a non-steroidal anti-inflammatory medication might also be recommended by your veterinarian. These decrease the swelling and inflammation associated with interdigital cysts. Not only will this reduce any self-trauma that can occur if your dog licks at a painful paw, but it will also help make your dog more comfortable.***

If your vet determines that the cause is a foreign object, it may need to be surgically removed, which is generally the case when a grass seed is involved.

Hot Spots (also known as 'Moist Dermatitis')

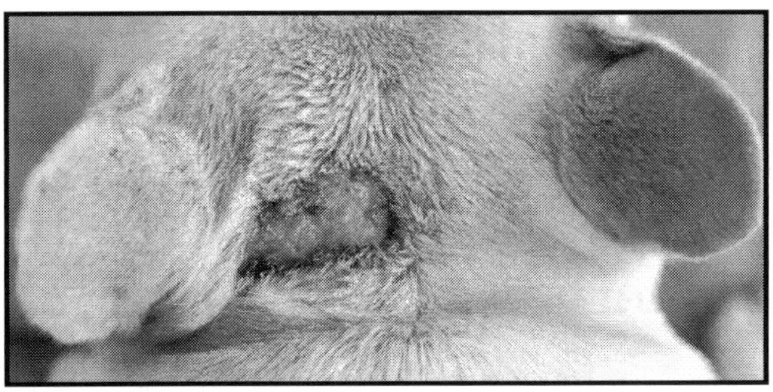

A hot spot (see picture) is an area of reddened skin that is itchy and painful. The problem can get worse if your golden's hair is matted and they lick it. Usually, a hot spot appears as a large, wet, oozing scab on an area of skin that looks raw and inflamed. Hot spots can bleed and might be due to an allergic reaction, infection, or lack of proper drying after your dog has been for a swim.

Hot spots are more prevalent in dogs with thick coats, such as golden retrievers, St. Bernards, German shepherds, Labrador retrievers, and Rottweilers, but any breed can suffer from them. One cause of hot spots is moisture getting trapped next to your dog's skin due to matted fur, a dog collar, or simply thick fur, creating ideal conditions for infection. Chronic hot spots often stem from an allergic condition.

These spots can appear anywhere on your golden retriever's body, but they are most frequently found on the hips, limbs, and head. When bacteria builds up in hot spots, it can quickly spread to other parts of the body. A dog with hot spots will suffer pain, and it is often difficult for them to heal naturally due to the tendency to lick, scratch, or bite at skin irritations.

A hot spot will usually dry out and start healing about a week after treatment begins. When it is dry and does not ooze, continue to keep the area clean and moisture-free. Your golden's fur will start growing back in about a fortnight. Talk to your veterinarian about essential fatty acids and dietary supplements to relieve itching and promote hair growth.

In general, hot spots improve when they are left to dry. Your vet can give you advice on how to proceed. Usually, this includes one or more of the following:

- Using clippers to shave the hot spot and surrounding area—this allows air to get to it.
- Bathing the hot spot frequently with a medicated shampoo (see picture).
- Applying a small amount of an over-the-counter hydrocortisone ointment to stop itching and aid healing.
- You might be advised to use an Elizabethan collar on your golden—also known as a buster collar or a cone—to stop them from irritating the area by licking, biting, and scratching.
- Oral antibiotics or a topical solution—spray, cream, or ointment—can be prescribed to kill bacteria, and an antihistamine can help reduce itchiness.

TIP ***The best ways to prevent hot spots are to maintain good hygiene, groom your retriever regularly, treat skin infections and parasites as soon as you notice them, and stay on top of allergies. Additionally, make sure your golden's coat is completely dry after swimming or bathing. Otherwise, the matted fur will trap moisture, creating ideal conditions for hot spots.***

Supplementary fatty acids can help prevent hot spots by building a healthy skin barrier and reducing inflammation. Fish oil is a great source of omega-3 fatty acids as it contains a lot of DHA and EPA. For more information on supplements and the correct dosage for your golden, contact your vet.

Harvest Mites ('Trombicula autumnalis')

These are seasonal, bright orange mites (see picture)—also known as 'chigger mites', 'scrub-itch mites, 'red bugs', and 'berry bugs'—active during the dry and sunny days of the late summer and autumn months. They can be found in gardens, the countryside, or the park. Large numbers of these voracious mites are usually found in areas with matted vegetation, long grass, or low-lying plants and bushes and on clumps of earth.

Whilst there is no specific breed predisposition, dogs who go to the mite's natural environment have a greater risk of encountering the larvae than dogs who are exercised on beaches or mown parks.

A retriever running through these locations can easily pick up mites as they prefer to congregate in areas that give them easy access to the skin, such as around the neck, margins of the ears, front legs, armpits, stomach, genitals, and between the toes. Mites latch on to your golden's skin with their hooked fangs and inject strong enzymes to break down and disintegrate the skin cells, making them easy to suck up.

Once firmly attached to your dog's skin, the mites stay on the same site for several days, feeding while they increase in size 3 to 4 times. Your dog will suffer an intense itching reaction to the mites' digestive enzymes, which could linger for many weeks.

Since harvest mites are quite small, it is difficult to find them. However, if your golden is scratching a particular area of their body, carefully examine the skin by spreading the hair and looking closely. This will help uncover the problem before it gets worse. If you find an irritated, crusted, or scabbed area with a red or orange-coloured 'dust', there is a good chance your retriever has harvest mites.

Diagnosis will usually be through taking a skin sample at the vet's that will be examined under a microscope. Your vet might recommend a spray to kill parasites, a shampoo to relieve itching, and a corticosteroid to reduce inflammation, as well as antibiotics if there is any secondary infection from scratching.

If left untreated, the harvest mites will drop off your golden once they've eaten their fill. However, even though they may no longer be around, your poor dog will still feel itchy for weeks.

Soothing baths with oatmeal and Epsom salts (see picture), applying calamine lotion or aloe vera to the crusted areas and adding a skin-supporting supplement can help soothe the itching.

Prevention is always better than cure. It's best to minimise the risk of your golden retriever encountering harvest mites. For instance, since the mite larvae are only active during the warmer hours of the day, walk your dog early in the morning or later in the evening and avoid areas with bushes, plants, long grasses, matted vegetation, or clods of earth. Also, if you have a garden where these biters can congregate, consider pest control to keep them out of your garden.

Sarcoptic Mange (also known as 'Scabies')

Sarcoptic mange comes from a parasitic mite—Sarcoptes scabiei (see picture)—that burrow just below the skin's surface. Sarcoptic mange should not be confused with with demodectic mange; the latter is caused by a different parasitic mite.

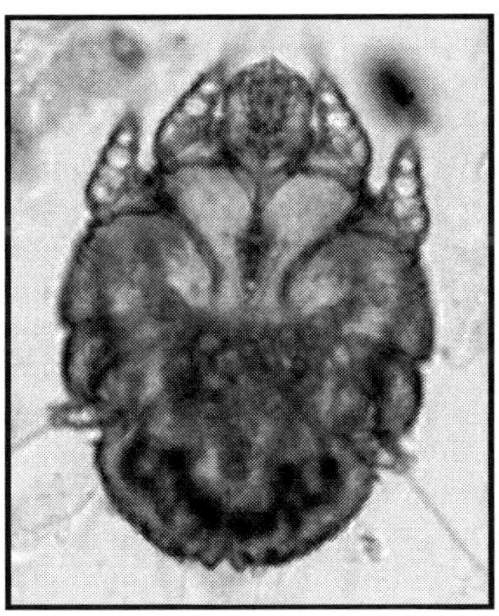

These mites bury themselves into the skin of healthy puppies and dogs, then feed on the material in and on the skin. It is zoonotic, meaning it is a disease transmissible from animals to humans. These mites prefer to infest hairless areas of the skin, making the abdomen, elbow, and ear flap most at risk.

According to the World Small Animal Veterinary Association World Congress Proceedings, 2004: 'There does not seem to be breed predispositions for scabies. Perhaps, Labradors, cocker spaniels and Doberman pinschers could be predisposed in North America.'

The main cause of infection is exposure to an infected animal or person. They may be encountered at dog parks, groomers, kennels, shelters, and daycares. Symptoms do not usually show until approximately two to six weeks after exposure.

It is normal not to see sarcoptic mange mites when performing a skin scraping on infected dogs. Instead, the skin scraping is examined under the microscope to make a diagnosis. This is because mites are tiny, burrow deep into the skin, and it only takes a few of them to create significant itching. On average, this test will confirm the presence of mites in 50% of examined affected dogs.

Just because you can't see any mites does not mean your golden doesn't have sarcoptic mange. This means a presumptive diagnosis must be made based on clinical signs. Sarcoptic mange can occur in any dog at any age.

While difficult to diagnose and highly contagious, this condition is easy to cure with the many scabicide treatments commonly found in flea, tick, and worming products. There are various treatments available, from medicated baths and dips to oral medications and injections. Many dogs require a combination of treatments to resolve this infection.

If any member of your family develops itching or a skin rash, contact your doctor immediately. Tell them you might have been exposed to sarcoptic mange or scabies. The mite is unable to complete its life cycle on humans, so it dies within a few days. However, during that time, it can cause intense itching requiring medical treatment.

Cheyletiella Mites

The clinical name for infection with cheyletiella mites is 'cheyletiellosis' and is sometimes referred to as 'cheyletiella mange' or 'walking dandruff' (see picture below) because the mites are white and look like dandruff as they crawl across the fur or skin. This infection is usually accompanied by large flakes of skin scaling, making it look even more like dandruff.

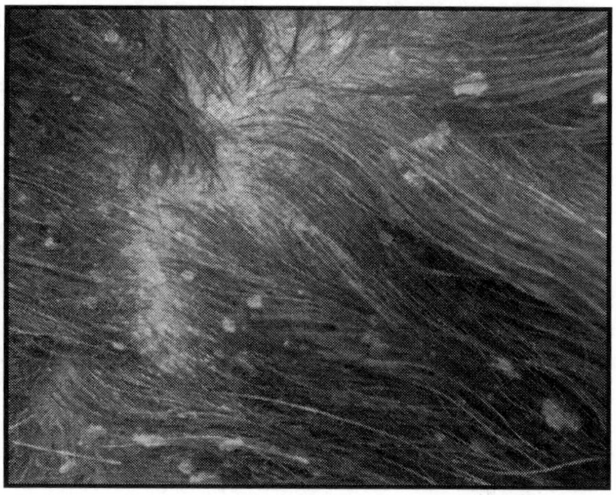

Cheyletiella is visible to the naked eye or with a magnifying glass. American cocker spaniels, King Charles spaniels, and boxers seem to be most susceptible to this mite. However, any dog who is groomed regularly, attends a dog daycare or frequents a place where there are other dogs can be at risk.

While uncommon—because of improved flea control medications—this is a highly contagious skin parasite that lives on the surface of the skin of its host as well as in the superficial skin layers. A dog can become infected with these large mites by encountering an infected animal. This typically happens when multiple dogs have contact with one another, such as in kennels, shelters, groomers, dog parks, and breeders.

If your golden retriever is infected with these mites, they might bite, scratch, or rub at the infected areas—often on your dog's back—or suffer swollen red skin or a red, bumpy rash followed by hair loss. Your veterinarian should be able to easily identify the infestation by taking a skin sample for microscopic examination.

Treatment usually involves clipping any long hair and then bathing to remove scaling skin. Next will be the application of a 'miticide'—a chemical used to kill mites—that is available as a lotion, ointment, spray, rinse, or dip. Oral medications may also be advised, such as milbemycin or ivermectin. Herding dog breeds are prone to developing 'ivermectin toxicity' and cannot be treated with this anti-mite medication.

Preventing re-infestation involves quarantining and then treating all your pets, before applying a strict cleaning protocol involving thorough cleaning of the surfaces your golden might have been in contact with—bed, bedding, furniture, carpets, flooring, clothing, kennel, and car. In other words, to eradicate this mite, you should thoroughly clean anywhere the dog has been at least once a week during your dog's treatment.

Since these mites live in the environment for up to ten days, complete elimination can take a while, which may necessitate multiple vet visits and treatment applications. It might take as long as a month or more to fully resolve.

Demodectic Mange

This skin disease is known by several names, including 'puppy mange', 'red mange', or 'follicular mange'. It is caused by one of three species of the Demodex mite (see picture below)—canis, cornei, and injai—usually found in young dogs or puppies. This disease results from a weak, poorly developed, or suppressed immune system that is unable to control the spread of these mites, which are passed from mother to puppy. Beagles, German shepherds, Doberman pinschers, Old English sheepdogs, collies, boxers, and shorthair brachycephalic breeds are predisposed to the generalised form of Demodex dermatitis.

FACT ***Small numbers of the Demodex mite are normally found living in harmony on the skin of every healthy dog, and it is believed they are simply part of the skin's 'microfauna'. It is only when your retriever has a compromised immune system—due to illness or advanced age—that the number of mites begins to multiply rapidly and inhabit your dog's skin and hair follicles, causing itching.***

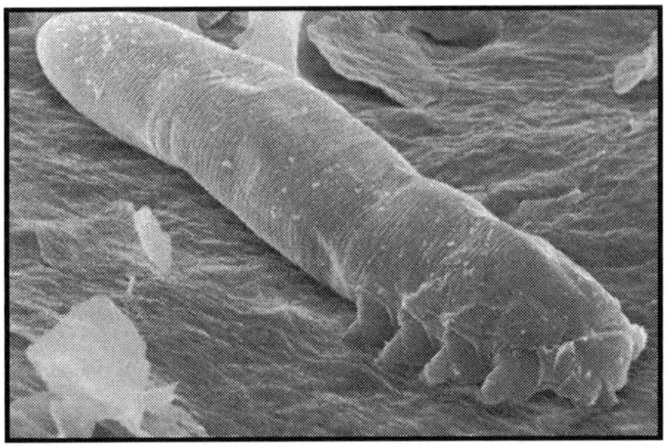

Most puppies are immune to the effect of these microscopic mites. The few who are not develop hair loss, or red, crusty lesions, usually around the head. In 90% of cases, a localised problem will heal naturally as your puppy matures and their immune system grows stronger. In persistent cases, you might need to apply topical medications to the skin.

There are three forms of Demodectic mange: 'localised', 'generalised', and 'pododermatitis'.

The localised form involves no more than two regions of your dog's body, with no more than four spots in total. It presents as one or two scaly, bald patches that are usually isolated on your golden's face and possibly a spot on their leg. Common in puppyhood, treatment is not necessary or recommended, as in most cases, it will resolve on its own.

The generalised form involves more extensive patches of your dog's skin. If left untreated, it can progress to cover all your retriever's skin. It often causes a smelly, highly itchy secondary bacterial infection that requires treatment with antibiotics.

Treatment in persistent cases can involve using 'isoxazoline' or other flea and tick medicine and management, which might need a visit to the vet for follow-up skin scrapings.

Pododermatitis is one of the most treatment-resistant forms of mange. Found only on a dog's paws, it can be very difficult to cure. Often a biopsy of the area is necessary since bacterial and fungal cultures might be required to confirm a correct diagnosis of the infection.

There can be many causes of this type of inflammation, including allergies, cancers, environmental toxins, hormonal problems, and tumours. Symptoms include red, inflamed paws and feet, itching, hair loss, constant licking, scabs, crusts, ulcerations or blisters, thickened foot pads, nodules, and darkened tissue.

Specific treatment of this type of mange depends on the cause. Your vet will first have to determine the underlying problem before a treatment plan can be put together. Possible treatments include foot soaks, wipes, shampoo washes, antibiotics, anti-fungal medications, and immune-modulating drug therapy.

While diagnosing the cause and then managing a treatment protocol can take some time, once the underlying reason has been identified and treatment starts, the prognosis for recovery is usually good.

Pyoderma

Pyoderma means 'pus in the skin', and it is a bacterial infection of the skin (see picture below) that can develop for many different reasons. It causes redness and itching that can lead to lesions on the skin similar to pimples. In young puppies, this might be called 'impetigo' and commonly presents as red and raised pustules on the skin of the armpits or groin filled with white pus. There can also be circular, flaky, and dry skin crusts or very itchy patches that cause hair loss.

FACT ***Pyoderma can occur for several reasons, including the surface of the skin being broken or damaged by scratching, impaired blood flow, or a change in the usual skin bacteria due to a compromised immune system. It may also be hereditary or triggered by hormone imbalances, thyroid disease, diabetes, fungal or yeast infections, parasites, some cancers, and some medications, including azathioprine, cyclosporine, or high steroid doses.***

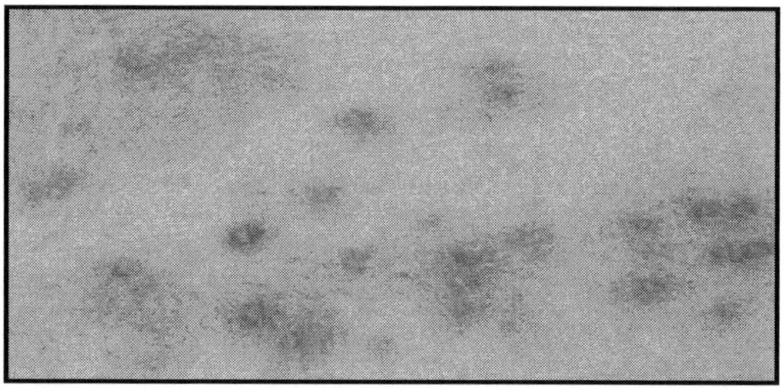

Pyoderma is often caused by staph bacteria that can be triggered by fleas or other irritants. Certain breeds with deep skin folds that create a warm, moist environment, such as bulldogs, pugs, and Chinese Shar Peis, are more prone to produce bacteria. The folds generate a large quantity of saliva, creating a hot, humid environment, making their mouth an ideal breeding ground for bacteria.

Pyoderma can present itself as yellow pimples of ulcerated skin with a red, scaling, or crusting rash that is itchy and sensitive to touch with a foul odour.

Diagnosis often includes skin scrapings, blood testing to rule out an underlying endocrine disease, and testing to determine drug sensitivity or other allergies.

Treatment usually involves bathing with an antibacterial shampoo two or three times a week at first, reducing to once a week until the infection resolves, as well as the application of antibiotic creams for approximately 3 to 4 weeks.

Never be tempted to pop your golden retriever's pimples. This will expose your dog to infection, which can make the problem worse.

Fleas

Dog fleas (see picture) are the most common parasites your golden retriever might pick up. They are usually brown, measure around 1-2 mm, and live for 7-14 days, during which time they stay and lay eggs on your dog. Flea eggs are white, oval-shaped, and about half a millimetre in length. The eggs hatch into tiny larvae, which burrow into your dog's bedding, carpets, and upholstery, where they develop into pupae.

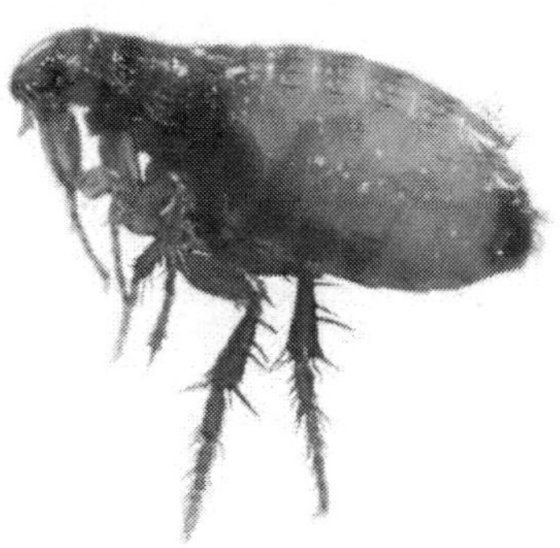

Fleas lie silent for many months, so you may not realise they are there until they sense heat and vibration. The adult fleas then emerge to jump onto a passing 'host'—in this case, your dog—to begin this cycle all over again. No matter how clean your house is, 100 more fleas could be around the home for every one you find on your dog.

Fleas spread diseases and are the leading cause of skin problems in dogs. All dogs itch after being bitten, and some can develop allergies, such as flea allergic dermatitis (FAD). The peak season for fleas is late summer due to the high humidity and warm temperatures. However, a cosy central heating system in the winter means you will need to de-flea all year.

Just because you don't see fleas doesn't mean they are not there. They can be easily detected by your retriever's persistent scratching, which can leave them with bald spots on their coat. If they have a flea allergy, your dog may also develop scabs and red, sore areas of skin. While regular dog grooming will not prevent fleas on your retriever, it will at least alert you to any symptoms so you can get treatment sooner rather than later.

You might find fleas in your carpet or see flea dirt in the fur of your dog when combing it. Test these specks by placing them onto some damp tissue paper. If it is flea dirt, the specks will turn red due to the digested blood they contain.

Always consult your vet about the most appropriate dog flea treatments, and only use vet-approved products that have been tested for safety and effectiveness. Using a flea comb helps but is unlikely to remove all fleas (see (see *Removing Parasites* in Chapter 9).

Powders are an old-fashioned and messy way to treat fleas on your dog. The powder needs to stay on your golden's coat to be effective and can be harmful if swallowed or inhaled.

Flea collars are not very effective in eliminating fleas on dogs since they only affect the area around the neck. Additionally, they might cause irritation or hair loss. However, there is a new generation of flea collars available that are much kinder to your dog's coat and skin. Your veterinarian can supply these, which work by dispersing the active ingredient throughout the body rather than sitting on the neck. Your golden's collar should always have a quick-release feature; otherwise, your dog may become tangled or caught on something.

TIP ***A spot-on treatment (see picture) is one of the easiest, most effective ways to prevent and treat dog fleas. A small amount of liquid is applied to the back of your golden's neck, killing fleas and preventing them from developing eggs. Several brands are available, so talk to your veterinarian about which one is right for your golden retriever.***

Dog flea treatment options also include tablets and liquids. These are absorbed into your dog's body, killing the fleas once they bite or sterilising them so they cannot reproduce.

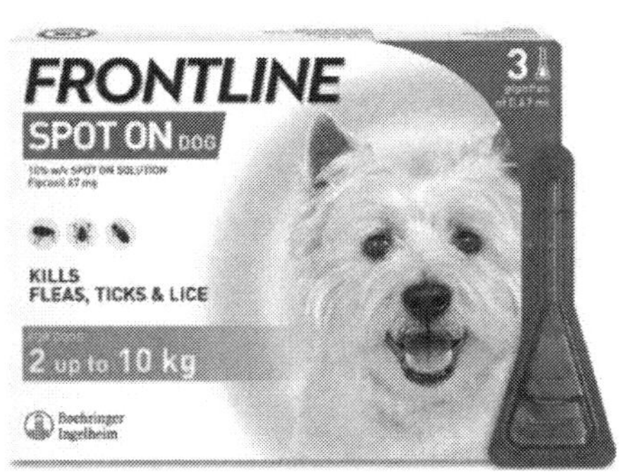

You must treat your house as well as your pet when you want to get rid of fleas. Use a combination of topical products to kill them, along with a treatment that prevents eggs from becoming adults. Always follow the manufacturer's instructions when using these products. This usually means hoovering your carpet first to bring fleas and eggs to the surface and then spraying your carpet thoroughly before hoovering your carpet again.

There is no magic solution to keep your golden flea-free forever. If you want to do your best to prevent fleas, here are some tips:

- Regularly wash their bedding.
- Reduce their contact with stray animals.
- Make sure you regularly brush your retriever.
- Follow your veterinarian's flea control recommendations.

Ticks

Adult ticks have eight legs and are classified as 'arachnids', which makes them relatives of mites, scorpions, and spiders. There are over 200 species of ticks, all of which feed on blood.

These bloodsucking parasites have a sticky secretion and crab-like legs that help them hold onto their host before they attach themselves to the skin by the harpoon-like barbs in their mouth. Ticks are usually not a problem during colder weather because they do not become active until the warmer spring weather when temperatures rise above 4 °C (40 °F).

Contrary to what some believe, ticks do not fly, jump, or drop from trees but live on the ground in wooded areas. They survive cold winter days by hiding underneath leaf litter, brush, and snow. Anyone taking their dog for walks through areas covered by leaf litter, tall grass, or wooded trails should regularly check their dog for ticks upon returning home.

Ticks on dogs are just large enough to be seen, especially if they have already bitten. At that point, they resemble small warts. If you look closer, you will also see their legs. Usually, you will find them on your golden's head and neck. Part your dog's fur and run your finger along their skin to check for them. A tick bite may cause irritation and redness, which can be visible.

Ticks can be difficult to remove from your golden (see *Removing Parasites* in Chapter 9 for tick removal instructions) since you need to get the whole tick out without leaving its mouth parts buried under the skin, as this could lead to reinfection. Take your dog to the vet if you are unsure how to remove the ticks or if you are having difficulty doing it yourself.

It is unlikely your golden will suffer any harm from having ticks. Ticks are not dangerous in and of themselves, but they may transmit diseases from other animals. For instance, they can pass on Lyme disease, which needs to be treated by a veterinarian. People can also contract Lyme disease, so if you were bitten by a tick and feel unwell, consult your doctor.

Check with your vet if you live in an area where ticks are common. You may be recommended some veterinary-approved treatments to prevent them. Various spot-on treatments, collars (see picture), and even tablets can be used to repel or kill ticks when they attach themselves to your retriever. Your vet can help you decide which option would be most suitable. You can obtain these preventatives from your veterinarian or, in some cases, from a pet store.

TIP ***Check for dog ticks as part of your dog-care routine. Keep an eye out for ticks when grooming your golden to detect them at an early stage.***

Heartworm

The thread-like heartworm only spreads through mosquito (see picture) bites. After a growth period of approximately six months, this parasite can reach up to 30 centimetres (12 inches). As the name suggests, this worm lives in the heart and the arteries that carry blood from the heart to the lungs.

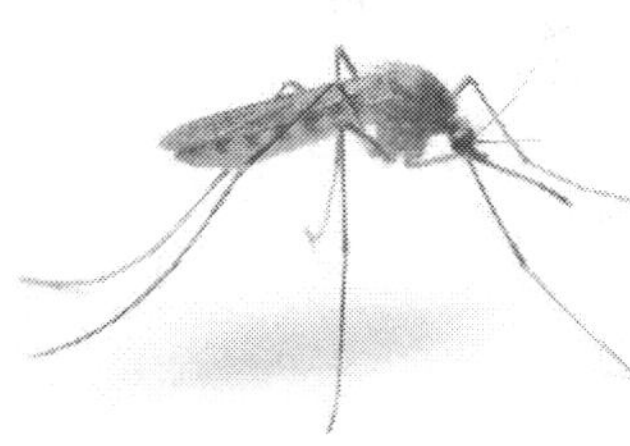

Once they reach maturation, they can live in your golden retriever's body for up to seven years, continuing to grow up to a length of one foot and continuously producing offspring. It is not uncommon for a dog to have hundreds of these parasites after a year, although the average number is 15. These worms cause inflammation and damage to the heart, arteries, and lungs. It is recommended that all dogs in the U.S. undergo an annual heartworm test, even if they are on heartworm prevention medication.

Symptoms in an infected dog include coughing, lethargy, weakness, anaemia, high blood pressure, abnormal heart rate, difficulty breathing, and fainting.

Whilst this parasite is not present in the United Kingdom, it is common in America, Australia, Spain, Italy, and southern France. Recent climate changes have seen the parasite spread closer to the U.K., and it has recently been reported as far north as Brittany in northern France. If you take your golden on holiday in any of these regions, they may become infected with heartworm.

There is no breed of dog particularly predisposed to heartworm. Dogs younger than six months are unlikely to have them as it takes approximately six months for a heartworm to develop from a microfilaria to an adult.

If left untreated, your dog's heart will eventually fail, and death will soon follow. The only good news about the heartworm parasite is that it can only be transmitted through mosquito bites. Taking steps to keep them away minimises the chance of your retriever becoming infected.

The FDA-approved treatment in the U.S. is melarsomine dihydrochloride. This medicine is sold under the brand names Immiticide and Diroban. A deep, intramuscular injection is administered to the lumbar region of the lower back of your dog, which is recommended if the parasite has not progressed too far.

Heartworm treatment is extremely painful, sometimes dangerous, and expensive. This is why good veterinarians insist on administering yearly tests and preventative compounds—what scientists call chemoprophylaxis. Guidelines from the American Heartworm Society include:

- Taking a heartworm prevention medication all year round.
- Strictly following your veterinarian's dosage schedule.
- Applying an FDA-approved mosquito repellent.
- Using environmental controls to reduce or eliminate mosquito breeding grounds—such as pools of standing water—using mosquito traps and limiting your retriever's outdoor activities during dawn and dusk, which are mosquito feeding times.

Ringworm

Despite its name, the ringworm (see picture) is a fungus, not a worm.

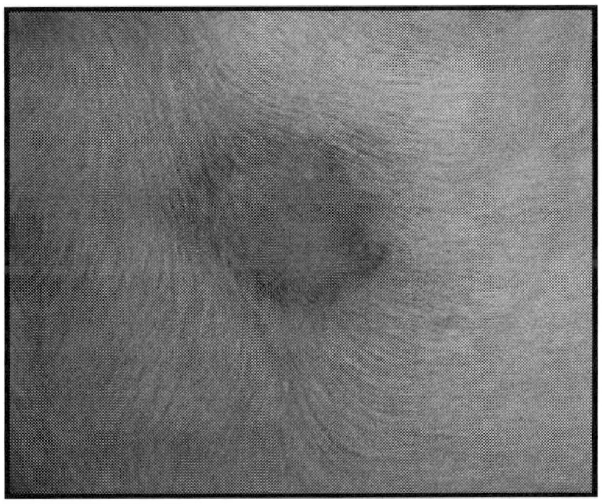

Ringworm is a common fungal infection affecting almost all domestic animals, including dogs. Its name derives from its round, raised, red ring appearance similar to that usually seen in human ringworm infections. Ringworm, scientifically called dermatophytes, is a pathogenic fungus. In 70% of cases, it is caused by microsporum canis, with 20% due to microsporum gypseum, and just 10% by trichophyton mentagrophytes.

Dogs with weaker immune systems tend to be susceptible to ringworm, such as very young or old dogs, dogs with diseases that weaken their immune systems, or dogs who have recently experienced long-term stays in kennels or shelters. Genetically, Boston terriers, Yorkshire terriers, and Jack Russell terriers are more prone to ringworm infections than other breeds.

Dogs with other skin conditions are also predisposed to ringworm. Normally, the skin functions as a protective barrier, but if your golden has fresh scratches, an open wound, fleas, or a chronic skin condition, they are more open to infection.

FACT ***Typically, ringworm develops in the outermost layer of your dog's skin, in the hair follicles, and occasionally in their nails. In most cases, the infection is superficial and will only affect a few parts of your golden's body.***

Ringworm is transmitted through direct contact with the fungus. Dogs get it if they meet an infected person or animal or touch something contaminated, such as a couch, comb, food bowls, bedding, or carpet. The condition usually manifests as circular areas of hair loss. The lesions may look patchy and can become inflamed or scabbed as they grow.

Ringworm does not usually itch. Hair follicles affected by the disease are brittle and easily break, which helps the disease spread. When the fungus infects the claws, they become brittle and rough.

In most cases, your vet will recommend a topical treatment, such as cream, ointment, and/or medicated shampoo (see picture). Sometimes, oral therapy is also required. Oral antifungal medications can help

fight infection, and, like topical therapy, are administered for a minimum of six weeks, although it might take months for positive results. The spores that reside inside hair follicles remain contagious for months at a time, living on couches, grooming tools, bedding, and furniture. Part of the treatment involves cleaning up all this hair, but, as many dog owners know, this can be challenging.

The best way to prevent reinfection is to thoroughly cleanse the home and any tools and bedding your retriever was in contact with. Follow your veterinarian's recommendations for other preventative measures.

Canine Acne ('Canine pimples')

Canine acne is an inflammatory disorder of your dog's lips and the skin of their muzzle (see picture below). If your golden has a mild case of acne, they will often have red bumps or pustules—pimples—on their skin. In more severe cases, this can lead to generalised swelling of the lips and muzzle, scabs on the face, or bleeding wounds. When left untreated, severe cases of canine acne can result in permanent scarring.

The basic cause of canine acne is not fully understood. Previously, it was believed to be related to human acne, which is hormone-induced. However, more recent evidence suggests this is not the case.

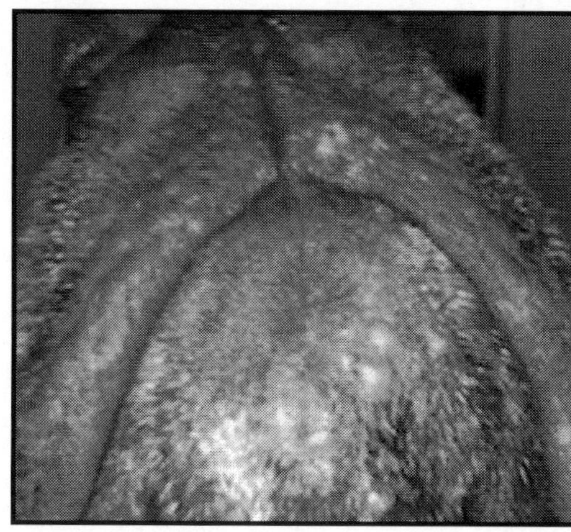

Trauma to the skin of the chin or muzzle is thought to be the trigger for many cases of canine acne. This trauma makes hairs break off near the surface of the skin, leading to inflammation in the hair follicle, which eventually ruptures. Once the hair follicle ruptures, it releases its contents into the surrounding skin. This further inflames the skin, as the surrounding tissues recognise the contents of the hair follicles as foreign.

In some instances, acne is associated with other underlying skin conditions and allergies. You should have your veterinarian assess your golden for possible environmental or food allergies. If your vet suspects allergies, managing them could reduce acne.

Genetics can also be a factor. Some breeds are more prone to acne than others, such as boxers, Doberman pinschers, English bulldogs, German shorthaired pointers, Great Danes, mastiffs, and Rottweilers.

Treating canine acne involves getting your vet to diagnose it. This might include taking a skin scraping and performing various tests to rule out possible causes—fungal infection, mange, parasites, allergies. Once a diagnosis is confirmed, treatment will typically include administering oral and/or topical medications.

Topical benzoyl peroxide is the most common treatment for canine acne. This medication is often available over the counter or can be bought from your veterinarian. It reduces bacterial contamination and helps flush out the hair follicles.

Steroids can also be prescribed to decrease inflammation. While topical steroids frequently have betamethasone or fluocinolone in them, oral steroids can include prednisolone or prednisone.

Top 10 Skin Care Tips

Here are some additional tips to bear in mind that will help keep your golden's skin healthy and nourished:

1. Keep your golden's skin clean and moisturised with regular baths every 4-6 weeks.
2. Only use dog shampoo and conditioner formulated for a dog's pH. Make sure to thoroughly rinse their coat so there is no residue remaining that could cause itching.
3. Do not bathe too often, as this dries out the skin, strips all the natural skin and coat oils, and causes itching.
4. In between baths, use moist wipes designed especially for dogs before bed. This is an easy way to remove daily dust and grime.
5. Feed them a high-quality diet that nourishes the skin. Inferior diets with inappropriate fillers can compromise your pooch's health and create itchy skin problems.
6. Feed organic, one-ingredient treats. Single-ingredient treats are free from additives that can cause allergies.
7. Regularly brush your golden's coat to remove debris, shedding hair, and mats that may irritate the skin.
8. Give an omega-3, vitamin E, or salmon oil supplement to make sure your retriever's skin is well nourished.
9. Avoid using toxic cleaning and deodorising products that can get on your golden's coat.
10. If you notice a problem, ask for professional help, especially if you are not certain about the cause.

15. Toxic Foods, Plants, and Products

'Money can buy you a fine dog, but only love can make him wag his tail.'

~ Kinky Friedman ~

Most owners know there are certain human foods, plants, and medications that are poisonous to dogs. However, they might not be aware of other toxic dangers found in plants, fertilisers, and cleaning products. Below is a list of some of the more common products easily found in our homes and gardens that can be harmful or toxic to your golden retriever.

Toxic Foods

Many foods can be toxic to dogs, depending on their age, size, current health, and how much they eat. While a good rule of thumb is to never give your golden human food, this is a list of the most widespread foods that dogs should never eat and what symptoms to watch out for if they do:

Alcohol – Alcohol has a huge impact on dogs, even in small doses. Not only does it intoxicate them, like it does humans, but it can also lead to sickness, diarrhoea, irregular heart rhythm, slowed heart rate, low body temperature, low blood sugar, and even damage the central nervous system.

Avocado – Avocados are poisonous to dogs. The avocado plant contains persin in its leaves, fruit, and seed, which can cause vomiting and diarrhoea in dogs.

Bread Dough – If your golden eats bread dough, their body heat will make the dough rise inside their stomach. As the dough expands, it produces. Dogs who eat bread dough can experience stomach bloating, abdominal pain, vomiting, disorientation, and depression. Since bread dough can rise to many times its original size, a small amount is enough to cause a problem.

Broccoli – The toxic ingredient in broccoli is isothiocyanate. While it may cause stomach upset, it probably will not be harmful unless the amount consumed is over 10% of your golden's daily diet.

Caffeine – Beverages containing caffeine, such as soda, tea, coffee, and chocolate, act as a stimulant and can accelerate your golden's heartbeat to a dangerous level. Dogs that have caffeine have been known to have seizures, which may be fatal.

Chocolate – Chocolate contains a chemical called theobromine, which is toxic to dogs in large enough quantities. It also contains caffeine, which should be avoided.

Different kinds of chocolate contain varying amounts of theobromine and caffeine. Dark chocolate, baking chocolate, and cocoa powder contain more of these compounds than milk chocolate, so your retriever would need to eat more milk chocolate to become ill. However, even a few ounces of chocolate could be enough to cause illness or even death in a puppy. No amount or type of chocolate is safe for a dog to eat.

FACT ***After eating chocolate, a dog could display symptoms including diarrhoea, vomiting, increased heart rate, restless behaviour, muscle tremors, or seizures. If they consume a large quantity, they could die within 24 hours***

Cooked Bones – These can be extremely hazardous for dogs because bones become brittle when cooked, which makes them splinter when a dog chews on them. The splinters have sharp edges that can puncture gums and become stuck in their teeth. They can also cause choking if caught in their throat or create a rupture or puncture of the stomach lining or intestinal tract.

Cooked turkey and chicken legs, pork chops, and veal bones are particularly dangerous. Symptoms of choking include pale or blue gums, dilated pupils, pawing at their face, gasping for air, or panting, unconsciousness, and collapse.

Dairy Products – Dairy products are a major source of food intolerance in dogs. Many dogs are lactose intolerant, which means they have difficulty digesting milk. Lactose-intolerant dogs can have trouble drinking milk but may be all right with other dairy products, such as cheese and plain yoghurt, which are normally easier to digest than plain milk. Other dogs can have an adverse reaction to all types of dairy.

If your golden is intolerant to dairy products, eating them could cause stomach pain, incontinence, bloating, diarrhoea, excessive thirst, vomiting, dehydration, weakness, or weight loss.

Grapes and Raisins – These foods could cause acute—sudden—kidney failure in your retriever. While the toxic agent in this fruit is unknown, clinical signs can occur within 24 hours of eating and include vomiting, diarrhoea, and tiredness with the eventual shutdown of the kidneys.

Garlic and Onions – The onion family is particularly toxic to dogs and can irritate the mouth, making your dog paw at their mouth or face, as well as causing stomach pain, excessive salivation, panting, weakness, refusal to exercise, rapid heart rate, pale or bluish gums, diarrhoea, vomiting, and collapse.

Mushrooms – Mushroom poisoning can be fatal if certain species of mushrooms are eaten by your golden. The most reported severely toxic species of mushroom in both the U.K. and the U.S. is the amanita phalloides, or death cap mushroom, but other amanita species are also toxic. This deadly mushroom is often found growing in grassy or wooded areas near various deciduous and coniferous trees, which means you might easily come across them when out walking your retriever.

Eating amanita mushrooms can cause severe liver disease and neurological disorders. If you suspect that your golden has consumed these mushrooms, you should take them to the veterinarian immediately. The recommended treatment is to induce vomiting straight away and give them activated charcoal. Further treatment for liver disease may also be required.

Pits and Seeds – Many seeds and pits found in a variety of fruits, such as apples, apricots, cherries, pears, and plums, contain cyanogenic glycosides that can cause cyanide poisoning in your golden retriever.

The symptoms of cyanide poisoning usually come on within 15-20 minutes to a few hours after eating and can include initial excitement, followed by rapid respiration rate, salivation, drooling, voiding of urine and faeces, vomiting, muscle spasm, staggering, and coma. If your dog experiences cyanide poisoning and survives more than 2 hours after the onset of symptoms, they will usually recover.

Raw Salmon – Never give your golden retriever raw or undercooked salmon. It could contain the neorickettsia helminthoeca parasite, which causes salmon poisoning disease. This can be fatal. Also, raw salmon contains many small bones. These are brittle and can lodge in their stomach or intestines or choke your dog. However, well-cooked, boneless salmon is on the list of safe food approved for dogs.

Macadamia nuts – This nut is extremely toxic to dogs. They can cause tremors, weakness, paralysis, and severe joint inflammation. If your retriever swallows or nibbles macadamia nuts, call your vet to ask about the best course of action.

Tomatoes – Ripe tomatoes can be fed in moderation as an occasional snack as they are non-toxic to dogs. However, unripe tomatoes and tomato plants should be avoided as they can cause tremors, seizures, stomach upset, and cardiac problems.

Either fence off the area in your garden with tomato plants or supervise your dog when they are in the garden to ensure they stay away from the plants.

Almonds, hazelnuts, walnuts – These are not technically toxic, so it is fine for your golden to occasionally eat them. However, their shape makes them a choking hazard, so they are best avoided.

Xylitol – This is an artificial sweetener often found in sweets, gums, breath mints, toothpaste, and mouthwashes. Xylitol is a poison risk to dogs.

FACT ***When puppies or dogs eat products containing xylitol, it creates a sudden release of insulin. This causes low blood sugar, which can damage the liver. Within 30 minutes, your golden might vomit, appear lethargic, and seem uncoordinated. However, some signs of toxicity can be delayed for hours or even days. Xylitol toxicity in dogs can be fatal if left untreated.***

Toxic Plants

Though some plants may only result in an upset stomach and mild diarrhoea for a day or two if eaten, others can cause more serious harm that could result in liver damage or even prove fatal. Plants differ in attractiveness to dogs. For example, a shrub might sit in your garden for many years and never be touched, while a fallen conker or acorn may appear enticing the moment it hits the ground. Therefore, deciding what to keep in your garden will not only depend on the toxicity of the plant, but also on how inquisitive your golden retriever is.

The following is a list from The Kennel Club in the United Kingdom of the most common plants found in homes and gardens which are poisonous to dogs:

- Aconitum.
- Amaryllis bulbs.
- Asparagus fern.
- Azalea.
- Bluebells.
- Cyclamen.
- Daffodil bulbs.
- Daylilies.
- Delphiniums.
- Dog's Mercury.
- Foxgloves.
- Hemlock.
- Hyacinth.
- Hydrangea.
- Ivy.
- Laburnum.
- Lily of the valley.
- Lupins.
- Morning glory.
- Nightshade.
- Oleander.
- Rhododendron.
- Rhubarb leaves.
- Sweet pea.
- Tulip bulbs.
- Umbrella plant.
- Wisteria.
- Yew.

This is not an exhaustive list. The American Kennel Club (AKC) website also contains a comprehensive listing of toxic plants, vines, trees, and flowers, along with pictures to help identify them.

Safe Garden Plants

There is no reason not to grow a variety of shrubs and scented flowers because you have a dog. The following plants, to name just a few, are not only beautiful, colourful, and fragrant, but they will also attract bees and birds. They are perfectly safe for your retriever:

- Camellia.
- Coral Bells.
- Cosmos.
- Creeping thyme.
- Dill.
- Fennel.
- Fuchsia.
- Honeysuckle.
- Marigold.
- Magnolia.
- Nasturtium.
- Pineapple sage.
- Polka dot.
- Purple basil.
- Roses.
- Rosemary.
- Snapdragon.
- Sunflower.

Safe Indoor Plants

Just because you have decided to share your home with a golden retriever does not mean you cannot have indoor plants. The following are just a few that are known to be safe for dogs who will eat anything:

- African violet.
- Areca palm.
- Boston fern.
- Cast-iron plant.
- Christmas cactus.
- Haworthia.
- Mini phalaenopsis orchid.
- Money tree.
- Moth orchid.
- Parlour palm.
- Peperomia caperata.
- Prayer plant.
- Spider plant.
- Swedish ivy.
- Wax plant.

Toxic Products

Human Medicines Toxic to Dogs

While you should always keep human medicines safely out of the reach of your retriever, some are more toxic than others, including:

- ADD/ADHD Medications.
- ACE Inhibitors.
- Acetaminophen—Tylenol, etc.
- Antidepressants—Cymbalta, Effexor, Lexapro, Prozac, etc.
- Beta Blockers.
- Birth Control Products.
- Cholesterol-Lowering Agents.
- Cough and Cold Medications.
- Non-steroidal anti-inflammatory drugs.
- Sleep Aids and Benzodiazepines—Xanax, etc.
- Thyroid Medications.

Toxic Household Products

Our beloved retrievers love to investigate everything with their mouth and taste it with their tongue. Since they don't wear shoes, our dogs are often directly in contact with products used to clean and moisturise ourselves, clean our homes, or applied to our lawns or gardens, such as:

- All-purpose cleaners.
- Antifreeze—used in car radiators.
- Bath and kitchen cleaners.
- Carpet cleaners.
- De-icing salts—used to melt ice.
- Dishwashing detergents.
- Disinfectant wipes.
- Fertilisers—for lawns and plants.
- Petrol
- Glues and varnishes
- Grass seeds
- Herbicides.
- Insecticides—used to kill insects.
- Laundry detergent.
- Lotions and moisturisers—for people.
- Mildew removers.
- Mothballs.
- Oven cleaners.
- Paints and polishes.
- Perfume—for people.
- Rodenticides—used to kill rodents.
- Shampoo and conditioner—for people.
- Slug poison.
- Toilet cleaners.
- Weed killer.
- Window cleaners.

As you can see, there are many hazardous products inside and outside your home that could seriously harm or even kill your golden. Always keep your home safe for your dog by placing all these products safely out of reach of your retriever.

Pet Poison Control Centres and Help Lines

If you suspect that your golden has ingested something that could be toxic, call a pet poison control line. These are centres for pet owners who need advice if they believe their pet has been in contact with something harmful. They should be able to tell you what symptoms to expect, if any, and if a visit to the vet is necessary. Where possible, give them the following information:

- Which poison your golden has been exposed to—e.g., chocolate, ibuprofen, etc.
- How much they consumed—e.g., 1000mg, 200ml, two tablets, etc. Even if you only have an approximation, this could help.
- The exact time when your dog was exposed to the poison.
- Whether your dog has been unwell, and if so, what symptoms have been observed.

TIP ***It is easier for your vet to successfully treat your poisoned retriever if they see them sooner rather than later. If you are in any doubt, do not wait for your dog to become severely unwell before calling for advice. Quick action could mean the difference between life and death!***

Here is how to help your dog while waiting for your vet:

- Never try to make your golden vomit. Don't administer salt water under any circumstances, as this is extremely dangerous.
- Do not attempt to medicate or treat your golden yourself. Some human and animal medicines can be poisonous to dogs.
- Keep your dog away from other animals to avoid cross-contamination.

If your golden's skin or fur is contaminated, wash it with a mild shampoo, rinse thoroughly, and then dry.

The Animal Poison Line is the United Kingdom's animal poison centre. This is a 24-hour, payable triage service for pet owners who need advice after a suspected poisoning. Call: 01202 509000.

The Animal Poison Control Center of the American Society for the Prevention of Cruelty to Animals (ASPCA) is staffed 24 hours a day, 365 days a year. It is a valuable resource for learning what can be toxic and possibly poisonous to a dog. Call: 1 (888) 426-4435.

The Pet Poison Helpline is a 24-hour payable service staffed by veterinary professionals in the U.S. Call: 0800-213-6680.

16. Keeping Your Golden Safe

'There's a saying. If you want someone to love you forever, buy a dog, feed it and keep it around.'

~ Dick Dale ~

Safe Travelling

Car Travel

Imagine you regularly drive your car without a seatbelt or airbag. Would you feel safe? Probably not. However, many of our furry friends aren't securely restrained in the car, which is unsafe not just for them but for the people around them as well. Never forget to think about vehicle safety for your golden. Keeping them safe is easy.

Owners often ask, 'Is my dog safe when they are buckled into a safety harness in my car?' Unfortunately, the harnesses available on the marketplace have a significant failure rate. Also, bear in mind that if your golden is travelling in the front passenger seat, even if they're secured with a fully tested safety harness, they can still sustain serious injuries if struck by the 100 kph force of the airbag.

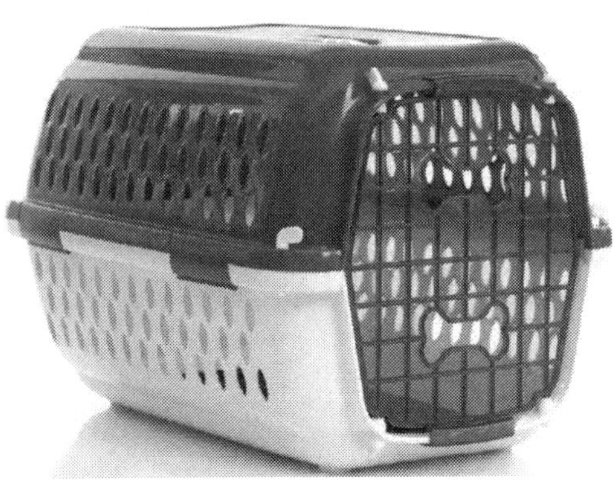

The safest way to transport your golden retriever is to secure them inside a kennel (see picture) bolted to the floor or use your vehicle's seatbelt system. A dog kennel will easily fit on the back seat of your car, where it can be secured with the restraint system. If you plan to have your golden drive with you, you should begin kennel training early on so your dog will calmly accept this travel arrangement.

When you secure your dog appropriately, not only are you providing a safe riding situation for your dog, but you will also avoid the fines which may be levied if you let them sit on your lap or roam freely inside the car. This is a distraction that could cause an accident.

Hot weather is very dangerous for a retriever puppy confined in a long car trip. Sunshades and opening the windows for a while can help. However, never allow them to travel with their head out the window.

Air Travel

Many airlines permit small dogs to travel with their owners in the plane's cabin if the carry bag fits under the seat. Call the airline in question in advance to confirm whether they will permit your golden to stay with you and also find out the size restriction of the carrier. You might have to book a space and pay a fee for transporting your golden retriever.

Most soft carriers are airline approved for the following under-seat dimensions:

Window Seat: 48 cm L x 35 cm W x 21 cm H (19 in L x 14 in W x 8.25 in H)

Middle Seat: 48 cm L x 48 cm W x 21 cm H (19 in L x 19 in W x 8.25 in H)

Aisle Seat: 48 cm L x 35 cm W x 21 cm H (19 in L x 14 in W x 8.25 in H)

While your golden retriever puppy might be small enough to fit into a soft carrier bag for travel inside a plane's cabin as carry-on luggage, they will be too large when they reach adult size. You must transport any puppies or dogs that are too large to fit comfortably inside a travel bag in a hard-sided crate or kennel in the heated cargo hold.

Bus Travel

Most public bus systems allow a small dog on board if they are in a carrier bag that will sit on the owner's lap or go underneath the seat, usually at no charge. Some countries—including the U.K.—permit any size dog to travel on the bus system either on a lead or in a carrier, unless there is a legitimate reason to refuse them.

Train Travel

Typically, every country has specific rules and regulations regarding pets travelling on trains. The following are general rules for train travel in the U.K., United States, and Canada:

National Rail, the train system in the United Kingdom, is very dog friendly. All dogs, no matter their size, can travel on a lead or inside a carrier. However, if travelling on Eurostar to France, dogs are not allowed at all.

Amtrak in the U.S. only permits a total of 5 pets per train, excluding service dogs. There is a small fee involved, so it is recommended to book well in advance. They allow small dogs to travel with their owners inside passenger cars if:

- The carrier will fit underneath the seat.
- The weight of the carrier and dog combined is no more than 9 kilograms (20 pounds).
- The trip is no longer than 7 hours.

Rail Canada allows small dogs to travel with their owners inside passenger cars if they stay inside an approved carrier that fits underneath the passenger seat. The weight of the carrier and pet combined must be no more than 10 kilograms (22 pounds), and there are a limited number of pets permitted on each train. You will be charged a small fee for your golden retriever. Reserving a space well ahead of travel time is advisable.

Ferry Travel

Many ferries have a specific area for dogs, either on lead on outside deck areas or inside the cabin if they are contained in a pet carrier. There is not usually an extra charge for your dog. However, if travelling from the U.K. to Europe on the cross-channel ferry, your golden will need an animal health certificate—or EU or Northern Ireland-issued pet passport—a microchip, and valid rabies vaccination from at least 21 days before your date of travel.

Identification

Thankfully, there are several effective choices, including tattooing, microchipping, and pet trackers to identify your golden retriever, so you can be reunited should they ever get lost. Read on to learn more.

Beware of dog theft

It can be a very scary time if your dog goes missing. Often your dog will simply have strayed a little too far away. Sadly, we know thieves target pet dogs either to sell them or as part of a scam to claim a reward for your dog's return.

If stolen, your retriever could easily be hidden and transported to another area, making it extremely difficult to find them. Prevention is the key to keeping your pet safe:

- Don't leave your golden retriever unsupervised in public. Never leave your dog tied up outside a shop or alone in your car while you run an errand.
- Secure your garden. When you let your dog out, keep them in sight. Make certain gates are locked, and there are no gaps in your fences or walls.
- If possible, vary your walking habits by using different routes. Avoid walking at the same time every day to prevent your activity from becoming predictable.
- Practise the Recall command to train your golden to come back when you call them. If you are unsure whether they will return when you want, keep them on a lead, especially in unfamiliar areas.
- Ensure that your microchip contact details are always up to date so that if your retriever does go missing, they can be traced back to you. In the U.K., it is a legal requirement for all canines aged eight weeks and over to be microchipped and registered on a compliant database.
- It is also a legal requirement for all dogs to wear a collar with an ID tag while out in public spaces. The tag should include your surname, house name or number, and postcode. You can also add your mobile number if you wish, but avoid putting your golden's name on the disc.

When it comes to dog theft, time is of the essence, so it is important to act immediately:

- Report your golden retriever missing to your local council's dog warden. You can find their contact details on your council's website.
- If you believe your golden has been stolen, contact the police and report the theft. You can call them or report it online.
- Contact the microchip database where your golden is registered on so they can record your dog as missing. You will then be contacted if anyone tries to change the chip details.
- Ask dog walkers in your area if they have seen your dog. Put up posters where allowed and post on local social media groups.

- There are many websites in the U.K. designed to help owners report their dogs as missing, including Dog Lost, Pets Reunited, and the National Pet Register. Use as many sites as possible to report your dog missing.
- Contact rescue centres in your area. If your golden retriever has strayed, they could be brought to a rescue. Several organisations, such as Battersea Dogs and Cats Home, have missing and found helplines.

Licensing

If your golden retriever is easily identifiable, they will be returned to you should they go missing. This is much better for your dog than leaving them for who knows how long behind bars at a rescue centre. In many U.S. states, it is compulsory to have your dog licensed yearly. There is no licence requirement in the U.K.

TIP ***The U. S. licence contains an identifying number and telephone number anyone can call if they find your lost dog wearing its tag. When the number is called and the tag number reported, it is identified with the owner, and your dog will be returned to you.***

Tattooing

Tattooing is another popular way to identify your dog if they are lost or stolen. Many dog owners like this safe, simple solution. Since a tattoo is visible, it is immediately recognisable and reported when a lost dog is found, making it a highly effective form of identification.

NATIONAL DOG TATTOO REGISTER

As a bonus, dog thieves are less likely to steal your golden if it has a permanent, visible means of identification. There are several registries for tattooed dogs, including the National Dog Tattoo Registry in the United Kingdom (see picture), which has a network of accredited tattooists across the country.

In the United States, the National Dog Registry (NDR) was founded in 1966. Since then, the NDR has supervised, directed, conducted, or overseen the tattooing of over 6 million animals.

Microchipping

A microchip (see picture) is an identification chip used to help return lost dogs to their owners.

The implant is a tiny integrated circuit, approximately twice the size of a grain of rice. The chip is enclosed in glass and implanted underneath the dog's skin with a syringe. The chip uses passive 'Radio Frequency Identification' (RFID) technology, also known as a Passive Integrated Transponder (PIT) tag.

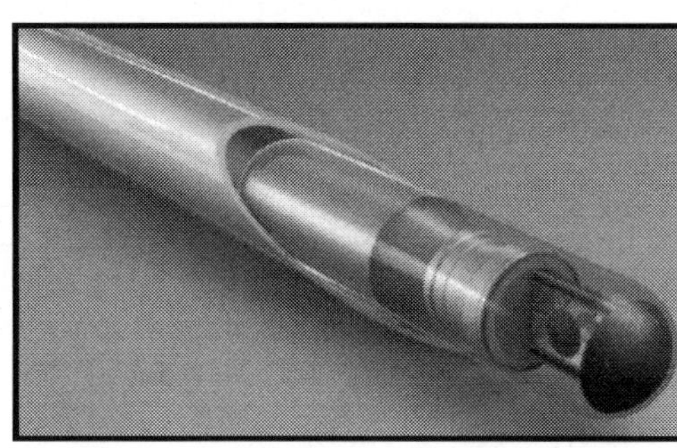

The microchip is usually implanted without anaesthetic into the scruff of your dog's neck by a veterinarian or rescue shelter. It does not have an internal power source. The chip is read by a scanner—also known as an 'interrogator'—that energises the capacitor inside the chip, sending radio signals back to the scanner so the identifying number can be read. Manufacturers of microchips often donate scanners to animal shelters, veterinarian clinics and hospitals.

If you live in the U.S., you are not obliged by law to microchip your retriever. However, in the United Kingdom, since 2016, it has been mandatory for those owning dogs over the age of 8 weeks to have them microchipped.

Microchipping is used by animal shelters, pounds, animal control officers, breeders, and vets to help return a higher percentage of lost canines. Some of the resistance to microchipping is due to problems correctly reading the implants. If the scanner is not tuned to the same frequency as the implanted microchip, it can't read it, rendering the process useless.

Microchips are manufactured with different frequencies, including 125 kHz, 128 kHz and 134.2 kHz. Approximately 98% of the pet microchips in the U.S. use 125 kHz, while those in Europe use 134.2 kHz. If the facility reading your golden's microchip does not have a compatible scanner—reading at the chip's frequency—your dog will not be identified.

Pet Trackers

While there are many pet trackers available, they tend to fall into two main categories:

- GPS Trackers.
- Radio Trackers.

A GPS Tracker can help you locate your retriever in real time by utilising cellular towers. It requires a SIM card or some sort of cellular service. Your dog will need to wear a collar or harness containing a tracking antenna (see picture).

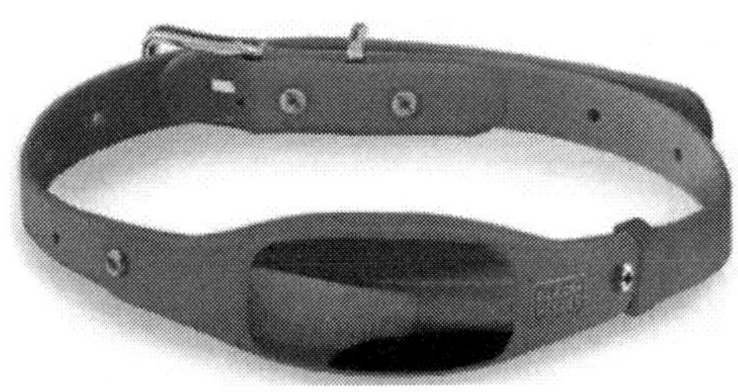

There is an app available for your smartphone or device designed to go with your GPS pet tracker, so you can get detailed location data. Some produce a map of where your pet is and offer directions to help you get there as fast as possible. Some companies selling GPS pet trackers do not provide apps, but you can obtain the same information by logging onto their website.

Radio Trackers have been used for decades and are often used with hunting dogs. They function over a limited range, much like a walkie-talkie. The dog wears a collar or harness containing a tag that can be read by RF (radio) signals. These devices operate like a compass, pointing you in the direction of your dog. Unfortunately, if your golden is out of range, you cannot receive any information. The more you spend on a radio tracker, the greater its range.

Where to Look

In the unfortunate event that your golden retriever goes missing, if you think they were stolen, see the above section 'Beware of Dog Theft'. If you think your dog has run away or gotten lost, there are many things you can do to locate your lost dog, including:

- Retrace your golden's last known location.
- Contact friends and neighbours.
- Place flyers on telephone poles throughout the neighbourhood with your contact details and your golden's photo. If you have insurance, your insurer may cover the cost of printing.
- Distribute flyers in all neighbourhood stores and businesses.
- Call all the local shelters and pounds every day.
- Contact local rescue organisations.
- Contact local schools—the children might have seen your retriever.
- Contact all businesses that deal with lost pets.
- Post a picture on social media.
- Ask the local radio station for help.
- Advertise in your local newspaper.

Health Insurance

Pet owners often wonder whether they can afford not to have medical insurance. Considering all the treatments and medications available for our dogs, which frequently come with a very high price tag, an increasing number of owners are deciding to get pet insurance. Some people feel that placing money into a savings account in case of unforeseen medical expenses makes more sense. Whether you start a savings account or purchase a health insurance plan, most dog owners will go to any lengths to save the life of their canine family member.

Dog insurance coverage can vary widely in cost, and over the average lifespan of your golden retriever can be anywhere from £1,640 to £6,300 ($2,150 to $8,000). These figures are based on the current average cost and depend on the level of coverage you have. Accident-only insurance is far cheaper than full accident and illness cover. Unless your dog contracts a life-threatening disease, you might never need to pay out much for treatment.

Having access to advanced technological tools and procedures means that your golden will be offered treatment options that were once only available to humans. Now, some canine conditions once considered fatal are being treated, although treatment can cost from £820 to £5,100 ($1,000 and $6,700) or more.

TIP ***Even though you might think pet insurance will cover the cost any time your dog needs a trip to the vet, be careful when considering an insurance plan. Many policies contain small print excluding certain ages and hereditary and chronic conditions.***

Some people do not consider dog insurance when their dog is healthy because they view it as paying for something they might never need. However, just like car insurance, after an accident has happened or your dog gets sick, it is too late to buy insurance.

For example, you might take your dog to the vet who discovers your golden has something wrong with their eyes. You decide to purchase insurance, but anything involving your dog's eye health will probably be excluded from the policy. Usually, when purchasing a pet insurance plan, you are required to provide the insuring company with a history of your retriever's health. In this example, the eye health issue will already be part of your dog's history. This means it's best to get pet insurance before any problems arise.

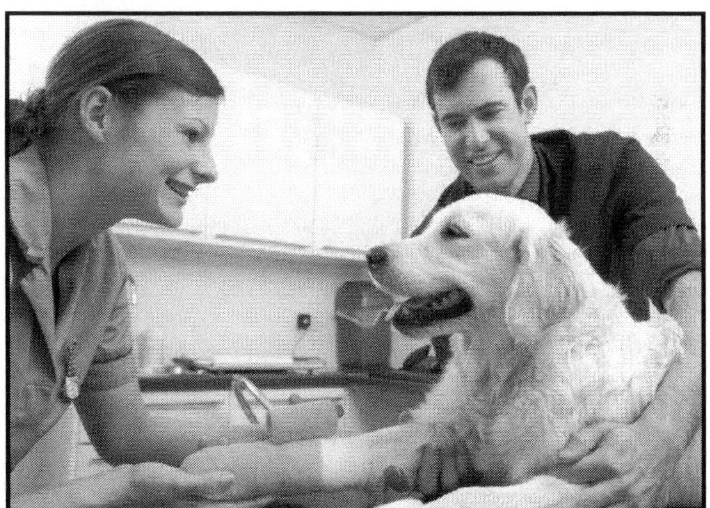

Also, bear in mind that canine health insurance rates increase as your dog gets older. When your golden is young, the policy might only cost £14 ($18) per month, but it will increase considerably to as much as £140 ($180) or more per month as your dog becomes middle or senior-aged, at around 8 to 10 years old.

Shop around. Pet insurance policies vary greatly between companies. The only way to know for certain exactly what sort of coverage you are buying is to get a copy of that policy, so you can read what will and won't be covered. Read the fine print carefully to avoid any nasty surprises. The middle of filing a claim is not a good time to find that a condition won't be covered.

A list of the cheapest and most expensive dog breeds to insure on accident-only policies and lifetime policies has been compiled by Manypets.com. The data comes from hundreds of thousands of quotes generated for real consumers. Here is the list of the five cheapest dog breeds to insure on accident-only policies:

1. Jack Russell—the cheapest.
2. Chihuahua.
3. Yorkshire terrier.
4. Shi Tzu.
5. Border collie.

Since many of us in today's uncertain economy might be hard-pressed to cover a high veterinarian bill, paying smaller monthly premiums can make it more affordable and provide peace of mind and improved veterinarian care for your retriever.

Before choosing your dog-insurance policy, there are several factors you must consider, such as:

- Will your retriever need a physical exam?
- Is there a waiting period before the policy becomes active?
- What percentage of the bill does the insurance company pay?
- Are payments limited or capped in any way?
- Are there excess pays—upfront costs to the owner?
- Does the plan cover pre-existing conditions?
- Does the plan cover chronic or recurring medical problems?
- Can you choose which vet or hospital will treat your golden retriever?
- Are prescription medications covered?
- Are you covered when travelling with your golden?
- Does the policy pay if your dog is being treated and then dies?

Insure your golden retriever when they are a young puppy. Waiting until they are older means your monthly premiums will be considerably higher.

First Aid

First Aid Kit

Do not forget to put together a canine first aid kit (see picture) in case of emergencies. Keep one at home and in your car. The following items should be included in the kit:

- Flannel.
- Blanket.
- Gauze bandaging.
- Styptic powder.
- Medical tape.
- Nail clippers.
- Non-stick pads for wounds.
- Scissors.
- Sterile eye wash.
- Tick twister.

- Towel.
- Tweezers.
- Antiseptic wash for wounds—hydrogen peroxide.

If you are in the United Kingdom, it would also be smart to keep a copy of the PDSA instructions on CPR for Dogs and Puppies in your first aid kit. In the States, you can find this in the American Red Cross emergency techniques called 'Saving Your Pet With CPR'. You familiarise yourself with the proper way to administer cardiopulmonary resuscitation (CPR) to your golden. You could also consider taking a CPR class; many courses are available through community educational systems and veterinary practices or online.

Of course, nobody wants to find themselves in a situation where the life of their dog is put at risk. However, the reality is that accidents happen. Knowing a little about how to save your dog—or maybe even someone else's—is time well spent.

TIP ***If your golden is injured, remember to always handle them carefully and gently. A dog who is traumatised, fearful, or in pain, even one who is usually gentle, might lash out and try to bite.***

Applying CPR and Artificial Respiration

If your dog becomes unconscious, depending upon the reason why, they could stop breathing. If they stop breathing, they will go into cardiac arrest when their heart stops beating. If this happens, your dog will die.

However, after breathing stops and before cardiac arrest, the heart can continue beating for several minutes. This is the window of opportunity when performing CPR and artificial respiration can save your golden's life. Ideally, one person does the artificial respiration while the other performs CPR.

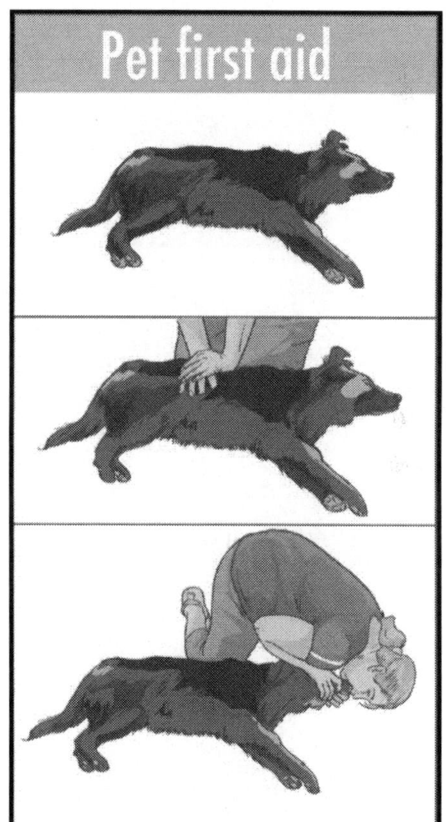

Here is how to perform CPR on your golden:

1. Put your retriever on their side on a flat surface.
2. Feel for their pulse or heartbeat by placing one hand over their left side, just behind the front leg.
3. Place the palm of your hand on your retriever's rib cage over their heart, with your other hand on top of the other hand. For puppies, put just your thumb on one side of their chest and the rest of your fingers on the other side.
4. Press down and release, compressing your dog's chest approximately 2-3 centimetres (1 inch). Repeat 80 to 100 times every minute.

Here are the steps needed to perform artificial respiration on your golden retriever:

1. Place your dog on their side on a flat surface.
2. Check to make sure your golden has stopped breathing by seeing if their chest rises and falls and feeling for their breath on your hand. Check the colour of their gums, as the lack of oxygen will make them turn blue.
3. Check your golden's airway is clear and that there is nothing stuck in their mouth or throat by extending the head and neck and opening the mouth.

4. If there is an object blocking your dog's throat, pull their tongue out and use your fingers or some pliers to get a firm grip on the object to pull it out. If you cannot reach the object, you will have to use the Heimlich manoeuvre to try to dislodge it (see below).
5. If your golden's airway is not blocked, lift their chin to straighten out the neck and begin rescue breathing.
6. Hold your dog's muzzle and close their mouth, put your mouth over the nose and blow gently—just enough to make your dog's chest rise.
7. Wait long enough for the air you just breathed into your dog's lungs to leave before repeating.
8. Continue giving one gentle breath every 3 seconds while their heart is still beating and until your dog starts to breathe on their own.

Choking dog

If an object is blocking your dog's airway and you cannot reach it with your fingers to remove it, you need to take immediate action to dislodge it. As with people, you will know your dog is choking because they will retch, gag and cough to try to expel the object. If this occurs, you may not have time to make it to your vet, so you should do the following:

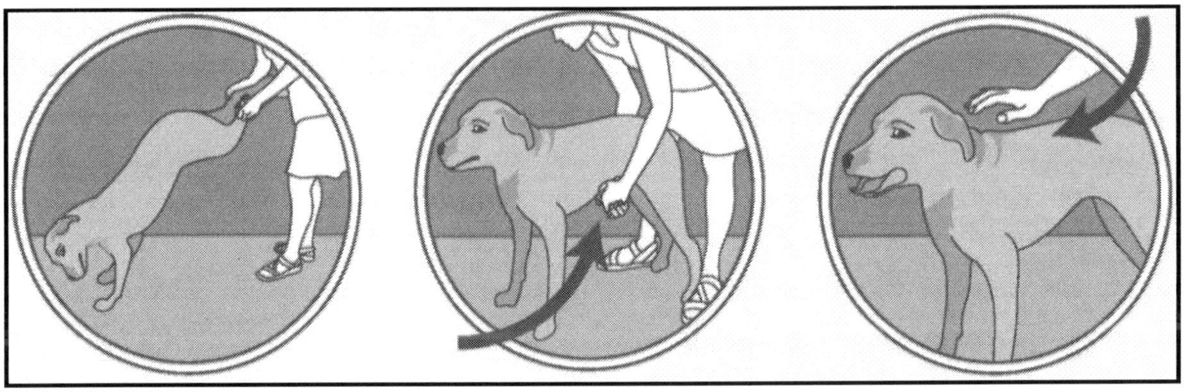

1. First, see if you can dislodge the object by opening your dog's mouth and sweeping from side to side. Take care not to be bitten or to push the object farther into their throat.
2. To help your golden's attempts to cough up the object, remove their collar. Then, lift them by their back legs and hold them vertically with their head down, like a wheelbarrow. This position might dislodge the object.
3. If the above steps do not work, try the dog Heimlich manoeuvre, as follows:
4. Put your arms around their waist with your golden retriever standing or lying down.
5. Close your fist and place it on the underside of their torso, where their ribs end just beneath the sternum.
6. Push up with your fist five times in rapid succession to compress the abdomen.
7. If your dog is not breathing, alternate this with CPR.
8. As a final solution, administer a sharp blow with the palm of your hand between your golden's shoulder blades. Then go back to step 3 and repeat the Heimlich manoeuvre.

It is relatively rare for dogs to choke, but some objects, such as golf balls or small rubber balls, can become stuck at the back of their throat. After performing the above steps, sweep your golden's mouth for the object. Once it is dislodged, immediately seek veterinary assistance.

17. Senior Dog Care

'Such short little lives our pets have to spend with us, and they spend most of it waiting for us to come home each day.'

~ John Grogan ~

Much like humans, when our dogs reach a certain age, they begin to experience behavioural and physical changes that are all part of their natural life circle. The following pages offer many suggestions about how to make your senior golden's years as pleasant as possible.

What Age is My Golden Retriever in Human Years?

We used to think that calculating a dog's age in human years was simple. All we had to do was multiply their age by 7. One reason for this formula is that the 7:1 ratio is based on the statistic that on average people live to about 70, and dogs live for about 10 years. Even though this theory has been around for ages, the reality isn't so straightforward.

Small dogs tend to live longer than bigger ones, and medium-sized dogs come somewhere in the middle. As a guideline, the American Veterinary Medical Association has proposed the following to calculate your dog's life in human years:

- The first year of your dog's life is equal to 15 human years.
- Year 2 for your dog is about 9 years for a human.
- After that, each human year is approximately five years for your dog.

We are always looking for ways to extend the time we have with our dogs and improve the quality of that time. Canine gerontology is an active field of science studying the ageing process in dogs, looking to delay ageing and promote healthy longevity.

Sometimes, you might not know the precise age of your golden if they've been rescued from a shelter or rescue centre. Or perhaps your retriever was found roaming the street with no identification, and they became a family member. Should you find yourself in this situation, your dog's teeth can offer a rough idea as to what their age might be. Of course, the accuracy of this estimate can vary from dog to dog depending on the dental care they received before they came into your life, but the following chart is a good starting point:

Age	Teeth Condition
8 weeks	All baby teeth are present
6-7 months	All white and clean adult teeth are present
1-2 years	Teeth are not so white, and back molars show some yellowing
3-5 years	Signs of tartar and some wear
5-10 years	Signs of wear, gum disease, some teeth might be loose
10-15 years	Teeth are worn, heavy tartar build-up, some teeth are missing

Signs of Aging

A vet can carry out an internal examination and perform various tests to determine the condition of the joints, bones, and organs of an elderly dog. In addition, you can assume your dog is in their senior years from their appearance if they have:

- Cloudy eyes.
- Grey hair around their muzzle.
- Loose skin.
- Stiff legs.

While many dogs retain their youthful vigour for many years, at some point, they will start to slow down. Some additional signs of ageing include:

- Easily tiring and needing shorter walks.
- Gaining weight.
- Not wanting to play.
- Panting more.
- Finding it difficult to jump up on a chair or sofa and being reluctant to jump back down.
- Being slower or a little unstable when climbing stairs or walking on uneven surfaces.
- Losing their hearing.
- Losing their eyesight.
- Becoming more dependent on you and not wanting to be alone.
- Sleeping more during the day.
- Getting colder and shivering.
- Losing bowel or bladder control.
- Needing to go outside more often.
- Accidentally peeing in their sleep or occasionally leaking urine.
- Showing signs of dementia or confusion and wandering aimlessly during the day or night.
- Declining appetite or becoming very picky about food.

- Refusing to eat or throwing up their food.
- Having difficulty jumping into the car.

Caring for your Senior Golden Retriever

The best way you can help your senior golden retriever when they might not be feeling their best is by giving them even more love, attention, affection, and companionship. They need to know you are there for them, so never leave them alone for long periods. They have been relying on you their whole life, and as they get older, they need you to be close to them.

There are many other things you can do to help your golden retriever be more comfortable and cared for during their senior years. Read on to find out what these are.

Feeding

While it is always best to give your dog the best diet possible, regardless of age, sometimes, your older retriever will have less of an appetite or little interest in the food they once loved. This can be because they are tired of eating the same food, or they do not need the same amount of food since their activity level has decreased.

TIP ***Often, senior dogs put on weight as they have a slower metabolic rate and their activity level has dropped significantly, yet they are still eating the same amount of food. Always keep an eye on your golden's weight as they age since overweight dogs age faster and have more health issues than lean dogs.***

If your senior golden tends to pack on the extra kilos, help them enjoy their healthiest years in later life by changing to a diet lower in calories. That way, they will not have to struggle with obesity. If your retriever seems to have lost interest in their food, switching to a more flavourful, aromatic home-cooked diet or adding a tasty topper can be more enticing and reignite their love of food.

Coat Care

Keeping your senior dog comfortable also means keeping them clean and well-groomed. If you have your retriever's coat clipped a little shorter, they won't need as much brushing to prevent painful mats.

Also, make sure your golden does not suffer from any sort of biting parasites that cause them the misery of constant chewing and scratching. At bath time, adjust the water so it is not too hot and dry their coat well afterwards since your older dog might be more sensitive to temperature changes.

Comfort, Convenience and Warmth

Just like people, older dogs can find it harder to maintain a comfortable body temperature. Keeping your senior golden warm during colder winter weather might mean a cosy coat when they go outside or even a sweater or T-shirt when inside. Make sure their crate or bed is not in a draughty location. You might like to raise it off the floor so they will not have to suffer cold draughts.

Though most dogs are fine sleeping on the floor, if they do not already have a comfy, padded bed, you might consider investing in one as they enter their senior years to make them more comfortable. A soft, cosy bed will keep them warm while alleviating joint pain and sore spots.

Also, if your golden is used to sleeping on a chair, sofa, or bed, and they are having difficulties jumping up, an easy solution is to purchase a soft set of foam stairs, so they can easily get to their favourite sleeping place.

Exercise

It is likely your senior golden will have health conditions or other problems that limit how much they can exercise. They are likely to slow down a little or need more rest, but it is still important to keep them active so they stay healthy. Here are some tips that apply to almost every senior dog:

- Exercise regularly but keep it gentle. This will help your senior retriever to remain active and help their muscles and joints. Little and often is better as their joints stiffen when they have not been used for a while. There are still plenty of exercises you can do with your senior dog. Just remember to go at their speed and stop if they look tired or are struggling.
- Do not stop walking. Your golden might not be able to go on long walks anymore, but they still like to go outdoors each day to sniff, stretch their legs, and get some fresh air. Choose to take a shorter route in case your golden becomes tired.
- Take the weather conditions into consideration when exercising your senior dog outdoors. Older retrievers do not cope as well with high or low temperatures. You might need to walk during the cooler times of the day if it is hot or put them in a dog coat when it is cold.
- If your golden has problems with their senses, try to stick to familiar routes and places. Like people, your dog could start to lose their eyesight and hearing as they get older. Walking somewhere familiar will stop them from becoming anxious and confused.
- If your golden's sight or hearing is deteriorating, sudden movements can take them by surprise and be extremely stressful. When you see something your dog might not have spotted, support them by petting and reassuring them.
- Always go at your golden's pace. Never rush them or make them exercise for longer than they can. If they lie down on a walk, it's a sign they need to rest.
- Your senior dog will benefit from indoor exercises if it is too hot or cold outside. Puzzle toys and indoor games are a wonderful way to keep your ageing dog happy and for you to enjoy quality time together.
- If your golden enjoys swimming, this is a great activity as it puts far less strain on sore joints. As soon as they come out of the water, remember to dry them thoroughly, so they do not get cold and only let them swim if it is safe. Be careful where you take them swimming. Outdoor pools or lakes can have high or steep sides that an older dog could struggle with.
- If their sense of smell is good, your golden will love scent games regardless of their age. It is an excellent way to keep both their body and brain in good condition.
- Even though their pace might have slowed down, your retriever will still love playing. Most dogs never seem to completely lose their fun-loving puppy nature and still enjoy playing with you,

even when they get older. Try to keep the games a little gentler, so they do not try to jump or twist for toys.

- Dogs are social creatures. While they might not have the stamina of younger dogs and often get frustrated by puppy antics, they will still enjoy seeing dogs their own age who they get on with, even if they do not play together.
- Contrary to popular belief, old dogs can still learn new tricks! Training is a fantastic way to keep your older retriever's mind active. They will enjoy every opportunity to get their brain working.

Always check with your vet that your dog is getting the right level of exercise so it won't cause them any problems. Ask your vet if you notice your dog having difficulties getting around or if they do not seem to enjoy exercising anymore. There might be things your vet can do to improve their quality of life and provide relief of any aches and pains preventing your golden from getting around.

Vet Check-ups

As your retriever ages, they might develop a weakened immune system or other conditions inherent to ageing. It is highly recommended to increase vet visits to keep an eye on the medical condition of your dog so that any changes that might cause problems can be detected early on.

Switch from a yearly check-up at the vet's to regular health check-ups every six months or more for your senior dog. More frequent visits can help diagnose problems and offer solutions that will help your golden live their best senior life.

Toilet Breaks

As your golden retriever enters their senior years, their ability to hold their bowels and bladder might begin to be compromised. Always be kind and do not shame them if accidents happen, as they will probably already be feeling bad enough about it.

Supporting your dog to deal with this could be as simple as taking them outside more frequently—the way you did when they were a puppy—or providing a toilet patch for them if they cannot get themselves outside quickly enough when nature calls.

Dealing with Diminished Eyesight

Even though there can be several different reasons for your golden's sight deteriorating, as they become senior-aged, most dogs will suffer from cataracts, macular degeneration, or glaucoma.

The first signs your retriever is losing their eyesight could be so subtle that you may not notice since dogs are used to negotiating their usual surroundings by smell alone. You might notice a reluctance to jump on or off their favourite chair under low light conditions or go outside for the last nighttime walk when it is dark.

As their eyesight deteriorates, they could start to bump into things or have difficulty finding toys. They may even begin to act in an uncharacteristically aggressive or defensive manner when startled by another dog or person since their loss of eyesight is making them feel vulnerable. Most likely, they will want to stay closer to their favourite person. If your golden retriever seems to be stubbornly ignoring hand signals, this can be a cue that they cannot see what you are showing them.

Although dogs adapt incredibly well to losing their eyesight, here is how you can help them safely navigate their home surroundings:

- Leave all the furniture in the same place.
- Do not leave things laying on the floor.
- Block off dangerous areas, such as stairs, where they might fall.
- Keep all passageways clear of debris.
- Keep their crate and/or bed in the same location.
- Remove any sharp or hazardous objects they might walk into.
- Keep their bowls in the same place.
- Use voice cues to announce your approach.
- Use a heavier step so they can feel the approaching vibration.

Above all, be patient and understanding. Always try to imagine what it must be like for your dog who is losing or has lost their eyesight.

Dealing with Diminished Hearing

Hearing loss is often attributable to slowly degenerating changes in the nerves inside the ears of an ageing golden retriever. Just as with failing eyesight, diminished hearing is typically a slow process that is not noticed immediately. Some of the symptoms of hearing loss include:

- Ignoring voice commands.
- Not coming when called.
- Not responding to squeaky toys.
- No longer reacting to fireworks.
- Not reacting to noisy neighbours.
- Not noticing a dog barking in the distance.
- Sleeping more soundly.
- Not hearing the key in the lock when you return home.

There are some workarounds to help a retriever who is going deaf understand what you are asking. For example, if your dog still has their eyesight, communication can easily be carried out with hand signals alone.

TIP ***Extra caution needs to be practised when walking your dog who has lost their hearing as they will be unable to hear cyclists, vehicles, or other approaching dangers. Keep your golden on a lead when outside so you can be certain their senior years can be as safe and stress-free as possible.***

Another alternative way to get the attention of a dog who is hard of hearing is stamping your foot on the floor. You can also teach them to come when they hear a loud whistle, a clicker, or loud hand clapping.

Just as a dog that is losing their eyesight can be startled by other dogs or people suddenly appearing, the same can happen to a dog with compromised hearing when someone or something suddenly appears without any sound to warn them.

Thankfully, when your dog begins to lose their eyesight and hearing, they usually retain their strongest sense - the smell - which they rely on to find their way and navigate the surroundings.

Dealing with Canine Dementia

As your golden retriever ages, they might show changes in brain function, which are normally displayed as unsteadiness or aimless wandering—signs of dementia. This type of behaviour often occurs during the night, especially if they are feeling pain, are confused, or are disoriented. If this is happening to your dog, sit with them until they relax and fall asleep again. Make sure they cannot accidentally fall down the stairs or harm themselves in any way. Take time to block off dangerous areas, so your confused dog will be safe from injury.

Mobility aids for your senior golden

If your golden's activity is being affected by their mobility for any reason, it is still important to keep them as active as possible and keep a watchful eye on their quality of life.

There are plenty of things that can help, so speak with your vet to see what options are available:

- Give them lots of brain games and stimulation to keep their minds healthy and active.
- Ask your vet about hydrotherapy, physiotherapy, or massage techniques that could help.

- It is often difficult to physically help a struggling larger senior dog because of their size. You might wish to consider buying a support harness or sling for walks.
- Consider using ramps around the home to help your dog get up steps to and from the house/garden or into the car.
- Sometimes, tiles and wood flooring can be quite slippery for our four-legged friends, especially if they are not as steady on their feet as they used to be. Consider putting down a mat or rug to make it easier for them to walk around.
- If they are still able to walk but just not very far, try to take them on shorter, flatter walking routes to allow them to go outside and stretch their legs. You might consider driving them to a park they used to enjoy walking to, where they can still sniff and walk around.

Remember, older dogs who struggle to get around can grow long nails since they are not wearing them down by walking. Check them regularly and have them trimmed when required.

Euthanasia

As difficult as it can be, the final act of kindness you can offer your golden retriever is to let them pass peacefully into the next world if they are suffering from old age or a debilitating injury that is seriously compromising their quality of life.

FACT ***Euthanasia is a painless, peaceful, and humane way of providing a gentle death to a dog suffering from chronic pain, incurable illness, or the ravages of old age. While this decision can truly be one of the hardest you ever have to make, it is also the kindest thing you can do if your golden is suffering.***

If you don't know whether the time has come to end your golden retriever's suffering, it can be helpful to keep a diary or daily log where you note how much of your dog's daily life is difficult for them. Your veterinarian can also help with this decision since regular check-ups will determine whether your golden is in pain and how badly.

Often, we cannot bear the thought of losing our canine friends and delay letting them go because we love them so much. However, you must be strong for your retriever and act in their best interests no matter how much it saddens you. In the end, you do not want to prolong their suffering.

Euthanasia is a procedure carried out by your dog's vet, either at their surgery or in the comfort of your home, if your vet offers house calls. Every veterinarian will have received special training to perform euthanasia.

When the time comes, it is usually a two-step process. First, your veterinarian injects the dog with a sedative to make them sleepy, calm, and comfortable. Second, a special drug is injected that will peacefully stop the dog's heart.

These drugs work in such a way that your dog will be unaware that they are transitioning towards a peaceful end. What they feel is very similar to what people experience when falling asleep under anaesthesia during a surgical procedure.

Once the second stage drug has been injected, the process takes about 10 to 20 seconds. Your vet will then check to make sure your dog's heart has stopped.

Memorials

There are many ways to honour the passing of your golden retriever. Each furry friend is uniquely special to their owners. For instance, you and your family might wish to have your companion cremated and keep their ashes in a special urn or sprinkle them along your dog's favourite walk, or across the lake where they loved to swim.

Perhaps you want to have a special marker, photo bereavement, photo engraved Rainbow Bridge poem, or wooden plaque created in honour of your passed friend. Another option would be to keep the memory of your dog close to you by having a DNA remembrance pendant or a bracelet made.

You might also choose a beautiful set of memorial wind chimes to remind you of your beloved golden every time you hear the chimes ring. There are even companies that will turn the ashes into a diamond that lasts forever.

Grieving a Lost Friend

Some people do not appreciate the extent of the terrible grief involved in losing a beloved canine companion, especially if they have not experienced it themselves. While some friends might give you pitying looks and attempt to cheer you up, if they have never lost a dog, they could be secretly thinking that you are making too much fuss over 'just a dog'.

However, for many people, the loss of their cherished golden retriever is so painful that they decide never to share their lives with another dog because they cannot bear the thought of going through such intense grief again.

When your faithful furry friend has passed on, it is normal to feel sad, tearful, and depressed. This kind of loss can be as acute as the loss of a human friend or life partner. The grieving process takes time to overcome. Some people never fully recover.

After the loss of your retriever, take care of yourself by making sure you keep eating and getting regular sleep, even though you might feel lonely and bereft. Losing your beloved dog is a serious shock to the system, which can affect concentration and the ability to find joy or willingness to participate in other activities that are part of daily life. During this early grieving time, take extra care while driving or performing tasks that need concentration, as you might find yourself distracted.

Many people do not give enough time before getting another golden and immediately go to a shelter to rescue a deserving dog. While this might help distract you from the grieving process, it is not fair to the new member of your family. Bringing a new dog into a grieving home can create behavioural problems for the new pet, who will have to learn all about their new home while dealing with the family's unstable, sad energy.

TIP ***If there are other dogs or pets in the home, they will also grieve the loss of a companion. This could manifest in their acting depressed, being off their food or showing little interest in play or games. You need to support your other pets through this grieving process by keeping them busy and interested, taking them for extra walks and spending more time with them.***

It is better to take the time to grieve properly by waiting a minimum of 3 to 6 months to allow everyone in the family to feel happier and more stable before sharing your home with another dog again. Of course, the grieving process is different for everyone. Only you can know when the time is right to consider another canine companion.

Rainbow Bridge

If you're struggling, there are support groups, such as Rainbow Bridge—a grief support community— to help you and your family through this painful period of loss and grief.

Anyone who has ever felt the intense, devastating grief of losing a much-loved pet will probably have heard of the *Rainbow Bridge*, a reference to the comforting belief that there is a heaven or otherworldly place that pets cross over to at the end of their life.

According to the poems anonymously written about Rainbow Bridge, this is a warm, lush green meadow where there is always fresh food and water, the sun shines all day, and healthy pets play with one another while they wait for their human family to join them.

While you are grieving an adored pet, the thought that they are in a beautiful place where they are well-fed, healthy, and happy while they wait for you to join them can offer much-needed comfort.

18. Holidays as a Golden Owner

'No matter how little money and how few possessions you own, having a dog makes you rich.'

~ Louis Sabin ~

Taking your dog with you

You don't need to leave your golden retriever at home if you are going on holiday. In fact, your dog can potentially make a great travel companion. With so many dog-friendly hotels and accommodation choices out there, it is easy to master the basics of travelling with your golden. Then the world is truly your oyster!

Going away with your dog is much easier if you prepare everything well in advance. Accommodation, travel arrangements, and paperwork can all be organised long before you go, which means less stress and more fun for both of you.

Things are even easier if you're staying somewhere closer to home rather than travelling overseas. Keeping a few simple things in mind will increase the ease of taking your golden on holiday. You'll need to consider everything in the following list:

Cover the basics – No matter how you choose to travel, there are a few essential things to bear in mind. Your golden can lose a considerable amount of body fluids through panting, so always have a bowl and many bottles of water with you to help them stay hydrated. Do not forget to pack plenty of poop bags for when your dog goes to the toilet.

Visit your vet a few months before travelling with your golden, especially if you're going abroad. Make sure you discuss your travel plans with your vet around six months in advance to give you plenty of time to comply with any extra requirements.

TIP ***Your dog's vaccinations will need to be up to date to go overseas, and there can also be specific vaccination requirements for the country you are visiting. It is also likely that you may need a certificate of vaccination, depending on where you are travelling.***

Dog insurance – Look for a policy that covers emergencies in the event of your golden needing vet care during your trip abroad. Some policies even contribute to the cost of a cancelled holiday or kennel fees if you are the one hospitalised.

Search for the nearest vet to your holiday stay – A nearby vet could be handy and can help with any health enquiries, big or small. Make sure you note down the address and contact details of the closest veterinary practice before you travel abroad with your golden.

Consider the current life stage and health condition of your golden retriever – You might miss out on sharing your best times with your four-legged family member, but sometimes it is better for them to skip some of the fun stuff, especially when travelling on a plane. If your dog is under 3 months old, senior, pregnant or ill, they will probably struggle to cope with a long journey. If in doubt, always check with your vet.

Accommodation tips – Whether you are holidaying with your dog at home or abroad, there are many dog-friendly hotels and accommodation options to suit every taste and budget. Your retriever might enjoy dog-training holidays, which provide the opportunity to experience canine activities and sports with other dog lovers under the guidance of a qualified trainer.

Be sure your accommodation is dog-friendly, and if you are staying at someone else's home, check ahead about the toilet facilities for your dog. Consider the possible presence of other pets—either during travel or at your destination—who might affect your golden's behaviour. For example, will your retriever want to chase the B&B owner's cat or bark at the dogs they are staying with?

Aeroplane travel – Make sure your airline is aware you will be bringing your dog on the trip. Consult them about carrier size and requirements, which may vary according to your retriever's height and weight. This will give you peace of mind and help you avoid a last-minute rush. Some companies will not allow dogs in the cabin with you, so make sure you are prepared to be apart from your golden for the length of the journey. It is always a good idea to include a feeding schedule note and any other relevant information just in case your dog does not make it to your destination at the same time as you.

If your golden is not already used to a carrier, take several weeks to introduce them to it before your trip. Leave it open and filled with soft bedding and an occasional hidden treat. Do not forget to put a small tag on your dog's collar showing the address at your destination, in case you are separated.

Leaving Your Golden Retriever Behind

Of course, while it would be wonderful if we could take our favourite furry friends with us on every holiday adventure, it's not always possible. Not all dogs are suited to travel. For example, if they are seniors or have a history of anxiety during confinement or travel, you should think about leaving them at home. There are several options to consider when you cannot take your retriever on holiday with you, including:

- Finding a trustworthy friend or neighbour who can look after your dog. Being away from their owner or changing their routine can be stressful for your golden. Usually, the best option is to have your friend, relative or neighbour look after your dog **in your home**. This allows you to keep things as familiar and stress-free as possible for your retriever. Also, leaving your furry friend with someone you know and trust will provide additional peace of mind while you are away.

- Locating a professional pet sitter who is available while you are travelling. The dogsitter will either stay in your home with your dog while you are away, or take your dog to their home. It is a good idea to ask for recommendations from other dog owners in your area when looking for a dog sitter (see below section).
- If you cannot find a friend, family or pet sitter, your other option is to locate a good dog boarding kennel. Take the time to find a place that is suitable for your golden retriever, they are all different and the environment could be stressful.

Pet sitter

Ask your friends and fellow dog owners if they can recommend someone, and do a bit of research to make sure it is the right choice for your golden retriever. Call your friends and ask the following questions:

- How much does their sitter charge?
- What experience do they have?
- Have they used them many times?
- How satisfied are they with their services?
- Do they come to you, or should your golden retriever go to them?

Remember, locating a professional dog sitter usually requires considerable advance notice, because they are trained and trusted professionals. Good ones will be booked well ahead on major holidays.

TIP ***Normally, the least stressful situation for your golden is to have the professional live with them in their usual home so their routine is not altered, and they can enjoy walks in their familiar neighbourhood. It could also benefit you to have someone living in your home while you are away, as this will deter intruders.***

If your dog is going to stay in their own home, you will need to show your professional sitter around the house and tell them about any household quirks or concerns.

Finding a suitable dog sitter can be a daunting task. You'll need reassurance that your golden retriever and property are looked after properly. In the United Kingdom, the National Association of Registered Pet Sitters can give you a list of their members.

Here is a checklist of questions to ask your potential dogsitter and some things to consider:

- If you are confident they can care for your golden's needs, meet the sitter before employing them.
- In the U.K., you can check the criminal record of someone applying for the position. This procedure is known as getting a Disclosure and Barring Service (DBS) check. In the U.S., you can see a copy of their police check or Criminal Records Bureau certificate to check that they have no criminal background.
- Having introductory sessions with your golden retriever's new carer will help them get comfortable and ready for when you are on holiday.
- Depending on your options, decide whether you would prefer the dog sitter to come to your house, or whether to take your dog to their home.

- Make sure they are reputable by asking for reviews or references from people in your area.
- Ask them for proof of insurance, including third-party, and preferably relevant qualifications such as dog first aid.
- If you plan to take your golden to the sitter's house, check whether they have their own dog or will be looking after other dogs. If so, it is a good idea for your golden to meet the other dogs on neutral ground before being in the home with them.
- Ask how the dog sitter is going to ensure the security of your home.
- Be certain to exchange details regarding vets and insurance in case your dog needs medical care while you are away.
- Decide whether you need regular updates on your golden, and who to contact in the event of an emergency.
- Most dog sitters will ask you to sign a contract stating what they will and will not do in your home.

Boarding Kennel

If it is your first time choosing a boarding kennel for your golden retriever, ask your vet or friends for recommendations. Alternatively, you can contact local councils or search online for local facilities. It is always recommended to visit the kennel beforehand and look for the following:

- An up-to-date licence.
- Proper insurance cover in case your golden retriever needs emergency care.
- Whether the facilities are clean, dry, draught-free, secure and provide shade.
- Will they exercise your golden and give them the space they need?
- Will the staff spend enough time with your golden every day and give them the social contact they need?

- Is there a system in place to monitor dogs during the day?
- Are they keeping predator and prey species separately to prevent stress?
- Do they ask for proof of vaccination? This is critical to prevent the spread of contagious diseases.
- Are there enough employees to take care of all the animals?
- Do they ask for details of your dog's diet and health?
- Can they accommodate any medical issues your retriever has?
- Do you feel welcome in the facilities and do the animals being hosted look clean and happy?
- Do the dogs and cats have up-to-date flea and worm treatment?

If the boarding kennel does not answer your questions or you are not convinced that they will care for your dog properly, find another reputable boarder who will.

Each kennel must provide a suitable environment, monitor your golden's behaviour and keep a record of your dog's stay. As a guideline, while staying in a boarding kennel, your dog should always have the following:

- Access to their own sleeping area at all times.
- Sufficient space to sit and stand at full height, lie down fully stretched out, wag their tail, walk and turn around.
- At least one daily walk outside their kennel.
- Their own kennel unit, unless you have given permission for your retriever to share with another dog from your household.
- Access to toys.

Boarders who aspire to higher standards typically offer two walks per day, each at least twenty minutes long. Finding a certified boarding kennel that can accommodate your retriever while you are away usually requires advance booking.

Generic Checklist

Whether a friend, dog sitter or kennel is looking after your golden, you should always ensure they have all the information and items needed to care for them while you are away. Here is a checklist so you don't miss anything:

- Details of your retriever's usual routine and the importance of sticking to this as much as possible.
- Their usual diet (including food and treats) with feeding instructions. If your dog normally eats fresh food, provide details of where to source it.
- Your emergency contact details.
- Your veterinarian's contact details, including out-of-hours service provided.
- It is a good idea to provide a familiar-smelling item, like a blanket or a worn item of your clothing to help your retriever to settle in an unfamiliar place.
- Important information regarding existing health issues, including a supply of any medication and clear instructions on how and when to take it.
- Information about your golden's behaviour and personality including their likes and dislikes.
- Details about when and how to exercise them.

- Supplies they will need during their stay, such as leads, collars, litter trays and toys.

Extra Expenses

While a close friend might look after your dog for free, if you send your retriever to a kennel or hire a professional sitter to care for them, you will incur extra expenses.

Professional sitter costs vary depending on location. On average, fees for dog sitting usually range between £20 and £27 per night in the U.K. and $20 and $40 in the U.S.

Boarding kennel costs also vary depending on what is included and their location. On average, fees for overnight dog boarding may range in price between £15 and £20 in the U.K. and in the U.S., from $30 to $50.

19. Breeding

'You know, a dog can snap you out of any kind of bad mood that you're in faster than you can think of.'

~ Jill Abramson ~

Anyone who has owned a female dog will usually think about whether to allow them to have a litter of puppies before having them spayed. There are many myths citing changes in personality or loss of happiness and contentment if you don't allow a female dog to give birth. These are all untrue. Your female golden retriever will live just as happily without having had puppies, and often longer, too. Whatever your decision on the subject, the following pages outline what is involved in the breeding process.

Female Heat

Female golden retrievers normally come into their first heat—oestrus— somewhere between 9 and 12 months of age, but this is not always the case. Depending on the dog, it may occur as late as 18 to 24 months.

Female breeding cycles

There are four stages in a female golden's breeding cycle:

1. **Proestrus** – The first signs of heat start to appear, comprising the swelling of the vulva and bloody vaginal discharge. This attracts males and lasts approximately 9 days—with a range of 2 to 22 days. Their oestrogen level rises, and their body prepares for ovulation. During this stage, the female will not permit males to breed.
2. **Oestrus** – Lasting approximately 9 days, the female is fertile during oestrus and will accept the male for breeding. This is when your golden retriever will fall pregnant. You might see them flagging—holding their tail to the side—or showing lordosis. This is when they arch their back and offer their hind end and vulva up for the male.

3. **Dioestrus** – This is a 60 to 90-day period when the progesterone hormone takes control of your female retriever's reproductive tract, and they aggressively prevent mating. During this time, they may display signs of a false pregnancy if they haven't conceived.
4. **Anoestrus** – No sexual activity takes place during this period, which lasts between 3 and 4 months. This is the inactive period until the start of the next cycle.

Behaviour during heat

If your female golden retriever is in heat, they might urinate more frequently or mark objects by peeing on them when out on a walk or even in the home. This signals to prospective mates that they are ready to reproduce since their urine contains hormones and pheromones highly attractive to males. Other changes in behaviour include:

- Being off their food or becoming hungrier.
- Being more affectionate.
- Paying more attention to male dogs.
- Tail tucking or sitting down when another dog approaches.
- Running away from male dogs.
- Becoming lazier.
- Lifting their leg when urinating or seeing a male dog.

How often?

On average, female golden retrievers go into heat every six months. This will continue every year until your female retriever dies or they are spayed.

Hormonal changes

During the first days of your female golden's heat cycle, there will be a significant increase in their oestrogen hormone. This causes swelling of your dog's vulva and creates a bloody discharge. Another hormonal change is the sudden surge of lutein, which is a heat-regulating hormone that causes ovulation. Finally, there is the production of corpus luteum to promote and maintain pregnancy, followed by an increase in progesterone, which makes the lining of your golden retriever's uterus receptive to implantation.

What to be aware of during a heat cycle

While you can still take your retriever out for their daily walks, they must always be kept securely on lead, as they might try to escape at any time to find a mate. They may also display aggression towards other dogs. You might also have to fight off male dogs who have a strong urge to mate with her.

TIP ***If you decide not to have your female dog spayed to prevent heat cycles, you need to be extra vigilant when they're in season. A dog in heat has only one thing on their mind—finding a mate. Your retriever may need to wear dog nappies for 1 to 3 weeks during each heat cycle to keep bloody mess to a minimum.***

The following steps can help to prevent unwanted pregnancy:

- Always closely supervise your female retriever.
- Remember that the urge to mate is so strong they could do whatever it takes to make it happen.

- If you cannot watch your female dog, place her in a secure crate.
- Keep her separated from all intact males.
- Keep all windows and doors securely closed—a male dog can smell the scent of a female in heat from over a mile away.

If your female golden retriever accidentally mates with an intact male during their heat cycle, you should immediately book an emergency consultation with your vet who can provide a morning-after injection to terminate an unwanted pregnancy.

Pregnancy

The ideal age for a female pregnancy will depend on their size and breed and the age they reach sexual maturity. While they can get pregnant during their very first heat cycle, this is not recommended, since they will still be growing. It is advised that you don't consider mating your dog until they have experienced their second or third heat cycle.

There are several methods for determining whether your female retriever is pregnant, all of which require a visit to the veterinarian, including:

Palpation – Approximately 30 days after you suspect your female retriever is pregnant, the veterinarian can perform an abdominal palpation. If they are pregnant, your vet will feel fluid-filled sacs surrounding the foetus the size of grapes or small golf balls. The timing of this manual test is critical, as the sacs begin to lose their distinctive shape after one month of pregnancy.

Blood test – Hormone levels can be measured by testing the blood at approximately 25 to 30 days after pregnancy is suspected. If the female is producing the hormone 'relaxin', this shows they are pregnant since this hormone is only produced during pregnancy.

Ultrasound – Your retriever's vet can perform an ultrasound between 25 to 35 days of suspected pregnancy to detect foetal heartbeats. This can also give an estimate of how many puppies your female is carrying.

X-ray – Taking your golden to the veterinarian for an x-ray is an effective way to determine if they are pregnant. It needs to be carried out at 55 or more days of a suspected pregnancy, as before that time their skeletons cannot be seen on an x-ray. This method gives a more accurate number of expected puppies.

TIP ***You need to check that your female retriever is healthy before you begin breeding to produce the healthiest offspring. This is easily accomplished with a pre-natal check-up at your vet's, where they can undergo a pre-breeding examination including testing for parasites and ensuring vaccines are up to date.***

Though some female retrievers experience morning sickness during the initial days of pregnancy and may lose their appetite for a few days, there are other signs to watch for, including:

- Swollen stomach.
- Enlarged mammary glands.
- Discharge of milk.
- Increased appetite.
- Increase in weight.
- Vomiting.

- Tiredness.
- Disinterest in exercising.
- Sleeping more.
- Depression.
- Restlessness.
- Becoming more affectionate or clingy.
- Hoarding and being protective of toys.
- Moving nesting material to create a den.
- Digging to create a nest.
- Acting more aggressively or irritable.
- Possible false labour contractions.

A canine pregnancy lasts approximately 63 days, and your retriever will go into labour within 56 to 66 days of becoming pregnant. If you notice signs of pregnancy, immediately take your dog to their veterinarian to confirm the pregnancy and receive instructions for their proper feeding and care.

Your vet might recommend increasing their food intake at around the 30-day mark or adding an egg to your golden retriever's meals as well as switching to puppy kibble, which is higher in protein. As your dog becomes heavier with the puppies, they will lose interest in exercising and other normal activities and need to sleep more.

When the time for birthing is drawing near, they start to display nesting characteristics, where they search for a warm and safe place to give birth. You can help by providing a nesting box. Your retriever will probably want to take things into the box to make it comfortable, such as towels or even a stuffed toy they start mothering.

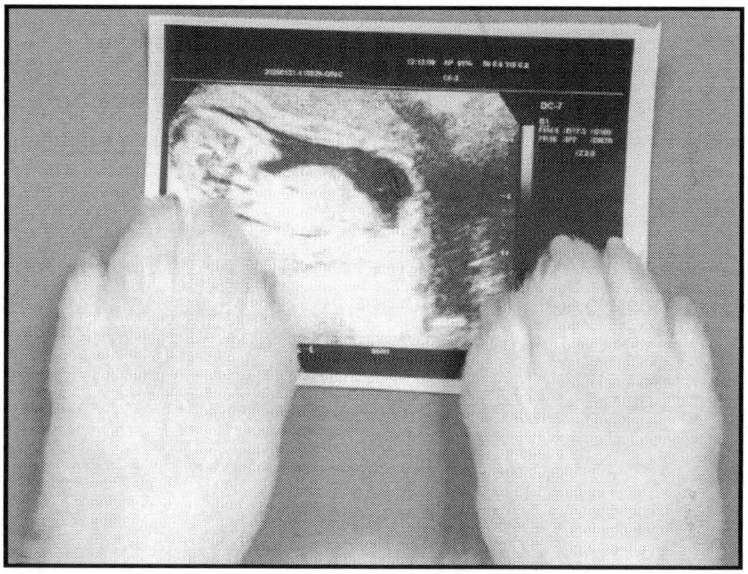

When they are close to whelping, your dog may completely lose their appetite and show distress by pacing, panting, and appearing uncomfortable. When the birthing time is near, their temperature needs to be checked. It should be about 37.9 to 38.2 °C (100.2 to 100.8 °F).

When their temperature drops to 36.7 to 37.4 °C (98 to 99.4 °F), the puppies will usually be born within 24 hours. If you are at all worried about the birthing process, take your mother dog immediately to your veterinarian.

If all goes well at home, within 5-6 hours of the last puppy's birth, you should take the mother and their puppies to their vet for a check-up. The vet will then make sure all puppies and placentas have been birthed and that the puppies are all healthy.

A false, pseudo or phantom pregnancy is a common condition that usually occurs between 4 and 9 weeks after a heat cycle. It simply means your non-spayed female is mimicking the behavioural and physical signs of carrying a litter of puppies as listed above.

Your non-spayed retriever might experience a false pregnancy because after your dog is old enough to be in a heat cycle, her ovaries produce hormones to prepare her body for pregnancy even if she has not been mated. These symptoms will usually subside on their own within a few weeks without any intervention.

Eclampsia

Eclampsia—hypocalcaemia or puerperal tetany—occurs in nursing mothers. This emergency medical condition is usually associated with a life-threatening drop in blood calcium levels. Eclampsia usually happens when the puppies are one to four weeks old, and the mother is producing the most milk.

Often, the cause of eclampsia is not found but can be due to the following:

- Excessive loss of calcium from the mother to the developing foetal skeletons.
- Calcium supplementation during pregnancy.
- Producing milk after birth.
- Not receiving a balanced, premium growth and development diet while pregnant and nursing.
- A hormonal problem with the parathyroid gland.

Signs the mother could be suffering from eclampsia include:

- Panting.
- Muscle spasms with arched back and rigid legs.
- Fever.
- Increased heart rate.
- Rubbing their face on the ground.
- Agitation and whining.
- Uncoordinated gait.
- Weakness.
- Rigid muscles.
- Seizures.

Treatment usually requires oral or intravenous calcium supplementation, anti-seizure medication, and cooling the body to reduce fever. While the mother is being treated, the puppies will need to be hand-fed with puppy formula and your vet might suggest earlier weaning to reduce stress on the mother.

FACT ***Eclampsia is a serious condition that can lead to coma and death if left untreated. It can be diagnosed using a simple blood test and can be easily cured with prompt veterinary intervention. Contact your veterinarian immediately if you think the mother is in trouble since eclampsia is a genuine medical emergency.***

When it comes to preventing eclampsia, calcium supplementation or feeding cottage cheese to pregnant and nursing dogs is not usually recommended, unless under the guidance of your vet. During pregnancy or nursing, excessive calcium intake can suppress production of parathyroid hormone, and increase the risk of developing low blood calcium levels or eclampsia. Your vet will advise whether your dog needs supplementation. Your pregnant retriever should eat a high-quality diet rich in essential vitamins and minerals formulated for pregnant and nursing mothers.

Pyometra

This is a serious and life-threatening infection of the uterus that occurs because of changes in your female golden retriever's reproductive tract during the heat cycle. The lining of the uterus gets thicker in preparation for pregnancy and if no pregnancy occurs during several cycles, the lining continues to thicken. Eventually, fluid-secreting cysts can begin to form, which creates an ideal breeding ground for bacteria to grow.

When this happens—2 to 8 weeks after the last heat cycle—your female's uterus becomes inflamed and distended with bacteria and pus that can discharge from the uterus, termed 'open pyometra', and through the vagina where it might be noticeable on their skin or hair under the tail.

If the pus is not able to drain to the outside ('closed pyometra'), their abdomen will distend, and the toxins released from the bacteria will enter the bloodstream. These toxins can quickly affect your retriever, and they can become very ill very fast. If your golden retriever is suffering from pyometra, they will exhibit the following symptoms:

- Increased water consumption.
- Increased urination.
- Slight vaginal discharge.
- Distended and painful abdomen.
- Vomiting.
- Diarrhoea.
- Listlessness.
- Depression.

Treatment involves the surgical removal of the infected uterus and ovaries by performing an ovariohysterectomy—spaying. Although hospitalisation can be required for longer than a routine spaying procedure, the prognosis for recovery is quite high when diagnosed during the early stages. Without prompt treatment, the chances for recovery decrease considerably, as the toxic effects created by the bacteria are usually fatal.

Mastitis

Canine mastitis is not a common breast infection but if your dog develops it, it will be within a few weeks of giving birth. This can be caused by puppies scratching with their claws, weaning the puppies too soon, or bacterial or fungal infection.

If your nursing retriever suffers from painful mastitis, they will present symptoms that include:

- Loss of appetite and listlessness.
- Fever.
- Refusing to allow puppies to nurse.
- Hard, almost black nipple segments.
- Red, dark, hot, or painful nipples.
- Irritation when the nipples are touched.
- Inflamed and swollen mammary glands.

Diagnosis includes blood work. Depending on the severity of the condition, antibiotics and pain medications will be prescribed. Other care includes applying warm compresses and expressing milk from the infected gland by hand every six hours to encourage blood flow and help diminish swelling and discomfort.

Early intervention can result in the affected gland returning to normal within several weeks. In other cases, the gland may be permanently damaged and unable to produce milk. Should a system-wide infection take hold, it is possible the female will die, even with aggressive treatment.

Female Dog Spaying

Spaying is performed via the surgical procedure called ovariohysterectomy. This is when the ovaries and uterus are completely removed to sterilise your female golden (see picture below). Some vets will now perform an ovariectomy where they only remove the ovaries.

There are many factors to consider to determine the best time to spay your retriever, including health and behavioural factors, together with your dog's environment. Consult your vet to determine the optimal time to spay your dog.

What's Involved?

Your veterinarian will examine your retriever and usually perform pre-anaesthetic blood tests. If everything is fine, your dog will be anaesthetised. Most dogs need an intravenous catheter to administer the anaesthetic and provide fluid therapy during the surgery.

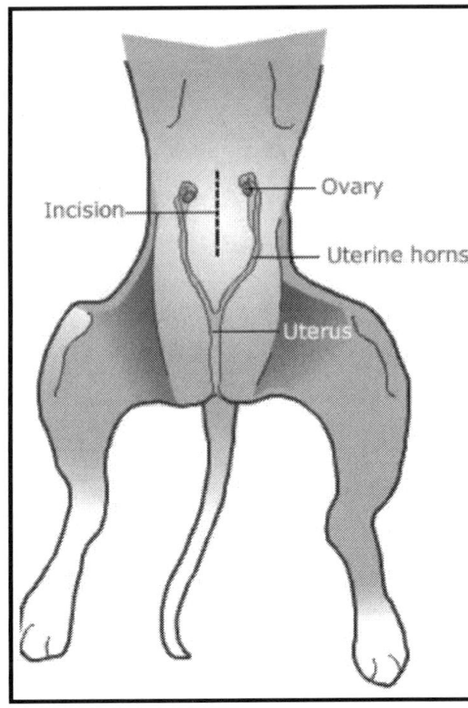

After your retriever has been anaesthetised, a breathing tube is placed in their trachea (windpipe). This allows oxygen and gas anaesthetic to be delivered directly into their lungs. The surgery comprises making an incision just below the umbilicus (belly button) before removing the ovaries and uterus, or just the ovaries, depending on your vet's technique. Most vets use absorbable sutures, which means you do not need to go back to have them removed.

If all goes well, your retriever will usually be able to return home the same day or the following day.

While the spaying process for a female dog is more invasive than neutering a male dog and takes a little longer to heal, the after-surgery protocol is much the same as it is for a male dog (see next section).

Pros and Cons

There are advantages and disadvantages to consider when thinking about spaying your golden retriever.

Potential advantages include:

- No accidental pregnancies.
- Reduced aggression or irritability.
- Zero desire to search for a mate.
- Lower risk of mammary cancer.
- No fluctuations in hormone levels causing false pregnancies after the heat cycle.
- Dogs spayed before their first heat cycle have a less than 0.5 % chance of developing mammary tumours.
- Lower risk of pyometra.
- No need to protect the female from males.
- None of the mess and odour involved in the heat cycle.
- An increased lifespan.

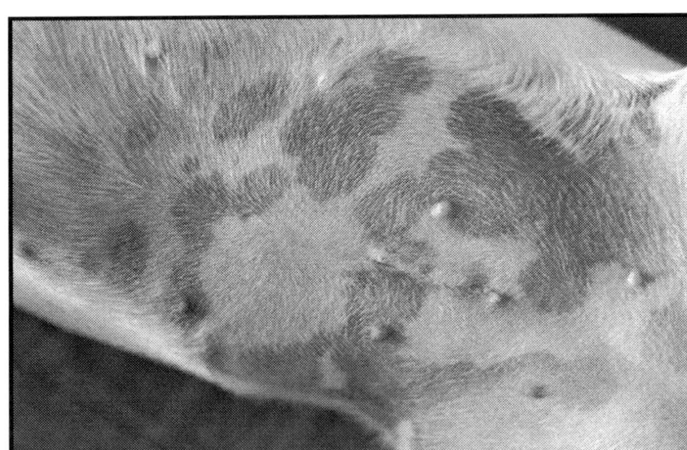

Potential disadvantages include:

- Spaying before maturity is linked to an increased risk of certain behaviours, such as noise phobia.
- Increased risk of hemangiosarcoma.
- Possible weight gain due to a reduced metabolism rate.
- Greater risk of hypothyroidism.

Spaying does not create a change in personality, intelligence, playfulness, or affection.

Male Dog Neutering

It is always important to discuss the decision to neuter your dog with your vet because exact timings are based on several distinct factors, such as weight, behaviour, health conditions, size, etc.

FACT ***Male dog neutering—or castration—is an operation to remove your retriever's testicles, after which your dog will no longer be able to father puppies. Dogs should not be neutered until they are at least 6-9 months old depending on size and breed.***

What is Involved?

This routine surgical procedure is conducted by your vet. Before surgery, your retriever will usually undergo a health check, which typically includes bloodwork.

During the operation, the vet will make a small incision in front of your golden's scrotum to allow access to the stalks of the testicles (see picture). These are severed and the testicles removed through the incision before it's stitched back up. The entire surgery usually takes 5 to 20 minutes.

In most cases, your retriever cannot eat for at least 8 hours before surgery since anaesthesia often causes vomiting. The operation is performed under anaesthetic, and the procedure is typically as follows:

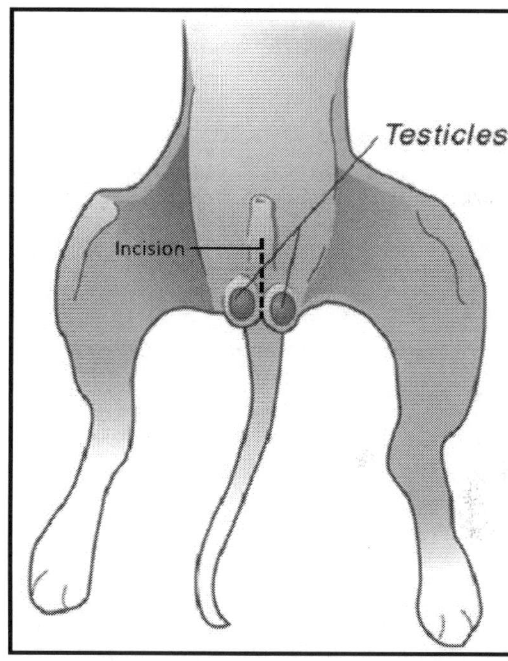

- Intravenous fluids and/or medications are injected to support circulation and blood pressure.
- An endotracheal tube is inserted in the trachea to deliver the anaesthetic gas and provide oxygen to the lungs.
- Pulse oximetry is initiated to measure the oxygenation of the blood.
- Blood pressure and temperature monitoring commenced.
- Warming blankets are used to prevent hypothermia.
- Electrocardiography is used to monitor their heart.
- Aftercare.

After surgery

Many dogs are fine to go home on the same day of the operation. When your golden retriever wakes up from their surgery, they will be in a crate where they are kept warm and monitored for problems. When you pick up your dog, they will probably still feel groggy and might whine when they first come home, as they will feel disoriented. Keep them quiet and warm, since it could take a little while for them to regain their normal temperature.

Your retriever will probably need to wear a buster collar or a cloud collar—a soft inflatable collar—to stop them licking the healing area.

Your vet will usually recommend your retriever to avoid vigorous exercise during the 10-day healing period, after which they can return to their normal activities. Note that it can be difficult to dampen your young golden's urge to run and play if they recover quicker than ten days.

Pros and Cons

There are both pros and cons you might want to consider when thinking about neutering your golden retriever. Reasons to book an appointment at the vet include:

- Prevents accidental, unwanted pregnancies.
- Reduces the risk of prostate disorders.
- Avoids testicular cancer.
- Eliminates the urge to run off in search of a female to mate with.
- Less likely to be aggressive with other male dogs.
- Reduces leg lifting or marking territory.
- Reduces sexual behaviour—humping other dogs, pillows, and legs.
- Lowers the risk of being attacked by another dog.
- Your golden retriever will often be calmer, more focused, and more loving with people.

Reasons to decide against the surgical procedure include:

- Possible weight gain.
- Increased risk of hemangiosarcoma.
- Increased risk of hypothyroidism.
- Increased risk of cognitive impairment during geriatric years.
- Possible complications during surgery.

Other Sterilisation Techniques

Zeutering is a new, non-surgical procedure designed to sterilise male dogs. Rather than removing your retriever's testicles, the chemical 'zeuterin' is injected into the testicles to render them sterile. This procedure is 99% effective, but since it is quite new, long-term effects have yet to be identified.

Furthermore, since this procedure does not remove the testicles, testosterone continues to be produced, which can cause aggressive tendencies towards other male dogs.

This type of sterilisation will not protect your male retriever from some health risks that neutering can eliminate, such as certain cancers. Research the subject thoroughly and discuss it with your veterinarian before proceeding.

A vasectomy procedure for your retriever involves removing a part of the tube that carries sperm from the testicle to impregnate the female dog. While this surgical procedure will leave your dog infertile, they will still produce testosterone. This means, they will still have an interest in females, mark territory, show aggression towards other males, and can develop the cancers that neutering prevents.

Should I Breed My Golden Retriever?

Whatever your reason, there are important factors to think about before breeding.

FACT ***Most owners find their golden retriever's companionship so rewarding they want to breed from their dog to continue the bloodline and/or keep a puppy. Others buy a female retriever specifically to breed them when they are old enough.***

If you're considering breeding, ask yourself:

- **Why do I want to breed my retriever?** Perhaps, you want to continue the bloodline of your wonderful dog and keep one of the puppies who will be just like their mother. Be aware that the odds are stacked against you getting another dog exactly the same as your beloved pet, as it is rare that any pup is exactly like their mother. If you want a dog with similar characteristics as your previous companion, it is better to contact the breeder or organisation you got your golden retriever. There is a possibility they might have a similar dog who would make an excellent addition to your family.

- **Will I be able to find homes for the puppies?** As the owner of the female golden retriever, you are responsible for finding homes for any puppies you do not wish to keep. The number of unwanted dogs in animal shelters should be enough to tell you that this is not always easy.
- **I wish to breed my dog to reduce their sexual activity. Does this work?** In actual fact, mating your retriever can make this behaviour worse. If you intend to control or curtail your dog's sexual behaviour or proclivities, breeding them will not fix it.
- **Will I be passing on any genetic defects or health concerns that could affect the puppies and weaken the breed?** This is always a possibility, but on the other hand, good breeders always make sure that no undesirable characteristics are being passed on because of their breeding programme.
- **Do I have the knowledge, time, and commitment required for successfully breeding my female?** Dog breeding takes a lot of work, research, and knowledge. Ethical and responsible breeders work with a mentor to teach them about breeding dogs and help them through breeding their first litter. Also, they will have done hours of research and know all the proper information needed before even deciding to mate their dog.
- Can I afford all the extra costs involved in breeding (see the section below)?

Breeding your female retriever is far more complicated than simply allowing them to have fun with any intact males you come across at the park and then waiting for the puppies to arrive a couple of months later. Beyond the initial expense of purchasing a purebred female, the costs involved in breeding can be as much as £2,700 in the United Kingdom based on a litter of four puppies. In the U.S., it can be as much as $4,500 or more. The sort of expenses you might incur include:

- Pre- and post-natal visits to the vet.
- Health tests and clearance.
- Stud-service fee.
- Progesterone tests.
- Ultrasound and x-rays.
- Food.
- Supplements.
- Whelping box.
- Whelping kit.
- Deworming for multiple puppies.
- Vaccinations for multiple puppies.
- Puppy food.
- Microchips.
- Possible C-section.
- Microchipping.
- Registration of the litter.

Breeding your dog is not something you should do on a whim. It is a huge responsibility, and you need to be certain you are doing the best for your retriever and their puppies. It is not just about finding two dogs who might create the perfect litter of puppies. Breeding requires all the knowledge and expertise of a responsible breeder.

Of course, the final decision is up to you. But once you consider all the factors and expenses involved in breeding, you might decide it's not something you want to get involved in.

20. Rescue Goldens

'You can tell by the kindness of a dog how a human should be.'

~ Captain Beefheart ~

If you have decided to share your home with a golden retriever, you don't necessarily have to go to a breeder. There is always the option to adopt from various rescue shelters in the United Kingdom, such as the RSPCA (SPCA facilities in the U.S.). While this means you'll probably get an older dog or puppy, there are many dogs who end up in shelters at a young age.

There are rescue and adoption facilities with almost every breed in most major cities around the globe. This means that if you want to adopt a golden retriever, all you need to do is carry out a Google search including your location, the name of the breed and the words 'rescue' or 'adoption'.

Also, many breeders can connect you with a dog who needs to be rehomed when one of theirs needs rehoming for whatever reason. Various social networking groups are also very willing to point you in the right direction.

Should I Adopt?

Deciding to adopt or rescue a retriever who needs to be rehomed is a very personal decision. There are several factors to consider when considering if it's right for you.

FACT ***Many dogs end up at a rescue facility or shelter during the adolescent phase of their life, between six months and a year old.***

Beyond getting lost or separated from their family, there are many reasons why a dog ends up in a rescue or shelter. For instance, shelters are overflowing with dogs who have not been properly house-trained, socialised, or taught basic obedience. Due to their previous owner's lack of care, they may have developed behavioural issues the owner didn't want to deal with. Other reasons that lead owners to surrender their dog to a shelter facility include:

Insufficient Research – Sometimes, deciding to get a dog is spontaneous rather than a well-thought-out, thoroughly researched decision. Careful research before bringing a dog home to your family ensures this will be a lifelong choice that makes everyone happy.

Energy Incompatibility – First-time owners might not be aware of how important it is to choose a breed that fits in with their lifestyle and energy level. For example, a family who spends their leisure time in front of the TV deciding to get a high-energy dog can spell disaster for everyone.

Training Inexperience – The amount of training involved in raising a dog to be a well-behaved family member is not always obvious to prospective dog owners. When it starts to become too much work, many owners decide to take their dog to a shelter.

Cost of Dog Ownership – Sometimes, people are not aware of the exact costs involved in properly caring for a dog until they get one. Food, toys, clothing, grooming, pet sitting, and vet bills can significantly add up, especially if your golden has added health issues.

Unforeseen Life Changes – Life happens, and often our circumstances can change dramatically. This can mean developing health issues that prevent you from being able to properly care for your dog, moving to a new home that does not allow dogs, getting a new job or having a baby who leaves little time for the dog.

Time Commitment – The amount of time you have available to care for your retriever can change as you become busier and other areas of your life take precedence. Sometimes, children beg for a dog and promise to care for them, only for their interests to change, so the dog's needs are neglected.

Allergies – The family might not have known that someone in the home is allergic to dogs, or a new baby or roommate could be allergic.

Unruly Behaviour – Though a dog's unruly behaviour might simply be down to their adolescent phase when they are biting or exhibiting other dangerous or aggressive tendencies, this is often when they find their way into a rescue shelter.

Health Problems – Sometimes, when a dog is injured or has chronic or age-related health issues, they could be surrendered to a shelter because the owner can't afford medications or does not have the time or patience to care for them.

FACT ***In the United Kingdom, it is estimated that there are over 600,000 homeless dogs in over 1,000 shelters at any given time. In the United States, there are over 10,000 shelter and rescue groups, sheltering over 3.1 million dogs each year.***

Most adopted dogs are physically healthy and might already be neutered, vaccinated, microchipped, and house-trained. All this reduces the initial cost of purchasing a golden retriever while giving a deserving dog a second chance. Rescued dogs can lack life experience and come with behavioural problems that need to be addressed. However, if you are patient, fair and consistent with their training, most dogs are eager to become affectionate and loyal family members. Rescuing a dog also means you will have helped to control the overflow of dogs abandoned to various organisations, which makes the choice to rescue a win-win for both the dog and you.

14 Shelter Dog Facts

Due to bad press and publicity, shelter dogs have often had an unearned bad rap. When some people think of shelter dogs—mostly non-animal lovers—they picture a vicious, volatile animal who has been surrendered to a shelter because it bit its owner. This couldn't be further from the truth. Here are some shelter dog facts that should allay any doubts you might have:

1. **Not every shelter dog is a mutt** – People believe the only way they will ever find a purebred golden retriever is through a breeder, but that is not the case. On the contrary, in the United States, DoSomething.org notes that an incredible 25% of all dogs in animal shelters are purebred.
2. **A huge problem is overpopulation** – Adorable as puppies are, there are simply too many of them compared to the current demand for dogs. Not only are most dogs not neutered, but on average, a fertile dog produces one litter a year, each litter having between four to six pups. When these puppies cannot find homes, they end up in shelters, creating a big problem for the small number of shelters.

3. **No neutering or spaying costs** – Having your dog neutered or spayed is expensive, but you don't have to worry about that if you adopt a shelter dog. Most shelters cover the cost of the procedure while the dog is in their care. These costs are then included in the fee you pay when adopting your new four-legged friend, which is frequently lower than purchasing a purebred retriever outright.
4. **Supporting a good cause** – By adopting, you are fighting against puppy mills, where dogs are kept in overcrowded, soiled cages, unable to socialise or roam.
5. **Shelter dogs are unique** – If you want a dog that is one of a kind, the shelter is the place to go. According to a study of over 900 puppies published in PLOS ONE, the average shelter dog is a mix of three different breeds!
6. **Shelter dogs love humans** – A recent study published in the Journal of Veterinary Behaviour: Clinical Applications and Research found that, compared to pet dogs, shelter dogs are 'more socially driven to gaze and interact with humans.' If you adopt instead of buying from a breeder, be prepared to receive all the affection in the world.
7. **Pit bulls are extremely misunderstood** – Pit bulls are the most common breed found in animal shelters, but that could be because they are stereotyped. While most people consider the breed to be vicious and aggressive, one study conducted by the website Dognition has found that out of 35 common breeds, the pit bull was ranked as one of the least aggressive. Note that despite this fact, it is illegal to own a pit bull in the U.K..
8. **There are more homeless animals than people** – Dogs suffer from vagrancy more than people. According to the DoSomething.org website, for every homeless human, there are five homeless animals on the street.

9. **You can live longer** – If you adopt a dog from the shelter, it is a win-win situation. According to a recent study published in Scientific Reports, out of 3.4 million individuals, single dog owners were 33 % less likely to die compared to their pet-free friends.
10. **Dogs provide children with a better home environment** – What they say about shelter dogs is true: You not only save them, but they save you, too. A University of Florida study found that having a dog around helps children to deal better with stress, preparing them for success in the future.
11. **People will still buy dogs from breeders instead of adopting them** – Although people are aware of how many dogs there are in shelters, the ASPCA stated that 34% of dogs are obtained from breeders, whereas only 23% are adopted from humane societies or animal shelters.

12. **All shelter dogs are carefully evaluated** – One thing stopping people from adopting a dog from a shelter is the worry that the dog will have hidden health or behavioural issues. However, this conception is far from truth. Not only do shelters evaluate every dog that comes into their care for behaviour and health, but they do so more thoroughly than most breeders and pet shops.
13. **Most shelter dogs end up euthanised** – It is sad but true. According to the PetFinder pet adoption website, approximately 60% of shelter dogs in the U.S. are euthanised every year because they cannot find a home.
14. **Most dogs do not find their forever home** – If you are still unsure about adopting a rescue dog, then consider this: According to the Mosby Foundation, a non-profit organisation that helps care for abused and injured animals, only 1 in every 10 dogs born is ever placed in a permanent, loving home.

If you decide you want to adopt a rescue dog, you can find a list of the main U.K. and U.S. rescue organisations after this chapter.

What to Expect When Adopting

Even though you might wish to save a retriever from a shelter or a rescue organisation, you need to be prepared to find that you are not a suitable candidate. Whilst it is true that countless puppies are waiting for an owner, dog shelters thoroughly assess people before letting them have a dog. Their goal is to ensure each dog up for adoption goes to a happy and loving family who will be a good match for their personality so they do not end up back in the shelter.

When it comes to adopting, most dog shelters have the same process:

- Submit an adoption application.
- Have an interview with one of the shelter's counsellors.
- Meet the rescue dog you have selected.
- If the interview is successful and the retriever you chose is the right fit for you and your family, you will need to pay a small adoption fee before taking them home.

By following these steps, shelters try to ensure people who adopt their dogs are not doing it impulsively and will provide love, care, and a long-term home for their new four-legged companion.

It is important to be aware that you may find the shelter interview questions to be personal and intrusive. Each shelter has its own specific interview process, but most tend to structure them like an informal, honest conversation instead of an exam you need to pass. Once you accept all those questions are only there to ensure your future canine family member is in the right hands, you won't mind answering them.

When it comes to the adoption interview, here are some of the questions you can expect:

- **What is your family situation?** How many children and how many adults are in your household? Does everyone within your household agree to adopt a dog?
- **What is your current housing situation?** Do you own your home, or are you renting? What type of property do you have? Are you planning to move soon?
- **What is your past experience with pets? Do you own any animals right now?** They will want to know the number of pets, your history of pet ownership, and what happened to each of them. Do you know how to socialise a retriever into their new family?
- **What is your work situation?** Can you afford to own and look after your new golden? How long are your work hours, and do you have to commute? Will you have to leave your dog alone for hours due to your work?

These questions determine if you are capable of taking on the responsibility of owning a dog. Although they might seem a bit too personal, they are essential. When you understand that moving away is one reason dogs are abandoned, as are strict property owners, financial issues, and lack of time due to work responsibilities, these probing questions make far more sense.

The next two questions are aimed at helping the counsellor understand whether you are the right personality match for the retriever you want to adopt and vice versa:

- **What is your lifestyle?** Are you an active, outdoorsy person, or will you take your dog with you on holiday, to social events, etc.? Are you currently in a relationship, and if so, how would your dog fit into it?
- **Do you have any knowledge about rescue dogs?** Will you train and socialise your retriever? Are you aware that dogs sometimes end up in a shelter because of abuse and neglect and never fully recover? What is your reason for adopting this dog?

Being honest when answering these questions is essential. Be truthful with yourself, and do not agree to something you don't know if you can see through. Nobody wants an adopted golden retriever to be unhappy or experience abandonment again.

Rescue Dog Special Needs

Unless a rescue dog has some form of medical or physical problem, they will not have any special needs beyond requiring time to get used to their new home. Often, people who rescue dogs can end up creating behavioural issues for their dogs because they feel sorry for their previous treatment.

A *feeling sorry* type of energy is not what a rescue dog requires since they could already be feeling nervous, confused, and uncertain. What will help them to acclimate to new people and surroundings is a kind, strong and confident owner who they can learn to trust and follow, so they can relax in their new home.

Plan to give your rescued golden retriever plenty of time to adjust to their new home and family. It can take anywhere from a few hours to several months for your dog to become used to living in a new home. During their adjustment period, do what you can to make your golden feel safe and comfortable. While they adjust, be patient and try to keep things consistent and predictable in their unfamiliar environment.

A retriever who has spent several weeks or more in a shelter might be stressed because their life has been so unpredictable. By establishing a feeding routine, with regular walks, playtime, and bedtime, you can provide them with some stability.

TIP ***Treat your rescue dog the same way you would any new puppy coming into your home. Assume they have never had any training. Even if your golden has had obedience training in the past, they may need a refresher after all they have been through.***

Your best approach is to expect your dog to know nothing. That way, you will be pleasantly surprised if they know some basic commands or are already house-trained. This means you will not be setting your retriever puppy up for failure by having too high expectations. Be certain to train your new retriever using positive reinforcement. Training sessions should be upbeat and stress-free.

Socialisation can be a challenge with adopted dogs. As with training, it is important to get your golden retriever used to their environment, as well as any people and other animals they may encounter in their new life. This should be done slowly, within your retriever's comfort level.

Assuming too much or too little about your dog's past is one of the most common mistakes new owners make with their rescue dog. Not every dog in the shelter has a traumatic past. Not all of them have been properly trained or socialised. As with every aspect of your retriever's care, take the attitude that they are a blank canvas waiting for your direction, training, and love.

Remember, training starts the day your new retriever comes home. It is tempting to coddle them at first to try to make up for their time spent in the shelter.

However, if you allow your shelter dog to engage in certain behaviour when you first bring them home, you might find it harder to train them to stop doing those things later. This includes annoyances such as jumping on the sofa, eliminating on the carpet, or chewing table legs. You need to establish your golden's boundaries early on and ensure the entire family enforces them.

As with a new puppy, it is important to introduce your shelter dog to crate training as soon as possible. That way, you can work on house training and know your golden retriever will not get into trouble when left unsupervised. A crate is helpful as it gives your shelter dog a place of their own. Between living in a shelter and coming to their new home, your golden might feel extremely stressed. Having a place to retreat to when they feel overwhelmed will go a long way towards helping your retriever feel at home.

Crates can be difficult for some dogs, especially if their previous owner used them as a place of punishment or they were left in one for too long. Never force them in if they are reluctant, so you can turn their crate training into a positive experience.

While your retriever is adjusting to their new home, be sure to always supervise them, especially when outside. Even if your garden is fully fenced, your dog could become curious about or startled by noises, sights, and smells outside the boundary. If they get loose, they will have a hard time finding their way back to their new home because they are unfamiliar with the area.

It is highly recommended you enrol your rescue dog in an obedience class. Regular training sessions help get your golden into a routine. Starting a training programme also helps establish boundaries for your dog from the start. An obedience class will set your retriever up for good behaviour and make it easier for them to be a happy and healthy member of your family. Remember, dogs are happiest when they know the rules. Training your new dog properly from the beginning is one of the best things you can do for them since dogs crave structure and predictability.

How to Choose a Rescue Dog

It can be difficult to choose the right dog for your family. Each dog has their own personality, so it is essential to find a dog that complements your character.

One of the biggest mistakes you can make is to fall in love with a dog for their looks. Yes, they might have the cutest puppy eyes in the world, but can you take care of all their needs? Will the dog you want get on well with your other pets or children? If you choose a retriever for adoption whose activity level and personality do not match yours, you are setting yourself up for trouble.

When you choose a rescue dog from your local shelter, bear in mind some dogs have a slim chance of being adopted.

Deciding which dog to take home can be something of an emotional rollercoaster. Seeing all those pleading eyes and so many gorgeous puppies and dogs can make you feel guilty that you can't take them all with you.

The best thing you can do is help as much as you can, whether by donating, volunteering your time, or spreading the word about available dogs and the shelters that have taken them in.

Final Thoughts

Regardless of whether you get them from a shelter or breeder, all dogs are loyal and loving. If you decide to adopt a dog, you will be saving a life. You might be a shelter dog's last chance for happiness. To be honest, there is nothing quite like the bond rescue dogs create with their families. They never forget their human is the one who gave them a second chance.

Although you cannot change a dog's past, you can help shape their future!

Helpful Links

Associations and Services

- Association for Pet Obesity Prevention: www.petobesityprevention.org
- Dog TV: www.dogtv.com
- Canine Journal: www.caninejournal.com
- International Boarding and Pet Services Association: www.ibpsa.com

Societies & Clubs

- American Kennel Club: www.akc.org
- The Kennel Club: www.thekennelclub.org.uk
- United Kennel Club: www.ukcdogs.com
- Royal Society for the Prevention of Cruelty to Animals: www.rspca.org.uk
- The Golden Retriever Club: www.thegoldenretrieverclub.co.uk
- Golden Retriever Club of America: www.grca.org
- Golden Retriever Breed Council: www.goldenretrieverbreedcouncil.co.uk

Forums

- Dog Forums: www.dogforums.com
- Pet Forums: www.petforums.co.uk
- Golden Retriever Forum: www.goldenretrieverforum.com
- Golden Retrievers UK Advice and Discussion Forum: www.facebook.com/groups/goldenretrieversuk

Golden Retriever Breeders

- Bonsaviour Retrievers: www.bonsaviour.uk
- Fallowfen Training Kennels: www.fallowfen.com
- Harmony Golden Retrievers: www.harmonygoldenretriever.com
- Haydengold Golden Retrievers: www.haydengold.com
- Gaytonwood: www.gaytonwood.co.uk
- Gaylan's Golden Retrievers: www.gaylans.com
- Amica Goldens: www.amicagoldens.com
- Sun-Golden Kennels: www.sungoldenkennels.com
- Syrah Goldens: www.syrahgoldens.com
- Chadwick's Goldens: www.chadwicksgoldens.com

Dog Trainers & Behaviourists

- Assistance Dogs International: www.assistancedogsinternational.org
- Dognition: www.dognition.com
- Animal Behaviour and Training Council: www.abtc.org.uk

Poison Control

- Animal Poison Line: www.animalpoisonline.co.uk
- Pet Poison Helpline: www.petpoisonhelpline.com

- American Society for Prevention of Cruelty to Animals – Poison Control: www.aspca.org

Rescues

- Southern Golden Retriever Rescue: www.sgrr.org.uk
- Happy Paws: www.happypawspuppyrescue.co.uk
- The Golden Retriever Club: www.thegoldenretrieverclub.co.uk/rescue-page
- Homeward Bound Golden Retriever Rescue: www.homewardboundgoldens.org
- Delaware Valley Golden Retriever Rescue: www.dvgrr.org
- As Good As Gold Retriever Rescue: www.asgoodasgold.org
- Dogs Trust: www.dogstrust.org.uk
- Golden Retriever Rescue of the Rockies: www.goldenrescue.com
- Retrieve a Golden of the Midwest: www.ragom.org

Resources (Informational)

- Vets4Pets: www.vets4pets.com
- Dog Food Advisor: www.dogfoodadvisor.com
- PDSA: www.pdsa.org.uk
- PetMD: www.petmd.com
- The Spruce Pets: www.thesprucepets.com
- Blue Cross: www.bluecross.org.uk
- Battersea: www.battersea.org.uk

Disclaimer and Legal Notice: This product is not medical or legal advice and should not be interpreted in that manner. You need to do your due diligence to determine if the content of this product is right for you. The authors and the affiliates of this product are not liable for any damages or losses associated with the content in this product.

While every attempt has been made to verify the information shared in this publication, neither the author nor the affiliates assume any responsibility for errors, omissions, or contrary interpretations of the subject matter herein. Any perceived slights to any specific person(s) or organisation(s) are purely unintentional. We have no control over the nature, content and availability of the websites listed in this book.

The accuracy and completeness of the information provided herein, and opinions stated herein are not guaranteed or warranted to produce any specific results, and the advice and strategies, contained herein may not be suitable for every dog or individual. The author shall not be liable for any loss incurred because of the use and application, directly or indirectly, of any information presented in this work. This publication is designed to provide information regarding the subject matter covered.

The information included in this book has been compiled to give as thorough an overview of the subject as possible and detail some of the symptoms, treatments etc. that are available. It is not intended to give medical advice. For a firm diagnosis of any health condition, and for a treatment plan suitable for you and your dog, you should consult your veterinarian or health care consultant.

The writer of this book and the publisher are not responsible for any damages or negative consequences that may arise because of following any of the treatments, suggestions or methods highlighted in this book.

The writer of this book understands and respects the many differing opinions regarding what may be considered appropriate choices when caring for any dog. Any identified products, suggestions, opinions, methods, or recommendations that may be noted here are simply based on professional experience, which may or may not agree with every reader and nothing written here is intended to be in any way adversarial or confrontational.

Printed in Great Britain
by Amazon

30827541R00183